Y0-BRM-330

LIBRARY
College of St. Scholastica
Duluth, Minnesota 55811

WITHDRAWN

WITHDRAWN

Minnesota 55431

Assessing Needs in Educational and Social Programs

Using Information
to Make Decisions,
Set Priorities,
and Allocate Resources

Belle Ruth Witkin

Assessing Needs in Educational and Social Programs

 Jossey-Bass Publishers

San Francisco • Washington • London • 1984

HV
11
.W67
1984

ASSESSING NEEDS IN EDUCATIONAL AND SOCIAL PROGRAMS
Using Information to Make Decisions, Set Priorities, and Allocate Resources
by Belle Ruth Witkin

Copyright © 1984 by: Jossey-Bass Inc., Publishers
433 California Street
San Francisco, California 94104

&

Jossey-Bass Limited
28 Banner Street
London EC1Y 8QE

Copyright under International, Pan American, and
Universal Copyright Conventions. All rights
reserved. No part of this book may be reproduced
in any form—except for brief quotation (not to
exceed 1,000 words) in a review or professional
work—without permission in writing from the publishers.

Library of Congress Cataloging in Publication Data

Witkin, Belle Ruth (date)
   Assessing needs in educational and social programs.

   (The Jossey-Bass social and behavioral science
series)
   Bibliography: p. 367
   Includes index.
   1. Evaluation research (Social action programs)
2. Social work administration—Planning.   3. Education—
Aims and objectives—Planning.   4. Social surveys.
5. Educational surveys.   6. Social service—Research.
7. Education—Research.   I. Title.   II. Series.
HV11.W67   1984   361'.0072   84-48002
ISBN 0-87589-634-0 (alk. paper)

Manufactured in the United States of America

The paper in this book meets the guidelines for
permanence and durability of the Committee on
Production Guidelines for Book Longevity of the
Council on Library Resources.

JACKET DESIGN BY WILLI BAUM

FIRST EDITION

Code 8434

The Jossey-Bass
Social and Behavioral Science Series

Preface

All organizations make plans, but not all of them may be said to engage in systematic planning. Plans are like a blueprint, showing how to reach an organization's goals. But how are decisions made as to what those goals should be? Social agencies must decide what people to serve and what kinds of programs are most appropriate to offer. School systems must decide what their curricula should be and how best to help students become self-sufficient, contributing adults. Businesses must decide what products to make for specific markets. Municipalities must decide what services to provide to community residents. The central decision for them all is What is the best way to portion out the available resources, including time, money, and organizational efforts, to meet all the demands—the needs—that compete for them?

Such decisions may be based on intuition, political pressures, past practices, or personal preferences, and they may be made by boards or managers. But the most effective way to decide such issues is to make needs assessment the first stage in planning. As used in this book, *needs assessment* is a generic term for any systematic approach to setting priorities for future action. It entails making choices among goals, based on shared values, and appraising gaps between those goals and the current reality. It seeks both facts and opinions from inside and outside the organization and establishes a solid data base. Above all, it enables the planner to look ahead and to provide a rational basis for the most productive use of the organization's resources.

Needs assessment is particularly important now, with increasing competition for shrinking resources. But it has also proved useful in times of expansion. Resources are never unlimited, societal values change, and neither society nor organizations remain static. Effective needs assessment provides the basis for decisions on priorities either for program development or retrenchment.

The principal intent of this book is to break new ground in the field—to bring together for the first time concepts and methods drawn from education, human services delivery, community planning, organizational and interpersonal communication, systems safety engineering, and forecasting. It presents a broad array of present and potential methods of gathering and analyzing data and setting priorities. *Assessing Needs in Educational and Social Programs* includes not only widely accepted models and methods but many less well known techniques that show promise. It focuses on models and practices in the United States and Canada, with brief references to developments elsewhere.

My thesis is that needs assessment is an essential part of an ongoing cycle of program planning, implementation, and evaluation; that its purpose is to make decisions about priorities; that it must be viewed in context; and that there is no one correct or definitive procedure for all situations. This is not to say, however, that all methods are equally valid. In this book, I point out many widely used but nonproductive methods, offer criteria for evaluating them, and suggest alternative practices. In the United States we have had about twenty years of experience in conducting formal, systematic needs assessments, and we now have a body of theory and practice to evaluate and build on. I hope that the book will stimulate additions to that body of knowledge as well as experiments to compare and validate alternative approaches.

Assessing Needs in Educational and Social Programs is

written for planners, evaluators, policy makers, administrators, and researchers in public and private settings, as a guide to present practices and future trends. The focus of the book is on methods and issues related to selecting data and converting data into decisions. While not a manual for doing needs assessment, it provides a reference to standard practices, as well as extensive descriptions of promising methods that are not readily available elsewhere.

This book grew out of my active involvement since 1966 in research and development of needs assessment models and instruments as well as my experiences directing or evaluating needs studies of varying degrees of complexity. It reflects both my interest in theory and system models and my bias toward the practical. It also reflects an urge toward synthesis, toward integrating knowledge from many disparate fields. The conceptual bases for the development efforts with which I have been associated owe much to the teaching and writing of Kaufman (1972, 1982; Kaufman and English, 1979); the practicality comes from years as an administrator and consultant in educational planning and evaluation and from the teachers and other practitioners who showed me what works and what doesn't in the world outside the laboratory.

As I see it, there have been two separate but parallel strands of development during the last twenty years, in education and in human services, in which I include community planning. Educational needs assessment has been strongly influenced by Kaufman's discrepancy model and his system approach to organizational problem solving and renewal. His methods have also influenced the more recent application of needs assessment to organizational problem solving and staff training in the private sector. On the one hand, the most favored approach of school systems has been to use specialized surveys and group decision techniques to achieve consensus on educational goals and on the needs of students. On the other hand, human service needs assessments have used social indicators, service statistics, social area analysis, and other techniques not used by schools, as well as the survey. My intent is to bridge the gap between these two strands, applying evaluative criteria, and drawing implications for policy and practice in educational and noneducational contexts.

Content and Organization

The book is organized in four parts. Part One defines the field and describes selected models. Chapter One gives a brief historical background and reviews the controversies about the terms *need* and *needs assessment,* the ways in which values influence standards of need, and the relationship of needs assessment to both program planning and evaluation. Chapter Two presents two methods for deciding how to choose a needs assessment approach, and describes eight models that were developed from different perspectives. The models were chosen as illustrative of varying approaches and contexts, ranging from Kaufman's Organizational Elements Model to a three-phase issues-based design to be incorporated into a management information system. Others deal with analysis of staff training needs, community college planning, an ecological approach to analyzing needs of a minority population, frameworks for integrating data from many sources for community decision making, and field analysis as a step beyond needs assessment.

Part Two reviews three general categories of methods and two special techniques for gathering data and raises issues connected with each. Chapter Three critically examines the types of survey questionnaires most widely used for needs assessment and finds most of them wanting. The chapter also discusses how the critical incident technique and behaviorally anchored rating scales could improve needs surveys.

The treatment of social indicators in Chapter Four includes social area analysis, rates under treatment, client analysis, service statistics, and spatial analysis. The application of social indicators to educational needs assessment draws heavily on the work of Rossi and Gilmartin (1980a) and of researchers at the University of British Columbia and the provincial Ministry of Education. Chapter Five discusses large and small group processes and games, including recently-developed models that demonstrate how to proceed from priorities to action planning.

In Chapter Six, methods of forecasting alternative futures are discussed for their relevance to needs assessment in long-range planning. Chapter Seven shows how the causal analysis phase of a needs study and the management of the study itself can be improved through the application of Fault Tree Analysis, an operations research technique adapted from systems safety engineering.

Part Three deals with methods and issues related to converting data to decisions. Chapter Eight is the first comprehensive review of methods of setting priorities from needs data and finds that the most commonly used techniques are the most simplistic and least valid. It includes discussion of recently developed models that use various decision rules to integrate and interpret the data. Chapter Nine places needs assessment in the context of organizational planning, and reviews recently published work on needs assessment in times of retrenchment. Chapter Ten discusses the significance of organizational and interpersonal communication factors that are frequently overlooked in planning and conducting needs assessments, including relevance to constituent groups with varying racial and linguistic backgrounds. In the treatment of strategies for communicating results of a needs assessment I draw on my own background in teaching communication as well as recent work on communicating results of evaluation studies (Smith, 1982a).

Part Four focuses on applying needs assessment to planning and evaluation. Chapter Eleven addresses the vexing problem of inadequate utilization of needs assessment results. It suggests that utilization may take many forms and discusses organizational and other factors that facilitate or inhibit the use of the findings, drawing extensively on the knowledge utilization studies of Rich (1981) and the two-worlds model of Rothman (1980). Chapter Twelve uses a case history of joint planning between a city and a school system as a springboard to discuss models and research on interagency cooperation. Chapter Thirteen describes a variety of both structured and informal methods for community-wide needs assessment.

Finally, Chapter Fourteen makes the case for increased attention to effective needs assessment, concerned with quality of life and the interaction of the organization with the larger environment. It closes with a discussion of the implications for needs assessment of certain predictions concerning social trends, population shifts, networking, changing public expectations for education and social services, and trends in methodology.

It is my hope that this book will open lines of communication between educational and human services planners and evaluators, and heighten their interest in the potential for better policy and management decisions through valid and effective needs assessment.

Acknowledgments

This book was written during a period when many changes were occurring in the role and utilization of needs assessment by educational and social agencies and governmental bodies. I am greatly indebted to the more than two score persons who supplied me with information about current developments in needs assessment in the United States and Canada and who graciously shared with me their recent publications and unpublished papers. I am also indebted to several people who kept me posted during the past two years on recent research and applications of social indicators to educational needs assessment, particularly Robert Rossi and Kevin Gilmartin, of the American Institutes for Research; Ronald Faris, executive director of the continuing education division of the Ministry of Education of British Columbia; and Thomas Sork, of the Faculty of Education at the University of British Columbia. I also wish to thank Cheryl Crowell, of the International City Management Association, who kindly supplied me with key documents on human services needs assessment.

The present organization and content owe a great deal to the recommendations of Scarvia Anderson, whose careful review of the first draft and insightful comments were invaluable. The manuscript also benefited at various stages from the suggestions of Roger Kaufman, and I thank him for his confidence in the book and his willingness to share information on his own work in progress.

I am especially grateful to Mae Lovern for the many hours she spent in carefully cross-checking the references with the manuscript through successive drafts. I also wish to thank Richard Knuth and George Swift for their considerable assistance with the literature search, and Phyllis Hatfield, who typed drafts of some chapters and suggested methods of dealing with the manuscript on my word processor. Particular thanks go to Jerald Smallidge, who cheerfully guided me through the intricacies of operating the word processor, and who devised special methods for enabling me to reorganize and edit large blocks of manuscript.

Most of all I am deeply grateful to my husband, Joseph Witkin, without whose patience, loving support, and encouragement this book could not have been written.

Renton, Washington   Belle Ruth Witkin
September 1984

Contents

The Author

Belle Ruth Witkin is an independent planning and evaluation consultant, living in Renton, Washington. She was formerly on the speech faculty at the University of Washington and was administrator of research and evaluation in the office of the Alameda County Superintendent of Schools in Hayward, California. She received her B.A. degree (1939) from the University of Puget Sound in English, her M.A. degree (1951) from the University of Washington in speech communication, and her Ph.D. degree (1962) from the University of Washington in speech science and communication disorders.

Witkin's main professional interests in the past fifteen years have been in applying systems analysis techniques to program planning and evaluation and in developing and refining methods of assessing needs and establishing organizational priorities. To this development she has brought many years of experience in small group and organizational communication in addition to research and consulting in planning and evaluation. She has published papers, technical reports, and monographs on needs assessment and planning. Her *Analysis of Needs Assessment Techniques for Edu-*

cational Planning at State, Intermediate, and District Levels (1977, revised) was the first comprehensive study of the state of the art in educational needs assessment.

Witkin's published work includes *Management Information Systems: Applications to Educational Administration* (1971), and a number of innovative needs assessment instruments. She directed the development of *A Comprehensive Needs Assessment Module* (1979a, revised), *A Model of Cyclical Needs Assessment for Management Information Systems* (1980), and *APEX Needs Assessment Surveys for Secondary Schools* (1983, with J. Richardson), as well as a decision model and a structured process for small groups. Together with K. G. Stephens she pioneered the adaptation of the Fault Tree Analysis technique from systems safety engineering to planning and evaluation in social systems. The principles are embodied in *Fault Tree Analysis: A Management Science Technique for Educational Planning and Evaluation* (1973, with K. G. Stephens). She later developed related causal analysis methods specifically for needs assessment.

Witkin organized the first national conference on needs assessment for all educational levels, held in 1976, and directed the first joint city-school district needs assessment, conducted in 1977-1978. She is active in a number of professional associations and has served as president of the California Association for Program Evaluation and as a member of the board of the International Society for Educational Planning.

Assessing Needs
in Educational
and Social Programs

Using Information
to Make Decisions,
Set Priorities,
and Allocate Resources

1

Relationship
of Needs Assessment
to Program Planning
and Evaluation

The widespread use of systematic processes of needs assessment for education and for health and human services in the United States dates to the 1960s and 1970s, when Congress passed a series of bills designed to bring about changes congruent with national goals. That legislation provided grants to states and local agencies. Most of those grants, which were allocated on either a formula or competitive basis, were administered by the then Department of Health, Education, and Welfare. More than thirty programs in the fifty-four largest pieces of legislation mandated needs assessment at the federal, state, or local level (Zangwill, 1977). Although the requirements for needs assessment were poorly defined, the legislation stimulated not only the development of numerous models and approaches to identifying and analyzing needs but also publications and national conferences on the topic. The movement also established the centrality of obtaining community consensus on goals and needs.

Other developments that encouraged needs assessment were the rise of interest in systems analysis and systematic planning; the accountability movement, with its emphasis on outputs of systems rather than inputs or processes; and new management techniques, particularly Planning-Programming-Budgeting Systems (PPBS)

1

and Management by Objectives (MBO). More recently, there has been a lively interest in strategic planning (or, as some prefer to call it, open-system planning), a major element of which is the open involvement of many constituencies in formulating directions for the future.

In 1981 the passage of the Omnibus Budget Reconciliation Act, which substituted block grants for many categorical aid programs and transferred responsibility for setting priorities and funding programs from the federal government to the states, eliminated about 80 percent of the laws that contained requirements for needs assessment. Nevertheless, school systems and social service agencies continue to conduct needs assessments, and several state educational agencies require that local educational agencies conduct needs assessments for their five-year plans. The consolidation of former categorical aid programs and the block grant provisions have also encouraged local agencies to examine their priorities closely and to document their needs, since they are now in competition with all other agencies in the state for their share of the state allocation.

Interest in needs assessment developed later in Canada than in the United States and was not supported by federal legislation or funding opportunities. Several provinces have recently developed new models and procedures for educational needs assessment, particularly for higher and continuing education. Other needs assessments have arisen from evaluation rather than planning efforts. Human services needs surveys are also done by Canadian social agencies, but not necessarily under government auspices. Needs assessments have also been undertaken in several developing countries, and studies of groups with special needs have been sponsored by the United Nations Educational, Scientific, and Cultural Organization (UNESCO).

Terminology and Scope

This book views needs assessment broadly as any systematic procedure for setting priorities and making decisions about programs and allocation of resources. The process is both objective and value laden. It involves the collection and analysis of data from many sources and the resolution of many viewpoints. It enlists the perceptions of constituent groups who are now, or who may potentially be, affected by decisions growing out of the needs assessment. Needs assessment is an integral part of organizational and community planning. It does not end with analysis of data but rightly extends into the program-planning phase, guiding the selection of alternative solutions. Its purpose is not to suggest solutions, however, but to identify those areas where solutions are most required and to set criteria for their resolution.

There is no good substitute for a systematic, reasonably objective way of assessing needs in order to make decisions about priorities for services or programs. The alternative is to leave decisions on priorities to the unverified judgments of decision makers, which are based on opinion, preference, bias, or the satisfaction of special interests. For all that, needs are ultimately questions of values and philosophy, and technical methods can neither identify nor analyze them completely. Quantitative methods of needs identification and analysis must be balanced by qualitative procedures that take values into consideration. This book offers both theoretical and applied approaches—concepts derived from model building and research but with due regard for the practicalities necessary when conducting assessments and utilizing the results in actual organizational and community settings.

The book discusses and synthesizes practices from many fields and in different settings—education, human services, government, community planning, and business. The terms used to indicate important constituent groups span the different types of settings. The process of needs assessment involves a partnership among three groups—service providers, service receivers, and stakeholders. The term *service* is used in a broad sense, to indicate not only the public sector but also business and industry, even when the latter are concerned with products rather than services. *Service providers* refers to agencies, institutions, organizations, and the people in them who offer services or develop programs and products and who conduct or sponsor the needs assessment. *Service receivers* are those persons, either inside or outside the organization or agency, who are the actual or potential beneficiaries of the services or products and whose needs are being assessed. *Stakeholders* are all other people, agencies (including regulatory government agencies), or organizations having an interest in the assessment and in those whose needs are being assessed.

In education, service providers are educational institutions and their teachers, administrators, counselors, and other staff; service receivers are students; and stakeholders are parents, employers, and other interested members of the community. In human services, service providers are agencies and their administrators and staff, service receivers are clients and patients, and stakeholders are other agencies, families of clients, and members of the community. In the private sector, service providers are businesses and industry, service receivers are consumers and clients, and stakeholders are the general public.

Another term used throughout this book is *needs assessor*, which indicates any individuals or groups who are in charge of the needs assessment. It is a shorthand term referring not only to the person who directs the assessment but also to committees, advisory groups, and others with responsibility for the design or conduct of the assessment.

The book refers many times to decision makers, planners, and policy boards. The viewpoint of the book is mainly from the perspective of planning rather than evaluation, although concepts from the latter perspective are also included. *Decision makers* are people within an organization, usually at the managerial level, who have the authority to approve a needs assessment and to make decisions about its utilization in program planning and resource allocation. *Planners* may or may not be decision makers in that sense, but they have responsibility for developing objectives and plans and are usually involved in the design and implementation of the needs assessment. *Policy boards* are school boards, agency boards, boards of trustees, and the like, who have the broad responsibility for authorizing the needs assessment and for adopting or rejecting recommendations from the assessment results.

Three other terms are also used in special ways throughout the book. *Primary needs assessment* focuses on needs of service receivers. *Secondary needs assessment* focuses on needs of the organization or of service providers. Finally, *needs study* is, in many places, used synonymously with *needs assessment*, particularly when the assessment has been undertaken as a project and is not an ongoing part of the planning process.

This chapter reviews how both theorists and practitioners define needs and needs assessment and the caveats they raise about those terms, discusses the purposes of needs assessments and the settings or contexts in which they typically occur, and places the process in a cycle of planning-implementation-evaluation of educational and human services programs.

Definitions of Need

What is a need? What does it mean to assess needs? For terms that have been in common use for a long time and have been linked to elaborate, often costly projects and studies, they are remarkably ambiguous. There is even controversy as to whether needs can be known or whether the term *needs assessment* should be discarded altogether.

Yet even if the terms were no longer used, the referents would still remain, and new terms would have to be invented. The *referent* is a complex of processes, sometimes not formalized, by which people decide, on behalf of an organization or a community, what goals to pursue, what their priorities are, and which ones have first claim on the pool of available resources. When those processes are systematic, when they are defined and delimited, and when they use data and opinions from sources other than the decision makers alone, that complex of processes is usually termed a *needs assessment*. Other terms proposed have been needs analysis, situational analysis, problem identification, forward planning, needs identification, needs sensing, and resource-allocation strategy. None of these are in widespread use, however, and some of them refer only to a part of the process.

In common usage, a *need* is "whatever is required for the health or well-being of a person," such as oxygen, food, or love (Gould and Kolb, 1964, p. 462). In personality theory, a need is "anything a person wants with sufficient consistency over time for this to be treated as a feature of his personality" (p. 462). Need is also generally understood to indicate a state or condition, such as Maslow's (1954) hierarchy of needs from the physical (at the lowest level of survival) to self-actualization (the highest level). When used as a verb, *need* means wants or requirements, as in the statements "He needs food," "The schools need more money," or "Poor people need better access to health care."

In the context of needs assessment, however, the term *need* is properly used only as a noun with the denotation of a discrepancy or gap between some desired or acceptable condition or state of affairs and the actual or observed or perceived condition or state of affairs (Kaufman, 1972; Witkin, 1977a; Anderson and Ball, 1978; Houston and others, 1978; Kaufman and English, 1979). Kaufman (1982a) defines it more precisely as a "gap between What Is and What Should Be in terms of *results*" (p. 73, Kaufman's emphasis). In this book the terms *status* and *standards* will often be used instead of "what is" and "what should be."

The type of discrepancy defined in the needs assessment depends on the level at which the needs are assessed. There are two levels—primary-level needs reside in individuals who are actual or potential receivers of educational, economic, or social services; secondary-level needs are in the institution, agency, or organization. At the individual level, the needs of students or clients or members of a community are assessed. At the organizational level, the needs of the agency or school system or government body and its resources, delivery systems, and personnel are assessed.

These levels can be made clearer by examples from the educational and human services fields. At the student level, especially in elementary and secondary schools, educators have generally defined a need as the discrepancy between a desired level of student performance (or ability, knowledge, skill, or attitude) and an actual or perceived level of student academic or other performance. At the institutional level, a need is the discrepancy between the resources required to meet the student needs and the actual resources available. Institutional needs relate to curricular and cocurricular programs, equipment and facilities, instructional materials, and personnel. In the latter category are in-service or staff-development needs.

The discrepancy definition of educational needs is sometimes modified or made more specific for particular purposes. Thus, when assessing the needs of the region served by the Appalachia Educational Laboratory and transmitting this information to the national research and development community, researchers defined need as "the discrepancy between current and desired status which is an unresolved educational concern, which emphasizes educational equity and improved educational practice, and which is eventually amenable to either short- or long-term R&D [research and development] solutions" (Shively, 1980, p. 10).

The discrepancy approach is also used to define human services needs, although the definition often combines both the individual and the institutional levels. "An identified service need coupled with an absence of a program to meet the need represents a gap, an 'unmet need.' High need, coupled with insufficient programs, documented low level of resources, and/or waiting lists, indicate that either additional services or improved efficiency of existing programs are called for" (Kamis, 1981, pp. 37–38). The discrepancy to be assessed is not in performance of clients but rather in the services or resources to be supplied to clients to meet their needs. An analogous situation exists when needs assessments are used to design or modify educational curricula, in which case there is an interaction between student needs and curriculum/resource needs. The two types of needs must be defined together.

Moroney (1977) identified four distinct categories of need in human services planning: normative, perceived, expressed, and relative. The normative definition proposes standards such as numbers of nursing-home beds or Meals on Wheels. Ratios of existing services are then compared with ratios proposed in the standards. Perceived needs are defined by what people consider their needs to be—the consumer point of view. Expressed need is revealed by the number of people who actually seek a service. Relative needs are measured by the "gap between services existing in different geographical areas, weighted to account for the differences in population and social pathology" (Moroney, 1977, p. 137). Relative need is concerned with equity of services to different population groups and geographical areas, not with desirable standards toward which to work.

A need may also be regarded as a set of problems perceived either by service receivers or by observers or service providers (Rossi, Freeman, and Wright, 1979). This definition implies a discrepancy but does not include it directly. In their discussion of assessing community-service needs, Siegel, Attkisson, and Carson (1978) remark that need is a relative concept at best and that "the definition of need depends primarily upon those who undertake the identification and assessment effort" (p. 216). They cite Nguyen, Attkisson, and Bottino (1976), who define an unmet need as a condition in which "a problem in living, a dysfunctional somatic or psychological state, or an undesirable social process is recognized, for which a satisfactory solution requires a major mobilization of additional resources and/or a major reallocation of existing resources" (Siegel, Attkisson, and Carson, p. 216).

Also departing from the discrepancy definition, Stufflebeam viewed a need as "something that can be shown to be necessary or useful for the fulfillment of some defensible purpose." He identified three viewpoints: the democratic, the diagnostic, and the analytic. In the democratic view, a need is "a change desired by the majority of some reference group." The diagnostic view considers a need as "something whose absence or deficiency proves harmful," while in the analytic view, a need is "the direction in which improvement can be predicted to occur, given information about current status." The analytic emphasis is on systematic problem solving and improvement (cited in Shively, 1980, pp. 7–8).

Although both the discrepancy and problem-identification definitions of need appear to be fairly straightforward, in practice there has been considerable ambiguity in the use of the term. In education, the term has often been used to describe a *problem* (such as vandalism or excessive absenteeism from school), a *program* (such as a remedial reading program), a *symptom* (such as low test scores in mathematics), a *resource* (such as teacher aides in the classroom or more money for instructional materials), and a *solution* to a problem (such as stricter disciplinary measures or a new method of teaching a basic skill). In fact, reports of needs assessments by school districts often contain a list of wants and wishes rather than a set of needs according to the discrepancy definition. Assessments of human services needs also frequently use the term *need* as synonymous with problems, programs, resources, and desires.

Some writers have felt that the term *education need* has been so overworked it has lost its precise meaning—if it ever had any

(Instructional Systems Group, 1974; Bank and Morris, 1979; Mattimore-Knudson, 1983). Misanchuk (1982b) found the literature of needs identification and assessment "awash with adjectives"; needs are described as basic, felt, expressed, normative, comparative, real, educational, real educational, symptomatic, universal, integrative, goal discrepancy, social discrepancy, wants or desired discrepancy, and expectancy discrepancy, among others (p. 1).

Moroney (1977) observes that in most social legislation, the concept of need is "often buried in phrases so global that it has little value for placing boundaries on the planning task [or is] . . . employed so narrowly that specific services are mandated. . . .[It] is rarely operationalized" (p. 133). In many needs assessment reports, the term *need* is used to indicate both the discrepancy and the desired state. In his wide-ranging critique, Kimmel (1977) insists that the term *need* is basically empty, "without conceptual boundaries. If the term is to have an operational meaning it must be defined in a specific context, usually by the use of absolute or relative (comparative) criteria or standards" (p. 11). In fact, Myers and Koenigs (1979) declare that a need is a function of the type of needs assessment being conducted, and until the type is defined, the need cannot be defined. The ambiguous nature of the concept can be seen in the fact that there are no commonly accepted standards of human need, other than for food; a widely cited global measure of need, the so-called poverty line, constantly fluctuates and is subject to much debate (Kimmel, 1977).

Among those who advocate discarding the term *need* altogether, because of its ambiguity and the fact that it never refers to a definite class of things, is Mattimore-Knudson (1983), who argues that, instead, one should use terms that simply describe a state of affairs. Thus, for adult education, "rather than doing 'needs assessments, identifications and analyses,' adult educators should do 'situation assessments, identifications, and analyses.' That is, they should, for example, investigate a community and make a report of what they observed, rather than impose a hollow concept like need by asking people what they do or do not need" (p. 119). He favors the term *situational analysis.* His criticism is really directed at the use of *need* as a verb, and his preferred term is limited to the status element in needs assessment.

Concurring in the criticism of the widespread imprecise and contradictory uses of the term *need*, Beatty (1981) proposes a definition of need as a foundation for social practice that modifies the discrepancy definition: "Need is the measurable discrepancy existing between a present state of affairs and a desired state of affairs as asserted either by an 'owner' of need or an 'authority' on need" (p. 40). The "owner's" need is described as motivational and the "authority's" as prescriptive. Her perspective is community development and adult education, but the definition is widely applicable.

A *prescriptive need* "is a discrepancy between a present state of affairs and a specific publicly prescribed goal for a given community" (p. 41). The goal may or may not be the same as the standard or norm within a given society or community. Beatty considers the differences among the three concepts (goal, standard, and norm) to be important in defining needs. "The standard is the lowest limit of a condition or situation held acceptable or tolerable by a society or community. The norm is the average or typical manifestation of a given condition or situation. . . . The goal is the asserted desired level of a given situation or condition" (p. 40). Both standards and norms in a given community or social setting must be taken into account when proclaiming goals.

A *motivational need* is "a deficiency relative to a specific individually defined and owned, desired end state or goal," but it is not synonymous with a want or desire, or with a present degraded condition (p. 42). Motivational and prescriptive needs are not mutually exclusive. Beatty has worked out a goal-state continuum that illustrates standards, norms, and goals in varying relationships to motivational and prescriptive needs. She proposes that the needs assessment process build a data base in which both kinds of need data are identified and their integrity is respected. Practitioners can then determine who are the owners and who are the authorities on need for any major goal domain or continuum.

In a different attempt to bring some specificity to the term, Roth (1978, pp. 32-33) posits five types of need based on the discrepancy formula $X - A = N$, where X is the target state, A is the actual state, and N is the need. She suggests that there are five different types of needs possible, depending on how the target state

X is defined. Thus, X could represent in ideal, desired, expected, norm, or minimally sufficient state, leading to the following types of deficits:

$$\text{ideal state} - \text{actual state} = \text{goal deficit}$$
$$\text{desired state} - \text{actual state} = \text{want deficit}$$
$$\text{expected state} - \text{actual state} = \text{expectancy deficit}$$
$$\text{norm} - \text{actual state} = \text{norm deficit}$$
$$\text{minimal sufficient state} - \text{actual state} = \text{essential deficit}$$

Roth drew upon earlier work by Scriven and Roth (1978) for the concept "A needs X." In that formulation, "a need is the gap between the actual and the satisfactory." Further, "A needs X means A is or would be in an unsatisfactory condition without X in a particular respect, and would or does significantly benefit from X in that respect; thereby moving towards or achieving but not surpassing a satisfactory condition in this respect" (p. 3). In other words, A is dependent on X, X's effect on A is beneficial, and an absence of X leaves A in an unsatisfactory condition.

This definition has the advantage of being more explicit than most, but it also shifts the meaning of *need* from a deficit or discrepancy state to that which will satisfy the need. This is partly because *need* as a noun is different from *need* as a verb. For example, as a noun, a need might be described by the statement that Jim, a seventh-grade student, is reading at a third-grade level; therefore there is a discrepancy of four grade levels between the desired (or normative) reading level for seventh-grade students and Jim's actual performance. But the verb usage "A needs X" implies that Jim would need something to overcome that discrepancy, perhaps remedial reading instruction. That, however, is a possible solution to the need; it is not the need itself. Jim might just as well "need" corrective glasses, in-depth diagnostic assessment, or special training geared to a learning disability—or all three. In fact, there are many semantic problems involved with the use of the term *need* as a noun or as a verb. In the Scriven and Roth (1978) formula A needs X, the need, or X, seems to be construed as a solution to the need rather than a discrepancy state. This is a confusion of means and ends (Kaufman, 1982b). The later formulation by Roth (1978), $X - A = N$, however, does clarify the discrepancy definition.

Frisbie (1981) argues that most presentations of the concept of need (as a change from the real to the ideal) do not represent the complexity of the needs-assessment process. Combining formulations by Roth (1978), Scriven and Roth (1977), and Guba and Lincoln (1981), Frisbie (pp. 3-4) constructed this test for a genuine need:

1. $Nc = Dt - Da$ [where Nc = a need candidate, Dt = some target state within a specified domain, and Da = some corresponding actual state within that specified domain]; and
2. with the Nc, a subject receives some otherwise unrealised benefit; and
3. without the Nc, the subject is in an unsatisfactory state.

The above formula is in the context of evaluation not of planning, and the Nc is a service, product, or program that would benefit someone—hence it represents a secondary-level need. The primary need and the two dimensions from which the discrepancy or need state is inferred are not specified.

Frisbie (p. 4) tested the formula by generating an exhaustive list of hypothetical cases that included all the possible combinations of events that can occur, using the generalized change formula

$\Delta D = D2 - D1$, where
ΔD = a change within a specified domain,
$D2$ = state 2 within a specified domain, and
$D1$ = state 1 within a specified domain.

Frisbie set three conditions to determine whether a change between states contitutes a need state, generating the list of hypothetical cases by systematically varying $D1$, $D2$, and T (the target state) in relation to each other. By graphing these relationships and applying the following criteria, he found that only two out of seventy-five relationships satisfied the definition of a need. Because

Frisbie found the match between the hypothetical cases and this definition of a need to be inadequate, he dropped the requirement for independently considering a target state (T) and defined need, opportunity, and cost in terms of the thirteen remaining cases:

> A *need* for a characterized change is said to exist if that change is appraised (a) to be beneficial and (b) to diminish the severity of an unacceptable condition. . . .
> An *opportunity* is said to be presented by a characterized change if that change is appraised (a) to be beneficial and (b) to enhance an acceptable condition. . . .
> A *cost* is said to accompany a characterized change if that change is appraised to be detrimental. This detrimental change may also be appraised to either (a) diminish an acceptable condition—an *acceptable* cost . . . or (b) increase the severity of an unacceptable condition—an *unacceptable* cost [pp. 9–10, Frisbie's emphases].

Frisbie solves the problem of distinguishing between changes that are needed and those that are wanted by noting that "without a needed change, the subject is in an unsatisfactory state, while without a wanted change, the subject would still be in a satisfactory state" (p. 10). To avoid the implication that a beneficial state is somehow self-indulgent, he uses the term *opportunity* rather than *want*.

In the human services field, the needs of individuals implicitly have to do with the quality of life. If one thinks in terms of either survival needs or Maslow's hierarchy of needs, the idea, as Moroney (1977) points out, is a "normative concept that is subject to temporal shifts" (p. 134). According to Moroney, the three facts that have influenced the definition of need—the standard of living, the sociopolitical environment, and the availability of resources and existence of technology—have all changed and shifted their bases with the passage of time. For example, as the cost of living has increased, the poverty line has had to be raised. A generation ago, universal daycare for working mothers was hardly considered whereas today it is accepted as normal and even desirable. And only after the public showed itself willing for government to allocate a greater portion of its resources to social needs did policies regarding the alleviation of poverty and problems of the elderly become viable.

Definitions of Needs Assessment

The most comprehensive definition of needs assessment is Kaufman's (1982a): "A needs assessment is a *formal* analysis that shows and documents the gaps between current results and desired results (ideally concerned with gaps in OUTCOMES), arranges the gaps (NEEDS) in priority order, selects the NEEDS to be resolved" (p. 75, Kaufman's emphasis). The needs assessment may identify gaps in results that show either too little or too much of something. Kaufman also views needs assessment as a tool for problem identification and justification, a tool that requires the consensus of partners in planning and setting priorities on needs (Kaufman and English, 1979).

Although the literature shows a certain consensus on the definition of a needs assessment, especially in the concept of a discrepancy, there is much less agreement on what elements or components comprise the assessment itself. In the mid 1970s, a comprehensive review of the state of the art in educational needs assessment found that methods ranged from simplistic public-opinion-type surveys to complex systems procedures of broad scope (Witkin, 1977a, 1977c). After reviewing human services needs studies from several sources, Kimmel (1977) found claims such as the following: It is a change-oriented process; it should attempt to define what is required "to insure that a population is able to function at an acceptable level in various domains of living"; it resolves many viewpoints on a state's high-priority or urgent needs; it provides a measure of demand for services "against which the service goals and objectives should be set"; it "identifies the incidence, prevalence, and nature of certain conditions within a community"; it assesses the adequacy of existing services and resources (pp. 8–9). He concluded that "the label 'needs assessment' may be applied to any approach, procedure, or method ranging from 'thinking sessions' to technically complicated surveys" (p. 33). Further, "the literature contains many varied views of needs assessment. It appears that needs assessment can be almost anything: a change-oriented *process,* a *method* for enumeration and description, an *analytical procedure,* a *decision-making* process, a process for the 'resolution of many viewpoints,' etc." (p. 8, Kimmel's emphasis).

Needs assessments can be categorized into two or more types, depending on the classification system. Roth (1978) recognizes two types: preparatory (when a product or program is being planned) and retrospective (when the product already exists or the program has been implemented). It is not clear from her discussion how a retrospective needs assessment differs from summative evaluation.

Kaufman and English (1979) recommend different categories: internal and external. The internal needs assessment is "a gap analysis which allows for the investigation and determination of needs to be restricted to the boundaries of the organization sponsoring the assessment. It assumes (knowingly or unknowingly) that the basic assumptions and ground rules of the organization are correct, or implies that they cannot be challenged" (p. 343). An external needs assessment is "a gap analysis which requires that the underlying basis for planning and accomplishment be the future survival and contribution in the world to which learners will go when they exit educational agencies and enter society. Any needs assessment has to consider both current societal requirements and future ones" (p. 342). Kaufman later used the term *self-sufficiency* instead of *survival.*

Another way of classifying needs assessments is by the focus of the assessment—whether the focus is on the needs of individuals (learners, clients) or on the needs of the organization (school system, human services agency). These types were described earlier as primary- and secondary-level needs assessments (Witkin, 1978; Kenworthy and others, 1980).

In her research on needs assessment in higher education, Roth (1978) used a factor analysis to identify six elements or stages of the needs assessment process: (1) educational goals or philosophy given as a point of departure, (2) need identification and need prioritization, (3) treatment selection, (4) treatment implementation, (5) evaluation, and (6) modification and recycle. Roth uses the term *needs assessment* in a special way: "It seems a better use of terminology to view needs assessment as *ending after treatment selection and implementation.* The stages of evaluation, modification, and recycle belong under the heading of evaluation. However, the fact that functionally these later stages are evaluation activities should not obscure the fact that they need to be included whenever a needs assessment is undertaken" (p. 130, my emphasis).

The Place of Values in Needs Assessment

The discrepancy definition of a need often specifies that "what is" and "what should be" are the two elements for which data should be gathered. But the very decisions as to what kinds of data to look for, and the appropriate indicators for the actual and desired states, involve the matter of values. Who should determine what should be? What types and quantities of data and opinions, from what sources, are sufficient to describe what is? Personal and social values enter into every step of the needs assessment process.

Needs assessment is also viewed as "primarily a political process in which the feasible, the opportunities, and the threats within the environment are carefully weighed and measured in light of existing value structures. *By avoiding the notion of absolute need,* the planner might focus on the more salient issue of determining which need can be legitimized. Although many problems have an array of powerful indicators, they could remain in a position of low priority until recognition legitimizes them" (Capoccia and Googins, 1982, p. 34; my emphasis).

The value-based nature of needs is emphasized by Siegel, Attkisson, and Carson (1978, p. 20), who recommend that the following factors be kept in mind when identifying human services needs:

1. Needs are relative to the perceiver and are based on values, culture, past history, and experiences of the individual and the community.
2. Human social-service needs are not singular, easily identifiable entities, but are diffuse and interrelated.
3. Communities and their needs are dynamic and in a state of constant flux.

4. The process of translating human services needs
    into community programs is influenced by char-
    acteristics of human resources, availability of
    adequate technology, and financing considera-
    tions.

From a somewhat different point of view, the question of
values is addressed by Mattimore-Knudson (1983) in relation to
what he calls the hedonistic nature of the concept of need. "In the
final analysis, it seems no matter how the term need is used, it
implies some degree of happiness, unhappiness, pleasure, or dis-
pleasure." Thus, program planners and evaluators "are faced with
the problem of determining *which* need and *whose* need should be
regarded as the basis of planning and evaluating programs" (p. 122,
Mattimore-Knudson's emphasis). Should the needs of learners or of
educators be of most importance, or does one group of needs have
greater value then another?

Guba and Lincoln (1982) have analyzed the place of values
in needs assessment more precisely. Building upon the work of
Roth and Scriven, they define need as "a requisite or desideratum
generated as a discrepancy between a target state and an actual state,
if and only if the presence of the conditions defined by the target
state can be shown significantly to benefit an S and the absence of
those conditions can be shown significantly to harm, indispose, or
constrain an S" (p. 313). The subject S may be an individual, family,
organization, group, or other need candidate.

With this definition of need, Guba and Lincoln deduce that
values enter into the process of needs assessment in six places: (1)
identification of the domain of the target state, (2) designation of
the target state to be used in determining the discrepancy between
T and A, (3) the operationalization of T and A, (4) the designation
of the difference $T - A$ that will be regarded as significant, (5) the
determination of what shall constitute a benefit, and (6) the
determination of what shall constitute an unsatisfactory state (pp.
313-316). They argue that "needs assessments in any particular
setting can have no meaning unless they are tied to local values"
and that "an approach to needs assessment that ignores the inescap-
able rooting of needs in values is a delusion at best and a snare at

worst," particularly because we live in a society with sharp variations in values among individuals or groups with a stake in the
needs assessment (p. 312).

Purposes and Settings of Needs Assessments

The needs assessment models and procedures described in
this book are intended to provide managers and policy makers with
data useful for decision making at the organizational, not the
individual, level. Thus, for example, the analysis should provide
the basis for decisions about services to developmentally disabled
adults or about adaptation of classroom instruction to children with
learning disabilities but not for decisions about what to do specifically about elderly Mrs. Jones or with Johnny in the eighth grade
who is reading at fourth-grade level. Needs studies provide group
data, not individual diagnoses.

Demone (1978, p. 73) offers two criteria for when to do a
needs assessment: (1) when there is great likelihood that it will
influence program decisions and (2) when resources to do an
adequate job can be generated. He recommends not doing a needs
assessment (1) when the data are likely to be irrelevant to critical
problems or policy issues, (2) when the potential user is strongly
resistant to the use of such data, (3) when the methodology is weak,
in that the methods chosen will not yield results that can be
usefully used for decisions, (4) when the results will be too late for
effective use, (5) when there are strong differences of opinion among
different management levels on the purpose and uses of the needs
assessment, and (6) when the organization lacks the capacity to
follow through in utilizing the results.

Moroney (1977) points out that analysis of needs linked with
long-range planning enables chief executives and agency heads to
balance political pressures for allocation of resources with objective
criteria on hierarchies of need and of priorities; and that lack of
needs assessment can cause an unnecessary waste of scarce resources.
Scriven (1981) notes instances in industry in which "sloppy needs
assessment" led to invalid conclusions about consumer needs. The
varying purposes and rationales for performing needs assessments

are illustrated by examining the settings in which they typically occur—education, human service agencies, government bodies, community action groups, and the private-sector.

Educational Settings. The education sector includes not only formal institutions and programs from preschool to university level and community-based adult education but also formal and informal programs (which could be labeled either education or training) for adults in many settings within the community: human services agencies, business and industry, hospitals, the military, libraries, trade institutions, professional associations, religious institutions, and community-service associations. In school systems, training needs are generally called in-service or staff-development needs.

The most common purposes for *local education agencies* (LEAs) to analyze needs at the school site or district level are (1) to satisfy requirements of federal or state funding sources for categorical and competitive programs—to document the application for funds and to show that the funded program will address critical unmet needs, (2) to identify those who comprise a target group of students, such as the handicapped, certain minorities, or the non-English-speaking, and to analyze their needs, (3) to reach a consensus on goals for districtwide master planning, (4) to identify where innovative programs could solve a problem or enhance learning and to justify support for such programs, (5) to improve existing curricula or to design new ones, (6) to provide a defensible basis for redistributing scarce resources among competing curricular and cocurricular programs and activities, and (7) to analyze in-service development needs for instructional and support staff.

A major impetus for *state educational agencies* (SEAs) to conduct statewide needs assessments came from legislation that required states to submit plans for disbursing funds for supplementary centers and innovative programs under Title III of the Elementary and Secondary Education Act of 1965 (ESEA, Public Law 89–10; see Beers and Campbell, 1973, and Zangwill, 1977). Even without the stimulus of federal laws or regulations, many states conduct periodic studies to assess needs of all students in the state and to set priorities for five-year planning by state boards. State-level assessments are also done to provide state legislatures with information about student achievement, which may then support new legislation. Statewide studies have ranged from enlisting public support for goals for public education to documenting needs through a variety of consensus-forming activities to testing all or a sample of students in communication skills and mathematics (for representative examples see Center for Statewide Educational Assessment, 1973, and Hershkowitz, 1974).

Needs assessments in *higher education* tend to focus less on discrepancy analyses at the student performance level and more on gathering data for institutional planning or on obtaining consensus on broad goals or on various aspects of the curricula or of university or college management. Community colleges are also interested in the relevance of their curricula to local and regional job markets. Regional planning is occasionally done through cooperative needs assessments of a university and its feeder community colleges. Community colleges in some provinces in Canada, in collaboration with universities, have recently undertaken broad-based assessments of community needs in order to develop more effective plans and programs for adult education throughout the province.

A specialized use of needs assessment at all educational levels is to develop or modify a *curriculum*. In that context English and Kaufman (1975) state that "needs assessment is a process of defining the desired end (or outcome, product, or result) of a given sequence of curriculum development. . . . It is neither a curriculum itself, nor should it embrace any set of assumptions or specifications about the type of curriculum which ought to be developed to best reach the ends desired and defined" (p. 34). Needs assessments are also used to identify curriculum needs of particular target groups—the differential English-language needs of foreign students in various major fields of study and academic levels in higher education, for example (Robertson, 1982).

Departing from the discrepancy, student-performance-centered concept, Cloud (1973, pp. 35-36) views curriculum development needs and priorities as "specific areas or parts of the curriculum which are cited by interviewees as needing expansion, revision, or deletion." Curriculum developers believe that a project to design a new curriculum should be undertaken only when a verified need is not being met (Pratt, 1980). Pratt includes in the needs assessment process the step of considering alternative ways of meeting needs and notes that a new curriculum should be designed only when it is a preferred alternative.

Another purpose of educational needs assessment is to analyze *information needs* rather than learner or program needs. An example is the analysis of needs for communicating information to the educational research and development community. The National Institute of Education set up a network of research and development exchanges with regional centers in various parts of the United States. A needs assessment is considered part of the feedforward process, which is defined as "the process of communicating practitioner needs and concerns to the R&D community with the intent of increasing the responsiveness of that community to those needs and concerns" (Sikorski, Oakley, and Lloyd-Kolkin, 1977, p. 1). The process attempts to synthesize existing data in order to "look for goals, trends, or projections of the future and the discrepancies or dissatisfactions that signal the existence of real educational needs" (p. 3). The information is intended to guide research and development planning and policies and thus to produce specific action.

Human Services Settings. The human services sector refers to "those publicly supported agencies which deliver health care, mental health care, social services, and special education" (Curtis, 1981, p. 2). Human services may be conceptualized either in their vertical structure (from the federal government down to local operations) or as a work force of professionals and paraprofessionals from such fields as medicine and social work. Curtis also suggests a third view, in which all agencies and professionals are conceptually consolidated into four organizational functions: (1) providing income for the poor, (2) creating households for those who cannot live independently, (3) reducing or helping individuals with impairments, and (4) training and placing the unemployed. This third view emphasizes not just public expenditures but also ways in which clients can participate actively in the process of change, especially in regard to their information-sharing role.

According to Kamis (1981, p. 28), "needs assessment data identify and describe health and social disabilities in a defined community in order that service providers plan and improve programs." It is also essential that any discussion of needs assessment in the human services sector include the concept of at-risk populations, which "has been inherent in such programs as Model Cities, maternal and infant care projects, services for school children and preschoolers, manpower, and the wide range of antipoverty programs. Those activities and efforts in the social services field are based on the principle of channeling resources to 'high risk' areas in which there are large concentrations of high risk families and individuals" (Moroney, 1977, p. 139).

Assessing human services needs is a complex task. Identification and assessment of human services needs are complicated by the facts that needs are relative to the perceiver, that they are diffuse and interrelated and in a state of constant flux, and that they cannot be translated into community programs without taking into consideration the technology, characteristics of human resources, and considerations of finance (Siegel, Attkisson, and Carson, 1978).

Human services needs assessment is often focused on resource assessment, in which the discrepancies of concern are those between the actual and a desired/optimal level of services, often for a specified population. Moroney (1977) raises the issue of distinguishing between planning for *services* and planning to meet human services *needs*. The danger of planning for services is that they "tend to take on a life of their own, thereby reducing their flexibility and inhibiting efforts to initiate change through experimentation" (p. 131). Thus, for example, the elderly may be thought to need homemaker care, or Meals on Wheels (a situation similar to that referred to earlier regarding a student's need for a remedial reading program). Moroney urges that the traditional approach of planning for services be replaced by a rational approach to problem analysis and assessment of need. The focus, which would then be on the needs of people rather than on the existing network of human services programs, would thus stimulate independence from the status quo.

Groups such as United Way also conduct needs studies, usually in their annual planning for the following year's budget. The assessment task is to gather data that will be useful in systematic planning and in determining the basis of allocations of funds to agencies with competing demands (United Way of King County, 1982).

Agencies often conduct a needs assessment not to uncover new problems but to justify the desirability of a program or social intervention that is already known. The study verifies the extent, nature, and conditions of the problem and identifies and locates target populations. The needs study is considered a critical first step in the design of a social intervention—to verify that a problem exists "in sufficient degree and extent to warrant an intervention" (Rossi, Freeman, and Wright, 1979, p. 86). Needs assessment in this context is defined as the verification and mapping out of the extent and location of a problem and its attendant target population.

Community and Government Settings. With the goal of setting priorities for new programs or services, many cities conduct comprehensive studies to elicit the concerns and needs of all segments of the population in the community. Since the data collected typically range over a broad spectrum of problems and services, the analyses can generate information useful not only to city government but also to public and private agencies that serve the city and its environs. The major purpose of community assessment is usually to enlist widespread support in identifying and helping to solve certain social problems or to set priorities for city or regional planning, where the cooperation of many agencies and voluntary groups is desired. Still other community-based needs assessments may be instigated by voluntary or officially constituted community action groups to serve a variety of social, economic, or political ends.

A comprehensive guidebook for community needs assessments states that the purpose of needs assessment is "to produce a basic understanding of the nature and extent of the various social problems confronting the city's citizens" (League of California Cities, 1975, p. 7). According to the guidebook, the three elements of the assessment are problem identification, resource identification, and problem analysis.

Community needs assessments often focus on one or more specific problems that have high visibility in the community and have aroused anxiety and concern; such problems include drug or alcohol abuse or vandalism among the school-age population. In such instances, the study is undertaken not so much to identify the problem or the need area as to investigate contributing factors and to raise the level of commitment of parents and community groups to one of alleviating the problem on a cooperative basis. Communities may also conduct needs assessments to define the scope of a problem (drug abuse, for example, and the ages and groups affected, along with the impact on families and the community) in order to qualify for funding for special programs. Sometimes special programs include broader-based community needs studies during the life of the program as part of the intervention strategy.

Needs assessment has been used by some departments of the federal government, such as the Department of Agriculture, which developed guidelines for assessing needs in nutrition education and training. Needs assessment techniques have also been used for establishing programs for the U.S. Army (Roberts, Daubek, and Johnston, 1977). In 1971, the Board for Dynamic Training did a complete assessment to identify discrepancies between army requirements in the training system and what it was then doing. Extensive solution strategies were developed based on system discrepancies that the board identified. The formal needs assessment of the army's training system was repeated four years later.

Private-Sector Settings. Business and industry also conduct needs assessments, which may take the form of reexamining organizational goals or "the utility and validity of the criteria used in planning," for the purpose of organizational renewal (Kaufman and English, 1979, p. 323). More often, however, business concerns equate needs assessment with market research to determine the potential market for a new or revised product or service. That is, they assess the needs of the organization to sell a product rather than the needs of citizens to determine what kind of product would satisfy their requirements. Kaufman and English (pp. 324–325) point out that needs assessments in business and industry, as elsewhere, should be based on *outcome gap* analysis "in which the gaps between current outcomes and desired outcomes are defined external to the corporation and its product line. . . . In order to be optimally responsive, a company must look at the society at large and determine the survival and contribution levels of the clients."

Hospitals, business firms, and other private organizations also use methods of needs assessment to elicit employee and management concerns, analyze communication networks and gaps, and identify areas in which meeting critical needs of people in the organization will result in greater productivity or higher profits. In recent years as well, more business organizations are doing studies to identify needs for employee and management training. Many professional associations conduct periodic needs assessments to identify their members' interests in new programs and services or in changes in organizational goals or structure.

Needs Assessment in the
Planning-Implementation-Evaluation Cycle

Needs assessment is an integral and indispensable part of a comprehensive, systematic program-planning-implementation-evaluation cycle. Initially, needs assessment serves the purpose of forward planning as part of a system approach that includes problem and needs identification, search for alternative solutions, selection of one or more solutions, program installation and implementation, and finally, evaluation. It is a circular relationship in which evaluation of the adequacy and effects of programs that were installed to meet the needs leads logically into a new phase of needs assessment and planning. In subsequent cycles, the core of a new needs assessment can be formed from evaluation data supplemented by other information to help managers decide whether new priorities should be set or programs should be modified to meet the needs more effectively.

As MacQuarrie (1982) has pointed out, however, this circular relationship is undoubtedly oversimplistic. The relationship is actually more complex and interrelated. The process should include not only the identification and measurement of discrepancies but also the identification of valid and available treatments and resources, comparing alternative solutions with needs to determine whether they are the most appropriate. Needs assessment can also occur at any stage in the cycle.

Planning is often described as having four components—problem definition, problem (need) assessment, problem analysis, and evaluation (Capoccia and Googins, 1982). In a system approach to planning, the first three elements are properly in the domain of needs assessment, but recently, some evaluation theorists have treated needs assessment primarily in the context of evaluation rather than of program planning (Roth, 1978; Scriven and Roth, 1978; Guba and Lincoln, 1981). Certainly there is a close relationship between needs assessment and evaluation, particularly in regard to analyzing data in order to make decisions about programs. From the perspective of the planner, however, needs assessment looks *forward* to identify critical or unmet needs that should be addressed by new or revised programs, services, organizational structure, and the like. After the programs and services have been implemented, the evaluation (summative) looks *backward* to see how well they met the needs and whether they should be continued, modified, or dropped. The purpose of both needs assessment and evaluation is to provide information for decision making, and they often use similar data. But their timing in the life of a program and the decisions made on the basis of the data are different. Also, planners have a greater tendency than evaluators to consider needs assessment in a broad organizational context rather than just at the program level.

The perspective shifts when needs assessment is viewed as a component of evaluation rather than of planning. Rossing (1982, p. 7) explains the importance of the two processes and their relationship thus: "Needs assessments are vital in establishing value claims with respect to program accomplishments. Program evaluation is essential in verifying that certain approaches can indeed meet specified needs." Rothman (1980, p. 18) views needs assessment as an element in evaluation research: "Evaluation research, as envisioned here, is broad in scope. It involves the conducting of any kind of research within an organization to improve its functioning. It overlaps with operations research in that it entails such organizational inquiries as needs assessments, descriptive information about services to clients, the tracking of clients, task analysis of professional activities, cost/benefit analysis, and so on . . . whatever research efforts contribute to the effectiveness of a particular organization's performance in serving clients and meeting community needs."

Some needs assessments also include descriptive information about services and tracking of clients as well, although Rothman considers them evaluation activities that are different from needs assessment. One may also perform an assessment to establish the need for an evaluation (MacQuarrie, 1982) or to identify what those evaluation needs are—"If the adequacy or impact of a new program is being evaluated, a needs assessment may be necessary" (Demone, 1978, p.74).

Guba and Lincoln (1981, p. 51) posit a relationship between formative and summative evaluation on the one hand and between merit and worth on the other: "The purpose of formative adoptive (or worth) evaluations is to fit or adapt the program or curriculum to a local context or situation. . . . The purpose of summative adoptive (or worth) evaluation is to certify or warrant the adapted program or curriculum for permanent local use." In their formulation, needs assessment serves as a source of standards to (1) assess local context and values in the formative stage and (2) certify and warrant, by means of a local needs assessment, an entity for local use for an audience of local decision makers. In this view, then, a needs assessment is integral to the justification of program activities.

We have briefly noted the importance of values in determining needs and the fact that evaluation includes the concepts of merit and worth—that is, that the process identifies strengths as well as weaknesses. But the terms *need* and *needs assessment* have carried the connotations of lack, deficit, and deficiency rather than of strength—connotations that have been encouraged by the discrepancy definition of a need. This fact has led many people to view needs assessment as a negative process.

In her study of assessment models and practices, Roth (1978) found almost no attention given to assessment of strengths in addition to assessment of deficits or weaknesses. Several of her informants, however, felt that strengths assessment would furnish important information for decision makers. Possibly one reason that the concept of strengths assessment has not received wide acceptance is that needs have typically been defined as deficiencies rather than discrepancies. In addition, strengths are difficult to assess; it is easier to set minimal standards than maximal ones. The cyclical MIS model described in Chapter Two (Witkin, 1979c) provides one way to include assessment of strengths—by defining three levels of discrepancies, one of which incorporates standards of excellence.

In theory, then, needs assessments should be conducted as an integral part of a cyclical planning-implementation-evaluation process. In practice, however, needs assessment is not always tied as closely as it should be to planning and evaluation. Identifying and analyzing needs does not always lead to new or improved programs, evaluation data are often ignored by those charged with the assessment, and evaluation reports often fail to mention the extent to which previously identified needs have in fact been met by the program, or whether other, more important needs emerged during program implementation.

Then too, it is rare that needs assessments take place on a periodic basis as a regular part of a planning cycle. More typical is the one-shot assessment that fulfills a specific purpose and is not repeated. Some examples of exceptions are community-funding agencies such as United Way, regional studies conducted by an educational laboratory (Shively and Holcomb, 1981, 1982), state departments of education such as those in South Carolina where needs assessments are updated every five years to identify priorities for five-year plans or those in Pennsylvania where annual needs assessment information is required from school districts, and school systems such as the one in Lansing, Michigan that conducts annual needs assessments (Lansing School District, 1977, 1979, 1983). Continuation proposals for certain grants under federally funded programs should give evidence of ongoing and updated analyses of needs, but many do not. Subsequent chapters will describe models and procedures for using needs assessment more effectively for both planning and evaluation decisions.

2

Models of Needs Assessment: Choosing the Best Approach

There is no one model or conceptual framework for needs assessment that has been universally accepted, and there is little empirical evidence of the superiority of one approach over another. Moreover, there often appears to be an inverse ratio between the elegance and completeness of a model and its widespread acceptance and implementation. The diversity of approaches to needs assessment can be understood better by examining a variety of needs assessment models that have been developed for different purposes and contexts.

Kamis (1981), an expert in the field of human services needs assessment and planning, believes that there is no single definitive method of needs assessment, but rather that a variety of strategies ranging from direct to indirect measures may be employed, utilizing any one or a combination of four generic methods:

1. Direct assessment of needs via an epidemiological household survey
2. Tapping the perception of needs of either key community people or of community residents [key informants]
3. Inferring needs from patterns of ongoing service utilization [rates-under-treatment approach]
4. Inferring needs from known associations between social area characteristics and the prevalence of social and health problems [social area analysis and social indicators] [pp. 28–32].

29

Finding advantages and disadvantages with each of these procedures, Kamis observes: "The community survey is most direct and probably most valid, but it is also complex, extensive, and expensive. The key informant survey provides for important input and is easy, quick, and inexpensive. It is likely, however, to be biased. Rates-under-treatment . . . is weak . . . in addressing and assessing unmet needs. The use of social indicators . . . is indirect and inferential, but lends itself to quantitative manipulations and analytical procedures that range from the simple to the sophisticated" (pp. 32–33).

Educational needs assessments, however, rely heavily on surveys of goal preferences and perceptions of adequacy of student attainment, on indicators such as standardized test scores, and on group processes to achieve consensus on priorities of need. Problems and issues in educational needs assessments are somewhat different from those undertaken to identify human services needs. In elementary and secondary schools, targets of the needs assessment are within the system; in human services needs assessment, they are outside the system; in higher education and community planning, they may be either inside or outside the system sponsoring the assessment. Degree of control over the target groups and responsibilities for meeting their needs differ greatly in the different contexts.

There is also a paradox regarding the focus of effort in building models. Reports of school-system needs assessments in the United States show among constituent groups and across disparate communities a high degree of consensus regarding the goals of education, yet a large percentage of the effort devoted to model-building and data-gathering techniques has focused on goal preferencing and methods of determining priorities of goal importance. In human services and community planning, however, where public consensus on goals is much more problematical, needs assessors must often, by necessity, use needs assessment to justify the way they are allocating their resources; this leaves little scope for consideration of goals, innovative program planning, or organizational renewal.

Educational models have been strongly influenced by Kaufman's system approach, described later, and by ESCO, one of the earliest discrepancy models (Sweigert, Jr., 1968; Sweigert, Jr., and Kase, 1971). ESCO is an acronym for Educators, Students, and Consumers of the educational product (the three principal reference groups for the assessment) and student learning Objectives. The ESCO model assumes that the focus of the assessment should be on student learning objectives and that evidence of the extent to which those objectives are functional in the school system is the agreement of the three reference groups, whose relationship is depicted as forming the sides of an equilateral triangle. The concept of a needs assessment as a three-way partnership among those reference groups—who in this book are called service providers, service receivers, and stakeholders—is generalizable to any needs assessment in the public interest and has become commonplace in both education and human services.

In the past two decades, researchers, planners, and evaluators have developed many models—mathematical, strategic, conceptual—as well as practical kits, collections of instruments, handbooks, and management plans for the needs assessor (Witkin, 1976a, 1976b). The term *model* as used in this chapter means a conceptual framework for planning and conducting needs assessments, sometimes with the inclusion of strategies for gathering and analyzing data and setting priorities. The models selected are representative of many different professional and academic perspectives. Some developed from attempts to build theory from a broad perspective, others from grappling with a more limited conceptual problem, and others from the viewpoint of practical operations. All data-gathering methods referred to in the models are described and evaluated in subsequent chapters.

Choosing a Needs Assessment Approach

Which approach to needs assessment should one choose? The choice of models, procedures, and instruments should be guided by the purposes and context of the assessment and the decisions to be made on the basis of the findings. Two decision models that pose key questions are presented here as a guide to the needs assessor. The first is particularly applicable to human services planning; the second is for educational needs assessment. The concepts from both can be applied to other contexts. Although they were developed independently, they are based on the same premises: that there is no one right way to conduct a needs assessment that is applicable to all cases; that the data should be related to the purposes of the assessment, the organization's present knowledge, and the decisions that will be made; that needs assessment is not an isolated activity but part of a broad planning or development effort; and that after answering key questions, the needs assessor will be in a better position to make an informed judgment regarding the choice of data-collection approaches and instruments.

The first decision model is from a 1981 position paper by Cohen of the Management and Behavioral Science Center of the University of Pennsylvania. The second (Witkin, 1978a,b) was developed in a project funded by the National Institute of Education, through the Center for Educational Policy and Management of the University of Oregon, with contributions by staff from the Oregon State Department of Education, the Far West Laboratory for Educational Research, the Center for the Study of Evaluation at University of California, Los Angeles, and the Alameda County (California) Office of Education.

Human Services Decision Model. Believing that needs assessments too often become ends in themselves, Cohen (1981) intended his model to give planners and program administrators a broad framework as a guide to looking at needs assessment in their own organizational and political context and to choosing among various approaches if they should decide a needs assessment would be beneficial.

Cohen defines needs assessment as a process synonymous with problem setting or problem identification. It "should be equally concerned with *describing* present conditions and with *envisioning* conditions that ought to exist in the future" (p. 4, Cohen's emphasis). Program administrators are advised to consider the following:

1. Purpose in conducting the assessment—political advocacy, community mobilization, production of knowledge, an aid to decision making, part of a planning process, or because of a mandate

2. Specification of whose needs are being assessed—whether it is a broad population or a specific target group (It is especially important to define the unit of analysis—the client, the client and the family, or service agencies—and to decide whether to assess the needs of only those clients being presently served, or of those in need and not currently served, or of the community in general. Answers to these questions guide the choice of data-gathering methods.)

3. Identification of the users of the needs assessment and the extent of their influence for implementing the needs assessment (A common criticism of needs assessments is that often their results are not used. Cohen furnishes an exercise for stakeholder analysis intended to enable designers of a needs assessment to think through issues related to use and influence.)

4. Appraisal of the worth of existing estimates of need before undertaking a new study

5. Specification of products or outcomes of the assessment

6. Decision about the time frame and the regularity of collecting needs data—whether short-term for grant applications or long-term on a regular basis for a management information system

7. Analysis of resources available to conduct the needs assessment—both inside and outside the organization

Cohen argues that scientific validity should not be the sole criterion for choosing needs assessment procedures (nor is it even particularly important in some cases) and that some approaches are more appropriate than others for a given context and purpose. He also counters the suggestion that "the best strategy is to use many different methods simultaneously" (p. 11). As an alternative strategy, he offers the decision model in Figure 1, which relates purposes, time frame, and target groups to data sources and methods.

Educational Decision Model. This model is incorporated in two documents: a guidebook that addresses nine key questions and contains worksheets for local planners (Witkin, 1978a), and the *Needs Assessment Product Locator,* to which the guidebook is keyed (Witkin, 1978b). These publications were in response to a strong

Figure 1. Decision Model For Selecting a Needs Assessment Approach.

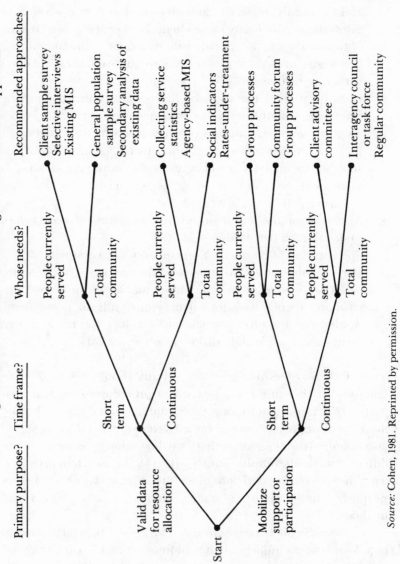

Source: Cohen, 1981. Reprinted by permission.

demand for materials that would relieve schools of the necessity for spending excessive time in product development, a task for which there was often little expertise. The definition of needs assessment is broad, going beyond discrepancy definitions: "any systematic procedure for setting priorities and making decisions about allocation of educational resources," the front end of educational planning, implementation, and evaluation (1978a, pp. iii–iv). The point of view is that needs assessments combine subjective judgments with empirical data to derive priorities.

Three of the nine key questions are similar to some in Cohen's model. As the needs assessment committee works through the questions in sequence, answering specifically for the local context, the focus of the assessment is sharpened to lead logically to the selection of an appropriate approach.

1. *Who wants a needs assessment?* There are two possible sources—external sources (such as requirements for funding, accrediting agencies, community pressure) or internal sources (such as desire for organizational change, staff pressures for system change, or change in patterns of student enrollment).

2. *Why is a needs assessment wanted?* Twenty sample reasons are given, including the usual ones of grant applications and planning for cutbacks in programs as well as some reasons that are not generally acknowledged, such as legitimizing what the schools are already doing, "getting the superintendent off the hook," continuing an established ritual of soliciting opinions before taking action, and raising the consciousness of constituent groups.

3. *What should be the scope of the assessment?* Scope has two dimensions—content and respondents—each of which may be broad or narrow. Scope of content may be broad (including all instructional components) or narrow (covering only certain programs such as reading and math). A broad scope of respondents could include the entire student body and community; a narrow scope might include only students in certain grades or only parents of students.

4. *On whose needs will you focus and at what level?* The three levels are the learner, the institution, and school-community

relationships; and in a K–12 district, the decision is whether to assess needs only at the elementary or secondary level or on all levels.

5. *What kinds and amounts of data should be collected for your purposes?* Three general types are discussed—descriptive, performance, and opinion data. Questions help focus the needs assessor on how to choose data that will help set priorities for the major focus, distinguish between what should be collected and what could be collected, and keep in mind the difference between wants and needs.

6. *What sources and methods might you use for data collection?* A matrix displays the relationship between client types (learner, institution, or school-community), data types, sources, and appropriate methods.

7. *What are your constraints on data collection?* Consideration is given to mandated requirements that allow little flexibility, data that are already available, standards of quality and amounts of data that must be met, data analysis, and balancing costs against requirements for the data.

8. *What can you invest in people, money, and time?* The needs assessor analyzes specifically (a) who will gather the data, compile and analyze the results, and report them and (b) the actual investments to be made in money and time.

9. *What needs assessment products meet your purposes, constraints, and resources?*

To answer the final question, the needs assessor turns to the product locator, which describes and compares thirty-four published needs assessment kits and instruments. The product locator is keyed to two factors: the scope of the assessment and the target or focus group. Products are organized by primary focus—learner, institution, or community—and are described twice: (1) by content descriptors of data types, sources, methods, and cost and (2) by graphic comparison of components. An index summarizes the focus, scope, levels, and salient features of each product.

The decision model can also be used to evaluate materials from other published sources or to design needs assessment procedures and instruments locally.

Organizational Elements Model

For nearly two decades, Kaufman, major contributor to both the theory and practice of needs assessment for education and training, has been conceptualizing and refining models (Kaufman, 1972, 1982a, 1982b; Kaufman and English, 1979; Kaufman and others, 1981). Recent work includes attention to diagnosing organizational needs (Kaufman, 1981; Kaufman, Johnston, and Nickols, 1979; Kaufman and Stone, 1983), needs assessment and holistic planning (Kaufman 1983a; Kaufman and Stakenas, 1981), and needs assessment in curriculum decisions (Kaufman, 1983b). His discrepancy definitions of need and needs assessment have become standard. (See Kaufman, 1983c, for his glossary of thirty-two components of a holistic system approach to needs assessment, planning, and evaluation.)

Kaufman's system approach puts needs assessment, the first stage of planning, in the context of organizational problem solving and renewal. The Organizational Elements Model (OEM) has both an internal and external frame of reference (Figure 2). Inputs and processes relate to internal organization *efforts;* products and outputs relate to internal organizational *results.* Products are en route results; outputs are the aggregated results that an organization can deliver outside of itself. Outcomes, a third type of result, are external to the organization and have impact in and for society. They are "those impacts which an organization can or will have for the success, self-sufficiency, self-reliance, and survival of itself and all individuals which it will or might affect" (Kaufman, 1983c, p. 13).

Inputs and processes, then, are means the organization employs to achieve the organizational results of products and outputs, which should lead ultimately to external results or outcomes. True needs are gaps between what is and what should be in terms of organizational results and societal impact. Quasi needs are gaps in organizational efforts. Thus, true needs assessment always begins with an external referent to determine what should be in terms of societal and organizational results.

This distinction between ends and means, organizational results and organizational efforts, is crucial to Kaufman's model. Realistic goal setting begins with stating current and desired

Figure 2. The Organizational Elements Model.

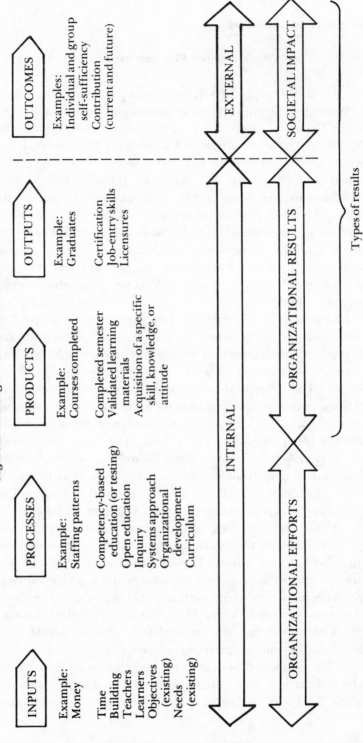

INPUTS

Example:
Money

Time
Building
Teachers
Learners
Objectives
(existing)
Needs
(existing)

PROCESSES

Example:
Staffing patterns

Competency-based
education (or testing)
Open education
Inquiry
Systems approach
Organizational
development
Curriculum

PRODUCTS

Example:
Courses completed

Completed semester
Validated learning
materials
Acquisition of a specific
skill, knowledge, or
attitude

OUTPUTS

Example:
Graduates

Certification
Job-entry skills
Licensures

OUTCOMES

Examples:
Individual and group
self-sufficiency
Contribution
(current and future)

EXTERNAL

SOCIETAL IMPACT

INTERNAL

ORGANIZATIONAL RESULTS

ORGANIZATIONAL EFFORTS

Types of results

Source: Kaufman, 1983b.

outcomes, or results, in measurable terms. Needs are assessed without making assumptions about what the resources or solutions should be or about which existing organizations or agencies could meet the identified needs. Once the needs are identified, the organization determines how to get from what is to what should be in terms of results, by identifying requirements for resolution and selecting solutions from identified alternatives. The complete process includes constructing a management plan and implementing, evaluating, and revising it as required. The model becomes cyclical by feeding data from outcomes back to the inputs.

The model also takes into account the frame of reference of constituent groups. In a school-system needs assessment, for example, the needs as perceived by learners, educators, and the community are combined with data about the external referent to identify needs. There may be differences between perceived needs and actual gaps. The only hard and fast requirements of the model are that it must "distinguish between means and ends and focus upon discrepancies in ends (outcomes); and use a referent external to the sponsoring or studied agency, especially referring to survival of the learners in the world to which they exit upon completion or release from the system under study" (Kaufman and English, 1979, p. 209).

In applying the model, what types of data are appropriate to depict what is and what should be? Following is an example of an extended statement about learner outcomes in which the overall minimal outcome for education is stated as "By the time the learner legally exits the educational agency he/she will be at the independent survival point or beyond" (p. 186). Data on "what is" for outcomes are gathered on demographics of recent graduates as well as such statistics as percentages of graduates who are currently unemployed, below poverty level, in college, in the contribution area, below norms on eleventh-grade reading and math tests, have jail records, or want more income. Representatives of constituent groups set standards of what should be:

> What Should Be (Outcomes): 100% of learners currently in the system and all graduates and those legally exiting want to be at the independent survival point or beyond as measured by their consumption at

least equaling their production; no bankruptcy for
any graduates or person legally exiting, no commitments to mental institutions, no person arrested and
found guilty of a felony, or misdemeanor which is
punishable by a fine of greater than $250.00, a divorce
rate which is significantly lower than the national
divorce rate, all of the above measured by a stratified
random sample certified as correct by a licensed psychometrician. There will be no significant difference
between those legally exiting from the educational
system on the above indicators which are attributable
to color, race, creed, sex, religion, or national origin
at or beyond the .05 level of confidence, as measured
by a stratified random sample of legally exiting people
as certified by a licensed psychometrician [Kaufman
and English, 1979, p. 195].

Such statements would grow out of earlier versions that
include the sources of data, such as specific government reports and
tests. They are refined several times before final acceptance by the
constituent groups working on the needs assessment. For example,
it may be necessary to resolve a considerable discrepancy in the
expectations of teachers and the community regarding the percentage of students who should and can get jobs after graduation, the
different expectancies obviously being based on differing experiences with the students and different views as to their potential.

This method of describing and analyzing discrepancies has
several strengths. Both status and standards are stated in verifiable
terms, and data on the two dimensions can be logically compared.
Data on status of high school students can be gathered from existing
records of many kinds, not only tests. For assessment of needs of
elementary and secondary school students, interim objectives can be
devised, and data gathered on the status of those objectives. The
level of standards, while based on the values of those setting them,
is explicit and provides an objective benchmark for identifying
needs.

How well does the model work in actual needs assessments
in school systems, particularly in regard to gathering data on status?
In practice, there is considerable difficulty with relating a discrepancy analysis to an independent survival point, except in a general
way. Population statistics for large metropolitan areas can be

gathered from social indicators supplied by government reports and the like, as described in Chapter Four, although they are often out of date. But data on graduates of specific school districts are very hard to come by. Schools find it difficult as well as costly to get follow-up data of any kind about former students due to high mobility, lack of interest of students in responding to queries, confidentiality of information, and data-gathering costs. Also, although the school system has the responsibility to educate students insofar as possible to the independent-survival point, survival in the world beyond high school for many students may have more to do with family background, health and personal abilities of the student, the state of the economy, and racial and gender bias than with preparation in the schools.

Butz (1983) proposes an interactive needs assessment between home, school, and community based on the OEM, which in part answers the above objection. Recognizing that it is difficult for school personnel to relate their functions to macrosocial indicators such as unemployment, divorce rates, and the like, he suggests that the constituent groups work together to develop enroute indicators representing both consuming and producing behavior. Vandalism, truancy, and substance abuse are examples of consuming behaviors; tutoring and volunteerism are examples of producing behaviors. Data on school and at-home behavior relevant to output indicators for high school students could be supplemented by student self-evaluations relevant to the curriculum, six-month postgraduation follow-up studies of college freshmen, and twelve-month postgraduate surveys of alumni employers.

The OEM concept of needs assessment as an outcome gap analysis is important for needs assessment in any setting. Many human services agencies and other organizations analyze needs primarily on the basis of discrepancies in services and resources rather than in client needs. This practice has recently been challenged by planners who cite the superiority of epidemiological and population-based needs assessment over service-based assessment. An understanding of the difference between gap analysis of inputs and outputs will prevent that confusion of means and ends, of needs and solutions, that has led to many of the criticisms about needs assessment cited in Chapter One.

The term *secondary needs assessment,* which was defined in Chapter One and is used throughout this book, is analogous to Kaufman's quasi-needs assessment. Secondary assessments (which focus on needs at the organizational level, identifying gaps in inputs and processes) serve an important function after primary-level needs (of service receivers) have been identified. That concept is elaborated on in the last model described in this chapter.

A Multicomponent Training Model

The widespread acceptance of the discrepancy model in theory encounters some barriers in practice. Although there are many techniques for determining the what-is dimension, the literature offers little help in determining what should be. Misanchuk (1982b) acknowledges that Kaufman's advice to focus on results or ends rather than means is pertinent, but that it presents problems. Kaufman's procedure of employing three partner groups "is sometimes difficult to implement in those situations involving learners outside the traditional K–12 school system, or indeed outside any formal educational institution. Furthermore, a constant concern with such partner groups would be whether or not truly representative data are being gathered: to be functional, the partner groups must be kept relatively small, thereby increasing the probability of biased information" (p. 2).

As a partial answer to a larger concern—the application of the empirical-analytic method to determine what should be— Misanchuk has developed an approach for assessing training needs in the business sector. A double question is involved: What do people do, and what do they value doing? Misanchuk's method of operationalizing this question forms the conceptual base for his needs assessment model.

Misanchuk uses two dimensions to define educational and training needs: the degree of "fuzziness" or "closedness" of the target group, or potential learners, and the degree of "freedom" or "captivity" of actual learners in the learning environment. Closed target groups are those "whose characteristics and roles are easily and precisely specified in such a way that group membership can be quite easily determined, and the members readily isolated." In fuzzy groups, the commonality of members "is operationally more difficult to describe with any degree of precision" (p. 3). Thus, for example, the schoolteachers in a given city or the operators of word-processing equipment in a particular office are closed groups—they are easily identified. On the other hand, the brown-eyed boys in the sixth grade of all schools in a county form a fuzzy group since it would not be possible to get that information from school records.

The determination of the captivity/freedom dimension hinges on the social, legal, financial, and other costs of not partaking of an educational experience. Children in elementary school classes are a captive audience, and secondary and technical school students only slightly less so. "But people attending a university extension course in Canadian literature, or a technical school night class in welding, or a church seminar on morality, form groups of relatively 'free' learners, since they will attend or not attend particular meetings at their discretion. . . . Neither subject matter nor host institution greatly influence 'freedom' " (pp. 4–5). For example, a person taking a university course as a hobby is free; someone else taking the same course to fulfill professional require-ments for updating of certification or because it was suggested by an employer is more or less captive.

The two dimensions serve to define two groups of learners for the needs assessment. Fuzziness and closedness "are characteris-tics associated with the group of *potential* learners (the target group), 'freedom' and 'captivity' are characteristics associated with the *actual* learners as they relate with the learning environment" (p. 5). The freedom/captivity dimension bears on where to start in determining what should be. Basic societal goals for elementary and secondary education change relatively slowly, whereas goals for career-related programs in higher education are likely to change more rapidly with changes in technology.

Once outside of a formal educational institution, the "ques-tion of fuzziness/closedness of the target group begins to intrude" (p. 6). It would be difficult to determine who should be invited to form a consensus group for *what should be* for a target population defined as "all the supervisory and managerial people in a city of 150,000," when the list includes private and technical schools, community colleges and universities, and provincial and civic agencies (p. 6).

Misanchuk provides six scenarios that vividly illustrate the elements of potential training contexts, each of which has varying combinations of degrees of freedom/captivity and fuzziness/closedness. He notes that "trying to apply existing conceptualizations of and approaches to needs assessment is fraught with problems in some of these real-life contexts" (p. 7). Since most of the educational needs assessments now in use deal with relatively closed and captive situations, other approaches are needed for contexts that are more open and fuzzier.

Misanchuk and Scissons (1978) introduced the idea of three need components—*relevance* of the task for the job role, *competence* of the individual in performing a task or skill, and *desire* of the individual to undertake education or training. Need can be defined by one to three components, depending upon the context. For example, an instructional developer in the closed, captive environment of industrial training would define need as high relevance plus low competence. One in a fuzzy, free university extension context would add high desire to the other two components. And still another in the fuzzy, reasonably captive context of a privately owned secretarial school would define need as high relevance plus high desire. High or low competence would not be an important factor.

The multicomponent (R-C-D) model is said to simplify data collection and interpretation and to focus on utility of knowledge rather than preference. Questions are specific to the task or skill and need little interpretation. Survey instruments have been devised for potential target groups, with self-reports of relevance and competence in one section and desire for the training component in another.

Schwier (1982) extends the R-C-D model to a situation in which an organization has decided to impose training and the needs assessment is undertaken to design an appropriate type. The proposed model is employee-centered in that employees are presumed to know both the relevance of a task and their own degree of competence. Situations occur, however, in which there is a disparity between an organization's and an employee's perception of what should be. For example, both office management and supervisors might recognize that word processors will eventually be introduced on a large scale, but supervisors might differ from management in their perception of whether related skills are secretarial or supervisory. With job relevance defined externally, a needs assessment might show low perceived job relevance.

Schwier worked out the training implications of each of the scales independently for all configurations possible from interaction of the three scales. The perceived relevance scale has valences of -1 (interference), 0 (irrelevance), and +1 (relevance). Different types of training experiences are indicated for each of the three types of groups. Perceived interference requires concrete experiences such as on-site practice and demonstrations; irrelevance calls for vicarious experiences using models and simulations; and relevance could accommodate abstract experiences such as independent study and classroom training.

A scale of perceived competence goes from lack of aptitude, through benign incompetence, to competence, with accompanying criteria for training experiences. The desire scale is from subversion, through apathy, to desire. Perceived subversion calls for exclusion from training, with apathy and desire requiring different kinds of organizational postures and reward systems.

Schwier's model permits analysis of the interaction of all three dimensions and their degrees in order to match learner needs with compensatory training modes. Some configurations do not indicate a need for training. The instructional developer's dream is the configuration of high desire, low competence, and high relevance. Schwier (1982, p. 15) notes that "full exploitation of the model would require parallel development of training modes to capitalize on the needs of individuals," that there are serious budget implications, and that it "would only be feasible in cases where there are sufficiently large subgroups of individuals to warrant parallel development."

Misanchuk's model and Schwier's extension of it are significant departures from the common practice of assessing training or staff development needs using only the dimension of desire. Misanchuk's observation about the slow rate of change of societal goals for elementary and secondary education also illuminates a characteristic of many educational needs assessments—the high degree of consensus and high ratings of importance of most educational goals, as revealed in reports of hundreds of needs studies. The most effective models are those that quickly get below the surface of general goal consensus to identify and analyze real needs within goal areas.

Field Analysis

As a solution to the difficulties inherent in many of the definitions of need discussed in Chapter One as well as in defining whether or not changes are beneficial and costs are acceptable, Frisbie (1981) proposes field analysis as a step beyond needs assessment. He employs a systems perspective, using the *field* as a unit of analysis that considers both the environment and the system or systems contained within it. The field takes into account changes in four factors: a specified domain within a system, the remainder of the system, a specified domain within the environment, and the remainder of the environment. "This approach is based on the perspective that the quality of 'need,' 'opportunity,' or 'cost' is not an inherent characteristic of a particular condition . . . [but] a function of the field within which that condition is described and the value structure against which it has been judged" (p. 15). Field analysis is "the process through which changes in a system and its environment are clearly described, so that these changes can then be judged to represent either needs, opportunities, or costs" (p. 16).

Frisbie considers needs assessment as a subset of field analysis, although many studies labeled *needs assessments* actually go beyond testing for genuine need and thus may be "virtually indistinguishable from field analysis" (p. 16). It is also closely related to context evaluation.

The basic steps in conducting field analysis are "defining the field, determining the changes to be considered, characterizing the change, and appraising the change. Four key elements in this process include the system, its environment, the domains of interest, and the phase shift between acceptable and unacceptable conditions. . . . [F]ield analysis could be thought of as an end in itself or as a springboard to further planning or problem solving activities" (p. 24).

The example used by Frisbie to illustrate the field-analysis orientation—determining the risks and opportunities to a strip-mining company deciding to buy out a credit card company—is at the secondary or organization level and is an assessment of solution requirements. The field analysis appears to be an evaluation or appraisal of the costs and benefits of a pre-determined planned change rather than an analysis of the need for a change. This perspective is characteristic of many models and theories of needs assessment that grow out of an evaluation (rather than a planning) perspective. It is analogous to needs assessment viewed as market research.

A Community College Model

A consortium of seven colleges in central Florida developed a model for assessing community occupational needs through intergovernmental data analysis, funded through Title III of the Higher Education Act and presented at the first national conference on needs assessment in 1975 (Tucker, 1973, 1974). The model focuses on the relationship of community college curricula to community educational needs, but the discrepancies are not between what is and what *should* be, but between what is and what *could* be. Tucker notes that "since the set of educational offerings identified as 'needed' in the future will always be based on some data derived from the present, and since there are many forces acting on the shape of the future, the set of needs identified must represent *alternatives* for future direction rather than what ideally should be" (1974, p. 1, Tucker's emphasis). The colleges wanted to offer the most relevant programs possible within their resource limitations as well as a consistent and dependable way of recognizing changing patterns and needs of potential students.

The model offers a planning technique to enable decision makers to

1. Rank the educational needs in their order of importance.
2. Develop alternative plans to meet those needs.

3. Determine budget allocation guidelines according to need priorities.
4. Monitor the benefit or value of a need as compared to its cost; that is, to discover if fulfilling a need justifies its cost.
5. Develop a continuing dynamic method to evaluate the educational systems' effectiveness in meeting community needs [Tucker, 1974, p. 6].

Each college in the consortium developed one module—a community awareness survey, a goal-setting model, a management analysis study, an employer survey, a student follow-up survey, a student characteristics profile, and a course-sample faculty evaluation. The modules can be used either independently or in combination. The heart of the model, however, and the feature that differentiated it from others at the time, is a computerized process that uses monthly status reports of jobs requested through the Florida state employment service to assess occupational needs for the service areas of the community colleges. (That capability is also present in other states.) The jobs are coded by occupation, and weightings are assigned based on net job openings for the month, average experience required, salary, and length of time the job is open. Using the composite weighting factors, the analyst sets priorities on need for jobs in the occupational codes, which are then matched as nearly as possible to college curricular programs.

The model was developed and field-tested in a preliminary needs study that integrated baseline data from the census, geocoding, future trends, historical data, and research statistical data. Using the data base, specialized analyses done over a two-year period yielded data for immediate decision making and analysis in planning and for later input to the needs assessment project planning center. The model calls for a major discrepancy analysis between the baseline data on community educational needs— present skill needs, social/cultural needs, special community interests, and priority of educational needs—and educational needs being met by colleges through their present courses and programs, enrollment patterns, budgeting, and community services. The analysis addresses the questions of why they differ, where and by how much they differ, and what can be done to change things.

Figure 3 depicts the data base for the model, showing the relationships of several sources and types of data to the needs of job applicants, workers, people in training, and employers and the relationship of the total data base to the needs assessment output.

The community needs assessment model is an illustration of how to operationalize the relationship between educational needs of

Figure 3. Florida Community College Model.

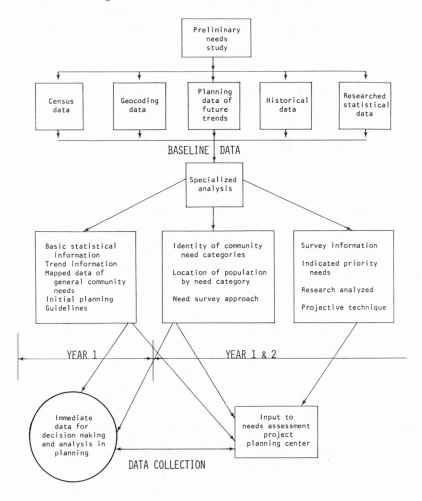

Source: Tucker, 1973.

students and requirements and opportunities in the external world. Tucker discusses the difficulties of acquiring local data for planning occupational training programs, since the scope and formats of data from different sources differ widely. The final decision was to use data from the state employment service job bank, supplemented with some state market trends and regional information, to give a range of number of occupations from a projected minimum to a projected maximum.

Tucker (pp. 200-201) views needs assessment as lying at the heart of humanistic planning for the future and the first step in a total management information system.

> Complicating factors to the educational system in analyzing the impact derived by the community as curriculum moves with the assessed needs (i.e., as data from the model are used to plan programs and monitoring and evaluation of the occupational training ensues), requires that the Needs Assessment Model not be used in a vacuum, but rather in conjunction with the total management information system.
>
> The need to bring to bear all available knowledge arises because no single educational institution is responsible for all career preparation. Often the training is shared among secondary schools, vocational centers, private schools and industries, community colleges in outlying areas, and universities.
>
> If the system could be totally comprehensive, we would need to include the number and size of educational institutions within an area and the nongeographic conformity of the areas with standard political and administrative geography, types of training programs being offered, resources being utilized inclusive of facilities and teachers, and most importantly characteristics of the students participating in the programs and the subsequent job market.
>
> Another complicating factor is that not all students participating in these programs intend to participate in the labor force with skills acquired in the occupational training program. Conversely, a student may be hired into the trained field even before he completes the total program—making it difficult to measure supply to demand. And he may be retraining while holding a job already.
>
> Consideration of these dimensions coupled with the need to longitudinally examine . . . the

occupational training being provided, labor market characteristics for subsequent job placement, and follow-up of trained persons in their career mobility will point up the need not only for these functions to be automated but in fact integrated into total long-range planning for the most effective benefit to future plans [Tucker, 1974, pp. 200–201].

Tucker recommended that the model be revised to do more job clustering and to relate those clusters to career objectives and college programs in order to provide students with the flexibility necessary to cope with the changing nature of the economy, technology, and the job market. The career concept embodied in the model can be applied to a useful core curriculum at any educational level from elementary school on up.

An Ecological Model

The Native Hawaiian Educational Assessment Project had two goals: to identify the unique educational needs of Native Hawaiians and to identify effective programs that could meet their unique educational needs (Kamehameha Schools . . . , 1983). The theoretical base was Bronfenbrenner's (1979) systems theory approach in which the " 'ecological model' encourages a researcher in human development to look at the interrelationships between variables at all levels of influence in a child's world. Beyond the immediate systems of which the child is a part, such as parent-child systems and teacher-child systems, there are higher-order systems which inter-relate to these. Events at the state or even national level have a definite interrelationship with the microsystem of the classroom. For the present Project, this meant that the search for educational needs of Hawaiian children had to be sensitive to historical as well as to other large-scale events and trends" (Kamehameha Schools . . . , 1983, p. iv).

The project investigated three areas of educational needs: parity in achievement as measured by standardized achievement tests, special educational needs, and needs related to the unique cultural background of the Native Hawaiian students. In addition to the test data, three other types of data were collected. *"Testimo-*

nial Data included written testimony presented before congressional hearings, quotations from interviews, and commentary offered by members of the Hawaiian community taken from a variety of sources. *Social Indicator Data* were numerical and statistical compilations of information from various institutions and agencies including the Department of Health, the Department of Social Services and Housing, and the Police Department. These data gave comparative figures for Hawaii's ethnic groups on standard indicators such as arrest rates, social welfare, and health. *Social Science Analysis* [provided] results of studies conducted by educators, psychologists, anthropologists, public health specialists, and so on. These studies generally contained some observational or experimental data along with analysis by the social scientists. From these sources of data, descriptions of needs were drawn and grouped into relevant categories" (pp. iv-v).

The categories for special educational needs were socioeconomic status, physical health, mental health, alienation, school-system barriers, and physical and built environments. Those for culturally related academic needs were problems at the interface, barriers in Hawaiian culture, barriers in the dominant culture, and cultural preservation. Each category of need area contained descriptions of relevant conditions for which data could be gathered. Conditions for problems at the interface, for example, were educators' perceptions of Hawaiian children, values and attitudes related to work, language, peer orientation, interaction with adults, learning style, achievement aspirations, preference for immediate gratification, male role development, and child-rearing patterns (p. v).

Bronfenbrenner's theoretical framework was chosen because it offered a structure for collecting and integrating data, analyzing patterns of educational needs, and formulating hypotheses of causal relationships. The ecological model has four levels of interaction that might enhance or inhibit learning in children—the microsystem, mesosystem, exosystem, and macrosystem. The microsystem includes the places that children live and the people (such as parents and teachers) with whom they have relationships. The mesosystem includes the relationships between the child's microsystems; these would include home-school or peer groups–school relationships. The number and quality of connections governs the richness of the mesosystems for the child. The exosystem includes systems (such as school boards and parents' work settings) that influence the children but in which they do not necessarily participate. The macrosystem refers to the broad ideological and institutional patterns of the culture, to the way the world is and might be organized. These levels are nested hierarchically in a complex, interrelated system.

The ecological model was chosen because the concepts avoided "some of the pitfalls of the traditional linear explanatory models. Cause and effect are not considered a one-way street: events at the mesosystem level, for example, contribute to the developing macrosystem just as events at the higher-system levels will inevitably have effects on the developing child" (Kamehameha Schools . . . , 1983, p. 4). The children whose needs were assessed by this project were considered at risk because of many factors in each of the four systems. Particularly, it was felt that needs could be better understood in the context of the macrosystem changes of the past two hundred years, which totally altered the world of Native Hawaiians.

The goal of identifying effective local and national educational programs that could be matched to the unique needs of Native Hawaiians led to general recommendations as guidelines for action initiatives in which interventions are targeted at specific systems levels. The project also includes provision for continuous needs assessment so that trends can be watched and indicators updated. The model offers interesting possibilities for needs assessment of other ethnic groups who, like the Native Hawaiian children, have experienced long-standing patterns of low educational achievement and high school alienation.

Community-Oriented Needs Assessment

A cooperative effort between a mental health agency and the research and public service center of a local university produced a model for Community-Oriented Needs Assessment (CONA), which was intended to supply a simple, inexpensive, consumer-oriented procedure using surveys and social indicators (Neuber and others, 1980). There are three sources of data in CONA: demographic statistical profiles, a mail questionnaire to key informants, and individual interviews with a random sample of citizens from the community. Eleven data-gathering instruments were developed for the model, two of which are reproduced in the guide.

A prime motivation for development of the model was a desire to increase community input into service delivery planning and evaluation. Traditionally, agency staffs collect the data and make important decisions about client needs and planning for service delivery. In the CONA model, citizens as consumers or potential consumers of mental health agency services are involved in the collection of data, not only as respondents but also as interviewers. The process of needs assessment, program planning and implementation, and evaluation is conceived of as a cycle, or wheel, in which the consumer is at the focal point, connected to each of the seven spokes of the wheel by information links of needs assessment.

The model suggests that needs assessment information be used in many ways: to identify needs for services, to support funding requests, to assist in establishing a goal for reducing the community need and planning to accomplish that goal, to serve as a basis for interagency cooperation in meeting the needs, and to provide data for funding and accountability. In regard to the last purpose, the data can be used to analyze existing services, identify needs for new services or for services in other areas, provide information to accrediting bodies, and evaluate programs that were instituted to reduce the community need.

The model offers no new methods for identifying needs. Its strength lies in providing a simple and feasible framework for integrating three types of data collection into a usable whole oriented to the needs of present and potential service receivers. The recommendations for multiple use of data and for working toward interagency cooperation in developing and delivering services put the needs assessment effort into a larger context.

A Community Youth Assessment Model

The Behavioral Research and Evaluation Corporation (BREC) developed a comprehensive approach to a communitywide youth assessment (Rossi, Freeman, and Wright, 1979). The first stage of the BREC strategy is to conduct a social area analysis to provide information on the social, demographic, and economic characteristics of the community as well as on its structure and organization. Indicators used are from census data, police and court records, school data, welfare, unemployment figures, and the like. BREC also developed a Youth Needs Assessment instrument to survey the needs of all youth in a population, not just those who receive services. Respondents are chosen by simple random sampling in the schools or cluster sampling in the schools or homes. The types of items developed for the survey were "(1) Problems, difficulties, and needs, specifying frequency of their occurrence, and perceived seriousness; (2) feelings, attitudes, and behavior regarding four factors: (a) perceived opportunities for achieving personal goals and desired social roles, (b) perceived negative labeling by parents, teachers, and friends, (c) feelings of alienation and rejection, and (d) self-reported involvement in delinquent behavior; (3) youths' perceptions and evaluation of available services and agencies; and (4) personal background and socioeconomic data of the respondents. In addition to uncovering needs, these measures also serve as baseline data for subsequent impact assessments" (p. 96). The same instrument can be used to gather perceptions of agency staff regarding youth needs. Agency personnel estimate the percentage of all youth having the problem and then assess the seriousness of the problem.

A Cyclical MIS Model

The model described here was developed in response to two identified school-system needs for which there were no existing models—a procedure for conducting needs assessment on a cyclical basis and a method of integrating multiple, disparate types of data and incorporating them into an ongoing educational management information system (MIS). It was designed and field-tested at Saratoga (California) High School (Witkin, 1979c; Kenworthy and others, 1980).

A major design requirement was to develop criteria for designing a data base of manageable proportions, consistent with ongoing needs assessment. One source furnished three useful ideas for that element—it was the Curriculum Management Information System (CURMIS), a project designed to evaluate a high school program in Madison, Wisconsin (Sapone, 1972). The basic concepts adapted from CURMIS were that the data collection should start with individual departments, rather than the entire school; that it be guided by a limited number of issues set by each department, and that there be three levels of standards for each issue. The concept of three levels overcomes the objections that a school's standards are too low or too high and that needs assessments look only at weaknesses and not at strengths. The standards are set before any data are collected.

The Saratoga model uses a system approach to provide a framework and methods for conducting ongoing, cyclical needs assessment in a high school so that planners and decision makers at the classroom, departmental, and schoolwide levels can (1) identify major unmet needs of students and support systems, (2) identify the criticality of those needs and set priorities for appropriate action, (3) sense when previous identified needs are being met and when new ones are emerging, and (4) use a rational and defensible method of weighing the merits of competing needs so that resources can be allocated where they will do the most to maintain and enhance the educational quality of the school.

Specifications for the model included (1) processes for communication and interaction strategies to promote a sense of ownership of the needs assessment and responsibility for taking appropriate action on the basis of the data, (2) the requirement that the data be relatively patterned and systematic over time in order to be used in a computerized MIS, and (3) provision of methods for determining potential consequences, both risks and payoffs, (a) if critical needs are not met and (b) if critical needs are met (that is, results of interaction with other needs or with other parts of the system).

The rationale for beginning the needs assessment at the departmental level and basing the data collection on a small number of issues arose from practical considerations. Schools have been called loosely coupled systems having a great deal of autonomy within units and little cohesion throughout their organizations. This is particularly true of high schools with strong curricular departments. Faculty of individual departments become much more aware of schoolwide issues and areas of need after working intensively with issues and concerns related to their own students. As for data collection, the potential number of indicators of need that might be entered in a data-based management system is tremendous. The indicators in the list developed by Houston and others (1978), for example, run to several hundred. Some guiding principle was required to select data types and sources that would indicate need, not just interesting information.

Conceptual Framework. The general theoretical base is a modification of Kaufman's system approach. As Figure 4 shows, the model has three phases. Specified issues derived from school and departmental objectives guide the collection of standards and status information on student outcomes; the discrepancies between the two are labeled *primary needs.* The output of Phase I is a list of primary needs, in order of priority, for each department. In Phase II, causal analyses specific to the primary needs identify input, process, and environmental barriers—those conditions or events that contributed to the existence of the needs or that had prevented them from being met in the past. The output of Phase II is a more definitive statement of each of the primary needs. Phase III consists of analysis of *secondary needs*—the discrepancies between resources required to meet the primary needs and those available in the system. A second causal analysis leads to the final output: both primary and secondary needs in order of priority.

Figure 5 is a functional flow chart of the cyclical process. Steps 1.0 through 12.0 should be completed in one school year, and steps 13.0 and 14.0 in the second.

Success and failure indicators of each department's program (step 2.0) are generated in brainstorming sessions. Key questions are: If you were an outsider observing your classes, how would you recognize a successful program? How would you recognize an unsuccessful program? Indicators of student outcomes should be observable behaviors as much as possible and be related to requirements and situations that students will meet after leaving school. To illustrate, some indicators of success in foreign language are for student *outcomes,* the ability to use the language in travel; for student *processes,* doing all homework assigned and oral practice;

Figure 4. Three-Phase Model of Needs Assessment.

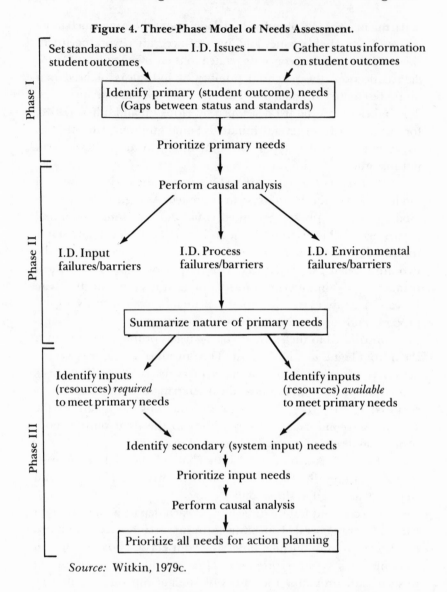

Source: Witkin, 1979c.

for *inputs* to the students, the ability of teachers to speak the language as well as read and write it and the quality of materials supplied for instruction. An indicator of an unsuccessful program might be a decline in number of students who enroll in advanced

Figure 5. Flow Chart of Cyclical Needs Assessment.

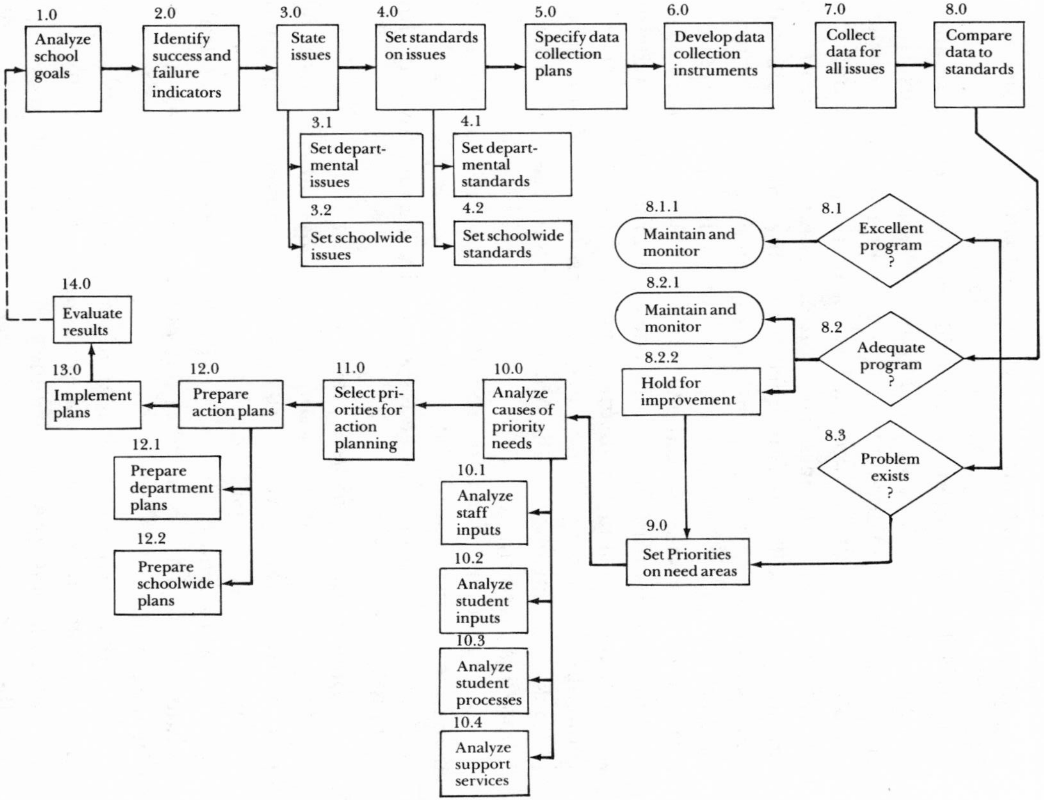

level courses. Causes of lack of success of the program could be due to failure of student inputs, teacher inputs, or student processing.

Issues (step 3.0) are derived from departmental objectives, schoolwide goals, and concerns that surface during the sessions of step 2.0. Select five to ten areas considered of greatest importance. For each issue, set three levels of standards—one for an excellent program, one for an adequate program, and one to indicate when a problem may exist (defining a level of need). Each set includes criterion levels of outcomes based on professional judgment and agreed upon by all staff concerned before any data are collected. Some sources of standards are norm- or criterion-referenced tests, statements of professional associations, university entrance requirements or criteria for advanced placement, skill levels related to out-of-school functioning, and competencies or proficiency standards set by the school and the district. Standards for support services could also draw on external sources such as the number and types of books recommended by the American Library Association for a school of a given size.

An issue and standards from the Saratoga physical education department illustrates step 4.0:

Issue: Do students take responsibility for their own health and physical fitness?

Standards: An *excellent* program exists if

1. at the end of the second year of physical education, 60 percent of the students voluntarily participate in a regular program of physical activity outside of school;

2. at the end of the fourth year, 60 percent of the students voluntarily participate in a regular program of physical activity outside of school;

3. five years after high school graduation, 50 percent of the graduates participate in a regular program of physical activity.

An *adequate* program met the same type of standards, except that the percentages of students meeting the criteria fell to 40 percent, 40 percent, and 30 percent for criteria 1, 2, and 3, respectively.

Criteria for a *need* were stated: "A problem may exist if, at the end of the second year of physical education, less than 40 percent of the students voluntarily participate in a regular program of physical activity outside of school," and so on for the other two criteria. The criticality of need is determined by the magnitude of the discrepancy between observed student behavior (outcomes) and the criteria for standards.

All departmental data-collection plans use a common framework to specify data to be gathered, sources of data, tasks necessary, outputs for each task, and target dates. The outputs are entered on a common format for the MIS. Insofar as possible, departments should gather data that are normally available to teachers in their daily instruction, devising checklists and forms to aid the aggregation of data from individual classes. Appropriate test and observational data are used, supplemented if necessary by short surveys. Schoolwide questionnaires can survey students, staff, and parents on issues not covered by departmental indicators such as school climate and morale, perceptions of overall school quality, and the kinds and quality of intraschool and school-community communication.

Priorities for action planning are set within each department separately and are based on that department's own data on criticality of needs. Thus, departments do not compete with each other for priorities. In the causal analysis, it is decided which factors can be modified or improved and which are beyond the control of the department or school and therefore resistant to change. If any of the latter contribute significantly to inadequate performance on high-priority need areas, both the issues and the standards should be reexamined. Are there ways of compensating for factors associated with low performance? Can extra resources be found? Were the standards unrealistic? What is the likelihood that change can take place?

After reviewing all the data at hand, select a new set of priorities, if necessary. One way of ordering the data is to cluster the need areas in a 2×2 matrix, with level of need on one dimension and resistance to change on the other. The four cells are (A) low-level needs, high resistance to change; (B) low-level needs, low resistance to change; (C) high-level needs, high resistance to change; and (D) high-level needs, low resistance to change. Whether program improvement starts with needs in cell C or D is a matter for departmental decision, aided by input from parents and students. Using the revised list of priorities, each department faculty or schoolwide committee designates those needs that should be addressed immediately, those to be addressed within the next couple of years, and those that must be postponed until later. Both the magnitude of the need and the likelihood that something can be done about it are taken into consideration.

Recycling. The model has two cyclic features. First, the needs assessment is conducted in the cyclic manner shown in Figure 5, with evaluation data feeding directly back into reanalysis of goals, issues, and needs. On highly critical issues with high-priority needs, the cycle may be a yearly one. Second, each department goes through the needs assessment process every third year, as follows:

Year 1.   Needs assessment completed in one third of the departments and on schoolwide issues.

Year 2.   Needs assessment conducted by another third of the departments, plus reassessment of high priority schoolwide issues. Year 1 departments implement and evaluate their action plans, reviewing and revising selected issues and indicators if needed.

Year 3.   Final third of the departments begin the process, and only highly critical schoolwide issues are reassessed. Year 2 departments begin implementation of action plans. Year 1 departments continue to monitor their plans.

Year 4.   The cycle starts again, but now there is a complete body of baseline data for both departmental and schoolwide issues. Trends are identified and long-range plans can be made for both curricular and other improvements desired by the school community. From the trends analysis, emerging needs may also be found for which preventive action can be taken.

The model is usable in other settings. In elementary schools, all issues can be on a schoolwide basis from the beginning, if desired. In noneducational settings, issues are derived from organizational or community goals, and appropriate criteria are set for indicators. The specific integration of causal analysis with primary- and secondary-needs analyses is a salient feature of the model and is essential for setting priorities.

3

Survey Methods: Questionnaires and Interviews

In its broadest sense, the term *survey* denotes the collection of many kinds of information, both facts and opinions, from a variety of sources, such as institutional records, the census, demographic and economic data reports, tests, case studies, and questionnaires. In needs assessment, however, *survey* generally refers to the gathering of opinions, preferences, and perceptions of fact, by means of written questionnaires or interviews. The discussion in this chapter is limited to the latter usage.

The survey is probably the most widely used procedure in needs assessment. It is frequently the sole element, but in comprehensive studies it is often combined with other data-collection methods, such as social indicators, group processes, trend analysis of demographic characteristics, resource inventories, and causal analysis. Needs surveys are most commonly used to gather facts, attitudes, and opinions at one point in time, but they can also be repeated over time to discover trends. Many large needs studies use both the questionnaire and the interview, with the interview used as a follow-up device to ensure a higher rate of response or as a means of probing certain questions in depth.

Needs assessment surveys often bear a superficial resemblance to public opinion polls or to questionnaires designed for survey research, but they differ from them both in purpose and in formal features. Needs surveys are intended to furnish data for situation-specific, time-based decisions about priorities for planning and resource allocation. Both the survey format and the methods of data analysis should allow inferences to be drawn about priorities and about the degree to which the needs are critical. There should be a theoretical framework—a discrepancy or problem-solving model—into which the data from the survey will fit.

The purpose of human services needs assessment surveys is to provide a valid description of a situation, the data of which are fed into the managerial and decision-making process. City managers in many large cities view citizen surveys "as a way to link governmental performance more closely to the government's 'customers,' the citizens" (Stipak, 1980, p. 523). The survey can also be used as a process tool—to heighten the awareness of a community, establish performance objectives, identify shortages or barriers to utilization of services (thus acting as a tool for action), legitimize change, stimulate support, and compare services over time. The community survey involves not only agency representatives but also community leaders and actual and potential consumers of the services.

Since the first systematic community survey (in Pittsburgh, in 1907) and the first modern school survey (in Boise, Idaho, in 1910), surveys have become an integral part of educational planning and policy development. Using status study and research findings to define both immediate and future needs was one of the four basic elements of school surveys. The terms *goal identification* and *needs assessment* were both used in school surveys. *Goals* referred to the missions and aims of public education, and *needs* referred to organizational or program inadequacies or deficiencies. Major reasons for conducting many surveys were issues of administrative efficiency and instructional effectiveness (Ignasias, Henkin, and Helms, 1982).

The most effective type of needs assessment survey asks respondents for informed opinion based on either personal experience or a background of expertise and knowledge, or for facts about themselves or others about which they have direct knowledge. It is not recommended that respondents be asked to make global judgments about the adequacy of community services or student achievement, for example, unless they have more than hearsay knowledge about the community or school system. Nor should they be asked for direct statements of needs, either their own or others', since those usually result in lists of preferences, desires, wants, goals, and the like. Data from the survey should be used, along with other data and causal analysis, to make *inferences* about needs. Both the wording of survey items and the instructions to respondents are all-important in clarifying the distinction between wants and needs.

Surveys can gather opinions about the two major elements of needs assessment: status and standards—what is and what should be (in terms of results). Surveys that merely solicit attitudes about education or human services are not complete needs assessments nor are goal-preference questionnaires. These types of surveys can, however, be used to identify needs if the responses are synthesized with other data that supply the missing dimensions. Surveys are often used to derive a broad community consensus on the standards dimension. But goal preferences alone are not standards.

If the survey is not the sole source of data, the needs assessor must decide when it should be used. If used at the beginning of the needs assessment, it is valuable for exploring areas that will be analyzed in more detail by other methods. If used later, its value lies in furnishing corroboration or refutation of needs identified by other means. The timing in the needs assessment should dictate, to a large extent, the content of the questions and the depth to which areas should be probed. Priorities for needs can rarely be established by a general, exploratory survey used as the sole data-gathering tool.

The scope of this chapter does not permit a step-by-step guide to designing and conducting surveys. Instead, the discussion centers on design elements characteristic of the written question-naire and interview that are specific to needs assessment. It also describes less frequently used techniques such as forced-choice methods, critical incidents, and behaviorally anchored scales. Additional topics are special aspects of interviewing and sampling, alternative methods of administration of written questionnaires, and issues involved in using the survey for needs assessment. Methods of deriving priorities from surveys are discussed in Chapter Eight. For detailed treatment of survey design, see Warwick and Lininger (1975), Alwin (1978), Orlich (1978), Demaline and Quinn (1979), and Sudman and Bradburn (1982); for telephone surveys see Frey (1983). Two sources of information on questionnaire design for educational needs assessment are Cox (1976) and Houston and others (1978).

Design of Survey Instruments

Needs assessors have essentially three options for sources of survey instruments: to use off-the-shelf questionnaires, to adapt published instruments for local use, or to design and develop their own. If survey instruments are developed locally, their construction should begin with staff involvement in defining a conceptual framework. Survey content and format should be chosen only after the needs assessor and survey committee clearly understand what types of decisions will be made on the basis of the data, what kinds of items will elicit usable data, and how the results will be analyzed in order to establish priorities. As a partial guide for those charged with selecting or designing needs survey instruments, this section treats four aspects of questionnaire construction that are particularly important for needs assessment: (1) identification of targets of the assessment, (2) identification of classes of respondents, (3) content of opinion scales, and (4) sources of scales.

Targets of the Assessment. The needs survey should be very clear about the focus or target of the assessment: Whose needs are being assessed—those of service receivers (primary level), or those of service providers (secondary level)? The focus in primary needs assessment is on products, outputs, and outcomes of the system. In secondary needs assessment (what Kaufman [1982a] terms quasi-needs assessment), the focus is on inputs and processes, including the programs and resources of the organization and the training needs of the staff. If these distinctions are kept in mind, the survey content will be less likely to confuse needs with solutions to those needs. The target of the assessment thus determines to a large extent the content of the survey. A given survey may, of course, include more than one target. But as a general rule, primary-level needs should be gathered before secondary-level needs.

In educational needs assessments, service receivers are generally *within* the system conducting the assessment. An exception is the community survey conducted by postsecondary institutions to identify needs of potential students for degree or continuing education programs. Receivers of health and human services are generally *outside* the system that is doing the assessment, as are the consumers who are targets of business needs assessments. In communitywide planning, the service receivers could be all residents of the community or particular target groups with common characteristics.

Classes of Respondents. Respondents to surveys may be service providers, service receivers, or stakeholders. They may be asked to answer questions about their own needs or about those of others, and they may be either within or outside the system conducting the assessment. The content and wording of the survey items should keep clear the distinction between primary and secondary needs assessment. For example, teachers may be asked to respond about needs of students (primary), about program or resource needs (secondary), or about their own needs for staff training (both primary and secondary). In the first case, teachers are service providers answering questions about service receivers. In the last case, they are responding both as service providers and service receivers. The survey developer should identify the sources that can give the best information about the needs of the target group. It must be assumed that respondents are knowledgeable enough and willing to provide the information, that they will understand the intent of the survey questions and answer them in the desired form, and that they will not lie or subvert the survey process or consider the survey an invasion of privacy (Demaline and Quinn, 1979).

Table 1 shows relationships among target groups, respondents, and sample-item content for a survey of needs in a school district. Item contents all relate to status, or what is. Items can be generated similarly for needs assessments conducted by human services agencies, where the service receivers are actual or potential clients and the service providers are the agency and its staff. Stakeholders could be relatives of service receivers as well as the general community, other public and private agencies, and appropriate departments in city or county government.

Inspection of Table 1 shows that the item-content samples are limited to self-reports or direct observations of others. Requests for general attitudes or opinions about a school system as a whole are rarely useful for identifying status. Parents should be asked to respond about their own children; teachers, about classes or groups that they have directly observed; and so on. With an adequate sample of respondents, a reliable picture of the entire system will emerge. Items for community respondents can be worded to elicit

Table 1. Survey Target Groups, Respondents, and Item-Content Relationships.

Target Group	Respondents	Sample Item Content
Service Receivers: Students	Service Receivers: Students	Attitudes about school, self, learning; self-reports of problems, need areas; opinions on achievement of objectives; facts about self
	Service Providers: Teachers, counselors, specialists	Direct observations about student achievement, behavior, problems, need areas
	Stakeholders: Parents	Direct observations about their children's need areas, problems, achievement
	Employers, community residents	Perceptions about student achievement, need areas in schools with which they are familiar
Service Providers: School system	Service Receivers: Students	Opinions about school climate, programs, services, learning conditions, curricular and cocurricular offerings
	Service Providers: Teachers, administrators, counselors, specialists	Observations on school climate, adequacy of programs to promote student learning, services, resources
	Stakeholders: Parents	Observations about their children's programs, resources, school climate
	Community	Perceptions about school climate, programs
Service Providers: Staff	Service Providers: Staff	Self-reports of need areas and problems in relation to instruction, classroom management, school goals
	Administrators	Self-reports of need areas; observations about staff needs
	Service Receivers: Students	Attitudes toward staff and administrators; observations about staff competency
	Stakeholders:	Observations on staff competencies in relation to their children's needs

perceptions about matters that are within their own experience in regard to the schools. Of course, there may be times when schools or service agencies wish to sample community attitudes regardless of their source. In such cases it is desirable to add questions to identify the sources of respondents' information or opinions—direct observation or experience, the press, television, friends' reports, and the like.

Content of Opinion Scales. Needs assessment questionnaires are often composed entirely of items requiring responses on category (ordinal or interval) scales. Lodge (1981, p. 5), observes that "the measurement technique most commonly used by social and behavioral scientists to determine the direction and strength of people's beliefs and preferences is one or another form of category scaling in which a respondent rates an item or expresses a judgment by selecting one of a fixed number of options." Needs surveys use questions or items that ask for opinions of the following:

1. *Importance* of educational or social goals, programs, services, types of learning or behaviors, conditions in the organization, and types and channels of communication. A variant is a scale of the degree to which a condition or goal *should exist.*
2. *Perceived performance* or achievement of specified objectives.
3. *Degree of agreement* with a set of goals or conditions or behaviors. Most agreement scales try to force a choice rather than leaving a middle ground of "not sure" or "no opinion."
4. *Frequency* with which some behavior occurs. The scales are usually anchored by "never" and "always." But sometimes the options are given in percentages of time, which has the advantage of providing a common referent for respondents, making the data easier to interpret.
5. Degree of *satisfaction* with services, courses, programs, communication types or channels, or any other inputs or processes in a system.
6. The level of *difficulty* that service receivers have with specified tasks.
7. *Preference* for a program or activity, such as how much respondents would like to do something, even if they don't do it now.

Surveys may also include requests for demographic information, past and present use of services, and other factual data. Due to the time needed for coding and analyzing responses, open-ended questions rarely constitute the major part of a written needs questionnaire. Many surveys do, however, include a few open-ended questions that invite comments on the items or addition of other opinions.

Sources of Scales. Needs assessors can find models and items for questionnaires in two general sources—those in which instruments were developed specifically for assessing needs, and those that were intended for other purposes, but that can be adapted. Since the mid 1960s, educational laboratories, university institutes, technical assistance centers, state departments of education, and independent consulting firms have produced models and instruments for educational needs assessment that have been widely used. (For descriptions and analyses, see Witkin, 1976c, 1977a, 1977c, and 1978. Some other sources are DeLorme, 1974; Arizona Department of Education, 1976; Glass, 1977; Crouthamel and Preston, 1979; Gable, 1980; Gable, Pecheone, and Gillung, 1981; Blair and Brewster, 1981; Hanley and Moore, 1979; Demaline, 1982; Hunt and others, 1982; and Radig, no date.) Reports from government bodies and social agencies often contain noncopyrighted questionnaires that can be used with permission.

A non-needs-assessment source of adaptable items and scales are the written questionnaires for students, teachers, parents, and the community that were used as one category of data source in a massive six-year project to investigate the state of the curriculum in elementary and secondary schools throughout the United States. It was conducted under the auspices of the Institute for Development of Educational Activities (I/D/E/A) and funded by two major federal agencies and ten private philanthropic foundations (Goodlad, Sirotnik, and Overman, 1979; Klein, Tye, and Wright, 1979; Benham, Giesen, and Oakes, 1980; and Bentzen, Williams, and Heckman, 1980). The surveys were intended to gather data for a national perspective on how the schools were operating vis-à-vis the curriculum, the environment of the students, and the environment of adults working in the school (Goodlad, Sirotnik, and Overman, 1979).

Other sources of survey instruments not developed specifically for needs assessment are attitude questionnaires, instruments
included in accreditation self-studies for school districts and universities, and a series on school evaluation offered by the National
School Public Relations Association.

Using published instruments that have been well designed
and validated often saves time and money and may be the best
option if the surveying organization has no staff skilled in survey
methodology. It is rare, however, that such instruments are completely appropriate to the local setting, purpose, or scope of the
assessment. An instrument can be *adapted* successfully if it fits in
with the conceptual framework of the local effort. The selection of
surveys for adaptation should be guided by the purpose of the
assessment and the need-to-know/nice-to-know distinction. The
cut-and-paste method of questionnaire construction, using unrelated items from several sources, is *not* recommended. *Copyrights
should be strictly observed,* and even with instruments in the public
domain, the source should be carefully credited.

Response Formats

Response formats for written questionnaires typically use
category scales that have an odd number of points (often five) and
that may be anchored with descriptors at each point or only at the
ends. Needs surveys given to elementary school children generally
use a format that requires little or no reading or writing. Questions
are read by the teacher or recorded on tape for playback in
classrooms. Responses can be made by marking a smiling, frown-
ing, or neutral face to indicate Yes/No/Don't Know or Not Sure.
Scales may employ different type sizes to indicate strength of
agreement or disagreement: YES yes no NO. There is a growing
trend to translate needs surveys into languages other than English in
communities with large non-English-speaking populations.

Many needs assessment questionnaires attempt to apply a
discrepancy model to the survey format by requiring two or more
responses to individual questions. Others request only one response
per item. This section discusses how surveys with different response
formats are designed to provide information on and comparisons

between status and standards. Their limitations for deriving priorities are discussed in Chapter Eight.

Single-Response Designs. Surveys requiring one response per question are used to collect either opinions about standards or perceptions/facts on status, but not to collect both at once. Such surveys typically ask for ratings of importance or degree of agreement with a list of goals or objectives, preference for services, frequency with which a problem has been experienced or degree of severity of a problem, or perceptions of extent to which students are achieving or to which a program has attained its goals. Responses are generally on four- or five-point category scales.

Some instruments seek more specific responses. For example, a survey of need for services for persons with developmental disabilities presents a list of eight services (including case management, vocational development, and legal counseling) and asks for one of these responses: wanted and did not receive, wanted and did receive, or received but did not want. Another section lists staff members (dentist, nurse, nutritionist, and the like) and the respondent checks one of the following for each person: saw at least once, would have liked to have seen more of, or did not see but would have liked to (Carlin and others, 1981). These response choices give information that is more specific than that obtained from category scales.

Many single-response questionnaires ask directly for the respondent's perception of degree or extent of need in specified areas. Present or potential service receivers are asked about their own needs or preferences for services, or service providers are asked their opinions about the needs of others. In this type of questionnaire, the separate status and standards dimensions have to be inferred. These surveys can be criticized on the grounds that they do not really identify or analyze needs but rather present wish lists or lists of solutions to needs.

Unless some source of standards is used for comparison, *the single-response instrument gives insufficient information about needs.* It is useful, however, when the survey data are compared with data gathered from other sources, such as social indicators or standards already set by some professional group. For example, if standards of health care are available for a particular population, then responses of a sample of that group to questions about their own health can be compared with the standards. The single-response design can also be used to identify perceived problem areas or to corroborate data gathered from other sources. The validity of the survey depends to a large extent not only on the content of the questions but also on how the data will be used in the overall design of the needs assessment.

Multiple-Response Designs. Questionnaires that seek to identify discrepancies directly from one instrument employ a design that requires two or more responses to each item. The two-response discrepancy survey asks for one opinion on existing conditions or states and another opinion on desired conditions or states.

The classic two-response school district questionnaire lists a set of goals, objectives, or conditions and requests two responses for each item: (1) its degree of importance on a five-point scale and (2) the degree to which the respondent believes that students have achieved the goal (or that the schools have been successful in helping students achieve the objective or that the stated condition exists). Possibly recognizing the lack of logic inherent in equating importance with what should exist (the desired state) as a standard with which to compare an existing state, some researchers have constructed surveys to elicit more direct opinions as to the desired state.

One such is the Battelle Institute survey (Mills and Hamilton, 1976), for secondary schools and colleges, which uses the scales "should exist" and "actually exists." Although the "should exist" scale appears superficially like the scale of importance, it actually taps a different opinion. A trait such as self-reliance might be deemed very important for students to exhibit, yet a statement such as "our schools teach students to be self-reliant" might not achieve a high rating *on the degree to which such teaching should exist in the school system where the needs are being analyzed*—in other words, it might be important to have, but not the responsibility of the school to teach.

Two-response surveys for human services generally focus on the delivery of services, using such statements as "I now receive" and "I would like to receive." Similar response choices are used for surveys of professional-staff-development needs in organizations.

Discrepancy items are usually displayed in a visual format that makes it easy for respondents to make direct comparisons of responses to the items. Occasionally a survey repeats the items in two sections, with questions regarding importance or desired states in one section and those regarding present states in another.

Some instruments are designed for three responses per question, such as one developed by the Westinghouse Learning Corporation for their needs assessment package offered to schools as part of an accountability program (Westinghouse Learning Corporation, 1973; Hansen and O'Neill, 1973). The format has been widely adopted by educational agencies. The survey contains fifty general educational goals for schools, each goal defined by one or more statements designed to clarify the intent of that goal. For example, the goal "Has a responsible attitude toward the environment" is accompanied by the statements, "Willingness to consider the consequences of various actions affecting the environment," "Willingness to change personal behaviors to protect environmental factors," and "Practice conservation of natural resources." Each goal is followed by three scales: a five-point scale of *importance,* a three-point scale of *extent of goal attainment,* and a five-point scale of the *school's responsibility for the goal.* The baseline data of perceived learner needs obtained from the survey could later be validated or examined in more depth by means of test data or other nonsurvey methods (Nichols, no date).

A similar three-response design can be used in surveys to determine what services should be offered in a community by health and social service agencies. Service providers and present and potential service receivers rate the importance of specified conditions to maintaining individual or family well-being, how well those conditions are now being met, and the responsibility of public and private agencies to meet individual or family needs related to those conditions. This format avoids the pitfall of asking for preferences for services and thus jumping to conclusions about solutions before analyzing the needs.

Forced-Choice Surveys

Although needs surveys most commonly use short category scales to establish strength or intensity of judgments, they may employ other response modes to force choices regarding the importance of goals or acceptability of services. The reason for doing so is that ratings of importance of educational goals, for example, all of which have high face validity and are educationally desirable, often cluster at the top of the scale, making it very difficult to establish priorities. To counter this tendency, some surveys call for ranking items in order of importance or preference, assigning only one rank to each item. This does not work well with more than eight or ten items, however. With longer lists, respondents may be instructed to choose the three most important and three least important items or to use card sorts to force choices.

Another type is the budget-allocation method, in which respondents allocate a fixed number of points, sometimes representing dollars, among a set of items such as goals or services—perhaps 100 points for ten items. The rules usually state that some points must be given to each item and that the amounts must vary among the items, but rules may be set as the needs assessor wishes. The budget-allocation method has the advantage of forcing respondents to think concretely about priorities, but it is harder to explain and more time consuming to respond to than questionnaires with category responses. The budget-allocation method is more feasible if respondents are brought together in a meeting rather than sent a mailed survey. The method works best with no more than fifteen or twenty items.

A variant of this method was used successfully by the Palo Alto, California, school district as part of a comprehensive communitywide needs assessment (McCollough, 1975). The survey furnishes respondents with a list of services offered by the schools and a brief explanation of each service. Using a system of points to represent actual dollar expenditures in the district budget, respondents make a series of decisions on which services to reduce or eliminate, which to maintain, and which to expand or add. The procedure partially simulates the decision-making process of a school board in making up the annual budget and clearly shows the relationships among district goals, the curriculum, support services, and expenditures. Respondents deal with varying amounts of money and must decide what allocations to make under conditions of varying reductions in the total amount of dollars available.

An important additional feature is that the survey supplies specific information about what the schools are doing—such as the number of hours per week devoted to reading instruction in the primary grades, the ratio of counselors to students in the high schools, or the percentage of students who achieve above the mean in a statewide math test. This feature can also be used in needs surveys that do not have the budget-allocation element. In that case, instead of merely listing goals or instructional conditions, the questionnaire supplies brief factual statements about each item, giving respondents a basis for judgments regarding the adequacy and desirability of the amount of effort devoted to selected components of the school program.

The budget-allocation method can be used by any organization that wants opinions from staff or stakeholders regarding allocation of effort and resources to programs and services. It makes more sense to use it with services than with goals since the former are more realistic and concrete. The method is particularly appropriate for assessing needs in a time of retrenchment, when priorities are a real concern. It should be recognized that the focus of the assessment is at the secondary (institutional or input) level rather than at the primary (or service receiver) level and further that, no matter how well the survey is designed, opinions about adequacy of services relate to solutions and do not analyze the needs themselves.

Critical-Incident Technique

Critical incidents (CI) are direct observations or self-reports of specific behaviors that relate directly to performance in a given situation or enterprise (Flanagan, 1954). The CI technique can be used to identify needs either at the service-receiver or the institutional level. A common CI method is to ask respondents to recall specific events or conditions, observed recently, that illustrate that the organization (service agency, school system) is doing an unsatisfactory job or that something about the system needs improving. They are also asked to recall other incidents about favorable situations that show that the system is doing a satisfactory job. Questions can be used to elicit CIs from all three classes of respondents—service providers, service receivers, and stakeholders.

Both positive and negative incidents are sorted according to program areas, and objectives and expectancies are determined (Witkin, 1977a).

CI technique has also been used to supply indicators or exemplars of the *attainment* of goals that are difficult to measure using standardized testing procedures. One such study identified behaviors of students enrolled in a comprehensive system of individualized education in the areas of personal and social behavior, especially self-management, initiative, responsibility, and resourcefulness. CIs were collected from teachers in the project and from self-reports of students. The data were gathered with a minimum of expense in a short period of time (Jung, 1971).

When used as an exploratory method in the early stages of a needs assessment, CIs help identify program areas that should later be explored in greater depth. CIs may also be used as a major element in a comprehensive needs assessment. The incidents can be collected for specific goals or problem areas (determined by other means) to supply indicators of present status.

Critical incidents can be incorporated into a needs assessment survey for any type of organization or purpose. In the organizational communication audit model developed by the International Communication Association (ICA), respondents to the survey questionnaire are asked for critical incidents that illustrate satisfactory and unsatisfactory communication in their organization (Goldhaber and Rogers, 1979). Results from an ICA communication audit at a large midwestern university illustrate the application of the CI technique (Goldhaber and Richetto, 1977). The 991 respondents to the survey reported a total of 566 incidents related to communication with immediate supervisor, subordinates, coworkers, and top management, which were analyzed for numbers and percentages of positive and negative incidents and divided into thirty-five subcategories, such as information adequacy, organizational roles, and interpersonal relationships. The analysis led to specific recommendations regarding needs at the organizational level as they existed in relationships among management, supervisors, and workers at different levels. It identified strengths as well.

In the ICA communication audit, the CI method forms one section of a validated survey questionnaire. A data bank contains norms for studies in seventeen large and small organizations in the United States and Canada (Porter, 1979). The 116 items in the questionnaire are in six sections related to information (receiving it, sending it, action or follow-up, sources, channels, and timeliness from key sources), organizational relationships, and organizational outcomes. Five sections use a discrepancy format for analyzing gaps between present and desired amounts of information.

Each section of the survey is followed by a request for critical incidents related to that section; these are called communicative experiences. The respondent briefly summarizes a recent work-related experience in which communication was particularly ineffective or effective. The respondent then indicates to whom the experience was primarily related (subordinate, coworker, immediate supervisor, middle or top management), rates the quality of the communication as effective or ineffective, and indicates the number of the survey item to which the incident applies. The description includes the communicative experience itself, the circumstances leading up to it, what the person did that made him or her an effective or ineffective communicator, and the results of what the person did.

Two important criteria for critical incidents are *specificity* and *recency*. Instructions to people reporting CIs in needs assessment should be very specific, or the incidents collected will be neither meaningful nor useful. The author's experience with using CIs in a variety of settings has shown that, if the request is worded too generally, the resulting incidents are difficult to interpret. For example, reports such as the following occurred in school surveys: "Students in this school have no respect for authority" or "Our principal never lets students take any responsibility; he treats us like babies." Such statements might be based on many specific incidents that rankle in the respondents' memories. Or they might simply be evidence of a general dissatisfaction with the school. The referents are unclear, leaving a good deal open to interpretation. For the purpose of more accurately identifying needs, it is better to collect a large number of *specific* behaviors and then to categorize them. Interpretations can be made after consultation with people at different levels in the system.

The following report from a CI-based needs assessment in a large school system illustrates the possibility of two opposite interpretations of the same incident. "A high school student is observed smoking just off campus; he puts out his cigarette before going on campus. Possible contradictory inferences are (1) *good*—he knows the rules; or (2) *bad*—the school should be teaching him not to smoke" (cited in Witkin, 1977a, p. 62).

The second criterion is recency—it is important to ask for a recollection of incidents that occurred within a recent specified period so that memories are sharp and the incidents reflect current situations.

Behaviorally Anchored Rating Scales

A major drawback to interpreting the results of most general discrepancy surveys using category scales is that the often abstract and ambiguous wording of statements and the limitations of the scales themselves make it difficult to judge the import of the responses. Interpretation of the operational meaning of the statements is left to the respondents, and the needs assessor must infer the meaning of the ratings. The consensus derived from such surveys may be more apparent than real.

In order to overcome these drawbacks, needs assessment surveys might use items based on the concept of behaviorally anchored rating scales (BARS), which attempt to define performance as carefully as possible in terms that leave little chance for misunderstanding in the mind of the respondent. BARS have been used to assist business in appraising managerial competence (Campbell and others, 1973) or employee performance (Kearney, 1979) or to measure obsolescence in performance and therefore to facilitate updating (Landy and Guion, 1970; Landy, 1974). Other applications reported in the literature are to measure selection and performance of pharmacists and motivation of engineers, assess rehabilitation counseling, evaluate college faculty teaching, assess readiness for the ministry, and evaluate training in chartered banks of Canada.

The scales consist of precise statements that describe behavior on a desired dimension, with different statements pegged at several points from the lowest to the highest points on a continuum. Thus, a scale of organizational identification reported by Landy (1974) had numerical values from 00 (very low) to 1.00 (moderate) to 2.00 (very high), with increments of .25 along the scale. Following are three representative statements from the scale:

> [Lowest point on scale]: "Organizational myopia: views his own activities with a kind of tunnel vision; unaware of broader organizational concerns."
> [Moderate point]: "Shows conscientious desire to further organizational objectives by fulfilling his own responsibilities."
> [Highest point]: "Shows broad concern for and acceptance of company goals as demonstrated by an alertness to possible organizational improvement beyond his own immediate responsibility" [p. 50].

Two other statements appeared between 00 and 1.00, and three others between 1.00 and 2.00, but not at equal intervals. The scale values were determined through a consensus process within the organization; this process is described in the following section.

A somewhat different type of scale, with a nine-point continuum, was developed for the major functions of the job of department manager in a retail store; among other things, the scales helped define training needs (Campbell and others, 1973). An example is a scaled expectations rating scale for the effectiveness with which the manager supervises sales personnel. Behaviors specified for five levels (level 9 is the highest) are

> Level 1: Could be expected to make promises to an individual about her/his salary being based on department sales even when she or he knew such a practice was against company policy.
> Level 3: Could be expected to tell an individual to come in anyway even though she/he called in to say she or he was ill.
> Level 5: Could be expected to remind sales personnel to wait on customers instead of conversing with each other.

Level 7: Could be expected *never* to fail to conduct training meetings with his people weekly at a scheduled hour and to convey to them exactly what he or she expects.

Level 9: Could be expected to conduct a full day's sales clinic with two new sales personnel and thereby develop them into top sales people in the department [p. 17].

Levels 2, 4, 6, and 8 are also specified in behavioral terms on the scale, which is displayed vertically with level 9 at the top. Similar behavioral rating scales were developed for other traits such as handling customer complaints, meeting deadlines, and ordering merchandise. A comparison study by Campbell confirmed the superiority of the behavioral scales over a rating procedure that was not behaviorally anchored.

Development of the Scales. Campbell and others regard the procedure for developing behavioral scales as a variant of critical incident methodology, since it requires people in the organization to consider in detail "the components of performance for the job in question and to define anchors for the performance continua in specific behavioral terms" (p. 15). As additional virtues, the people who will use the scales participate in their development, and the resulting language is that of the organization.

BARS go through several phases of development. The final decisions on items and their positions on the scale (different for each dimension being studied) are made after several rounds of judging by different groups. Various writers list either four or five steps. The following summary is adapted from Landy (1974), and Schwab, Heneman, and DeCotiis (1975).

1. Derive a pool of *critical incidents,* or specific illustrations of effective and ineffective performance behavior, from persons with knowledge of the job to be investigated.
2. Determine the *performance dimensions,* or facets of the problem, by clustering the critical incidents into a smaller set and establishing broad definitions of high, moderate, and low amounts of the trait.

3. Verify the dimensions and scales through a *retranslation* process with a different group of judges, who eliminate ambiguous and useless items and place the definitions and behavioral items in the appropriate categories. A retranslation criterion is set—for example, that 50 to 80 percent of the group must assign an incident to the same dimension as did the group in step 2.

4. Convert the items into *scales* on each dimension. The third group of judges rates the amount of a particular trait represented by a given item. The final scale is constructed after analysis of the means and standard deviations of the judgments for the items on each dimension. The scale must be anchored along its entire length and must have high agreement among the judges as to the scale values of the items, the agreement being determined by low standard deviations on the items.

5. Construct the *final instrument,* which consists of a series of vertical scales (one for each dimension) anchored by the retained incidents. The rating for each incident in step 4 establishes its location on the scale. Incidents are not necessarily located at equal intervals. The scales are tested by triads of judges. In the case of organizational effectiveness, for example, the judges might be two supervisors and a subordinate. Correlations of the supervisors' ratings of the subordinate on the scales give a measure of interrater reliability.

BARS in Needs Assessment. To test the feasibility of adapting behavioral scales to needs assessment, Witkin, Richardson, and Sherman (1982) designed three secondary school surveys (the APEX surveys) that use a variation of BARS. The survey instruments use a two-response discrepancy format with content suitable for assessing needs of students in grades six to twelve; the items are descriptive, specific, and easy to understand. Unlike the BARS scales for employee performance appraisal, the content is not intended for only one setting but rather is broadly applicable to junior and senior high schools anywhere. Respondents, however, answer for their own specific situations.

The APEX surveys for students and parents have three parts. The student survey elicits self-reports from students, and the parent survey requests observational data on their children. Part A is on student performance; Part B on attitudes, knowledge, and health; and Part C on help for students. Parts A and B use behavioral scales, and Parts A and C use a two-response discrepancy format. The staff survey elicits observational reports about students on items identical to the other two surveys for Parts A and B, but Part C is a self-report on help for teachers. Schools may delete or add items.

The behavioral scales can be illustrated by examples from Part A of the student survey. Each item consists of statements descriptive of a behavior at three levels—the lowest (or least difficult), a medium level, and a high (or difficult) level. The scales also contain two intermediate, but not described, levels of difficulty—between the low and medium levels of difficulty and between the medium and high. Thus five levels of difficulty are provided, with three descriptive phrases as anchors. The student gives two responses to each item: the behavior he or she usually exhibits and the behavior students in that grade should exhibit. Figure 6 shows the format and response modes for the first four items in the student survey.

The statement preceding each item establishes the domain of the behavior and asks for a self-report of existing state, or *status*. The statement following each item asks for a judgment of desired state, or *standard*, for the same item. Corresponding surveys for parents and instructional staff contain the same scaled items as those in the student survey with slight variations in wording of the introductory phrases for existing conditions preceding the behavioral scales. Teachers respond on status for students in specified classes, and parents respond on status for their own son or daughter. The parent responds for only one child—instructions are furnished on how to select that child if there are two or more students in that family in the same school.

The behaviors chosen for the least difficult end of the scale are generally typical of average students in middle or upper elementary grades. Those at the most difficult end could be exhibited by high school seniors. Thus the range of behaviors goes below as well as above the expected behaviors for average students in junior and senior high schools. Schools may add items to or delete items from the surveys, or they may construct their own items on the same model. The scales can also be used by and for students

Figure 6. Behaviorally Anchored Rating Scales, APEX Student Survey.

REMEMBER

Circle **two** answers for each item:

WHAT YOU ARE DOING NOW . . . . A   B   C   D   E

WHAT STUDENTS IN YOUR GRADE SHOULD BE DOING. . . . A   B   C   D   E

1

WHEN TRYING TO READ, I USUALLY...

| A | have trouble understanding school books. | B | Between A and C | C | understand school books. | D | Between C and E | E | understand school books without trying very hard. |

A B C D E

WHEN TRYING TO READ, STUDENTS IN MY GRADE SHOULD...

A B C D E

2

OUTSIDE SCHOOL, I USUALLY READ...

| A | comic books and magazines for teenagers. | B | Between A and C | C | newspapers, popular novels, and news magazines. | D | Between C and E | E | classical novels, technical books, and journals. |

A B C D E

OUTSIDE SCHOOL, STUDENTS IN MY GRADE SHOULD READ...

A B C D E

3

WHEN FINDING AN UNKNOWN WORD, I USUALLY...

| A | skip the word. | B | Between A and C | C | sound the word out and guess its meaning from the other words in the sentence. | D | Between C and E | E | sound the word out, look it up in the dictionary, and add it to a written vocabulary list. |

A B C D E

WHEN FINDING AN UNKNOWN WORD, STUDENTS IN MY GRADE SHOULD...

A B C D E

4

WHEN FINDING A CONFUSING PAGE IN A BOOK, I USUALLY...

| A | go on to the next page. | B | Between A and C | C | read the page quickly a second time. | D | Between C and E | E | reread the page carefully until it's understood. |

A B C D E

WHEN FINDING A CONFUSING PAGE IN A BOOK, STUDENTS IN THIS GRADE SHOULD...

A B C D E

2

with language or learning disabilities, comparing their perceived needs and expectations with those of other students (Witkin and Richardson, 1983).

The development process of the APEX surveys was modified from that recommended by Campbell and others (1973) and Landy (1974). The domains for the scales were derived from examining the educational literature for broad categories of school goals; the behavioral items assigned to each domain were based on expectations set forth in many sources, including courses of study, state assessment programs, and subject matter frameworks. Items were validated by groups of high school students and teachers and then revised for content and clarity of language.

In contrast with the scales of eight to ten items usually found in BARS, the APEX scales contain only three descriptive behaviors for each domain in order to provide a feasible task for junior and senior high school students and their parents. The developers felt that scales with more than three behavioral levels would present too long and difficult a task for the respondents, since each survey contains eighty-seven items, including the thirty-three discrepancy items in Part A.

There is another major difference between needs surveys using BARS and scales developed for employee performance appraisal or individual diagnosis and evaluation. Needs surveys generate group data. Their purpose is not to evaluate individual performance or to diagnose individual needs but to gather facts and judgments that will assist in identifying and analyzing group needs for priorities. They aggregate individual data in order to develop a profile of the critical needs of the target group.

Analysis of data from APEX scales in school districts that field-tested the instruments in California showed fewer problems with unrealistic or meaningless levels of standards than the typical needs assessment scales. In addition, it is easier to define actual discrepancies from the two-response APEX items than from category scales or forced-choice instruments. The APEX scales also serve a purpose beyond the data-gathering phase of the needs assessment. Following the data analysis, teachers and students can use the items to develop individual and group objectives for instructional improvement based on the identified critical needs.

Also, because of the specificity of the items in the scales, the data provide a focus for causal analysis.

Interviews

Individual interviews are often favored as an alternative to written surveys. Two important considerations when deciding whether to use interviews are the time taken to schedule and conduct them and the importance of training people to conduct them in an objective, standardized manner.

Characteristics and Training of Interviewers. Cities, human services agencies, and large school districts often retain consultants or professional polling organizations. Some schools have successfully used parents or students as interviewers. Other methods are to hire interviewers through newspaper advertisements (Cates, 1977); to use college students who are majoring in educational or public administration or evaluation (Witkin, Richardson, and Wickens, 1979); to solicit volunteers from advisory committees, boards, or other interested stakeholders; or to develop an in-house capability with staff.

Social-survey researchers have found that the best results are obtained by interviewers with whom respondents can identify, especially when ethnicity, language, cultural background, or age could make a difference. Thus, for a survey of elderly people in publicly assisted housing, the interviewers were women in their late fifties or older who were retired or displaced homemakers. One of the most effective was seventy-one years old—the respondents trusted her, and she was very good with probes on open-ended questions (A. Kethley, personal communication with author, July 7, 1982; see Evashwick, Oatis, and Herriott, 1980).

It is essential to train interviewers for the specific survey instrument. This can be done in group sessions, which may last from half a day to several days. If the agency doing the assessment does not have a staff person trained in interview methods, departments of speech communication or sociology in the nearest university may be able to supply someone to train others. Sometimes a graduate student intern with the requisite background can be found through such groups as the Western Interstate Commission on

Higher Education (WICHE). In an interagency needs assessment project, two WICHE interns were hired to develop survey protocols and to train interviewers (Witkin, Richardson, and Wickens, 1979). In addition to receiving modest honoraria at rates set by WICHE, the interns also received graduate credit through the University of California.

The best training includes both practice and supervision. Interviewers for a model project conducted by the University of Washington Institute on Aging had a five-day training period. Topics included information on the aging process, the interviewing process, and the specific contents of the survey. The interviewers then practiced on each other and on older people at senior centers and nutrition centers. The project director and a graduate student were present every day at the building sites where the interviews were conducted, to answer questions that might arise (A. Kethley, personal communication with author, July 7, 1982).

Interview Formats. Interviews can be either structured or open-ended. The structured format generally contains a list of specific questions of fact or opinion which can be answered with a simple yes or no, by choosing from a multiple-choice set, or by ratings on a category scale. Interviewers use a standard format and procedure so that all respondents are taken through the questions in the same sequence. There may also be one or more questions of a general nature, leaving room for an open-ended response as well as providing the opportunity for the interviewee to add comments.

Open-ended interviews are sometimes used in the early stages of a needs assessment to identify broad need areas for later exploration in depth by other means. The interviewer uses a general guide that outlines a set of issues to be addressed in a semi-structured fashion during the interview. The interviewer is trained to ask the issue question, then to follow up with probes to clarify the respondent's meaning and to be sure that there is understanding on both sides. The interview may be tape-recorded and later analyzed for content. Sometimes there are two interviewers, one to ask the questions and guide the discussion and the other to take notes.

In order to cover many topics and keep confusion to a minimum, interview protocols normally require only one response per question. Some needs assessment surveys that have been reported, however, have used a two-response discrepancy mode. The Wisconsin Department of Public Instruction (1977) conducted a telephone survey of local district needs that included one set of discrepancy questions. They were designed to elicit opinions on student performance, skills, attitudes, and values. Respondents rated each statement twice: first on a five-point scale of importance and then on a four-point scale of degree of emphasis that the school should place on the item. Other questions in the survey used category scales for ratings of importance and approval of various organizational matters. All questions required respondents to keep in mind from three to five response options.

Focus-Group Interview. The focus-group interview, which has been used successfully in market research to explore public opinion prior to the design of a new product, is an alternative to individual interviews for gathering information in depth. "Usually two interviewers are present to guide the group, but not to interfere with their discussion. They tape the proceedings and also take notes. Immediately after the session the interviewers transcribe the tapes and analyze the contents. Ideas brought up in the interview are categorized, and the classification scheme is reviewed by both interviewers to eliminate bias.

"Sessions typically include eight to twelve participants and last about two hours. Many such sessions can be held to reach large numbers of people, and the results of the different groups are compared and synthesized" (Witkin, 1977a, p. 111).

Other focus interviews have been used to identify the educational needs of American Indian students and in a statewide study in Washington (Consulting Services Corporation, 1969, 1970). In the latter, thirty-four group interviews were held to probe into needs that became evident from a statewide questionnaire. Blackwell and Joniak (1974) conducted three research studies to refine the focus-group interview method.

The focus-group interview differs from other group needs assessment methods both in its purpose and in the role and skills of the interviewer. The object of the interview is not primarily to obtain group *consensus* on needs, goals, and concerns but rather to discover and draw out important themes or strands. The focus interview is not structured, and in order to follow up leads and to probe promising avenues in depth without coloring the discussion with her or his opinions, the interviewer must be able to sense what the participants in the group are really saying. The interviewer must be alert and objective and must know enough about the subject of the interview and the frame of reference of the group members to be able to gain their confidence and to ask appropriate questions.

When handled well, the focus-group interview is excellent for uncovering attitudes and problems that would not surface in other needs assessment methods. When handled poorly, the results can be disastrous. An example is a two-hour focus interview with a group of eight high school students that had unfortunate repercussions with the school administration. The interview was one element in a multiphased needs assessment for district master planning. Previous stages included planning sessions with faculty and students and a written questionnaire survey, with students actively participating in the administration and data interpretation of the interview. The students selected for the focus-group interview included some leaders from the earlier stages as well as others chosen by the principal to represent different groups in the school. They thus spoke not only from personal experience but as representatives of the student body.

The interviewer, an external consultant who was highly skilled in market research and the focus interview, was so bent on encouraging the students to express their negative feelings toward the school, the school climate, and the administration that he skewed the course of the second hour. These negative feelings were highlighted in the oral report the consultant gave to the principal and other administrators, who were unhappy with the whole effort. Several months later, the eight students saw a videotape replay of the interview and discussed its content as well as changes that had occurred since the interview. Several students stated that they felt the interviewer had wanted to know only about their negative experiences and that they had many good things to say about the school that they never had the chance to express.

Despite the adverse reaction of the administration, the interview and follow-up discussion did throw into relief both student values and problems and strengths in the school. The interview data also contradicted some of the conclusions from the earlier survey, especially regarding racial isolation and school-community relations.

Observers of the process concluded: "It appears that if focus-group interviews are done well enough to probe deeply, not just to skim the surface, the results may be too uncomfortable to deal with—and in many instances, there will be no easy solutions because the problems are symptomatic of deeper social problems beyond the ability of the school to solve. On the other hand, if the interviews are less threatening, they may also be too superficial to be of value in identifying real needs" (Lehnen and Witkin, 1977a).

With skilled leadership, however, the focus-group interview is useful in the exploratory stages of a needs assessment. Few other needs assessment processes provide as good an opportunity to explore feelings in depth. Unlike the individual interview and most of the group methods described in Chapter Five, the pace and direction of the focus-group interview are set by the group. Strengths as well as weaknesses can be assessed. When used in conjunction with other data-gathering methods, the process offers an effective alternative for identifying educational and human services needs.

Administering the Survey

This section deals briefly with methods of choosing respondents, followed by discussion of alternative methods of distributing and administering the written questionnaire. The scope of this chapter does not include instructions about how to draw a sample. For good nontechnical explanations of sample selection for surveys, see McCallon and McClaran (1974) or Orlich (1978, chap. 5).

Selecting Respondents. Three methods used in needs assessments are to survey the total population of interest, to draw a sample, and to survey key informants. In small and medium-sized school districts, needs assessors often survey the entire student body and faculty. Even in larger schools, the survey is usually given to all instructional staff rather than sampling them. School administrators often feel there would be negative attitudinal factors if only a portion of the student body were surveyed. If costs are not excessive and large amounts of data can be processed, many school districts opt for surveying the entire student population.

For surveys of a community or in large districts, *random* or *stratified random samples* are drawn. School surveys often use samples stratified by grade level. For example, a high school wishing to investigate instructional needs of students could survey a sample randomly selected in each of grades nine, ten, eleven, and twelve; the parents of students in the sample (not a random sample of all parents); and all teaching staff, department chairpersons, counselors or psychologists, and other instructional support staff. If the assessment is intended to identify other needs, such as those related to school climate, vandalism, and abuse of alcohol and drugs, the survey could be extended to a sample of residents of the school's attendance area.

The parent sample should be composed of parents of those in the student sample so that data between the two groups can be compared meaningfully. If students answer questions about *themselves* and parents answer about their *own children* (*not* about the school or district in general), the responses can be compared for degrees of agreement or disagreement in the need areas. Only group data are compared since both parent and student responses should be anonymous.

The main considerations in drawing a sample are that it be representative of the different respondent groups and that it be large enough so that generalizations about the needs identified in the survey can be drawn to the target population. An invalid method of sampling often used in schools is to select every third or fifth name from a student roster. This procedure violates the criterion that each member of the population subgroup should have an equal chance of being included in the sample. It is also not recommended that parent respondents be chosen simply from those who are most active in school affairs or from volunteers since there is no way to judge their representativeness. They could, however, form a pool from which to select key informants, as described later in this chapter.

Samples for community surveys have been drawn from voter registration lists and utility billing lists (Cates, 1977); a city telephone directory, where a written questionnaire was followed up by telephone interviews; street directories; and census tract information, among others.

Many needs assessments survey *key informants* instead of, or in addition to, a random sample. The key-informant survey is often classified as a distinct type of human services needs assessment, but it is simply a method of purposeful sampling. Key informants are "spokespersons who can articulately and adequately represent school staff, parents, other community members, or whatever sources of information you have selected" (Hunt and others, 1982, p. 57). They can represent groups with special needs or be representative of organizations or subgroups identified as typical to show the needs of similar groups (Hunt and others, 1982). They can also be people with special local knowledge or with particular expertise in a field. Typical key informants in a community are public officials, administrators and staff of human services agencies, public and private sector health personnel, clergymen, clinical staff of community mental health centers, and staff of guidance clinics and vocational rehabilitation organizations (Warheit, Bell, and Schwab, 1977).

Advantages of using key informants are that the method is relatively inexpensive and simple to implement and, in the process of interaction, lines of communication among agencies and influential individuals can be established or strengthened. Disadvantages are the built-in bias of those who see the community solely from their own or their organization's perspective and therefore may not be truly representative of the needs of the community (Warheit, Bell, and Schwab, 1977; Rossi, Freeman, and Wright, 1979).

The key-informant survey is particularly recommended in the exploratory phase of a needs assessment to identify needs and issues that should be assessed in greater depth by other means. For that purpose, open-ended interviews with twelve or fifteen key informants are often sufficient to indicate the direction and scope of problems. After analyzing the information, the needs assessor can gather more specific data from social indicators, sample surveys, or group processes targeted to the issues raised. If the key-informant survey is the main component of the needs assessment, about fifty people should be surveyed, either through interviews or written questionnaires. Rossi, Freeman, and Wright (1979) recommend that the questions call for specific and concrete information. For example, don't ask about serious social problems in the community; rather, ask how many families are located within a block of public transportation lines.

Distribution and Administration of Surveys. The choice of methods of distributing and administering written questionnaires is important in order to assure the highest rate of return consistent with time and budget constraints. Communitywide citizen surveys for human services needs assessment are usually mailed, with a return rate of from 30 to 60 percent. The mailing may be followed up by telephone calls. Surveys in school systems are administered to students and school staff during class time or at meetings designated for the purpose. Parent surveys are often sent home with students. Less frequently, students or parent volunteers leave the questionnaires at respondents' homes or places of business, to be picked up later. In one district, three hundred parents distributed a thousand surveys door-to-door one evening and picked them up the next evening (Glass, 1977).

Brief surveys that seek public reaction to, or support for, educational goals have been published in local newspapers. A city recreation department in California included a questionnaire in its newsletter to the community. Lucco (1980) reports using a full-page newspaper advertisement that included a draft of a set of district goals, with boxes to check off indicating, for each goal, the type of respondent (parent, educator, student, and the like) and the choice of one of the three options: (1) I strongly support these goals; (2) I support these goals with the following exceptions; or (3) I cannot support these goals for the following reasons. Some writers recommend leaving survey forms at public offices or in heavily traveled areas such as supermarkets, banks, and post offices. These methods often result in good community response, but there is no way of verifying how representative of the community the respondents are.

Group administration of written questionnaire surveys is a desirable alternative to individual administration. Research with both group and individual administration for the survey and critical incidents in the communication audit of large organizations showed that the group method is faster, results in a high percentage of completion, allows for clarification of items, limits the opportunity for participants to bias the results by discussing items with each other, and has greater perceived trust and anonymity. Some disadvantages are time away from the job, logistics of finding meeting rooms, and fatigue. The individual method overcomes the disadvantages of logistics and time away from the job, but there is also a greater turnaround time to completion and an uncontrolled return rate (Goldhaber and Rogers, 1979). Group administration of student and staff surveys in schools is preferable, although problems of logistics and time away from class arise if the survey is given to a sample rather than to the entire student body.

Surveys in school districts often require special effort to ensure that the needs-assessment process does not engender negative reactions among respondents because of time requirements or interference with other activities and that neither teachers nor students regard the instruments as tests. On this latter point, needs assessors have sometimes found it necessary to assure respondents that the surveys seek opinions or facts within their experience, that there are no right or wrong answers, and that answers will have no effect on student grades. Additionally, in order to obtain a representative sample and a high return rate, it is desirable to use more than one method of distributing the survey to parents.

Table 2 summarizes the principal advantages and disadvantages of seven methods of distributing and administering educational surveys to parents and other stakeholders. Alternatives to mailed surveys are particularly desirable when the instruments have unusual formats, such as the APEX. Small group methods might also work for surveys in other than educational settings.

Mailed or hand-delivered surveys have higher rates of return if a return date is specified and if addressed envelopes are included with the questionnaire. The envelopes also protect identity of respondents when the surveys are administered by any of the methods using home visits. If surveys are administered anywhere other than at school meetings or by mail, parent volunteers should be trained to explain the purpose of the survey and how it fits into the needs assessment, how to answer questions about items, and to know what kinds of additional information to gather.

Table 2. Advantages and Disadvantages of Methods of Distributing and Administering Educational Surveys to Parents.

Method	Advantages	Disadvantages
Student delivery to their parents	Inexpensive; quick; students can explain items and answer questions	Students may forget or ignore the survey
Mailing	Reaches parents at a distance; seems more confidential; district has control of process	Returns often low; more expensive; no chance to clarify questions; time lag
Mailed survey and follow up visit by parent volunteers	Volunteer can clarify items, ensure prompt return	May seem to destroy anonymity of responses
Parents administer survey to others in home visits	High credibility if sponsored by school council or PTA; good for reaching parents who rarely participate; can use interpreters for parents who speak little or no English	Requires large group to administer survey; time consuming to schedule, have meetings
School meetings—at evening meeting with potluck dinner	Survey completed under expert supervision; parents can comment, discuss student needs; 100% return; short time frame	Difficult if attendance area is large; need pool of alternate parents for sample if many cannot attend
Neighborhood meetings: parents host small meetings in their homes; host takes notes of items discussed, returns completed surveys	Less intimidating for many than meetings at school; can give informal feedback; encourages parents to complete survey; opportunity to meet new people	Takes considerable planning; needs cooperation of many host parents; might not be feasible in large districts
Oral interviews: written questionnaire is administered item by item in home visit or at school	Good for using with respondents who speak little or no English; good if survey has unusual format, or if parents have little experience with surveys	Time-consuming and may be cumbersome; some parents may object to lack of anonymity

Adapted from Witkin and Richardson, 1983, pp. 12–13.

Issues in Using the Survey

In many quarters, the written questionnaire survey has become synonymous with needs assessment, but often, because of design limitations, the data do not furnish an adequate basis for establishing priorities. Chapter Eight discusses issues concerning validation of survey instruments and methods and problems of setting priorities from survey data. Here we summarize the principal advantages and disadvantages of using survey methods, particularly the written questionnaire and interview.

Bell and others (1978) note several advantages of citizen surveys that are carefully designed and conducted. The information on needs and patterns of utilization is direct and valid; they can clarify and corroborate the relevance of information obtained through other approaches and sources; and they are flexible in design, item and instrument construction, and sampling techniques. The survey can also "identify needs among residents who have not, for lack of awareness about services and for other reasons, contacted existing health and human service programs in the community" (p. 287).

The interview has several advantages over the mailed survey. The response rate is usually close to 100 percent, and the personal contact allows immediate clarification of questions and the opportunity to probe for implications of the answers. The respondent is free to reveal feelings, discuss causes of problems, and provide additional personal information and has a high sense of participation. The interviewer can observe and record nonverbal behaviors and ask follow-up questions. In addition, individuals with low literacy skills or visual impairment can participate (Orlich, 1978).

General disadvantages of interviews are that they take much longer to complete than written questionnaires, scheduling and transportation may be difficult, interviewers may consciously or inadvertently bias the responses, and the cost of interviewers' time and training can be prohibitive. Some administrative costs may be reduced by using telephone surveys.

An important consideration when planning interviews is the method of recording responses. A taped record increases accuracy, but the interviewer should not use a tape recorder or take auxiliary notes without asking permission. Listening to taped answers and comments after the interview is also time consuming.

Advantages of the mailed questionnaire over the interview, whether conducted in person or by telephone, are anonymity of respondents, no special training required to administer the survey, economy, and the potential for repeating the survey with the same or different populations in order to establish a normative data base (Bell and others, 1978). Disadvantages of mail surveys, in addition to possible low rate of return, are

1. Questionnaires sent through the mail may be answered by persons other than intended respondents.
2. Respondents may not report spontaneous, first reactions since they may take time to think things out or to consult with others for appropriate or desirable responses.
3. Respondents may not follow the order of the questions—a fact that precludes the sequencing of questions.
4. Respondents may find it difficult to follow complex questions or instructions—a fact that reduces the design flexibility of the questionnaire.
5. It is not possible to secure observational, corroborative information on the respondent's immediate environment, such as type of neighborhood, household living conditions and arrangement, or family atmosphere [Scott, 1961, cited by Bell and others, 1978, p. 282].

Several factors are strongly influenced by each of these survey techniques (mailed questionnaire or interview): sampling procedures and size; length of questionnaire or interview schedule; format for asking, recording, and coding the questions; amount of time required for responding; rates of nonreturn or refusal to participate; costs in money and time; and validity of the findings (Bell and others, 1978).

Despite the popularity of surveys both for human services and educational needs assessment, some voices have been raised in caution. Critics claim that surveys "suffer a not entirely undeserved reputation as a 'stall' tactic to defer action," especially when repeated studies have been made of certain neighborhoods or groups (Salvatore, 1978, p. 4). Furthermore, unless surveys are conducted in a time frame that coincides with the opportunity to do something tangible about the needs, the survey can become an end in itself, without implementation. Salvatore also comments on the frequent inaccessibility of respondents in low income areas, which reduces reliability of results; the rapid rate of obsolescence of the findings due to the transiency of many needs based upon services; and the fact that needs are multifaceted and multicausal, whereas surveys are by their nature superficial.

As with any other method of gathering data for needs assessment, the survey approach is only as good as the content of the questions. Constraints of time, format, and data processing often lead to using items that are too general, simplistic, or superficial; to confusing opinions with facts, and needs with solutions; and to basing the survey on present services and programs rather than on identifying needs and problems.

Sometimes so much effort and time are expended on a comprehensive survey that there is no energy left for utilizing the recommendations. Also, too much sophistication in the survey sometimes sidetracks agency councils and staff. For example, in her comparison of citizen surveys in three cities, Cates (1977) reported some staff dissatisfaction with the effort to keep the survey process objective. One administrator was so concerned with the integrity and objectivity of the survey that he practically eliminated partic- ipation of the staff. In the largest city, which used a polling firm, management felt they should have involved the staff earlier and more fully in the process.

Noting that sample surveys of citizens are "increasingly advocated as an important data-gathering technique for local public officials," Stipak (1980) provides a set of rules for the critical manager. Three that apply to needs surveys are

1. Do not judge program effectiveness only on the distribution of citizen responses to a subjective evaluation or satisfaction question.
2. Be alert for especially high or especially low citizen expecta- tions for service levels.

3. Look out for factors, such as widespread publicity about the high cost of a program, that may cause citizens to give negative evaluations despite their perceptions that the program is effective.

Probably the best use of the written questionnaire is neither at the beginning of a needs assessment nor as its sole component. Rather, after need areas have been identified by examining available data and perhaps interviewing a few key informants, the survey is useful for filling in gaps in information, corroborating data gathered by other means, and exploring in depth critical need areas and their implications. This procedure saves time and other costs and helps focus the needs study most effectively for making valid program-planning decisions.

4

Social Indicators: Using Demographic and Other Statistical Data

Social indicators are demographic and statistical data that identify the size and characteristics of population groups with particular needs, the symptoms of those needs, and the scope of a problem. Indicators in themselves do not establish needs, but when combined with other information and with goals or standards, they can show evidence of need. They are also useful for establishing a data base from existing sources prior to conducting surveys or using other methods of collecting new data.

Indicators are generally based on data already existing in various forms in many locations, although new data are sometimes gathered by means of interviews from key informants. Indicators, however, are based on hard data, as distinct from the opinions and preferences generally elicited from survey questionnaires. Social indicators are most useful as inputs to the what-is or status component of needs assessment, whereas surveys are most useful for establishing the what-should-be or standards component.

This chapter discusses several different approaches under the general rubric of social indicators. In human services planning they are social area analysis, rates under treatment, client analysis, service statistics, and spatial analysis. In educational planning they are goal indicators; test and performance data; indicators related to people, program, and organizational variables; and indicators of training needs.

Definitions

Reports of studies using social indicators for needs assessment show that the term *social indicator* is used with varying degrees of rigor. One definition is "a measure reflecting a problem or condition and for which time series information is available" (Rossi, Freeman, and Wright, 1979, p. 82). Rossi and Gilmartin (1980a) note, "Social indicators are disaggregatable time series that measure social conditions. Some researchers in the social indicators field think that social indicators should be related to social welfare and should display a historical pattern of covariation with social change. Although it has been proposed that social indicators must measure welfare or system outputs only, must be direct measures of the variable they represent, and must be defined so that change in one direction is always considered to be 'good,' these components of the definition of social indicators are not generally supported" (p. 29).

Ascher (1978, p. 207) defines social indicators as "summary measures, usually of societywide phenomena, such as the distribution of wealth, levels of satisfaction or alienation, consumption patterns, and broad aspects of the 'political climate.' . . . [They] standardize the outcomes of diverse social structures just as functional capabilities standardize the performance of diverse inventions."

A distinction should be made between indicators (which are data that have been selected, corrected, and refined) and indices (which are composed of a weighted combination of two or more indicators). Social indicators may be either objective or subjective, direct or indirect measures of variables. They may measure "any part of a theoretical framework: either input, process, output, or contextual variables; variables under policy control and those that are not; and intended or unintended outcomes" (Rossi and Gilmartin, 1980a, p. 29).

Social indicators may be classified as descriptive or analytical (Clark, 1973). Descriptive indicators provide information about societal dimensions but do not show relationships of the dimensions. Analytical indicators are integrated into a model of the causes and/or consequences of changes in indicators. A common misconception is that all variables are indicators. Rubenson (1982, p. 6) points out that "although all indicators are variables not all variables are indicators. An indicator is an observable trait of a thing that is rightly or wrongly assumed to point to the value of some other trait, usually an unobservable one." Indicators usually combine more than one variable in order to formulate a theoretical construct to measure some phenomenon. The construct summarizes large amounts of data that are a part of those phenomena (Moroney, 1977).

Cochran (1979) identifies three kinds of social indicators. (1) Social statistics include population characteristics, such as mobility and family patterns, and economic indicators, such as unemployment data and the Gross National Product. (2) Indicators can also include implications of the economic and geographic data along with the data themselves. And (3) one can focus directly on subjective, or quality-of-life indicators. For example, work might be assessed not from employment statistics but by asking workers about their physical surroundings, whether the work was pleasant, and if they had enough time to get their work done.

Types and Sources of Indicators

Social indicators are derived from the collection, correlation, review, and analysis of materials from studies, reports, agency records, the census bureau, and similar sources. Generally the data are routinely recorded for other purposes, or are contained in reports of one-time studies that are already on file. Nonquantitative items such as minutes of meetings, complaint reports, newspaper articles, and waiting lists for agency services are also useful (Salvatore, 1978).

Educators can find much information pertinent to needs assessment already collected at the school site or on the district level. This includes student test scores, reports of previous needs studies, self-studies for accreditation purposes, records of complaints by students and parents, evaluation reports of special programs funded by federal and state sources, enrollment figures and demands over several years for required and elective courses, dropout rates, and teacher records. When the data-collection effort is focused by means of issues related to student performance or school instructional and support services, the data gathered from in-school records provide highly useful indicators for analyzing current and potential needs.

Primary sources of social and health indicators are city and county planning departments, state and local health departments, state and local mental health associations, federations of social or health agencies such as United Way, comprehensive health planning agencies, universities, and staff members of both state and federal funding agencies. The Office of Management and Budget publishes in tabular form data acquired from existing sources and covering eight areas: health, public safety, education, employment, income, housing, leisure and recreation, and population. (For comprehensive lists of data sources see League of California Cities, 1975, pp. 53–58; Siegel, Attkisson, and Carson, 1978, pp. 231–232; and Rossi, Freeman, and Wright, 1979, pp. 110–112.)

Other sources of indicators are fertility and mortality rates, population censuses and large-scale sample surveys, data generated by various governmental agencies, and population and housing composition of states, local jurisdictions, and census tracts within urban areas—data types that are available in the form of published summaries and public-use computer tapes (Rossi, Freeman, and Wright, 1979). The National Center for Health Statistics is one of the statistical agencies of the federal government charged with collecting, analyzing, and publishing data for general use. The center has three major survey programs that provide estimates of the prevalence of specific diseases and disabilities in the United States. Other surveys cover child abuse, children, the elderly, the mentally retarded, delinquency, and mental illness.

A good source of indicator data for social area analysis is the mental health Demographic Profile System (DPS) of the National Institutes of Mental Health, which describes the demographic, social, and economic characteristics of all census tracts, minor civil divisions, and counties in the United States. The 161 indicators were taken from the 1970 census tapes and are the most comprehensive measures of selected contextual variables for the U.S. population (Rossi, 1979). In view of the difficulty of retrieving information from the 1980 census (see p. 127), the DPS could continue to be a prime data source for several years.

In 1979, researchers at the University of New Hampshire began to compile a comprehensive archive of data on American states and regions (Straus, 1980). The State and Regional Data Archives (SRDA) identified over 3,000 variables in the preliminary search. The SRDA has two overlapping archives—one for each of the 50 states and the District of Columbia, and a regional archive based on the nine regional divisions used in the United States census. The file contains some 2,000 variables to which education variables can be related. Among other data bases being developed are one at the University of North Carolina at Chapel Hill, the economic and social data bank of the United States Agency for International Development, and those of many departments of the federal government, such as Education, Health and Human Services, and Justice.

Social Indicators in Human Services

The social indicators approach in human services is based on *inferences* of need drawn from descriptive statistics (Bell and others, 1978, pp. 266-268):

> The use of social indicators to assess the relative distribution of service needs in a community stems from two important investigative traditions: epidemiological research and social area analysis. . . . [E]pidemiology is the study of the distribution of physical and mental disorders in human population and an analysis of the factors that determine that distribution. . . . [The fundamental orientation of social area analysis research is] that of describing human habitats and environments and analyzing the interrelationships among the characteristic descriptors of such environments. . . . The two research orientations . . . differ in many respects. . . . [T]he primary focus of traditional epidemiological research is the individual or a group of individuals. . . . Social area research . . . focuses specifically on the description and assessment of human habitats and environments, typically in terms of social and economic characteristics. . . . [Both types of studies] have consistently demonstrated . . . [a] correlation between proximity to the urban core and rates of social and psychological dysfunction

[which] is a key relationship in the social indicators approach to need assessment.

These empirical relationships make it possible to establish links between place of residence and needs for service and between residence and service utilization patterns.

Social Area Analysis. Social area analysis is defined as "the statistical treatment, usually by means of factor or cluster analysis, of demographic data describing the population within a defined geographic region in order to develop summary indices of social characteristics for various subpopulations within the region," such as counties, civil divisions within a county, or census tracts in a city or catchment area (Kay, 1978, p. 65).

Although many researchers who use social area analysis are interested in establishing either causal or associative relationships between demographic characteristics and other attributes of a population, the technique is also useful as a planning tool apart from the study of relationship. "For the planner, social area analysis summarizes the salient demographic features of a region in a succinct and comprehensible set of major indices" (p. 66). Steps in conducting a social area analysis are (1) develop a demographic data base for each subpopulation within the area of interest, (2) consolidate the large array of descriptive variables into a small number of meaningful aggregate measures, and (3) group the subpopulations that share similar composite measures of demographic variability, in order to discover how various social areas are arranged within a larger geographic region. Kay illustrates how cluster analysis can be used to develop profiles of each census tract in terms of three major dimensions of demographic variation—socioeconomic independence, family life, and assimilation.

The social area analysis can conclude at that point, but to assess the service needs of a population, researchers take the further step of assembling several incidence or prevalence measures corresponding to relevant physical or social dysfunction in the community, which can then be analyzed by the cluster technique. Kay notes that the DPS (referred to earlier) includes demographic descriptions and need measures for each catchment area in the country and that the data can be accessed by county and census tract as well. The

Bureau of the Census has also prepared an Urban Atlas series that is helpful for people who need data for urbanized regions.

Rates Under Treatment. Rossi, Freeman, and Wright (1979, p. 105) distinguish between using indicators and using rates under treatment, which "estimates target populations via the services utilized for that particular target problem in a similar community. The assumption underlying this approach is that the characteristics of the desired target population and its size will parallel closely the attributes of those who have already received treatment. . . . In communities where there were no previous interventions, estimates may be derived from one or more geographical areas that resemble the proposed project site." The term *rates under treatment* refers to service statistics and records of treated populations. But such statistics must be used with caution. Rossi, Freeman, and Wright (p. 105) cite the use of *Uniform Crime Reports,* published by the Department of Justice, based on crimes reported to the police, then transmitted to the Federal Bureau of Investigation. When these crime rates are compared with crimes reported in surveys of victims, it is found that the *Uniform Crime Reports* "significantly underestimates (by a factor of about 4) the total number of crimes in which a victim is involved."

Client Analysis and Service Statistics. The client analysis method "begins with a review of legislation, regulations, and guidelines, and an attempt to calculate the size of the potential consumer population. Actual utilization is then estimated. The resources necessary to close the gap are costed out and future targets are developed" (Moroney, 1977, p. 138).

"The service statistics approach utilizes the concept of expressed need and is based on the periodic accumulation of service reports from direct service agencies. These reports can provide a rough measure of the agency effort expended and are valuable in maintaining support activities and establishing monitoring procedures" (p. 144). Advantages are the availability and accessibility of data, economy in use of resources and time, the fact that it is a low-profile activity that does not raise hopes for increased services from present or potential recipients, and that it allows time-series analyses for trends. Disadvantages are that it may be difficult to preserve confidentiality of sources and that it does not provide information about the prevalence of unmet needs. The reports give numbers of people who have already used the services, who have been placed on waiting lists, or who have attempted unsuccessfully to receive services, and these demand statistics may reflect "only the tip of the iceberg as far as need is concerned" (p. 144).

Spatial Analysis. There are two aspects to use of indicators in assessing human services needs. One is to find out the characteristics and numbers of people in specific groups that constitute a high-risk population, such as the handicapped or the elderly. The other task is to "*locate* concentrations of high risk groups by carrying out a spatial, or geographic, analysis" (p. 148, Moroney's emphasis). Spatial analysis is the use of social indicators to classify geographic areas into typologies so that managers may determine extent of need. These have been generally carried out in metropolitan areas. "In deriving social indicators, small-area analysis does not establish baseline indicators of quality of life or levels of absolute need but rather attempts to compare relative need by area or population group" (p. 149). Since indicators usually combine more than one variable, "a health status indicator might include a combination of such factors as mortality rates, morbidity rates, and accessibility of medical care. An indicator of social equality might include measures of access to educational resources, employment, housing availability, and community participation in decision making" (p. 149).

In order to develop a coherent picture of a geographic area from large amounts of data, planners sometimes use factor analysis to identify clusters of highly correlated variables that may have an underlying factor in common. Moroney warns however that, if the factors cannot be interpreted because the related variables do not make sense conceptually, it is of little value to use factor analysis for identifying priority needs for planning.

Predictive Value. An assumption underlying the use of social indicators is that social statistics are accurate predictors of level of need. One method for establishing that level is to assign to each census tract a percent of the total needs of people in that area. "This method takes into account the fact that the strongest indicator of need is the number of persons who live in each tract" (Rossi, Freeman, and Wright, 1979, p. 108). The level of need of each census tract identified by the rates-under-treatment method is multiplied by the number of people in the tract, using absolute numbers such as the number on welfare and the number of unemployed. To illustrate, one study used three indicators: the number of people below poverty level, the number of probation cases, and the number of families with a female head of household. These indicators were assumed to be related to a need for mental health resources. The numbers were then converted into percentages. In Census Tract 1, for example, the percentages were 20, 13, and 17, respectively, making an average of 17 percent for the predictor variables. The inference was that the tract had 17 percent of the needs and should get 17 percent of the resources for the geographic area (Stewart and Poaster, 1975).

A drawback to the use of small-area statistics is that they may not accurately predict mental health needs. Nevertheless, it is felt that such statistics tend to be relatively stable in character, even though there may be a high turnover of individuals. For many kinds of social needs, the number of cases in each tract should be proportional to the number of people in the tract, although there is the possibility that some tracts would have a higher proportion of certain cases, such as poverty.

To the extent that social indicators represent observations over time, they can be used to identify trends and to predict related problems that might arise. "Sudden and sharp changes in these indicators are often useful signals about the emergence of phenomena that require action programs. For example, since there is a known correlation between unemployment and suicide rates, and the time-series data on unemployment point to a sharp rise in the number of unemployed workers, it can be anticipated that likewise there will be a marked increase in the number of persons who may want the services of a suicide intervention unit" (Rossi, Freeman, and Wright, 1979, p. 110).

Social Indicators in City Planning

For municipalities and community planning, two crucial indicators are policy outputs (the products of collective decisions) and policy impacts (the changes brought about as a consequence of policy outputs) (Clark, 1973). Social indicators contribute to city and community needs assessment and planning by providing a picture of important characteristics, neighborhood by neighborhood, categorized by age, sex, income, and ethnic membership, in order to determine where and to whom programs should be directed. Data should be organized to indicate both the extent and severity of problems in various parts of the city. Comparisons should be made with data from previous years (to determine trends) and with other cities and geographical regions. The League of California Cities (1975, p. 55) strongly recommends that cities study the relationships between problems: "A great mistake has been forcing people to fragment themselves by defining them separately as health, economic, welfare and recreation needs. If unemployment, drug abuse, alcoholism, crime and infant mortality problems are all located in one census tract or among one population group, it is essential that methods be devised to treat the neighborhood or group on a coordinated basis. Consequently, data should be collected so that the relationships between social problems can be identified."

There are three major sources of social indicators for city planning—the census, social service agencies, and private industry. Census data provide information on housing and population characteristics such as density, mobility, age, race, sex, educational and income levels, family structure, type of work, number of occupants, age of dwelling, characteristics and condition of structures, and financing arrangements. Indicators derived from public and private social service agencies and churches are health, crime and delinquency, environmental health, transportation, business activity, housing and land use, income, recreation, education, and basic needs. Some sources are clearinghouses for information from a variety of services, such as community-action agencies, local United Way organizations, councils of governments, and county and state human resources agencies.

The third source, private industry, can often supply such indicators of social well-being as employment, housing conditions, population, and education. Typical business data sources are banks, associated building industry, real estate research councils, and city directories (League of California Cities, 1975).

The Community Analysis Research Project of the University of Texas (1973, cited in League of California Cities, 1975, p. 77), suggested these criteria for selecting indicators:

1. The indicator set should facilitate inferences about actual conditions in the community . . . not simply describe governmental activities. [The set should be] capable of being improved with use.
2. The indicator set should bring together a comprehensive picture of all the most significant conditions relating to the quality of life in a community.
3. The indicator set should be simple enough so that city staff personnel can collect and present the information, and local officials will not get difficult explanations and ambiguous interpretations.
4. The indicator set should be useful to local officials in describing subcity areas of concern, in helping to set priorities, and in helping to allocate resources.
5. The indicators should require only data that is already available.

Social Indicators in Education

Social indicators of the type used for human services planning have not been widely used in educational needs assessment. In education, the term *indicators* is often used to mean "references to a domain which all will agree represents the array of desired behaviors or outcomes" (Kaufman and English, 1979, p. 212). Indicators are representative of the outcomes desired rather than complete evidence of accomplishment: "An indicator of 'increased love for learning' might be an increase in books taken out of the library during the period under study. An indicator of 'ability to survive and contribute in the external world' might be an individual who gets and keeps a job for six months or more which would place him or her above the poverty level for that community during that period of time. . . . [I]ndicators allow for our fallibility in identifying all of the important behaviors which constitute an educational enterprise. We cannot reasonably measure everything, so we reference those indicators which are, by agreement important and representative" (p. 212).

In this sense, indicators are not so much a construct for identifying the nature and location of problems and needs, as they are a means of clarifying educational goals and objectives stated in broad terms. Indicators may be derived from school-based statistics, such as the checkout of library cards, or from teacher observations, follow-up studies of former students, and the like.

Taking the lead in conceptualizing and applying social indicators to education have been researchers at American Institutes for Research in the Behavioral Sciences (AIR) in Palo Alto, who have published papers on using a social-indicators approach to youth development and educational performance (Rossi and Gilmartin, 1980a), a handbook on social indicators (Rossi and Gilmartin, 1980a), and a series of monthly bulletins on social indicators in education. Rossi and Gilmartin also established a special interest group on social-indicators research, which is now under the sponsorship of AIR.

Rossi and Gilmartin (1980a, p. 158) delineate the advantages of establishing and maintaining a data base on specific aspects of education system performance composed of relevant statistical time series:

1. Social indicators constructed from time-series data would provide a baseline (past years) against which the current status of educational performance in a variety of areas can be compared.
2. Time series would allow the identification of long-term trends, periodic changes, and fluctuations in rate of change. When deteriorating trends are identified, educational conditions that might affect these trends can be examined more closely in terms of relations among variables in the data base.
3. A social indicators data base would allow researchers and theoreticians to begin testing currently proposed theories of youth development and educational achievement (for example, which variables they would expect to be associated with other variables and with how much of a time lag).
4. Social indicator models of aspects of youth development and of school-youth interactions could be constructed using time-series data.

5. Social indicatoɪ models would permit conditional
    forecasts of key indicators. Such forecasts can serve
    the needs of educational planners and practi-
    tioners in that they allow for actions to be taken
    before the problems facing youth become severe.
    [Rossi and Gilmartin, 1980a, p. 158]

A Conceptual Framework. Rossi and Gilmartin (1980a) propose a conceptual framework for the establishment of a social-
indicators data base for education. They point to the need to
construct social-indicators models to interpret trends and changes
in social conditions since isolated social indicators usually raise
many more questions than they answer. Their informal model
focuses on developmental processes of youth and the outcomes of
those processes that could be affected by the educational system.
This model shows how educational system inputs could increase
opportunities for development by augmenting youth resources, by
decreasing the amount of youth resources required, or by providing
additional incentives for the application of resources.

The model relates four variables—status-descriptive, developmental, personal investment, and contextual—to fifteen areas of
concern in the development of youth. For example, in the intellectual development area of concern, indicators for each of the four
variables might be *status-descriptive:* functional literacy rate, *developmental:* tested level of academic knowledge and cognitive abilities, *personal investment:* percent reading literature or nonfiction
outside of school, and *contextual:* the educational level of parents
(p. 18). Other areas of concern are health and personal safety;
personal understanding and planning; relations with parents, si-
blings, or other relatives; relations with friends; relations with
spouse or girl- or boyfriend; socializing; having and raising children; creativity and personal expression; passive and observational
recreational activities; active and participatory recreational activities; occupational role; material well-being and financial security;
activities relating to local and national governments; and activities
related to helping or encouraging other people.

Applications in Education. Despite the advantages of time-
series data bases, educational planners seldom draw upon them to
furnish indicators of educational needs. One reason may be that

educational needs assessments focus on those areas about which the
school system can take some action, such as the cognitive realm and
the control of student behaviors related to learning and functioning
in a school environment—data that are internal to the system. It is
often difficult to obtain social statistics (external data) relevant to
decision making at the school or district level. Indicators aggregated
by census tract are often not descriptive of conditions or trends
within a district's boundaries, since the census tract may include
more than one district, or parts of several, or the data may be
disaggregated on a regional basis that is too general for identifying
local needs. Finally, few school systems have the resources or
expertise to seek out indicators and to establish time-series data that
would be helpful in identifying emerging needs, or changes in
needs over time.

Social indicators are used to a limited extent for certain
aspects of needs assessment. Allocation of funds under Chapter 1
(formerly Title I) of the Elementary and Secondary Education Act
is made on the basis of indicators of poverty, such as the number
of students in a school whose families receive AFDC (Aid to
Families with Dependent Children) funds or who are eligible for
school lunches. Such indicators define the population in need.
Further analysis of their needs is usually based on test scores or
other performance indicators of achievement in the basic skills of
reading, writing, and mathematics.

Certain social indicators are used in the California Assessment Program (CAP), a statewide annual testing program, as
covariants to establish performance expectations about the basic
skills levels for students in all school districts in the state. Indicators
used, varying somewhat with the grade level tested, are socioeconomic index based on parent occupation, percent AFDC families,
percent of limited- or non-English-speaking pupils, and parent
education index (for grade 12 only; California State Department of
Education, 1983). Annual test results reported to each district show
comparisons of actual performance on specified objectives to expected performance based on the indicators. Two districts with very
different socioeconomic indicators would have different ranges of
expected test scores. Needs can be identified by examining the
differences between predicted and actual scores in the general areas

of reading and mathematics, as well as in specific objectives for which test scores are furnished.

According to Rossi and Gilmartin (1980a), the use of tests and social indicators are "mutually supportive procedures for assessing effects of an educational system": "Social indicators, when used in coordination with either criterion-referenced or norm-referenced tests, can strengthen or throw into question the validity of test results by providing independent verification regarding whether or not students' successes and failures at life tasks are related to test results. Comparisons of performances measured with social indicators to reported test score trends permit the assessment of what significance these scores have for students' personal and career development, and monitoring educational achievement in terms of life experiences allows these score trends to be characterized in ways the public can easily understand" (1980a, pp. 158–159). These researchers suggest that reports of basic mathematics test scores would be more meaningful if "augmented by the actual rates of mathematical errors by present and former students on income tax forms that resulted in the person being called in by the revenue agency" (p. 158). They do not comment, however, on the difficulty of getting such information.

The following steps for generating social indicators for educational needs assessment are adapted from Rossi and Gilmartin: (1) Develop a conceptual framework by means of an interactive process with people who have key relationships with youth, determining the content areas and types of variables to be monitored; (2) identify and interrelate specific variables to be monitored, relating them to needs assessment issues; (3) identify and screen existing data sources; (4) identify and screen statistics from existing data sources; (5) access statistics from existing data sources; (6) prepare and issue social-indicators reports; and (7) perform time-series analyses and develop social-indicators models.

Houston and others (1978) propose that data be collected on variables associated with three targets of educational needs assessment: people, programs, and the organization. The collection procedure uses information already available in some form, such as products, vital statistics, court proceedings, or census and school records. This documentary analysis focuses on events that have already occurred.

The categories of variables that they suggest for the *people* area are (1) student variables—personal characteristics, attitudes, values and interests, goals and priorities, behavior, knowledge, and sociological context; (2) teacher and professor variables—personal characteristics, behavior, goals and priorities, competence, and attitudes toward students, school, and programs; (3) administrators—personal characteristics, competence, and attitude toward students, school, and programs; and (4) parents and community—personal characteristics, current conditions, attitude toward students and schools, goals and priorities, and sociological context.

Variables suggested for *programs* are (1) curricular programs—content and sequences, strategies and methods, and resources and (2) lesson, unit, and module—content and sequence, strategies and methods, and resources. For the *organization,* variables are (1) governance—policies and composition; (2) administration—personnel, facilities, students, and instruction; and (3) management climate—school satisfaction and interpersonal relations (Houston and others, 1978).

The foregoing variables are further subdivided into specific indicators, with a checklist provided so that those planning the needs assessment can choose variables most relevant to their situation. For example, variables listed under the category of "people, student variables, behavior" are "signs of overt and latent hostility, incidence of laughter and anger, disturbance in class, vandalism, withdrawal and nonparticipation, response to strangers in school environment, behavior in peer group in classroom and on the playground, participation in school activities, fighting, harassment, swearing, name-calling, and arrests" (p. 266).

Several questions arise about such behavioral indicators. What is their meaning? How can the data be gathered? What are the dangers in using and interpreting them? What inferences about needs can be drawn from the data? And further, how does one choose among the hundreds of indicators that are possible? Clearly, there should be some conceptual framework for gathering and interpreting such data in a needs assessment.

The cyclical MIS model described in Chapter Two bases its plan for collecting indicators on departmental and schoolwide issues (Kenworthy and others, 1980). This procedure provides a focus for the needs assessment, narrows the scope of the data gathering to manageable proportions, and ensures that the indicators will have relevance for the identification and analysis of needs.

A school district self-study that used indicators to develop a district profile was done in Jacksonville, Florida (Roberson and Kees, 1982). The study, which developed a large data base and which is also generalizable to other school systems, involved 134 schools at all grade levels. The profile was based on seventy-seven variables in four categories, with data collected over an eighteen-month period. The categories were students, instructional staff, parents, and facilities. Major determinants for selection of the variables were relevance to pupil achievement and centralized availability of data concerning selected institutional elements. The profile provided a data base for the variables, a data processing system, and a methodology for modifying the data base. Results of standardized and district tests were also used to assess academic strengths and weaknesses for the district as well as for individual schools.

Direct and Indirect Indicators. Social indicators are often direct indicators of need for health or welfare services, but most indicators that can be gathered from existing sources outside of schools are only indirect indicators of educational needs. Statistics on family composition and income, employment, community health, and population mobility, for example, can be correlated with such factors as educational achievement and resources available to the schools, but they need interpretation to be useful to decision makers for needs assessment and program planning. Even indicators of student abilities and achievement, such as reports of the National Assessment of Educational Progress, are not sufficient as they stand for setting educational policy on the local level. Schools do, of course, make inferences of educational need from such indicators as test scores, vandalism, absenteeism, and the like. But for needs assessment purposes a distinction should be made between descriptive statistics (sociodemographic factors), observable behaviors (violence, absenteeism), and performance/achievement (test scores, grades).

Toledo Catalog. Most schools that use test scores for needs assessments rely on general, standardized or norm-referenced achievement tests. Often neither the items nor the reported scores can be easily interpreted to throw light upon student needs, partly because they were not designed for that purpose and partly because the test items sample only a very few domains—usually reading, writing, and mathematics.

A resource that can be used to help school districts develop indices of student performance in seven growth areas is the Toledo Catalog, developed jointly by the Toledo public schools and the Evaluation Center at Western Michigan University (Nowakowski, 1983). Volume 1 of the catalog contains descriptions of 147 measures for students, cross-indexed to seven growth areas: intellectual, emotional, physical and recreational, aesthetic and cultural, moral, vocational, and social. Each of the growth areas, called classes, is divided into categories, which are further subdivided into student traits. The development of the catalog was guided by the principle that school evaluation systems should be based on characteristics the district wishes to develop in students, characteristics that are pervasive in nature and affect all levels in the district.

Volume 2 contains key evaluation concerns and assessment information that can assist in evaluating administrative functions that facilitate student development: staff personnel, curriculum and instruction, business and finance, pupil personnel, facilities, school-community relations, and policy. Each key evaluation concern is followed by assessment information with examples that elaborate on the type of information that could be considered or gathered. The entries are also cross-indexed by topic. The Toledo Catalog is "intended to provide a more complex view of the administration of a school district than can be obtained using any single set of criteria presently available or by using student achievement as the sole guide to judgments concerning administration" (vol. 2, pp. 2-3).

In his foreword to the catalogs, Stufflebeam (1983) notes that users "will be less likely to concentrate on student test scores to the exclusion of other important developmental variables such as emotional stability, physical well-being, and social maturity. . . .

They will be more likely to consider excellence as well as efficiency and student needs as well as equity."

Training Needs Indicators Model. A different application of indicators for an educational purpose is that of identifying needs for staff training in a school or agency, as in the comprehensive model developed for assessing training needs for children's services in Ohio and Wisconsin (Rindfleisch, Toomey, and Soldano, 1980). The model uses a questionnaire format for deriving indicators from five data sources: front-line workers (13 indicators), supervisors (4), administrators (4), case records (5), and special data collection (2). Most of the indicators were tested in Ohio, and all but one of those tested produced the desired results. The format for each indicator can be illustrated by item 5 of the front-line workers' questionnaire:

> *Name of Indicator:* Availability of training on a case-by-case basis.
> *Question:* How many planned conferences have you had during the past month in which you discussed your cases with your supervisor?
> *Analysis:* Total the number of case conferences for all workers in the agency and divide that total by the number of workers. The result will be the average number of case conferences in the agency.
> *Interpretation:* Case conferences are said to be an essential component of the training of frontline workers. The higher the average number of case conferences, the lower the number of courses attended [p. 62].

Indicators in Higher Education. Sizer (1981) has identified partial indicators for assessing performance for institutions of higher education, drawing on perspectives from Western Europe as well as North America. He offers a matrix that plots focus of the measure—such as availability, awareness, accessibility, and effectiveness—against conceptual content and indicated results. He asserts that "a whole range of process, outcome, and progress performance indicators should be considered when establishing appropriate indicators for the research, teaching, and central service functions within an institution of higher education. . . . [H]igher education abounds with joint inputs and multiple outputs and outcomes, and the ultimate impact of many of the outcomes is long term and extremely difficult to measure . . ." (pp. 74-75). To identify appropriate performance indicators for institutions of higher education, he recommends the application of six tests or standards by which to judge whether indicators are appropriate: relevance, verifiability, freedom from bias, quantifiability, economic feasibility, and institutional acceptability.

International Use of Indicators

The international program of UNESCO provides that case studies be undertaken to illustrate the way in which indicators of social factors linked with development can serve nationally to illuminate and solve problems inherent in rapid socioeconomic change. The program, in cooperation with the World Health Organization, includes studies on the theory and practice of using indicators regarding the disabled and elderly and ethnic and cultural minorities (Canadian Commission for UNESCO, 1982). UNESCO has also sponsored international meetings on the use of social indicators of disabled persons and of ethnic and cultural minorities, and has commissioned case studies of social indicators in Mauritania, Peru, Singapore, Yugoslavia, and Canada.

A study done in rural Jordan illustrates the use of social indicators to assess needs in developing countries (Dajani and Murdoch, 1978). The purpose was to evaluate the basic human needs of the population of rural Jordan—basic material needs, health, education, income and economic opportunity, and personal adjustment and social participation—and to propose priorities and courses of action that could make the villages more productive and liveable. Performance and input indicators were used to compare the extent to which the needs were satisfied, with the level of effort directed to their satisfaction. The study was hampered by the fact that data were unavailable for some of the categories, particularly at local levels. But data on health and education were available at the national level and for the five administrative Governates. Regional differences among the Governates were examined to identify differing levels of need.

Social Indicators in Canadian Education. Several Canadian provinces have used social and economic indicators to set priorities for planning for adult and continuing education. The Ministry of Education of British Columbia, in cooperation with the University of British Columbia, undertook a project to gather data that would be useful to community colleges in the province (Dickinson, 1981). In 1982 the University of British Columbia contracted with Okanogan College to test the use of indicators for five-year planning. The indicators were selected following a survey of people associated with various aspects of community and adult education. Respondents judged the usefulness for planning purposes of fifty-six potential indicators, and added forty others. The analysis grouped indicators in categories of demography, education, family life, health, economy, and community life. The unit of analysis was the school district. The indicator report contains a description of each indicator, its uses, and data for the indicator for each geographical area and district in the province.

Following the initial study, additional research was done to validate the indicators, to determine those categories most useful to college planners, and to revise the geographical boundaries for the data groups in order to provide more specific data for decision making (Ish, 1982). Many census tracts that were used in the original analysis were too large for the college district, and therefore the statistics were too general to be applied meaningfully.

Case Study of Use of Social Indicators

Social indicators constituted one of four types of data collection for a joint city–school district needs assessment, the LINC project (Scarborough, Fraser, and Witkin, 1978, see Chapter Twelve). The project staff designed a social indicators matrix to guide the collection of data in five areas and to serve as a transferable model. Examples from two areas—childcare and mental health—will show the types of indicators used and their rationale.

The general need for childcare services had already been established by other means, but documentation was required on the population characteristics of persons potentially needing childcare, the number of children served by existing childcare facilities, the number of requests for childcare referrals, and the number of children potentially needing specific types of childcare. The indicators were number of licensed childcare facilities within the city, number of children served by childcare facilities, number of city referrals for childcare, number and percent of women in the labor force who had children, number of female-headed families with children under six years of age, number of children under thirteen years, number of children under eighteen, total number of poverty families with children, children under six in poverty families, total number of poverty families headed by females, and number of mothers receiving AFDC. Sources of data were the 1970 census, a county social service agency, a regional childcare referral service, and school principals.

To document the level of mental health, statistics were provided on alcoholism, drug abuse, family problems, and deaths by suicide. The social indicators used were estimated number of alcoholics, calculated by the Jellinek formula: cirrhosis of liver as cause of death, as an indicator of alcohol abuse; alcohol-related arrests; drug law violations; cases of serum hepatitis, as an indicator of drug abuse; numbers of deaths by drugs; number of reported child abuse/neglect cases; juvenile delinquent tendencies and arrests; and deaths by suicide. Data were gathered from the county children's protective service, county health department mortality reports, and department of criminal justice reports.

Data for each indicator were transformed into rates and percentages and organized into tables. Each indicator was reported separately, using a standard format, and both factual and interpretive summaries were compiled for each need area. When possible, data items were presented with a comparison figure for the entire county, which provided a point of reference for interpretation. Statistics used were raw numbers (a straightforward count of people, incidents, or client cases), percentages, rates (expressed in terms of a common numerical base, such as cases per 1,000 population), and ratios (to show the quantitative relationship between two different groups or populations, such as the ratio of physicians to the general population). Percentages, rates, and ratios were used to compare the city indicators with those of other jurisdictions, such as the county as a whole. Statistics used to summarize groups of numbers were the median, the mean, and estimates derived from formulas. Estimates were used when the raw numbers were not directly available. For example, since there was no direct count of the number of residents in the city who were alcoholics, an estimate was computed using the Jellinek formula, which is based on the number of deaths in a population due to cirrhosis of the liver.

The following illustrates the format for reporting a single indicator for Elson (a fictitious name), the project city:

> *Indicator:* Number of Elson referrals for child care.
> *Description:* The number of Elson residents who have sought and received direction to potential child care services.
> *Source:* Bananas [address and phone], a child care information and referral service agency in the area outside of the city.
> *Methodology:* Information was requested and received by telephone call to Bananas.
> *Statistical information available:* Bananas, the child care referral agency, estimates about 10 requests for referrals for child care services from Elson residents are made per month.
> *Analysis:* There are an estimated 10 Elson residents per month requesting referrals for child care from Bananas. This implies 120 request per year, which is a rate of one request per five children under 13 in Elson every year. Since not everyone seeking child care would enlist the services offered by Bananas, the total number of referrals or requests for referrals in Elson is probably higher. The data point to a high percentage of the families of children under 13 seeking child care information.
> *Limitations:* The data from Bananas were an estimate. Also there are no data available on the number of referrals which may be made informally through the schools, churches, neighbors, and other sources [Scarborough, Fraser, and Witkin, 1978, pp. 9–10].

Issues in Use of Social Indicators

By the late 1970s social indicators had become highly important in human services program planning, not only in the United States but in twenty-nine other countries (Cochran, 1979). Although there is general agreement that measuring social processes provides needed information and opens up new decision-making options for administrators and policy makers, Cochran emphasizes the shortsightedness of treating data as if technical adequacy and availability were the only criteria of usefulness.

Cochran (p. 2) argues that, although we recognize that subjective measures such as self-reports are value laden, we "are less inclined to recognize that the compilation of data with physical exemplars like number (in the population) or amount (of income) is value laden also." She points out that *all* indicators are value laden because we choose to collect particular data and to compile them in particular ways. Values are as implicit in social statistics such as census data as they are in quality-of-life assessments. The needs assessor might well heed her warning of the possibility that "the availability of data helped define the problem as well as provide information about it."

In discussions up to this point, we have noted the assumption that social indicators can be related to other data to indicate needs for program or policy decisions. Cochran asserts that "the weakness of any data-collection procedure is that society cannot necessarily translate data that developed from one set of values into information that is organized to support a different set of values. The structure of data—the way it is collected, aggregated, and juxtaposed with other data—is not easily altered" (p. 3). For assessing needs and planning programs and interventions, it might be much more meaningful to ask questions about quality of life, the answers to which cannot be inferred from statistical information alone. Cochran does not condemn current strategies of collecting social indicators, but she does emphasize that measurement strategies have consequences and that they restrict as well as expand our perceptions. Data are not neutral, and critical appraisals about the assumptions on which they are based may be as useful as the data themselves.

Misconceptions abound regarding the role of social indicators (Johansson, 1979). They can show how many people are affected; specify which groups are involved by sex, age, region, and social class; show the connection between different problems; and serve as a warning signal. But indicators *cannot* specify which problems are the most urgent, show causes of problems, state what actions should be taken, or show if a reform has been successful. Ultimately, political decisions govern the selection of which problems and needs are most urgent and the actions that will be taken.

Rubenson (1982) considers that the most critical issues regarding social indicators are value neutrality, the theoretical base, and data availability.

Often there is no firm basis for the hypotheses regarding the relationship of social indicators to other variables important for planning, on which subsequent action is based. For example, the indicators judged most useful in the British Columbia project on adult education included population change in the next five years, percentage of adults with grade eight or less, and unemployment (Dickinson, 1981, p. 16). But the relationship of these indicators to the educational sector is problematic. Rubenson (1982, p. 7) asks, "Is a high unemployment rate an indicator of the educational status of the region? . . . [D]oes more adult education increase a person's employment possibilities, and if so, what kind of education is most effective?"

Assessing needs for adult education involves understanding the relationships among objective needs for education in order to participate fully in society's resources, the individual's perceived need of adult education, and the educational resources available now or potentially available. According to Rubenson (pp. 16–17), "results from welfare surveys and adult education participation research bluntly reveal that demands are negatively related to objective needs of education (i.e., being under-privileged). Put very simplistically, there is a vicious circle: poor childhood conditions, short formal education, low educational standard in adult life, no influence through participation, no improvement of the educational standard, etc." Commonly used indicators such as number of years of formal schooling are not sufficient to identify objective need for adult education, nor is self-selection adequate to indicate actual demand, given the differing values on education that occur among adults with different backgrounds of socialization.

Another important consideration in using social indicators in community or human services planning is to identify the unit for analysis. In the past, most studies have utilized existing area units such as census tracts, enumeration districts (ED), block groupings, or minor civil divisions. Warheit, Bell, and Schwab (1979, p. 33) argue that "it is better to gather data at the enumeration-district level than at the census-tract level because enumeration districts are subdivisions of census tracts and the characteristics of the tract can be obtained by aggregating the ED data. On the other hand, data obtained at the tract level cannot be reduced to the ED without considerable additional work."

Mention was made earlier of surveys published by the National Center for Health Statistics. Moroney (1977) points out that service agency managers should be aware of two important qualifications in their use: (1) Data from the surveys are not specific to the geographic area of concern, so population characteristics of the survey must be compared with population characteristics of the area of concern. (2) The conceptual approach of the survey and the operational definition of the problem or condition are important. For example, the definition of *impairment* of elderly differed in two national surveys. One study tested actual ability while the other asked for respondent reports on ability to carry out certain functions. The survey based on self-reports found double the percentage of elderly "impaired" as the other.

Moroney suggests that indicators from such surveys can be combined with local patterns of resources and services and compared with standards to derive normative needs. This approach has the strength of short time involvement and relatively low cost. Its limitation is in possible biases of professionals toward particular solutions. Moroney recommends that this bias can be countered by consulting with experts after a basic strategy for meeting the needs has been outlined. The professionals can then assist by estimating the numbers of population at risk, establishing feasible targets, and helping with programmatic development. This procedure, however, confuses needs with solutions. The basic strategy for meeting the needs should be determined *after* the population estimates and targets have been determined.

In their comprehensive and systematic analysis of social indicators, Rossi and Gilmartin (1980a) stress the importance of a conceptual framework and offer critical appraisals of methodology as well as consideration of important issues such as standards. The following discussion is based on their handbook.

In the matter of standards, rather than being guided by an explicit concept, many indicators are chosen because the available statistics are easy to collect. Since there is no standard with which to compare it, the social indicator cannot be validated, evaluated, or improved. According to Rossi and Gilmartin (pp. 66–67), "although some researchers have advocated the use of standards, or threshold values, in reporting indicators (that is, reporting the proportion above or below the standard rather than reporting the mean value of the population on the indicator), the disadvantages of standards usually outweigh their advantages. The disadvantages are that (1) it is difficult to reach a consensus on a standard; (2) the standard will have to be redefined as public perceptions change concerning what is an appropriate standard, and (3) the indicator is only sensitive to cases crossing the threshold not to changes in values that take place above or below the threshold."

Three principal disadvantages to the use of existing data sources in constructing social indicators are agency or institutional biases in the data, unreliability of data, and obsolescence of data. Data may be unreliable, for example, because there were changes in the way statistics and records were produced or recorded, and therefore the measurements of variables over time are not comparable to each other. It is essential to have data that are *exactly comparable* for variables measured over time.

In order to avoid unnecessary overlap, it is helpful to use a measurement rationale as the basis for selecting both direct and indirect indicators. For example, public involvement in local schools could be indicated either by attendance at school board meetings or at parent-teacher-association meetings—both indicators have the same measurement rationale. A different type of indicator for the same variable, however, might be the percentage of voters in the last election who approved a school bond issue—the latter indicator has a different measurement rationale for public involvement.

When using social indicators to study trends, it is important to know whether there have been interventions that have affected a time series. There may be abrupt, delayed, or temporary changes in level or direction of indicator values that have occurred because of some intervention. For example, laws regarding the use of seat belts may change the level of automobile fatalities over time.

Rossi and Gilmartin (1980a, pp. 167–168) conclude their extensive treatment of social indicators with this warning: "Social indicators structure our perceptions of the real world, and in so doing, they affect which conditions are salient and how we interpret them. Depending upon which indicators are being reported, certain societal problems may be underestimated or ignored, and possible solutions may not be considered. Developers and users of social indicators must be careful that all the major aspects of social welfare are being measured."

The LINC project cited earlier illustrates the problem of obsolete data. Since much of the information had to be extracted from the 1970 census, the figures were seven years old when the study was undertaken. Also, information on poverty families and mothers in the labor force might not have been accurate, due to changing economic conditions. By comparing the size of kindergarten enrollment for 1970–1971 and 1977–1978 (the year of the LINC study), researchers found that there was a similar number of children in the same age brackets in the two time periods and that, therefore, the number of children from poverty families was probably correct.

In addition to the fact that census data quickly become obsolete, there are serious problems for planners needing access to data from the 1980 U.S. census. Instead of issuing printed reports immediately, as has been done after collecting census data in the past, the Census Bureau now puts its highest priority on furnishing computer tapes to large corporations supplying market research to distributors of products (Hacker, 1983). These tapes are expensive and are not easily accessible to individuals or to agencies that might need certain breakdowns of information. Unless the Bureau's priorities change, the 1980 census data may never be available in a form to supply adequate social indicators for human services and educational needs assessment.

There are complex social policy, conceptual, and statistical problems associated with developing and using social indicators. The needs assessor should be aware of these problems and of the limitations as well as the advantages of using social indicators to identify needs. In most of the literature on using social indicators for needs assessment and planning, little attention is paid to the technical problems or the matter of using time-series data. In fact, many needs assessments use social indicators more as snapshots of current situations than as analyses of trends over time. The time-series aspect of social indicators is especially useful in the context of an ongoing needs assessment that is an integral part of a management information system. Social indicators are best used within the conceptual framework of a comprehensive needs assessment. Even if it is not feasible to use social indicators in that sense, however, needs assessors should consider the merit of consulting available data before designing new data collection instruments, conducting surveys, or assessing needs through group processes.

5

Group Processes:
Public Hearings, Forums,
and Small Groups

Group processes provide a qualitative method to supplement quantitative means of needs identification and problem analysis. Most types of data collected in surveys can also be gathered through group processes either as the principal means of identifying needs and setting priorities or as part of a larger assessment model. Groups may be convened to validate existing data or to provide new information. But group processes also add another, often critical dimension to a needs assessment—the active, public involvement of service receivers or stakeholders in the selection of priorities for public services.

This chapter describes and illustrates procedures that involve both large and small groups in face-to-face interaction at some stage in the needs assessment. Forms discussed are public hearings and forums, nominal and other small group processes, games and simulations, and the focus group process. The chapter concludes with a discussion of advantages and disadvantages of group processes, and issues involved in using them for needs assessment.

Public Hearings and Forums

The public hearing is an open meeting to which the general public is invited and where people are asked to give testimony about needs of the area. The principal characteristics are that all interested residents may attend and that large numbers of people are brought together for a limited period of time with a limited agenda. There are several formats for public hearings: (1) the hearing where people can talk as long as they wish and the forum ends when all have spoken, (2) the hearing where each speaker is limited to five or ten minutes and given the option of supplying additional comments in writing, (3) the group survey in which participants are given a list of questions or items and asked to rank them or to indicate agreement or disagreement, and (4) the small group approach, in which participants are divided into a number of small groups and each group discusses a set of issues, and reports back to the total group (Hunt and others, 1982). "Ideally, those attending the meetings are able to articulate their own needs, to represent the concerns of their neighbors, and in some instances, to speak for an organized constituency. Needs and priorities are then determined by a consensus of those involved in the process or through tabulation of articulated concerns to be prioritized at a later time" (Moroney, 1977, p. 147).

The community forum may consist of a series of public meetings to which all residents are invited. Or it may be structured to assure the attendance of *key informants* from specific age, racial, ethnic, or other groups with special needs. Large group sessions alternate with small group meetings. In the large assembly, the objectives of the forum are outlined and ground rules established. The small groups discuss whatever issues have been decided upon by the needs assessment steering committee and record the results for later review. The group processes chosen help focus the discussions on the issues yet also provide opportunity for candor and spontaneity on the part of the participants (Warheit, Bell, and Schwab, 1979).

Community meetings can be used for such diverse purposes as identifying general need areas, furnishing to the sponsoring agency information regarding specific needs of the conference participants, or achieving a consensus on the importance of goals and objectives. In the community-forum approach suggested by Warheit, Bell, and Schwab (pp. 111–112) for identifying the mental health needs of a community, the participants are supplied with a structured interview form that contains items on demographics, the individuals' perceptions of their own as well as others' mental health needs, their experiences with community agencies, and suggestions for ways that specific agencies—such as schools, churches, daycare centers, family service groups, and hospitals— could improve their services in meeting mental health needs.

The interagency LINC project (Witkin, Richardson, and Wickens, 1979; see Chapter Twelve) exemplifies the usefulness of a community conference to identify general need areas prior to more formal methods of data collection. A one-day community meeting was held before the official beginning of the needs assessment. At that meeting, representatives of all stakeholder groups in the school district and the community generated a list of concerns from the "grass roots." Shortly thereafter, a Needs Assessment Committee (NAC) representing all organizations and official bodies in the community was formed. Most NAC members had been actively involved in the community forum. Input from the forum and subsequent NAC meetings contributed valuable data to the process of selecting areas on which to target the data gathering.

For general community or city planning, the League of California Cities (1975, pp. 69–70) recommends that different meetings be held with different groups of informants, particularly at the beginning of the needs assessment process: "In dealing with agency representatives, it is best to meet separately with county representatives, private sector voluntary agencies and community action agencies. This will allow you to focus upon the particular experiences and insights of each sector without running the risk of sparking interagency conflicts. Similarly, it is wise, if possible, to hold meetings of citizens separately and under separate format from the agency meetings . . . on an open public basis in different sections of the city. These meetings should be conducted in an open style soliciting a wide variety of suggestions, comments and ideas although some effort should be made to make sure that the purposes, methods and expectations of the city are made clear."

An effective use of public meetings as an integral part of a comprehensive needs assessment with extensive citizen participation is illustrated by a study done between 1973 and 1975 in Alameda, California (Schoenberger and Williamson, 1977). To determine the problem areas to be addressed, mail questionnaires were sent to Alameda's 27,000 households. The preliminary results of the survey were presented to the community at a citywide congress held three months later. Nearly 1,300 residents attended the congress, and more than 400 signed up to serve on task forces organized around the nine crucial issues revealed by the survey. The task forces met weekly for the next three months to develop a series of preliminary goal statements for each area; these they presented at a second meeting of the citywide congress. Finally, personal interviews were conducted with a random sample of 1,000 residents to validate the goals and to set priorities among them.

Small Group Processes

Small group processes for needs assessment, which can be used alone or in conjunction with community forums, use structured or semistructured meetings that range in length from short sessions of one or two hours to multisession meetings held over several days or weeks. They vary considerably in degree of interaction among participants, but they share the element of leading a group to focus directly on one or more specified stages of the needs assessment, with written products expected at the conclusion of the group work.

Group Discussion. Problem-solving group discussion may be used in any phase of needs assessment. Indeed, the stages of a well-conducted discussion could be the paradigm for needs assessment, program selection, and evaluation. These stages are identification of the problem, analysis of causes, setting criteria for solutions, identification of alternative solutions, evaluation of each solution in the light of the criteria, consideration of resources needed, and final selection of a solution. Creative thinking can be encouraged through the use of brainstorming, lateral thinking, and other methods that depart from linear logic in order to free the mind for innovative approaches.

Group discussion depends heavily on the skills of the leader, as well as on the willingness of members to focus on the task at hand and to subordinate individual agendas to the group. Group discussion is most likely to be successful with highly trained leaders who have a broad understanding of discussion and group decision-making processes and whose knowledge and experience encompass more than a few prescribed techniques. (See Scheidel and Crowell, 1979, for an excellent handbook for group leaders and members; and Ferguson and Ferguson, 1980, particularly parts 9-11, for chapters on group conferencing, decision making, and creative problem solving.)

Nominal Group Process. The nominal group process was developed at the University of Wisconsin for problem identification and program planning (Delbecq and Van de Ven, 1971). It has been described as "a noninteractive workshop designed to maximize creativity and productivity and to minimize the argumentative style of problem-solving and competitive discussion" (Siegel, Attkisson, and Carson, 1978). The technique employs a number of diverse features including brainstorming and pooled individual effort, that have been derived from research on small group dynamics.

In its original form, five to ten individuals assemble in a nominal group—that is, a group in name only—and follow a highly structured, noninteracting format to achieve an assigned goal (Green and Pietri, 1980). Each group meets with a trained leader, sometimes called a grouper or, more commonly, a facilitator, because the role and responsibilities are different from those of the traditional discussion leader. The process can be used with a large group of people as long as there are enough rooms and trained facilitators for the small groups. Schoenberger and Williamson (1977, p. 2) describe the three phases of the nominal group meeting—listing, recording, and voting:

> Participants are asked to write down their needs. These individual lists are combined into a single list for each group. After clarification and discussion of each of the needs listed, group members write down their top five priority items. The leader tallies these votes and prepares a list of the group's top five priorities.
>
> The list of each of the groups is posted on a wall where all the participants may view them. Reporters explain briefly each item and then all vote on the top five priority items from each of the group lists. Votes are tallied and reported as the consensus of the group.

The foregoing description should be amended to note that, in order not to confuse needs with wants or solutions, it is preferable to list *elements* of potential needs—such as goal preferences, concerns, or problem statements—rather than *needs* as such.

Many needs assessments employ the nominal group process as one element but add other features of an interactive nature. A common technique is *brainstorming*, in which many items are quickly suggested, with all criticism reserved until later in order to encourage innovative ideas. Some methods alternate periods of brainstorming with periods of evaluation. Others use a different panel to evaluate the original list and select the most promising (Scheidel and Crowell, 1979).

An adaptation of the nominal group process is used in the one-day community conference format developed by the Fresno, California Unified School District (Jordan, 1973). Teachers, students, parents, and interested community members meet in groups of five or six to consider two questions: "What are the things that are keeping our school from doing the job it should for the students?" and "What are the things that our school should be doing for the students of this community?" Each group generates as many statements as possible, records them on large sheets of paper, and then passes them to other groups that rank them for priority, from most to least important. This procedure is repeated four or five times. Following the conference, the needs assessment steering committee transfers all statements to cards, clusters them into categories, and then writes composite statements of need. The results are given to a working committee of teachers, parents, and students who meet several times to delineate the needs more explicitly. These are further refined, priorities are assigned, and the statement of needs is published. In the final stage, the need statements are converted to goals, and the goals are presented to the school board for action. When the needs assessment is undertaken at the school site rather than the district level, the committee might also meet with members of the school's curriculum committee to translate the goals into program objectives for curriculum planning.

The so-called modified Delphi, as used in needs assessment, has some features of the nominal group process. (See Chapter Six for a description of the Delphi and its use in forecasting.) Instead of answering mail questionnaires, the participants meet in one session, but anonymity of responses is preserved. In one version, TARGET (Wishart, 1972), group members gather in a large meeting but individually write statements related to five indices: educational goals, quality of life, perceived achievement of students, priorities, and educational trends. The statements are sorted and categorized through a forced-choice group procedure, and the outputs for each index are ranked for importance.

Concerns Analysis Conference. The Concerns Analysis Conference is an important element of a comprehensive systems model for educational needs assessment (Eastmond, 1974). The conference uses a structured group process for reviewing and integrating facts, values, and policies in order to arrive at carefully formulated objectives. It is preceded by a public opinion poll and a preliminary analysis of concerns and available data.

At the conference, committees of up to fifteen citizens are appointed for each level of learners—that is, elementary, junior high school, and so on. They work separately for two days to study the concerns in detail; to review the results of the opinion poll, test scores, and other available data; and to separate facts from policies and values. Their recommendations are developed from statements of validated need, each of which specifies the learner need, target population, criterion for resolution, level of criticality, and the date projected for resolution. Results are documented and presented to the board of education. The Worldwide model was later modified for higher education, substituting a multivariate statistical analysis for the concerns analysis and relying more heavily on the survey questionnaire data than did the original model (Eastmond, 1976).

CSE Model. The Center for the Study of Evaluation (CSE) at the University of California, Los Angeles, has prepared a kit containing detailed instructions and scenarios to guide the needs assessor in using four different interactive group methods for obtaining educational goal preferences from the school community (Bank and Morris, 1979). Group meetings constitute the first stage in the needs assessment, which is selecting high priority goals. (The second stage calls for collecting baseline data related to the goals, and the third stage relates the goals to the baseline data resulting in judgments about the feasibility of attaining each of the goals.)

The goal-preferencing stage is usually carried out in a single meeting two and a half to three and a half hours long. Four different techniques are offered: (1) *Select the Goals,* in which participants work with pre-prepared goal statements related to elementary and secondary subject matter areas, scoring the goals according to importance; (2) *Values Clarification,* in which participants use interpersonal exercises to explore their own values and those they would like children to possess, then translate the values into student goals; (3) *Futuring for Goals,* in which the participants use guided fantasy and discussion about the future to decide on appropriate goals for the present; and (4) *Problem Snapshots,* in which participants generate goals based on identified problems. The scripts for the leader show how to use a number of techniques, including nominal group process, team discussions, advocacy, bargaining, two-person interactions, and methods of synthesizing and ordering the data.

Needs assessors in education have shown considerable interest in structured group processes, and many manuals and kits of materials have been published to meet their needs. Although the examples in this section were drawn from education, the processes can be adapted for almost any organizational or community setting. For more detailed descriptions of these and other procedures, see Witkin (1977a, 1977c, and 1978b).

Games and Simulations

In order to provide structure along with high interest, group processes that employ various combinations of decision-making techniques have been packaged in game form for needs assessments. Some games use simulations in which participants take the roles of service providers, receivers, and stakeholders and make decisions regarding goals and needs based on their perception of those roles. In other games, the participants take no roles other than their own. The players are selected to ensure a representative cross section of those who have knowledge useful to the needs assessment. For maximum utilization of the needs assessment results, the players should also include people who will be responsible for implementing the recommendations for program planning or renewal.

An approach that combines elements of the community conference with game procedures was developed in the 1960s at the Northern California Program Development Center in Chico and subsequently distributed to thousands of educators throughout the country by Phi Delta Kappa (PDK) through its twenty-three training and dissemination centers. In Phase I of the PDK model, educators and citizens meet to rate the importance of a preselected set of eighteen educational goals. The goal statements and descriptions are listed on individual cards and rating sheets. Participants are divided into small groups (each with a game board and colored discs) and use a forced-choice procedure to determine group ratings of the goals on a five-point scale. The data from each group are displayed, and the differences among groups are reconciled for the final criticality ratings. A committee chosen to represent the community also ranks the goals independently, using a card-sorting procedure and arriving at consensus in small group sessions. The full model includes procedures for rating the status of objectives, setting priorities, writing performance objectives and developing plans for implementation (Commission on Educational Planning—Phi Delta Kappa, 1978); and ten tests related to the goal attainment, grades seven through twelve, in English and Spanish (Tuckman and Montare, 1975).

A highly structured series of decision-making procedures for needs assessment is "Games People Oughta Play," which was developed and field-tested by this author and the staff of the Alameda County (California) Office of Education (Wickens, 1980). Strategies used are the nominal group process, concerns analysis, brainstorming, advocacy, clustering, paired-weighting, and consensus formation. The rest of this section describes this game's activities and their outcomes.

In three group sessions, a facilitator guides participants through a series of activities in which they identify concerns about the educational program, areas where program improvement is needed, probable causes of needs, resources that are being used in relation to the needs, and currently unavailable or unidentified resources that could be used to meet the needs. The sessions are designed for teachers, students (in high schools), parents, and other adults who have input to the needs assessment and concern for improving the educational program. Total time for the sessions is about five hours. The sessions can be held on one day or spread out over two or three days, with the latter option being preferable in order to give participants time for gathering data in the intervals.

Sessions are conducted alternately with the total group and with small groups of six to eight, each with a facilitator and a recorder. The manual (Wickens, 1980) gives detailed instructions.

Procedures for Identifying Needs, Causes, and Resources. Session 1 produces up to ten categories of need areas, in order of priority, by means of eight separate activities in two hours. A brief description of each activity illustrates the process.

1. 10 minutes—overview of each game (activity) and its products, and definitions of facilitator and recorder roles.
2. 20 minutes—brainstorming topic: "What students in this school are doing well." Items recorded on large sheets.
3. 20 minutes—brainstorming topic: "What students in this school are not doing well." Second list recorded. The topics in activities 2 and 3 relate to personal growth, academic achievement, and all student activities before, during, and after school.
4. 15 minutes—two small subcommittees cluster items from the two topics into ten or fewer categories, and the synthesized list is posted for the large group.
5. 10 minutes—whole group reconvenes to approve, revise, or reword the categories. This list becomes the agenda for later sessions.
6. 10 to 20 minutes—advocacy period. Each speaker has 30 seconds to advocate why a single category is or is not important as a need area to be addressed later.
7. 20 minutes—individuals independently assign ratings of importance to the categories, using a paired-weighting procedure. Ratings are summated on a master list displayed to the group and held for later analysis. (The paired-weighting procedure is described below.)
8. 10 minutes—the whole group selects the categories to be used in session 2, in order of the priorities established by the paired-

weighting. The group then quickly brainstorms for sources of data that can be gathered for each category. Participants volunteer for or are assigned data-gathering responsibilities, and the time and place are set for the next session.

Session 1 has several distinctive features. The tempo is purposely kept very fast in order to generate as many ideas as possible and to keep the session moving without getting bogged down in lengthy discussions. During brainstorming, all suggestions are accepted without comment or criticism. The items called out are very specific. The clustering procedure enables the group to deal with a manageable number of need areas, and the advocacy time permits people to state reasons why the categories are important. Thus the *generation* of ideas is separated from the *analysis* of ideas.

In the interval between sessions 1 and 2, participants gather as much data as they can regarding the priority categories. For example, if "reading achievement" was selected, those assigned to that category might seek information about the school's standing in annual statewide achievement testing, what remedial or developmental programs the school offers in reading, what teachers say about students' ability to read textbooks and related materials, and the results of any previous needs assessments or program-evaluation studies that would add specifics to the general notions of how well students in the school are reading.

Session 2 produces problem statements for each category and probable causes of each problem. Small, *heterogeneous* groups—with staff, students, and parents in each—define the problem statements and brainstorm for contributing causes. Problem statements relate to student behaviors and do not include mention of resources or what the staff or school does or does not do. Examples of problem statements are "Students in this school are dropping out in increasing numbers before completing the tenth grade" or "Over one half of the students in this school are reading below acceptable levels" (p. 27). The statements of problems and causes draw as much as possible on the research done by the participants between sessions 1 and 2. All statements are recorded on large charts.

Following a break, the participants meet in three *homogeneous* groups (all staff, all students, and so forth), to review the lists generated by the heterogeneous groups and to add causes that might have been overlooked. This provides the opportunity for each group to examine the problems and causes from its particular point of view and to draw on their group experience to throw light upon the problems. The total group then convenes to review the lists from the small groups, to achieve consensus on the causes of the problems, and to rank them for importance.

Session 3 produces lists of resources to meet the identified needs. First, the total group identifies resources that are currently being used to reduce or eliminate the causes of the problems, discussing them in the order of priority previously assigned. Then small homogeneous groups generate lists of resources that are currently unavailable but that could be used to deal with each of the causes. The facilitator and recorder then make up a large chart listing for each cause available resources and potential resources. The total group reviews the chart and makes additions if necessary. A summary is prepared. The facilitator and needs-assessment committee later prepare an outcome report and submit it to those groups responsible for planning programs to meet the identified needs.

Procedures for Setting Priorities. The two methods for rank-ordering items for priority are group consensus and paired-weighting procedure (PWP). The group consensus method uses the "rule of three" in which each participant chooses one third of the total number of items (such as causes) on the list, rather than ranking all items. If ten items are to be ranked, each group member selects the three that appear to be the most important. For twelve or thirteen items, each selects four; for fourteen or fifteen items, each selects five; and so on. Voting is by show of hands.

In PWP, each item is compared for importance with every other item on the list, one pair at a time. Each participant uses an individual rating form like the one for ten items shown in Figure 7 (minus the bars and marginal comments, which have been added to clarify the weighting process). Similar forms can be made for any number of items, but the procedure works best for no more than fifteen.

In row 1, item 1 is compared with items 2-10; in row 2, item 2 is compared with items 3-10, and so on. The rater circles the item

Figure 7. Tallying Weights on the Paired-Weighting Procedure Form.

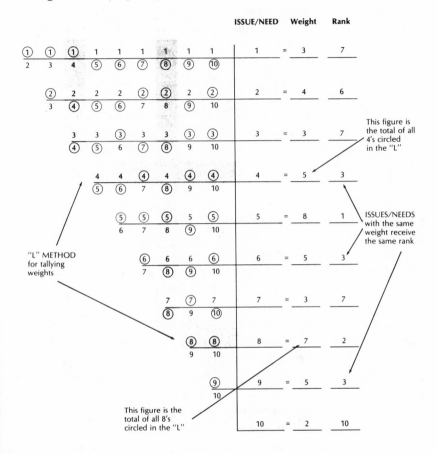

Source: Wickens, 1980.

in each pair that seems more important. In the example of Figure 7, in row 1, item 1 is considered more important than items 2, 3, and 4, but not more important than items 5–10. The weight for item 1 is thus 3. The weight for each item is the number of times the item has been chosen in comparison with all other items. Ranks are assigned based on the magnitude of the weights. Group weights are calculated by adding all individual weights, and group rank orders are then calculated.

There are several methods for deriving paired-comparison rankings. In "Games People Oughta Play," it is done as a group process in which the facilitator reads each pair of items aloud and, in order to get first impressions, paces the group rapidly in rating each pair. The items are displayed on a large chart or provided to the participants on individual printed sheets, but responses are made on separate forms, like that of Figure 7.

"Games People Oughta Play" can be adapted for assessing needs in other than school settings by changing the content of the questions in the first session. The procedures have been used successfully with community groups dealing with many different kinds of problems.

Focus Group Process

A focus group process is useful when a school system or agency wishes to narrow the scope and focus of a needs assessment and to use time and money most efficiently in the planning stage. It works best when an external consultant is available to facilitate the process. The qualitative methods of small group interaction are used to identify what is already known or believed to be true about educational or human services needs and to pave the way for gathering specific quantitative data through surveys or social indicators.

The following account illustrates how the Livermore (California) School District used a focus group process in the exploratory phase of its needs assessment and how the outputs from the sessions were integrated with other data-gathering procedures. Two consultants—a colleague and I—from the county office of education met with the district needs assessment steering committee in structured meetings to (1) define and delimit the areas for needs assessment and (2) generate a base of facts prior to developing survey questionnaires for in-depth analysis of high-priority need areas identified through the focus group process. The process was carried out in three sessions held over a two-month period. Intersessions of about three weeks each allowed time to gather data and prepare worksheets. The sessions used both highly structured group processes (designed to move the committee systematically through certain decision stages) and less formal small group work. The other consultant and I alternated roles as facilitators, recorders, and data sources, using both group processes and technical knowledge about needs assessment to keep the group work focused on the tasks at hand.

Session 1. The committee of twelve people, representing teachers, administrators, parents, and special education staff, met first for a half day. One consultant introduced the process with a statement about the purpose of needs assessment and of the sessions, emphasizing that they were not to suggest solutions but to identify those areas where solutions were most needed.

Session 1 had four stages: examine district goals, generate and share concerns about achievement of those goals, set priorities on goals and concerns, and suggest data items and data sources for the highest-priority areas. In the first stage, participants studied the eighteen goals of the district, identified the key idea of each goal, and clustered the goals into a smaller number of categories. In the second stage, a nominal group process was used to generate between sixty and seventy-five concerns, with each individual writing concerns on separate cards. Card sorts reduced the concerns to five for each goal. These were posted on wall charts and reviewed for group consensus on criticality of the concerns for needs assessment.

The third stage was an advocacy period, when the group set priorities by voting for top concerns using the "rule of three" and came to agreement on ten major concerns. In stage four, the goals with their concerns were assigned to two-person teams, who listed all they knew of (1) facts and opinions presently available for their areas and (2) facts and opinions that would have to be gathered to analyze the needs. For example, a curriculum goal elicited concerns that declining enrollment was causing program cuts and that budget reductions were affecting programs and extracurricular activities. The team working on that goal had to decide what was actually known about enrollments, budget reductions, and so on and what data would have to be gathered in order to clarify the concerns. Each member of the group took an assignment to gather specific information before the next session.

In the interim, the chairman of the steering committee organized the outputs from session 1 into separate charts, each of which contained a statement of a high-priority concern for a given goal along with items in four parallel columns—facts available, opinions available, facts needed, and opinions needed.

Session 2. The steering committee reviewed the charts and added items in both the fact and opinion columns. Charts were annotated for additional information to be gathered, such as definitions, statistics, present efforts to meet a need through curricular programs or special services, and results from district testing and other evaluation activities. Each member took an assignment to gather specific data. Further discussion identified resources available and resources required in specific areas of concern.

Before the next session, the two consultants produced a design for questionnaire surveys of parents, students, and staff, with sample items for different purposes: attitudes, perceptions of importance, verification of existence and/or extent of a problem, degree of support for stated policies or programs, and reasons for degree of support.

Session 3. The consultants and steering committee refined and edited the draft versions of the surveys, discussed how to administer them in group sessions at the schools, and settled on the outline of a report to the school board, which would be presented by the chairman of the committee.

When the survey instruments were completed, the focus turned out to be quite different from that advocated originally by the committee. Also, the research to find existing facts about the needs led the committee to decide to append statements of fact to questions about the criticality or importance of needs or program solutions. Thus the respondents' degree of agreement or support for an item would be based on a shared knowledge base, making the results of the survey easier to interpret.

Issues in Using Group Processes

The advantages of inviting people to public hearings or small group meetings to identify and analyze needs rather than using written surveys or interviews are psychological as well as practical. Even with the nominal group process, which is essentially noninteractive, group members generally have a lively feeling of involvement. Needs assessment group processes give people the opportunity to voice their concerns, and the problem-solving techniques employed often result in genuinely creative and sometimes surprising outcomes.

A major attraction of the Fresno model, for example, is that the community conference generates an enthusiasm for the needs assessment and a sense of commitment to taking steps to improve the school program. Regardless of the size of the total group in attendance (it may run to several hundred) the small groups meeting at tables throughout the conference room develop a strong sense of group ownership of the statements of concerns and needs. Further advantages are that the group process can involve hundreds of people at very little cost and the time commitments for follow-up work by committees are not onerous.

There are many disadvantages, as well, to relying on group processes for needs assessment. Public hearings pose special problems. Major issues for small group meetings center around the selection of participants, the necessity for skilled leadership, the structure of the thinking of the group, and use of the results to establish priorities of needs.

Issues Related to Public Hearings. Public hearings have been popular because they employ democratic decision-making processes, they are more economical in costs and time than the survey method, they encourage lively interaction and interchange of ideas, and no one who is interested is excluded from the process. If the planners are careful to include representatives of all segments of the community, the meetings may result in input on previously unrecognized needs, as well as identifying citizens who could be valuable resources in later phases of the needs assessment or in implementation of the results (Moroney, 1977; Warheit, Bell, and Schwab, 1979).

It is important, however, that public meetings not be taken over by groups that have their own agendas. According to Warheit, Bell, and Schwab (1979, p. 24), "The forum may be transformed from a positive seeking of information on the part of agency personnel to a generalized grievance session if some group in the community takes over the meetings in a physical or organizational sense and uses them to express disenchantment with real or perceived injustices beyond the scope or control of the local agency. While all persons in a community ought to have an opportunity to express their feelings regarding social, political, economic or other perceived injustices, or to freely voice their concerns about the inadequacy of the human services system, it must be recognized that individual local agencies are relatively powerless to alter the institutional arrangements of a community or society. It is important for those conducting the forum to know the program's purposes may be lost if the meetings become focused on problems for which the agency has no responsibility."

In addition to providing a forum for airing grievances, the public meeting may also furnish the opportunity for individuals or groups to lobby for particular programs that they want to see installed. Thus the purpose of the meeting is altered from an analysis of needs to a premature consideration of solutions. A further disadvantage is that those attending the meeting may leave with expectations that cannot be met by the sponsors, either because of lack of resources or because the solution to the problem is not within their control. Finally, unless special methods are used, the subjective and impressionistic data obtained in public forums do not lend themselves to systematic analysis "nor is there guarantee that input is accurate or representative of all groups in the community" (p. 25).

Selection of Participants. For public hearings and community forums, it is customary to issue a general invitation to the community. When small groups are convened, as in the nominal group process, it is customary to use key informants selected on some specific basis—people who represent elements in the community that can provide information or have a stake in the needs assessment. There are two important considerations in the selection of participants when the results are to be used to establish priorities among competing needs: whether they are representative of actual or potential service receivers and stakeholders and whether the groups include an adequate degree of expertise. The former criterion is more commonly mentioned: "The success of the effort in a communitywide needs assessment or goal-setting process depends to a large degree on the representativeness of the group participating and on its willingness to 'trust' the process established by the community" (Schoenberger and Williamson, 1977, p. 163).

If the public hearing or forum is the principal source of data for the needs assessment, it is even more essential to ensure that a representative cross section of the community attends the meetings. Groups such as the elderly, welfare recipients, or ethnic minorities might find it difficult to attend meetings about human services needs. School districts often schedule needs assessment meetings during the day, thus excluding working parents. Transportation may also be a problem for some. In communities with a high percentage of adults whose English is limited or who do not speak English at all, interpreters should be provided (and that fact should be publicized). If the meeting is announced mainly through the mass media, attendance of groups most in need may be minimal. Moroney (1977) recommends that resources, including the use of outreach and community organization activities, be allocated to reach important target groups.

Representativeness is not always easy to achieve, however. In some widely used procedures, such as the community conference of the Fresno model, it is advocated that all *interested* persons in the district attend. In practice, however, the participants are usually people who have been active to some extent in school matters, who have strong ideas about quality of education, and who like to attend meetings. Typically, the needs assessment steering committee invites people they know to be interested, and these may in turn invite others. Representativeness can be improved by adding criteria other than *interest* and by making a special effort to ensure attendance on the part of all segments of the community served.

On the other hand, the group may be representative of the stakeholders and service receivers yet be lacking in certain types of expertise. One solution is to use sampling to ensure the representativeness of participants and also include key informants with special knowledge in the social services or educational areas being assessed. The use of experts may not be as crucial in the needs-identification stage (if the process carefully distinguishes between status and standards and between facts and opinions) as in the exploration of causes and criteria for solutions.

Leadership of Groups. Scheidel and Crowell (1979) view every discussion group as a task group in which the role of the leader is to help the group to focus on its task. The leader must also reconcile the group goal and individual member goals. If members are working from different value systems, the group goal may have to provide motivation for them to resolve conflicts. The leader must understand her or his role, which is to help the group move systematically through the phases of the discussion, not allowing the most verbal individuals to dominate, and not contributing or advocating personal ideas and opinions. The leader or facilitator must thoroughly understand the task, know how to sort out appropriate from inappropriate contributions without discouraging individual participation, and keep the group thinking on the task at hand. The leader should be trained in discussion methods, be familiar with the needs assessment purposes to be served by the group sessions, and be able to manage conflicts and strong differences of opinion and values among the group members.

Maier (1980) likens the leader's role to "that of the nerve ring in the starfish which permits the rays to execute a unified response. If the leader can contribute the integrative requirement, group problem solving may emerge as a unique type of group function" (p. 287). The leader "must be receptive to information contributed, accept contributions without evaluating them (posting contributions on a chalk board to keep them alive), summarize information to facilitate integration, stimulate exploratory behavior, create awareness of problems of one member by others, and detect when the group is ready to resolve differences and agree to a unified solution . . . [and] he must clearly distinguish between supplying information and promoting a solution" (p. 286).

Quality of the Group Thought Processes. A third factor crucial to the success of group processes is the nature of the group's thinking. As Scheidel and Crowell (1979) put it, "To be effective for group thinking, communication needs to be characterized by *sound* thinking and *systematic* thinking. For sound thinking the group needs reliable information, a group thought-line developed by cooperative idea-production and idea-correction, and appropriate use of levels in resolving differences. At certain points, tests of evidence and reasoning need to be applied in detail; at other points, where understanding and agreement can be more readily reached, the group will need less rigorous use of these tools. . . . [The group] should consistently give attention to describing and analyzing a problem thoroughly before seeking out ways to manage it and choosing the best among the alternatives by careful comparison on standards they have formulated" (p. 52, their emphasis).

Recent research on problem-solving effectiveness of groups has found that successful groups tend to begin discussion by trying to analyze a problem before searching for solutions, while unsuccessful groups tend to begin discussion by searching for solutions before attempting to analyze the problem (Hirokawa, 1983). It is precisely in the group-thinking processes, however, that many needs assessments break down. Even when the group follows a structured format such as those described in this chapter, the temptation is strong to jump to solutions rather than to focus on identifying problems and needs. Unfortunately, many published needs assessment manuals and guidelines for group processes do little or nothing to clarify the distinction between needs and programs or solutions. This makes it all the more important that the leader/facilitator understand the requirements of needs assessments as well as basic discussion techniques.

Maier (1980) has examined the assets and liabilities of group problem solving. He finds assets to be that the group has a greater sum total of knowledge and information and a greater number of approaches to a problem than any of its members, that participation in problem solving increases acceptance and support for the solutions, and that the people affected by the decisions have a better comprehension of them if they have participated in the processes leading to those decisions thus reducing the chances for communication failures. Liabilities of groups are social pressure to accept majority opinions regardless of their objective value; possibility that skilled manipulators will influence the group unduly; influence of a dominant individual, who may be the leader; and desire to win arguments rather than find the best solution.

Factors that may be either assets or liabilities are disagreement among members, conflicting interests versus mutual interests, risk taking, time requirements, and the question of who changes views during the group deliberations. The leader can turn any of these factors into assets by playing a constructive role to facilitate communication and reduce misunderstandings. But if the leader suppresses minority views, promotes his or her own views, fails to utilize discussion time effectively, and fails to identify mutual interests, the group process will deteriorate.

Use of the Data. Both qualitative and quantitative data are possible from group needs assessments, but caution must be observed, especially if the meetings are the sole source of data or form the principal basis for establishing priorities. Groups commonly use card sorts, rankings, paired comparisons, and the like, all of which are subject to procedural problems and possible bias (see Chapter Eight). Lists developed in the nominal group process and its variants frequently confuse ends and means. Final lists of priority needs submitted for board approval all too often contain a bewildering mixture of problems, symptoms, causes, concerns, and solutions. The results are impossible to use as a basis for rational program planning.

To correct for the often fuzzy nature of group-derived needs statements and analyses, needs assessors can use social indicators and other types of factual data to validate or clarify the needs. Methods of synthesizing different kinds of data are discussed in Chapter Eight. Provision should also be made for reconciling the often conflicting views of different groups.

Many of the foregoing problems can be prevented or alleviated by careful advance planning. Those in charge should be quite clear about the purpose of the meetings, why particular group processes are employed, what outcomes are expected, how the results will be used, and what the processes are intended to accomplish in the framework of the total needs assessment plan. A good procedure is to use a focus group process early in the planning stage to delimit the needs assessment and to identify critical areas of concern that should be assessed in depth, and later to use structured group processes to provide qualitative analyses of those areas. It is also wise to provide some training for the group leaders, briefing them on the purposes of the assessment and discussing how to avoid the pitfalls of confusing means with ends while not discouraging lively participation.

6

Futures Methods: Forecasts, Scenarios, and the Delphi Method

Most needs assessments are done for immediate or short-term planning, although organizations that use a comprehensive systems approach sometimes take a longer view, perhaps three to five years. Institutional planners charting new courses for organizational renewal or facilities expansion may use needs assessments for longer-range planning, setting new goals and priorities that are expected to guide general policy for several years. They may consult demographic data projections and other social indicators to analyze trends. But often the projections have few dimensions, and the needs thus identified take few variables into account. Some needs assessments, however, attempt to look farther into the future to identify potential changes in present needs or the emergence of new ones.

The desirability of accurate long-range projections is illustrated by the familiar case of structures planned for populations that have changed by the time the building is completed. Some five or six years ago a large, handsome facility was designed for a community college in western Canada. As this is written, the college has just opened, but it is nearly twice as large as it needs to be to accommodate its daytime enrollment. What happened? The suburb of the metropolitan area where the college is situated is losing population, and instead of many young families with children, the area now has a much larger percentage of older people who are not

151

as interested in what the college has to offer. Similarly, a large county education office in a western state recently completed a building that was designed seven years ago and is now one third too large for its needs because of severe retrenchment in staffing.

For the past several years, most school districts in the United States have been faced with steadily shrinking enrollments that have necessitated the closing of many schools. At the same time, the nature of the school population has often changed racially and ethnically, calling for different kinds of programs to meet student needs. Community colleges have seen their nighttime and part-time enrollments grow much faster than enrollment in daytime courses leading to two-year degrees or transfer status. Yet often the colleges have not been adequately prepared to meet the needs of older adults and of those who must work at jobs while pursuing a degree on the side.

In the social services, the focus on present needs may also blind an agency to what should be done to prepare for needs of a changing population. As the percentage of older people has increased in relation to the whole population, for example, human services needs have changed as well. Although there is a growing awareness of this fact, the present widely used methods of needs assessment often serve to obscure real needs in favor of increasing or extending well-established existing services.

This chapter presents an overview of the application of futures techniques and forecasting to needs assessment. Several methods are described and illustrated by applications to planning in different settings, technical issues are discussed, and issues are raised regarding the validity of forecasts and problems associated with using futures methods for needs assessment.

Futures Methods in Needs Assessment

Futures methods in needs assessment can be illustrated by examining those methods a regional educational laboratory has found appropriate and feasible for use by schools (Research for Better Schools, 1977; Heathers, Roberts, and Weinberger, 1977). Listed here in approximate order of difficulty, these methods, with suitable variations, can be applied in almost any needs assessment setting.

> Future Wheel (diagrammatic): To determine needs and consequences of a given development.
>
> Scenarios (narrative): To generate alternative future histories, integrating factors of society.
>
> Decision Tree (diagrammatic): To analyze alternative possibilities resulting from a sequence of decisions.
>
> Simulation and gaming (computer analogs, role-play): To determine possible, probable, and preferable futures of a given system or group of interrelated developments.
>
> Delphi (survey): To determine consensus of opinion among experts as to the desirability and probable date of occurrence for given devlopments.
>
> Cross-Impact Analysis (diagrammatic): To determine the impact of one group of factors upon another group of factors.
>
> Trend extrapolation (graphic): To determine probable alternative futures by extending a graphed trend in several ways, relating each extension to appropriate influential factors.

The foregoing techniques can be used alone or in combination to serve specific purposes and to make findings more useful. They can also be used with other methods of needs assessment in order to furnish a different perspective. The scenario, decision tree, Delphi, and cross-impact analysis are described here in more detail.

Scenario. A scenario is an integrated set of events or conditions (Ascher, 1978), a story about how a possible future state of affairs might occur. Scenario writing is not a separate forecasting method. Rather, it is a device for giving substance to alternative futures once they have been identified by forecasting methods such as the Delphi. It is useful for communicating possible futures in terms understandable to nonexperts, investigating trade-offs among alternatives, speculating about alternative futures, and postulating future consequences of current technological and social policies.

Decision Tree. The decision tree is a network planning tool used by organizations to make decisions about instituting programs or building facilities when it is important to anticipate the impact of future events on alternative choices made in the present. The method uses a branching diagram to depict probable results of present decisions, given the occurrence of other events at stated times in the future (Archibald and Villoria, 1967). Decision trees are probably less helpful for assessing future needs than for evaluating alternative programs for meeting those needs.

Delphi. The Delphi technique seeks to achieve consensus on goals, concerns, or potential needs. The method was developed at the Rand Corporation as a means of organizing expert opinion and sharing their forecasts about the future (Helmer, 1966). Typically, a sequence of three questionnaires is mailed to respondents who remain anonymous to each other: "Respondents first generate several rather concise statements of events, and in the second round give estimates as to the probability of each event occurring at a given date in the future. . . . [The] responses are collated and returned to each respondent who then is invited to revise his estimates. The third-round responses are made with the knowledge of how others felt regarding the occurrence of each event. Again, the responses are assembled and reported back to the participants. If a respondent's estimate does not fall within the interquartile range of all conjectures, he is asked to justify his position, whether or not he wishes to change his position" (Weaver, 1971, p. 267).

The Delphi has been popular in educational needs assessments. A model developed by Research for Better Schools and used in Pennsylvania and other states employs a six-step process: identify experts, ask them to identify trends likely to shape the future, develop a Delphi questionnaire, establish a response panel, administer the questionnaire to develop consensus, and finally, use the Delphi data to identify alternative futures, trends, perceptions, and/ or preferences (Research for Better Schools, 1977).

In a needs assessment kit developed at the Center for the Study of Evaluation, Bank and Morris (1979) give guidelines on using a two-round Delphi in a "Postal Polling" technique to elicit preferences for educational goals at the level of the school, the district, or the state. "The goals . . . will be greatly influenced by the directions provided in the instructions accompanying the mailed forms. The Needs Assessor will determine whether goals are to be stated very generally or narrowly, whether they are to be affective or cognitive or a combination of these" (Section 8, p. 2).

A modified Delphi, described in Chapter Five, uses small group processes rather than mailed questionnaires mainly to avoid both the costs and time delays of mailing and the problem of attrition in the returns.

The underlying assumptions of the Delphi are that data will be more believable if participants agree and move closer to a central position or consensus and that anonymous responses, such as those from the Delphi process, are more likely to lead to reasonable and objective input than are the activities of interpersonal conferencing (Weaver, 1971). Rasp (1972) considers that the Delphi survey process is valuable in all stages of educational planning: identifying desired future conditions, assessing current conditions, establishing indicators of progress toward the desired future, and identifying necessary resources. The technique can be modified to suit the situation and requirements of the needs assessors. It can also be combined effectively with other approaches to futuring, especially cross-impact analysis and the scenario (Research for Better Schools, 1977).

Limitations of the Delphi are that it is weak in comparison with performance and outcome measures for evaluation; the problems of questionnaire construction are great, particularly for the second round; there is little explanatory power in the responses; and it is difficult to know why participants move to consensus. An important consideration that is often overlooked in Delphi studies is the measure of central tendency to be used to indicate consensus on the third questionnaire. The mean is generally not appropriate since few response scales in Delphi instruments assume equal intervals. The mode is often used when eliciting opinions about desired future conditions. The main point is that the decision must be made in advance because it affects both the calculated consensus and the style of statistical treatment to be used if further analysis is desired (Rasp, 1974).

The adequacy of using the Delphi to establish educational goals for the future was investigated as one research phase in the Atlanta Assessment Project, which is described later in this chapter (Sweigert and Schabacker, 1974). More than a thousand community leaders, educators, and high school students completed three

rounds, either through interviews or administration of questionnaires individually or in groups. The investigators found convergence in perception over the three rounds, greater convergence in
the second than in the third round, and a high reliability of goal
rankings. The study did not confirm the necessity of at least three
rounds or the desirability of feedback of own responses to participants. If it is considered desirable to produce convergence, however,
a three-round study is in order, but feedback of own last responses
should be omitted.

Cross-Impact Analysis. This method permits the study of
complex relationships among possible future events. With the use
of a matrix, each event is considered in relation to all other
predicated events. A grid of impact squares is constructed. Along
axis A, topics or developments are listed. Along axis B, the same or
different topics or developments are given, depending on the
purpose of the analysis.

In the first type of analysis, for example, the following
statements could be placed along both axes of the grid:

- Society will become more open-minded toward the teaching of
  different standards in morals, ethics, and culture.
- Parents will demand a larger role in making decisions about
  educational goals and needs.
- The state legislature will enact statutes dealing with curricula.

Other statements of a similar nature could be added. The
analysis consists of forecasting the impact of each of these attitudes
and developments on every other, thus identifying areas of potential
agreement or conflict among various stakeholders that could signal
future changes in needs and priorities.

In the second type of analysis, the items along axis A are
different from items along axis B, and two analyses are made for
each set of relationships. For example, one could study the impact
of a number of educational developments (E) on a set of social
developments (S), and vice versa: E_1—competency-based education
for students, with proficiency examinations required for graduation; E_2—busing for desegregation; E_3—bilingual education for
non-English-speaking students; S_1—health; S_2—welfare; S_3—rec-

reation. If the educational developments were a reality, what would be the impact on the social developments? And if the social developments were a reality, what would be the impact on the educational developments? Needs assessment participants analyze the potential impact of E_1 on S_1 and S_1 on E_1, the impact of E_1 on S_2 and S_2 on E_1, and so on for each pair.

The Center for Future Research at the University of Southern California has developed a sophisticated cross-impact model that allows for complex interactions of hundreds of elements of continuity and change as well as choice. Analysts play the roles of key decision makers, choosing new policies in response to scenarios created by the computer (O'Toole, 1982). O'Toole illustrates how a cross-impact matrix could be used to forecast the probability of different combinations of events for assessing work changes in the 1980s. Five events are postulated for 1989: a 4 percent annual inflation rate, a 2 percent annual productivity increase, a 25 percent increase in business automation over the 1981 level, 40 percent of all workers participating in managerial decisions and quality control, and 40 percent of all workers owning shares in the companies in which they work.

Each event is given a probability of occurrence by 1989. In the cross-impact matrix, each event is analyzed in conjunction with every other and given a new probability of the event's occurring as a consequence of the interaction. For example, a 2 percent annual productivity increase is given only a 10 percent chance of occurrence by 1989. But *if* there is also a 4 percent annual inflation rate, the probability of the 2 percent annual productivity increase goes up to 40 percent. Some events would have no effect on others—for instance, the annual inflation rate would have no impact on workers participating in managerial decisions or owning shares in their companies.

Cross-impact analysis provides projections of needs at the system level rather than the individual level and is therefore more appropriate for secondary than for primary needs assessment. When combined with social-indicators data and other futuring methods, the technique can identify potential new need areas as well as show the consequences of possible present developments in the future. It can also identify areas where the level of need might drop in the future, forcing cuts in programs or services.

Applications of Futures Methods

This section presents both general and specific applications of futures methods in different settings. They illustrate how the techniques are adapted and combined with others in making decisions about needs and priorities for planning.

Forecasting in the Corporate Setting. Forecasts are considered a precious commodity in the corporate setting, where both inside and outside forecasts are used and often jealously guarded. Companies using a corporate planning model employ sets of equations and other formal procedures to project corporation performance for some period into the future—one study found that the average was eight years. The models used by top-level management not only forecast trends but also assess the impact of trends outside the corporation on the corporation's performance. The models provide a structure of information and relationships upon which decision makers can trace the impact of alternative executive strategies and link the forecasts to outcomes relevant to the goals of the organization.

Forecasting in the Governmental Setting. In considering the actual or potential uses of forecasting for needs assessment purposes, a distinction should be made between situations in which development of forecasts is a goal in itself and those in which forecasts are used in an incidental way to provide one kind of input among others for agency or organizational planning.

In the United States, forecasting at the national level as a goal in itself has been viewed with a good deal of suspicion. The basis for this is a general opposition to *planning* by governmental agencies, which to many people signals governmental (hence unwanted) intervention. For example, the National Resources Planning Board (NRPB), which was established in 1934 as a coordinating agency for the executive branch of government, published many reports on energy, population, and natural resources that contained forecasts of future supplies and demands. Although the reports were written by prominent economists, sociologists, and demographers, the NRPB came under heavy criticism from other executive agencies because of its potential power to plan. It was assumed that "a systematic investigation of future resources and needs might promote the government's predisposition and authority to further control the public and private uses of resources" (Ascher, 1978, p. 25).

Another example of failure to incorporate forecasting into governmental decision making was the Planning-Programming-Budgeting System (PPBS), developed originally for the Department of Defense but extended to other executive agencies as part of the federal budgetary process from 1965 to 1971. Forecasts were used to project the "magnitude of problems and contextual factors affecting the implementation of programs" as well as the impact of proposed programs (p. 26). In a sense, PPBS was the governmental counterpart to planning models in corporations. Shortly after it was introduced into federal procedures, many states adopted it for educational planning. For instance, the state department of education in California instituted a multiphase program for incorporating PPBS into school district planning. Pilot programs were funded, workshops and other training sessions for administrators were held throughout the state, and both school personnel and community stakeholders were involved in generating goals and identifying needs for the planning aspect of the system. Forecasts were used to the extent that PPBS was intended for multiyear planning.

The use of PPBS for governmental planning was abruptly discontinued in 1971 when the Office of Management and Budget (OMB) ceased to require the reports for budget applications. In educational planning, PPBS also quickly lost favor, although many educators still use some of the concepts in their planning. Ascher points out that two fundamental weaknesses of PPBS were related to the use of forecasts. "As in the case of the studies produced by the NRPB, the PPBS forecasts were tied to *planning*. The rationale behind analyzing the context of three or five years into the future was to formulate programs that would be coherent over the time span of the analysis. Yet the OMB continued to make bugetary decisions in the traditional way—through incremental decisions based on the one-year time frame. The unwillingness or inability to utilize the PPBS reports for longer-term planning in individual agencies, or for the coordination of governmental programs, reduced the value of the forecasts for the OMB as well as for the specific agencies" (pp. 27–28, Ascher's emphasis).

The same problem faces school districts that try to make use of forecasts for multiyear planning. Their budgets must be made up year by year, and often the exact amounts of income are not known until the school year has started. Therefore forecasts that might indicate *future changes* in needs, or the *future impact of present decisions,* tend to look problematic at best to education boards and administrators who must cope with the realities of present needs competing for ever more limited resources.

On the other hand, there has been one highly successful forecasting institution in the federal government—the Census Bureau, which is the national clearinghouse for demographic information. The forecasts of the Census Bureau are not looked upon as a threat to other government agencies because they do not deal directly with policy choices, nor do they impose any assumptions on the user of the forecasts. Therefore they tend to be seen as primarily informational and noncontroversial. Population projections are an important source of input for decisions about facilities and programs for schools, social services, community mental health care, and hospitals; but as the forecasts are not developed specifically for such purposes, they are free from suspicion that they will serve goals other than those of the local planners. In addition, the Census Bureau uses a multiple-projection approach, and thus policy makers can choose the series that suit them best.

Forecasts have different implications for government than they do for the private sector because of the political facets of government planning as well as differences in consensus on goals and priorities. "Because of the lack of goal consensus in the public arena, expert advice of any sort is suspect to the extent that the experts may be thought to be pushing their own goals" (p. 19). To be acceptable to government, a forecast must be perceived to be not only accurate and plausible but also in line with the priorities of those using the forecasts. "It is hard to imagine that a believable forecast would be deliberately disregarded by corporate decision makers. Governmental decision makers may have quite good reasons for disregarding believable forecasts that conflict with their goal priorities" (p. 20).

Global Forecasting. The UNESCO Project on Research and Human Needs used forecasting on a global level to work out a coherent policy for relating science and technology to solving human problems. The program provided "for elaborating the concept of 'human needs' as a dynamic and complex system. . . . [Tasks to be performed were] to compare global models in order to determine the critical problems with which mankind is confronted . . . [and] to devise methods of making an integrated and overall assessment of the real development of countries and regions by working out a system of appropriate socio-economic indicators and using data banks" (Petrovskiy and Khairov, 1979, pp. 191–192). The project was concerned with evaluating the practical importance of a scientific finding by analyzing the needs it was meant to satisfy and the extent to which it in fact did so.

Petrovskiy and Khairov describe a comparatively new method called Problem Network Analysis. It is based on the principles of the man-machine relationship and "takes the form of a series of dialogues between a group of experts and a computer concerning the problems being studied" (p. 198). A network is developed for studying all the problems and all the links among them, and after all information in the network has been fed into the computer according to the principals of a metamodel, a suitable concrete model is then built. In this model, the term *problem* is understood in a broad sense, and it may be qualitative as well as quantitative.

Using Futures Techniques in Education. The *Delphi* has been used extensively in educational needs assessment, with scenarios and cross-impact analysis also playing an important role. For several years, Research for Better Schools (RBS) was engaged in developing materials and workshops to train educators in using the futures techniques listed previously. RBS also developed ideas for a futures curriculum in the schools. All the methods listed earlier have been used with students in grades eight through twelve, and they can be adapted for younger students above the third grade.

The Delphi technique was part of a three-phase statewide needs study in Washington state (Rasp, 1972) and was used to assess future needs of industrial education (Cunico, 1973). A modified Delphi was used in a statewide survey of vocational problems and needs perceived by educators and lay citizens in Kentucky (Schneider, 1975). In the latter, the five groups of respondents represented various sectors of the economy, levels of the vocational educational system, and geographic areas of the state.

In 1973 the Dallas (Texas) school district used a set of modified Delphi procedures and other futures techniques to evolve the Skyline Wide Educational Plan (SWEP) as a guide to planning secondary education in the Dallas–Fort Worth metroplex for the years 1980 to 2000 based on societal needs to be met by the school (Burns, 1974). Data were gathered and synthesized on student population trends, metroplex manpower needs, facility and site considerations, and analyses of the future society. Political, legal, and demographic facets of a multidistrict schooling venture were considered. The study also included forecasts of student enroll-ments, population ethnicity, holding power of future schools, and pupil and family metroplex socioeconomic status.

A communitywide survey investigated the likelihood of occurrence of fourteen possible developments in the future and the degree of educational impact that each would have. Results were analyzed using a nine-cell double-axis matrix, which produced a consensus concerning the likelihood of social propositions and their impact on education in the areas of technology, population, life style, careers, and education. Many other school districts have since used the propositional statements from the SWEP study for their own needs assessments.

A different use of futures projections was made by the Atlanta Assessment Project where the technique was used as a basis for developing goals, objectives, and evaluation measures for secondary education in the 1980s (Sweigert, 1973; Atlanta Public Schools, 1980). Using as a starting point the set of educational goals for Georgia adopted by the state board of education in 1970, the project (which ran for seven and a half years) used a series of Delphi studies to validate the goals for 1985. The questions were (1) What will young people in the Atlanta area need to know, be able to do, and value in order to cope successfully with life in 1985 and after? (2) Where are young people in the Atlanta area today in achieving these things? And (3) To what extent are the assessment instruments and techniques developed to answer the first two questions applicable to statewide testing in Georgia?

Three Delphi studies produced consensus on validation, importance ratings, and priority rankings of 85 goal statements (all but 1 from the original set) and added thirty-five new goals. The 120 statements were then organizd into fourteen goal areas grouped in five major categories; and a task force of teachers developed behavioral objectives that represented the goals and the competencies needed for high school graduation. Finally, test items and procedures to measure achievement of the objectives were developed and tested statewide. The Atlanta Assessment Project was one of the most ambitious and thorough in translating futures methods into concepts immediately usable by the schools.

The *scenario* approach to futuring was used by the Palo Alto Unified School District as part of Project Redesign, a comprehensive school-community needs assessment (McCollough, 1975). Participants created three scenarios, any one of which might be a plausible aspect of the society and the school district in the future. The scenarios were dubbed Status Quo Extended, Economic Disappointment, and Culture Transformation. They were based on a representative sampling of about forty alternative future histories, which emerged from apparent future trends, describing the worldwide spread of industrialism and an increasing rate of change and consumption of energy and other resources.

The Status Quo Extended scenario assumed that current trends would continue to represent the predominant goals of society. The Economic Disappointment scenario posited that the combined effects of various problems would make it impossible to stave off a rather severe economic depression shortly after the elections of 1976. The Cultural Transformation scenario assumed that the depression that occurs in the Economic Disappointment alternative provides a positive stimulus for the reshaping of national priorities rather than stimulating retrenchment. The scenarios projected actual "events" for "The View from 1985." These included the development of an extensive computer- and credit card–based system of doing accounting and quality-of-life measurements and the development of a workable conferencing technique

that synthesized the best elements of the Japanese martial art of
Aikido, the group-dynamics art of organizational development, and
the Quaker silent-meeting method of gaining group consensus.

It is interesting to note that the Economic Disappointment
scenario was only a couple of years off in predicting severe economic depression. To date, however, the response in the United
States has been retrenchment rather than cultural transformation.
Perhaps a wide dissemination of some of the creative responses
envisioned in the Cultural Transformation scenario might stimulate thinking about needs and priorities in a way that frees us from
preconceived notions about how to cope with severe societal
changes.

Cross-impact analysis was used in a needs assessment conducted jointly by a city council and a small school district to
facilitate interagency planning (Witkin, Richardson, and Wickens,
1979; see description of the LINC project in Chapter Twelve). One
area identified as important for cooperative planning was health.
On the educational side, health services currently offered by the
district were health screening, immunizations, referrals, and limited
emergency care. The curriculum incorporated health concepts in
health education, science, physical education, and some adaptations
for handicapped students. Community services available (mostly in
neighboring cities) were inpatient and outpatient care in a hospital,
public health and private clinics, private health services, and police
and fire services. Needs were identified by considering the interrelationships of each pair of educational and community services and
analyzing the impact in both directions and by identifying overlaps
and gaps in service areas.

A project carried out in southwest Virginia in a rural
Appalachian school district illustrates the use of three types of
futures techniques as a prologue to long-range planning and staff
development. The immediate objective was to develop a set of
propositional statements relative to the year 1989, which was
thirteen years in the future from the project's beginning. One reason
for this time span was that it designated the school life cycle of a
child. The propositional statements were intended to lead to
writing futures histories, goal and policy formulation, policy
planning, and eventually a long-range plan for the district (John-

ston, 1976). The project also used techniques of participatory planning and the nominal group process described in Chapter Five. Johnston's report includes a useful evaluation of the whole process. There were three rounds of futures statements:

1. intuitive writing of propositional statements regarding what can be, will be, and should be in both the school district and the county by the year 1989 (Participants were to use their own knowledge and not consider likelihood or desirability.)
2. writing of wide-angle propositional statements, based on participants' reviews of what others were saying about the future— in books, journals, and films (Materials included all items from the SWEP project, discussed earlier in this chapter.)
3. extrapolations and propositional statements based on local data (Data from 1950 to 1976 were reviewed, and projections were made forward to 1989. Both desirability and feasibility were considered.)

Participants rated each item for impact (importance of the item to the future), likelihood (the degree of probability that the event could occur), and desirability (value or positive effects). Study groups reviewed the propositions as rated, and finally reached consensus on a shorter, revised list that was delivered to the district for more general response. The final phase was to subject the items to cross-impact analysis prior to writing future histories from which district goals would later be written. From that point, administrators would assess policy impacts and begin long-range planning.

To assist school districts in using futures techniques, several research laboratories and institutes and state departments of education published background materials. Using trends analysis, Stanford Research Institute (1973) issued memoranda on socioeconomic and other issues affecting education that planners and policy makers might anticipate over the next two decades. These predictions were used in futures workshops such as those developed at RBS.

The Piedmont Virginia Community College (PVCC) used *future-trends analysis* in a community-based needs assessment of its five-county service area (Askegaard, 1982). The analysis, labeled

Piedmont 2000, was based on interviews with key informants who supplied twenty-year projections in their areas of specialization and in a general area as well. Prior to the interviews, researchers identified thirteen sectors to describe PVCC's service area. Eight were specialized, such as medicine and law; five were general, such as work environment and culture/leisure. The sectors were organized into an 8 × 5 matrix that was used as the basis for selection of key informants.

After interview results were content-analyzed and summarized by sector and cross-sector themes, key informants met at a forum to review the results. Small discussion groups considered the specific implications of the portrait of the future community for education—what and whom should be taught, and who should teach.

In order to prepare respondents to make twenty-year projections, interviewers briefly described the purpose of the interview when they telephoned to set up schedules. At the beginning of each interview, they gave examples of current trends and held a brief discussion as to the extent to which trends such as the computer revolution could have been anticipated in 1962.

Human Services Applications. All the futures methods discussed so far are appropriate for human services needs assessment, although trend projections are probably more widely used than other techniques. In addition to the Delphi method and the development of scenarios for alternative futures, Bolen (1977) suggests technological assessment (similar to cross-impact analysis), which traces the impacts of a given technological improvement (such as television or automobiles) on American society. He observes, "A thorough assessment of drug therapy and its impact at all levels of the community may have revealed many of the problems now being experienced as state and local governments attempt to deinstitutionalize patients and put them under the care of local community services" (p. 109).

Demone (1978) also feels that it is important for human services planners to study the future in order to identify potential trouble spots, particularly in the context of four interacting influences: changing social values and ideologies, technologies, administrative practices, and program patterns. Demone differentiates between forecasting techniques commonly used by professional futurists and scholars and those available to the human services worker and manager. Four techniques useful to the practitioner are simulation, the Delphi, scenarios, and extrapolations from present data. He points out, however, that extrapolations, which are essentially oriented to demand, generally assume "that current trends will continue relatively unchanged in the future" (p. 106).

The University of Akron maintains an Institute for Futures Studies and Research, which conducts various types of studies for planning purposes and offers workshops on alternative futures. One such study was done for the Children's Services Board (CSB) of Summit County, Ohio. The project included trends analysis, needs assessment surveys, and the development of five different models of alternative futures for the board to consider (Clough and Gappert, 1981). The needs assessment work, with its futures applications, was done within a context of strategic planning that included a concern with environmental forces, organizational issues and policies, and professional concerns and orientations.

The trends analysis considered both impacts from the external environment (such as birth rate and economic stress) and internal factors (such as policy decisions and response to legislation). Needs-assessment surveys of the community covered such objectives as community perception of the role of CSB, priorities for current services and emerging needs for services, and new alternatives for future services.

The alternative futures models were developed in a strategic-planning workshop the Institute held in cooperation with CSB. Five groups were assigned the task of developing a model that would represent their perceptions of CSB in the year 2000. The groups were formed on the basis of their similarities of preferences for problem solving, which were determined by means of the Myers-Briggs instrument—a self-administered, self-scoring questionnaire. Each group developed distinctive models that reflected the group combinations of elements of sensing, thinking, feeling, and intuition. Although the groups had differing conceptions of the role of CSB in the future, they had many factors in common, such as agreeing that the focus of services would move from the child to the family.

Further work included identification of significant issues for CSB over the next five years and the establishment of a needs assessment committee to review the needs research and discuss priorities for services. The Institute then offered four different, alternative planning orientations to be incorporated in the development of a new five-year plan for the CSB. The Clough and Gappert study shows explicitly how several futures methods can be integrated in a logical and systematic fashion with long-range strategic planning for human services.

Criteria and Classifications

Forecasts can be projections or predictions. "A projection is a mathematical exercise, and a forecast [prediction] makes a judgment about future possibilities. Forecasts use projections as tools to extend trends, but judgments about what trends to use and how likely they are to continue are part of the forecasting process" (Hoaglin and others, 1982, p. 220).

In using forecasts for projecting needs, it is essential to have criteria by which to judge the accuracy or credibility of the forecasts. Toffler (1980, p. 21) contends that "Social forecasts . . . are never value-free or scientific, no matter how much computerized data they use." Ascher (1978) offers criteria for analyzing and appraising forecasting methods used in both corporate and government settings. He suggests that forecasts can be evaluated by taking two approaches—the insider's and the outsider's. In the former, the relevant factors are adequacy of data, a priori validity of assumptions, biases inherent in the techniques, and logical consistency. In the latter, forecasts are evaluated in terms of the record of accuracy of forecasters in the past, taking into account known biases such as overestimation.

In addition to the above criteria, Hoaglin and others (1982) propose a quality checklist that includes appropriateness of the components and level of aggregation, scope of the forecasting model, how the forecast compares with other related work, and the remoteness of the target date (the closer the date, the more accuracy, in general). Other criteria are stability of the trends, and the forecaster's training, track record, and biases. They believe that the most neutral use of project models is in planning school closings, evaluating the merits of competing city zoning plans, and the like.

Ascher (1978) gives several correlates of accuracy, in three general categories: (1) relevance of methodology—the use of components of trends, whether scope is comprehensive or limited, whether to adopt a consensus from previous forecasts, and reliance on the forecaster's judgment; (2) relevance of context—remoteness of target date, structural stability of the trend in relation to other trends, and complexity of the context; and (3) relevance of the forecaster's characteristics—the institutional base and the discipline in which training was received.

Ascher concludes: "The core assumptions underlying a forecast, which represent the forecaster's basic outlook on the context within which the specific forecasted trend develops, are the major determinants of forecast accuracy. . . . When the core assumptions are valid, the choice of methodology is either secondary or obvious. When the core assumptions fail to capture the reality of the future context, other factors such as methodology make little difference; they cannot 'save' the forecast" (p. 199). He also considers that expert judgment is often as good as or even better than sophisticated methods of forecasting and that, on the whole, forecasting accuracy has been poor, especially for more than five years into the future, despite sophisticated technologies.

Ascher suggests that sociopolitical forecasting can be made more meaningful through the use of scenarios and social indicators. For future planning, social indicators are generally widely applicable: They can be used with relatively little contextual information, they are explicit, and they can be appraised and interpreted in a straightforward manner. A disadvantage is that they do not paint a full contextual picture in the way that scenarios do; thus they fail to clarify the relationships among elements of the context.

Forecasts can be strengthened through making a clear statement of assumptions; using good leading indicators, time series analyses, the proper level of aggregation of data, and the Delphi technique; and doing a sensitivity analysis, which is a systematic exploration of the way forecast results depend on assumptions about background variables (Hoaglin and others, 1982).

Ayres (1979) classifies forecasts on three dimensions: (1) conservative versus radical, or alpha-omega, (2) the use or nonuse of quantitative data, and (3) the subjectivity or objectivity of the rationale or method.

1. Conservative versus radical, or alpha-omega: "The *alpha* forecaster believes, essentially, that the future will be very much like the past, only 'more so.' . . . He expects no major change in [present] trends—only minor adjustments in the *rates* of change" (p. 2, Ayres's emphases).

    The *omega* position is "characterized by a tendency to minimize (or even overlook) institutional and psychological rigidities and political-economic constraints. It visualizes a utopian future and leaps over all the difficulties and problems of getting there from here. It ignores the complex dynamics that characterize the real world. . . . [The viewpoint is] that almost anything which the mind of man can envisage (as long as it does not violate natural laws) can be implemented by a sufficiently concentrated engineering effort" (p. 5).

2. Use or nonuse of quantitative data: The people who use quantitative data are concerned with very different things from those who use qualitative judgments, insights, and values. *Quantitative* forecasts "measure trends, formulate relationships between variables, and attempt to interpret what will happen in the future in terms of amounts and sizes" (p. 12). The future is charted in terms of shifts between such variables as income, urbanization, resources, and life expectancy.

    Qualitative studies of the future often emphasize a perceived change in the quality of life. Optimists focus attention on the capability of technology "to solve 'problems' such as good health, housing, and transportation/communications." Pessimists tend to be concerned with "'alienation,' crime, social disorder and dissent, the decline in the work ethic, [and] the overpreoccupation of the society with material comforts" (p. 12).

3. Subjectivity or objectivity of the rationale or method: Objectivity is the dimension of indeterminacy-causality. In *subjective* forecasts "the forecaster *cannot* really explain how

he reaches his conclusions, nor would another individual necessarily arrive at the same ones. They arise out of a 'gestalt,' an intuitive, holistic vision, which is itself a natural consequence of the inherited nature and accumulated life experiences of the individual. The forecast is a kind of work of art" (p. 14, Ayres's emphasis).

The *objective* forecaster uses the paradigm of science, in which "All phenomena are assumed to have definite causes, at least in the sense of being explainable in terms of [knowable, physical] principles. Living organisms, including man, are viewed as parts of this great evolving system" (p. 14). In objective forecasting, "trends or events will not be projected in the absence of ascertainable and understandable connections between cause and effect. . . . I do not make forecasts based on desirability or possibility (the omega position) in the absence of a conceivable and plausible cause-and-effect mechanism for achieving the end result" (p. 16).

Ayres recognizes that many nonscientists are offended by this point of view because it seems to rule out the role of human values and man's intuitive, spiritual, and artistic nature. He points out, however, that the scientific determinism of the nineteenth century has been substantially modified by the concepts of relativity and quantum mechanics, in which cause-and-effect relations become probabilistic (statistical) in nature as the basic phenomena are viewed under greater magnification.

Two implications follow: (1) "that one cannot know everything about the past, present, or the future even in *principle*" (following the Heisenberg principle) and (2) that "*indeterminacy* is not the same thing as and does not imply *unpredictability*. It means merely that predictability has intrinsic limits" (pp. 17–18, Ayres's emphases). Ayres's conclusion regarding forecasting methodology, then, is "Since it is a fundamental tenet of the paradigm of science that every event has a set of real causes, the problem seems to be to structure the causal relationships in a useful way. That is, one would like to sort out the consequences of unidentifiable, unmeasurable, and predictable ones. And one would like to concentrate attention on the latter" (p. 18).

From the needs assessor's point of view, the concern here is not primarily with the dynamics of forecasting and the merits of the various approaches of the three dimensions that Ayres postulates. Rather, it is to point out factors that must be taken into account by policy makers who wish to use forecasts for anticipating human services or educational needs. Both the enthusiastic embrace of futures methods and their outright dismissal are often based on a narrow view of a highly complex and multidimensional process. By considering the purposes for which the forecasts will be used and the data sources and points of view of those who prepared the forecasts, planners will be in a better position to appraise the usefulness of forecasting for considering probable or alternative futures related to the organization's goals and potential needs.

For those wishing more technical background, publications of the World Future Society—*The Futurist* and *Future Survey*—deal with topics such as world futures, energy, environment and resources, national and global economies, cities, transportation, education, health, communications, and science and technology. Recent books of interest to planners are *The United States in the 1980s* (Duignan and Rabushka, 1980) published by the Hoover Institution at Stanford University, *The Third Wave* (Toffler, 1980), *Megatrends* (Naisbitt, 1982), and *Looking Forward: A Guide to Futures Research* by the coinventor of the Delphi technique (Helmer, 1983).

Issues in Using Futures Techniques

There are several misconceptions regarding the role that futuring can play in needs assessment and planning. The primary objective is not to predict the reality of the future but to determine possible states of knowledge or of uncertainty and thus to infer early warning signals for change. Forecasts, analyses, and scenarios do not in themselves provide decisions about needs. They can only give perspectives and data as background for the decision makers. Unless a conscious effort is made to incorporate the concepts into a comprehensive plan that identifies probable future needs and provides alternative ways of meeting them, the futures exercises will be wasted.

As we saw in the previous section, however, determining the usefulness of forecasts demands appropriate criteria for accuracy and a knowledge of the forecaster's point of view and basic assumptions. Critical examination of forecasts is essential for needs assessors, who are generally in the role of consumers rather than producers of forecasts and have little control over methodology. Nevertheless, needs assessors should be alert to the validity of futures methods and to technical problems in applying them to needs assessment.

Validity of Forecasts. There are many problems involved in surmising about the future. Writing in 1967, Kahn and Wiener and their colleagues at the Hudson Institute were speculating on the shape of things in the year 2000. They felt that, if conditions could be predicted in reasonable detail, it might be possible to change the future through appropriate policy changes in the present. Unfortunately, "the uncertainties in any study looking more than five or ten years ahead are usually so great that the simple chain of prediction, policy change, and new prediction is very tenuous indeed" (p. 1). In their view, it is too difficult to do long-range predictions well and "even more difficult to estimate how this relatively distant future depends on current policies" (p. 1). Nevertheless, long-range studies provided a context at the Institute in which to do five- to ten-year studies that could and did influence policy choices. The long-range perspective was useful to planners and research analysts, less useful to line decision makers in government and industry.

More to the point for needs assessment, an important objective for long-range study is to anticipate problems early enough for effective planning. "Trends or events that depend on large, aggregative phenomena are often more amenable to long-range planning than those that depend on unique circumstances or special sequences of events. Projects, such as educating an individual, carrying out city planning, projecting recreational demands . . . can normally be usefully considered much further in advance than problems of international relations or subtle and complex national security issues. This is true because gross, long-term trends are far more recognizable and projectable than complex sequences of unique events, such as those that will determine tomorrow morning's headlines" (p. 2). Greater flexibility should be built into both systems and programs, even though it may be difficult to achieve. A range of futures should be considered. Even though one may not be able to affect the likelihood of various futures by decisions made today, "one attempts to design programs able to cope more or less well with possibilities that are less likely but that would present important problems, dangers, or opportunities if they materialized" (p. 3).

Critics of futuring techniques used for planning have pointed to the dismal failure of many predictions made in the past, particularly certain technological developments. Yet often the reason they did not occur was that political or other social conditions were not right. Scenarios need to be multidimensional and take into consideration the interaction of many different factors.

For example, in the decade following the passage of the Elementary and Secondary Education Act of 1965, a number of large-scale experiments showed the desirability of Computer-Assisted Instruction (CAI) in the schools. Computers were programmed to perform many routine instructional tasks, to keep track of pupil progress, to give overnight feedback to teachers and students on progress toward specific objectives, and to provide to students individual tests that would diagnose their own strengths and weaknesses. It was predicted that CAI would soon become an important part of the instructional resources of most school districts since it would free teachers to do more complex teaching tasks rather than rote jobs of monitoring and record keeping. Furthermore, instruction could be more effectively tailored to individual student needs, and progress could be monitored continuously, rather than sporadically through occasional testing. Research was also done (for example, at Stanford Research Institute) on man-machine interfaces, where youngsters were taught to interact directly with computers and teachers were taught to write programs for them.

Because of the enormous capital investment demanded, both in computers and in software, CAI did not become widely adopted and much of the early enthusiasm faded. With the recent advent of the small, versatile computers made possible by integrated circuits, however, there has been an explosion in the use of computers for all kinds of educational purposes. Probably few people in the mid 1960s could have foreseen the advent of the microchip. Yet when the computer revolution became apparent to school planners, many high schools rushed to provide computer science courses for their students, and some elementary schools are teaching computer literacy to first graders. In a short time, the school computer has come to be taken so much for granted that several nationally syndicated comic strips have used story lines based on use of computers by elementary school youngsters; one such use was the foiling of a principal's attempt to promote his own career by doctoring the students' grades entered into the school computer.

There have been scathing denunciations of futures planning. Nisbet (1982, pp. 237–238) excoriates the "monstrosity known as futurology" and comments:

> The fundamental assumption of this ill-named and ill-conceived "discipline" is that the future is contained in the present, and therefore, if we but examine the present with all the thoroughness that the computer revolution makes possible, we shall find the embryo of the future and then, with that embryo as a guide, extend it into the full growth that is the future ahead of us. There are computer fanatics who do not doubt for a moment that if we intensify and multiply our use of computers, we shall we able to foresee the future with the same accuracy that now goes into our recovery of the past. . . . That no one economist of record in the early 1970s was able to forecast correctly what actually happened to the American economy in the final years of that decade of stagflation, high interest rates, and the like seems to have not one iota of effect on the businessman's confidence in the models and numbers that futurology, under whatever name, comes up with.
>
> The blunt and inescapable fact is that the future is not in the present. Nor is the present to be found by searching the past. . . . The science of 1980 was not in the science of the 1930s. The science of the year 2025 . . . is not to be found in potential and embryonic shape in our present. Futurologists, whether unwittingly or calculatedly, confuse continuity of time with continuity of history. And for all their parading of mathematical models and computerware, their forecasts and predictions come down literally to simple extrapolation, extension of some real or imaginary trend in the present into the future.

Perhaps the forecasting of needs should not be simplemind-edly thought of as *predicting* events, or even trends, but as *imagin-ing* alternative futures and their consequences—given that this or that might happen, what would be the effect on certain aspects of education or human services? Other implications are

- In a volatile and rapidly changing environment, institutions should avoid being locked into planning facilities or programs that are too rigid to be modified without great expenditure and trauma.
- Some events in the present do give lead time for planning to meet changed needs. A sharp drop or increase in the birth rate can enable school systems to predict fairly accurately what the size of the school population will be at given times in the future as new cohorts enter. But that factor must be balanced off against in-migration and out-migration to urban centers. Health and mental health agencies can anticipate changing needs for services to children or the elderly from population trends. As another example, after a massive rubella epidemic in the United States that affected many women in their first trimester of pregnancy, speech and hearing clinics were able to forecast the need for specialized services to increased numbers of multiply handicapped children a certain number of years in the future and to plan appropriate programs.
- Sometimes a look into the future, even if problematical, can lead to rephrasing a problem or a need, putting it into a different context or a larger framework. Extrapolating present reductions in federal grants to agencies, for instance, might lead to future planning that includes more interagency cooperation (see Chap-ter Twelve), sharing facilities, or moving from service planning to strategic planning. Such steps might also help cushion the impact of needs that cannot be anticipated because they stem from international dislocations, such as the sudden influx into the United States of refugees from Indochinese countries with their attendant linguistic, educational, and social needs.

Kamis (1981, p. 32) believes that the most accurate predic-tions of future service utilization "are based on trends derived from the patterns of past utilization." But that claim is often disputed. It depends on whether one is projecting for the short or the long term. The patterns of needs could be affected by changes in demographic and economic factors, structural changes in society and organizations, changing expectations of present and potential clients, and even political and social factors on the global scene.

Aside from the fact that most people believe we cannot predict the future, many administrators find themselves so occupied with putting out present fires that they have no inclination to look ahead for signs of conflagrations down the line. The span of control that managers can exercise over events is usually short, and therefore most planning is done for no more than a three-year cycle. Sometimes, however, the shape of the future can be seen without complex scenarios. For example, once the black-power movement— with its demands not only for civil rights legislation but also for black studies in the curriculum, affirmative action to hire minority instructors, and the addition of soul food in school and college cafeterias—had attained prominence in the United States in the mid 1960s, it might have been anticipated that other minority groups would at some point follow suit. And that in fact happened, especially in states like California with large minority populations. Hard on the heels of the black power movement came the Chicano movement, then the Native Americans and other minority groups, all asking for their fair share of recognition in the educational processes and curriculum. Yet as each new group asserted its needs and wants, school systems were time and again caught without programs or resources with which to meet the needs.

As another instance, at a time when the young of an affluent society were roaming the globe as never before, and when international understanding and communication were becoming increasingly urgent, school systems were reducing or eliminating foreign language instruction. (A recent report on preparing students for college urges schools to begin teaching foreign languages again [College Entrance Examination Board, 1983].) In fact, by failing to speculate about future needs or to look to external societal requirements, most needs assessments of the past fifteen years did little to prepare school systems for the changes that their graduates would encounter in the adult world.

Technical Problems. There is little guidance for the practitioner in recognizing and avoiding pitfalls of using futures methods for needs assessment. Mention has been made of the research on the Delphi process that was done by the Atlanta Assessment Project, but there are few other critical appraisals of the application of futures techniques. An important question is that of who should be consulted about possible futures. Some studies have used key informants rather than a population sample. In the Piedmont 2000 study described earlier, key informants were used because it was felt that "only expert practitioners with significant experience would be in a position to accurately estimate future directions and to identify the pressures pushing in those directions" (Askegaard, 1982, p. 10). Even though chief executive officers of human services organizations say that they do not know what the future holds, the decisions they make in the present play an important part in constructing the future.

An important consideration, however, is the *selection* of key informants. The Piedmont 2000 study made the assumption that present needs were possibly not congruent with needs twenty years hence. The needs-assessment researchers did not collect information from community college clients or prospective students because (1) they did not expect the clients to know what their specific future needs would be; (2) the makeup of the community college population would probably change drastically in the next twenty years, as it had in the past two decades; and (3) the college had a responsibility to play a leadership role, leading students into nontraditional programs even though their importance might not be generally recognized (Askegaard, 1982).

A second issue that arose was how to summarize *differences* among key informants, all of whom have specialized knowledge. A divergence among medical respondents illustrates the dilemma: "The majority of physicians and administrators projected that a local health maintenance organization (HMO) would probably not develop in the next 20 years because the population wasn't large enough. One respondent, a state legislator, expressed certainty that an HMO would be organized. When asked why, he produced a folder of detailed plans and agreements, smiled, and said, 'Because we're just about ready to start.' The point is that consensus per se is not an adequate criterion for inclusion of a projection since one or two key informants may be in a position to know something of a certainty" (p. 9).

To solve the problem, interviewers asked respondents for rationales for their projections, especially if the interviewers knew that there were discrepancies among the projections given by different informants. If projections fell into two or three scenarios, those were reported with competing rationales. Where there was total lack of consensus, that information itself was significant. A final solution was to report majority consensus, adding the proviso that there was some dissension.

Capoccia and Googins (1982, p. 34) sum up what is perhaps the most persistent dilemma in futures planning. "As a future-oriented activity, the planning process ideally seeks to predict and determine the future. It is essentially proactive. In some cases, however, past practice has served as the principal guide to future action, losing sight of the concept of future in the process. The predominance of compliance planning in the public sector over the past decade is a case in point. The future is often defined by interests that are external to the planner. In this case, a variety of active futures are presented from different sources, each of which need to be explored and eventually resolved into a desirable course of action."

7

Causal Analysis:
Ways to Determine
the Causes of Needs

An essential step in a complete needs assessment is the analysis of causes. What has prevented the needs from being met? What factors have operated to perpetuate an unsatisfactory situation? Often what appear to be needs are actually symptoms of a problem. Causal analysis uncovers the factors underlying the symptoms and so brings planners and evaluators closer to the real needs. It is an important stage between analysis of data and consideration of alternative solutions.

According to Heise (1975), a causal relation exists when "the occurrence of one event is reason enough to expect the production of another" (p. 11), but "only if some operator effects the transformation" (p. 10). Warwick and Lininger (1975) note that the terms *explanation* and *cause* have both had a stormy history in the social sciences as well as in philosophy. The two terms are often linked together, and many social scientists find that "the most convincing evidence of explanation is the establishment of a causal relationship between two or more variables" (p 49). To infer the existence of a causal relationship, however, there must be covariation between the two variables, a time ordering or sequence where the cause precedes the effect or at least the effect does not precede the cause, and the elimination of other possible causal factors that might produce the observed relationship between the two (Warwick and Lininger, 1975; Asher, 1976).

Keeping in mind those criteria, the needs assessor will find that a causal analysis, broadly conceived, will help analysts and policy makers avoid jumping from data to unwarranted conclusions about solutions. A typical instance is the study that surveyed the intentions of students regarding their post-high-school plans. Results showed that senior boys were more interested in going on to higher education than senior girls and that the boys had identified their plans earlier than the girls. The analyst concluded that more vocational and educational counseling was needed for the girls so they might formulate postsecondary plans earlier in their high school years. The data alone, however, did not lead inescapably to that conclusion. A causal analysis might have identified contributing factors that would point the way to a different solution. The needs assessor assumed a need for counseling, whereas counseling was one possible solution to an inadequately analyzed need.

In their work on systematic thinking and problem solving for groups, Scheidel and Crowell (1979) show the desirability of searching out causes and underlying conditions in the analysis step of their Problem Management Sequence. They suggest listing not only all significant causes but also any conditions in the problem situation that allow, invite, or precipitate the operation of the causes without themselves actually producing the problem. In needs assessment, the analysis should lead smoothly into a plan of action. Ideally, the program of action (solution) should attack or master the problem and thus reduce or eliminate the need. But they point out:

> Planning the approach for managing the problem begins with the choice of a *major cause* of the symptoms discovered—a highly important and somewhat lengthy task. Deciding which of the important causes to strike at is important because here is determined *which* of the symptoms will—it is to be hoped—be reduced or eliminated; in the meantime, all other symptoms (though perhaps weakened in their effect by successes in the attack upon these) will continue their harm as before.
> In some situations, however, the symptoms are so intolerable or are increasing so rapidly or the opportunities for their correction are diminishing so rapidly that the first attack must be launched directly

at the most harmful symptoms rather than at the underlying causes. . . . A detailed examination of the causes (and conditions) on the basis of the symptoms for which they are largely responsible should reveal the most central of the causes and thus the appropriate DIRECTION for attack, an attack to be made by means of the plan chosen in subsequent steps [pp. 32–33, Scheidel and Crowell's emphases].

Causal analysis is used in this book to refer broadly to techniques that seek contributing factors or preexisting conditions that have explanatory value for the needs being examined. This chapter presents some general approaches to incorporating causal analysis in a needs assessment and describes in detail a specific logic method, Fault Tree Analysis. The chapter offers methods of varying degrees of difficulty and rigor that can be used by needs assessors without an extensive knowledge of mathematical models.

General Approaches to Causality

The concept of causal analysis enters into the design for program planning by local governments suggested by Schoenberger and Williamson (1977), who note that the manager must be able to analyze and understand six factors: severity and extent of problems, interrelationships and connections between problems in one area and those in another, underlying causes, barriers to solution, previous efforts, and the current situation. It is important to know in what neighborhoods or among what socioeconomic or age groups a problem is most severe and whether it is rising sharply in incidence. Interrelationships among problems should be noted. For example, members of families with certain problems, such as poverty and health difficulties, may also have educational problems and experience drug abuse. By examining relationships among problems, program planners may be able to adopt an interagency approach, such as using existing school counseling services to help with juvenile crime or drug abuse (Schoenberger and Williamson, 1977). Although it is rarely possible to work with root causes of social problems at the local level, Schoenberger and Williamson suggest that it is useful to understand how national patterns of poverty, race prejudice, and the like operate in the local community.

Problem analysis and needs assessment can be made even more meaningful by putting the problem in the framework of a cause-and-effect analysis. Researchers at the Far West Laboratory for Educational Research and Development have shown that problems can sometimes be viewed as causes and sometimes as effects, but in any event, they cannot be viewed in isolation (Sikorski, Oakley, and Lloyd-Kolkin, 1977). In deciding how to attack a problem one must consider both the antecedents and the consequences. A problem of discipline in the schools, for example, "requires attention to an immediate cause ('angry, apathetic children') which in turn is apparently influenced by 'hopelessly poor' achievement among certain students, which in turn is traced to automatic promotions, themselves one result of a conveyor-belt mentality which itself may be a defense mechanism in response to schools' inability to deal with problems of teacher education, selection of principals, motivating the unmotivated, achieving educational equality . . . and so forth. And probably each problem-solution has multiple, sometimes unanticipated effects and relationships with other conditions and problems" (p. 16). Furthermore, programs to decrease dropouts have had the effect that students stay in school but do not master basic skills, which in turn brings a new set of problems, such as angry children and poor discipline.

Sikorski and her colleagues contrast this perspective on educational problems with the usual needs assessment. They liken the totality of information sources on needs to a prism that refracts educational problems and needs in a variety of directions. A school district has a "bundle" of problems and needs that are complex, highly interrelated, and interdependent. Any one needs assessment study tends to isolate one need or a subset and view it from a particular perspective. They rarely "capture the totality or gestalt which is the 'real' situation that the LEA faces and must deal with" (p. 18). Not only will solutions then be totally inadequate to the complex situation but also they may make the problem worse. If problems are systemic but the solutions are aimed at a subsystem level, "there will be unaccounted for (and usually unanticipated) effects throughout the system" (p. 18).

The following sections describe three specific methods of employing causal analysis within a system approach to assessing needs and indicate how each can be used to set priorities on needs as well as offering directions for planning solution strategies.

Causal Analysis in a Six Step Model. The Research and Development Utilization Project (RDU) of the Georgia Department of Education developed a six-step model of needs assessment in which the last step is the conduct of a causal analysis of the need to be improved (Crouthamel and Preston, 1979). In the RDU model, causal analysis is used to delimit or redefine systemwide needs that were given high priority for program improvement in steps 4 and 5 of the analysis. Each need is analyzed in relation to six causal areas—students, teachers, curriculum, resources, management, and the community—for factors that might have caused the identified need. Representatives from the need areas that are affected participate in the causal analysis; they describe desired conditions in each area and examine interrelationships across the six areas. The needs assessment committee then decides which of the six areas or subareas that can be affected by improvement efforts might be contributing causes of the problem. New data are gathered or existing data reexamined, and if necessary, instruments are used that are of a more diagnostic nature than those used for identifying needs in the earlier stages of the assessment.

Causal Analysis in a Cyclical Model. Causal analysis is performed in two stages in the three-phase, cyclical, management-information-system model described in Chapter Two (Witkin, 1979; see Figures 4 and 5 in Chapter Two). The causal procedure is carried out within an information-processing framework.

The output of Phase I is a set of primary needs, in order of priority, based upon discrepancies between standards and status of student performance. At this stage, priorities are tentative and are listed in order of magnitude of discrepancy.

Phase II consists of the first causal analysis. Considering each need area separately, participants in the assessment analyze three different kinds of failures or barriers—in inputs to students (opportunities that were not provided), in student processes (failures to use the opportunities provided), and in environmental factors (constraints or barriers in the school/community context that contribute to the identified needs, prevent the needs from being met, or raise barriers to student performance). For example, an important need might be inability to converse adequately in a foreign language. Causes related to *inputs* might be too few assignments in speaking and listening in the language (the emphasis being on reading and writing). Causes related to *processes* might be poor class attendance during oral lessons or failure to practice orally outside of class. Causes related to *environmental* factors might be lack of native speakers of the language in the area or lack of foreign films to attend. The output of Phase II is a revised summary of primary needs that takes the causal factors into account.

Phase III consists of identification of secondary, or system input needs, which are also analyzed for causes. Inputs are the resources required to meet the primary needs. A discrepancy analysis is performed between those resources *required* and those *available* to meet the needs. Using the example of oral proficiency in a foreign language, it might be determined that important resources are teachers trained in speaking the language and a language laboratory with listening booths and tapes. The analysis might show that the language laboratory is adequate but that the teachers have inadequate training or lack interest in the oral use of the language. Causal analysis can be carried out to whatever levels are necessary to establish the nature of the factors that produced the primary and secondary needs and the barriers that have prevented them from being met thus far.

Final priorities for action are arrived at by considering the nature of the needs themselves, the magnitudes of the discrepancies, and the likelihood of reducing the magnitudes by eliminating or diminishing the impact of the causal factors.

Cause and Consequence Analysis. This type of analysis can be used with any needs assessment model after major needs have been identified. It works best with small groups of key informants who have varying perspectives on the system and its needs.

All items are entered on large charts ruled off into five columns. In column 1, list the concerns or needs that were previously identified. In column 2, list separately all possible *causes* of each concern or need. A given need may have more than one cause. In column 3, again considering each need separately, list the *consequences* if the need is not met or the problem not ameliorated. In column 4, enter a rating—on a scale of low, medium, or high— of the difficulty of correcting the problem once it has occurred. And in column 5, enter a rating—using a five-point scale—of the degree of criticality of the need if it is not met.

If a large group is convened, the process is first explained and illustrated to the group as a whole. Then the causal analysis is carried out in small groups of between five and eight people, each group working with its own chart on which the needs have been entered in column 1 and generating the entries for causes and consequences. After the inputs from all groups have been synthesized on a master chart, the entire group is assembled to make judgments regarding "difficulty to correct" and "degree of criticality," using any of the consensus-formation techniques described in Chapter Five.

An alternate procedure for establishing consensus on the last two items is to have each group member make individual judgments using rating sheets with numbers corresponding to the numbered needs or concerns on the master chart. The modal response of the members is recorded as the group judgment. Although any need may have several sets of causes and consequences, only the need itself is judged for difficulty to correct and degree of criticality.

To set priorities on needs, combine the data from the last two columns. The highest rank is given to those needs that have both a high rating of difficulty to correct and a rating of 4 or 5 on the scale of criticality. These rankings are then synthesized with other data from the needs assessment, such as magnitude of discrepancies. If desired, the highest-priority needs can be further analyzed by having groups generate suggestions for offsetting strategies that would not only address the need but also attack one or more causes or prevent undesirable consequences from occurring.

The remaining sections of this chapter describe a method of causal analysis that uses both qualitative and quantitative methods. Fault Tree Analysis combines logic diagramming, expert judgments, and quantitative analysis in a systems approach that makes it possible to interrelate hundreds of causal factors and to establish priorities of critical needs.

Fault Tree Analysis

Fault Tree Analysis (FTA) was developed in order to predict the most probable ways a system might fail, thus providing a basis on which to redesign or monitor the system so as to prevent the failure from occurring. It is also used to analyze the causes of events that have already occurred. Since the 1960s it has been an important part of systems-safety analysis and design in aerospace engineering, nuclear reactor studies, industrial accidents, and highway safety, among others (Haasl, 1965; Ericson, 1970; Driessen, 1970; Lambert, 1975; Salem, 1976; Roberts and others, 1980). The technique was adapted to nonengineering systems by Witkin and Stephens (1968, 1973a), who modified both the qualitative and quantitative methodology (Stephens, 1972). Since 1967, they and others have applied FTA to hundreds of planning, management, and evaluation problems in educational and other social systems (Witkin, 1973, 1975, 1977b, 1979c, 1982; Witkin and Stephens, 1972, 1973b; Torres and others, 1970; Long, 1976; Cummins, 1977).

The term *fault* may be misleading. The method of diagramming and quantifying in a typical FTA—considering multiple causality and comparing the contribution of each causal sequence to all other causal sequences—can be used to analyze any event (Driessen, 1970). Because of its broad generality, Driessen prefers the term *Cause Tree Analysis*. Stephens, who (under the auspices of his Sage Institute) has applied the technique extensively to large-scale policy decisions in industry, government, and the armed services, now labels his approach Sage Analysis and includes a number of management techniques in addition to the logic diagramming. The term *Fault Tree Analysis* is widely used in the literature, however, and retained in the present discussion.

FTA Methodology—Qualitative Analysis

FTA uses logic diagramming to relate combinations of possible events, or subsystems within a system, to show how they interact to produce a predefined *undesired* event (UE). The UE is the problem or event analyzed by the fault tree. FTA provides two types of analysis: (1) qualitative, in which carefully defined inputs are related in a systematic fashion in a logic diagram or fault tree, and (2) quantitative, in which the analyst identifies strategic paths—those sequences of events by which failure is most likely to occur—in order of probability. In needs assessment, the strategic paths indicate priorities of needs for action planning.

Any complex system can be analyzed in terms of success or failure—the accomplishment or nonaccomplishment of the system's mission. A systems approach may utilize either success or failure analysis. Success analysis, however, is much more problematic than failure analysis. It is often difficult to achieve consensus as to those factors most crucial for system success; it is much easier to describe and achieve consensus on the factors that will produce failure. In fact, it is usually harder to identify when a system has achieved its purposes than when it has not. This proposition can be tested by trying to define wellness versus illness, literacy versus illiteracy, or mathematics competence versus incompetence.

When program planners set out to improve educational methods or social and health services, they generally focus on those elements necessary for the success of their plans. In the FTA approach, the analyst studies those postulated success factors and then asks how they could fail to occur or fail to achieve their purposes. The method identifies actual or potential problems in a system and their modes of occurrence. FTA can be used either to *identify* critical needs in a system, or to *analyze the causes* of needs that were previously identified by other means.

This section presents the principal qualitative steps in FTA, with specific applications to needs assessment. There are two possible approaches to the first step. We will call them steps 1a and 1b.

Step 1a. *Success analysis.* In a comprehensive FTA, the analyst, working with key informants, may begin the process with a success analysis, using functional flow charts in order to grasp the system configuration and understand how policy makers and managers view system success. This step converts the general goals and objectives to activity flows that show graphically how the system is supposed to work to achieve its goals. Analysis by means of fault trees then proceeds backward through the system flow. The event to be analyzed by FTA—the undesired event or UE—may be the failure of the major goal of the organization, or there may be a series of UEs derived from subsystem failures about which the informants already have knowledge or concern. (An alternative approach is to begin with step 1b.)

Step 1b. *Gather perceptions of concerns, needs, or problems from service providers and receivers and from stakeholders.* This can be done by means of individual interviews with key informants or in small group sessions. For an exploratory needs assessment when the areas of need have not been previously established, the concerns analysis is focused by framing one or two questions based on social or performance indicators that indicate areas where problems are known to exist. If the FTA is used for causal analysis within the framework of a systems model, the gathering of concerns is focused on needs that were identified in earlier phases of the assessment.

For both primary and secondary needs assessment, concerns may be elicited in the general categories of input, process, and environmental failures or barriers, as described earlier (Causal Analysis in a Cyclical Model). Both present and past factors are considered, as well as trends that portend future problems. If desired, the concerns may then be organized in a preliminary failure analysis, using the format described above for Cause and Consequence Analysis.

Step 2. *Select one or more UEs for the FTA.* The major UE may be derived directly from a success analysis (step 1a) or from a concerns analysis (step 1b). In either method, the analyst works with a group of key informants. If method 1b is used, the group reviews the probable *consequences* of the events in the preliminary failure analysis and notes those events that have both a high rating of difficulty to correct and a rating of 4 or 5 on the scale of criticality. If the analysis was organized around inputs, processes, and contextual failures related to identified need areas, a UE can be selected for each type of failure. Because of the system nature of FTA, however, the analysis of any UE will generally encompass concerns of all three types. That is, if a UE is selected that relates to a *process* failure, the subsequent analysis usually uncovers contributing causes that relate to both inputs and environmental failures as well.

Step 3. *Gather from another sample of key informants, additional concerns focused on the UE* if steps 1 and 2 did not yield sufficient material for an in-depth analysis. The analyst may seek additional information selectively from people who are most knowledgeable about a particular aspect of the UE. Such individuals may be able to suggest more failure events or contribute special knowledge that adds perspectives on causes, consequences, and criticality of events already considered.

Step 4. *Synthesize the analysis by constructing a fault tree.*

Fault Tree Construction

A fault tree is a logic diagram consisting of statements of events interrelated by logic gates and resulting in complex pathways. The analysis begins at the top with the major UE and proceeds downward. Inputs to the UE are contributing failure events in a cause-and-effect relationship. The events are depicted by boxes in the shape of a rectangle, circle, or rhombus. The relationships among events are depicted by logic gates—this is a principal feature of the fault tree that distinguishes it from other forms of graphic analyses including functional flow charts and decision trees.

Event Symbols. Input and output events are classified according to their nature, which is symbolized by the shape of the box. The *rectangle* identifies an event that results from a combination of less general fault events through an associated logic gate. All events symbolized by rectangles have additional development in the fault tree. The *circle* identifies a basic failure event that requires no further development because it represents a primary failure of a component (analogous to a power failure in a telephone system) or because the definition of an event is sufficiently explicit to satisfy the purpose of the analysis. The *rhombus* identifies an event that is not developed further in the tree because of either lack of information or a very remote likelihood of occurrence or because constraints of time or money preclude further analysis.

Logic Gates. The two principal types of logic gates are the AND gate and the OR gate. The OR gate is used when *any one alone* of two or more possible inputs to an event could produce the output event. The AND gate is used when two or more events *must coexist* to produce the UE. With either AND or OR gates, more than two inputs may exist. Variations of these two gates allow for the depiction of complex relationships—there are inhibit gates, priority AND gates that specify sequence of events, matrix gates, and conditional gates. The analysis thus specifies precise conditions as well as modes of relationships, all of which can be expressed mathematically.

Fault Tree Examples. Basic uses of the AND and OR gates are illustrated in the descriptions and figures that follow. Readers wishing more detailed explanations of the variations are referred to Witkin and Stephens (1968 and 1973a), Stephens (1972), and Witkin (1977b).

Figure 8 shows two input events related to an output event through an OR gate. It is read: The undesired event can be caused *either* by event A *or* by event B, or both. An alternate reading is: *Either* event A *or* event B alone will produce the UE.

Figure 9 shows two input events related to an output event through an AND gate. It is read: The undesired event can be caused only if events A *and* B *both* occur, or events A *and* B must *coexist* to produce the UE, or The output can occur only if the inputs A and B coexist.

Figure 8. Illustration of an OR Gate.

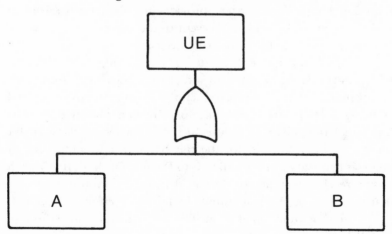

Figure 9. Illustration of an AND Gate.

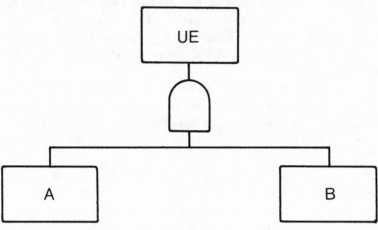

In social and behavioral systems the AND relationship most commonly occurs when backup systems or components exist or are possible within the design of the system. In other words, if a system allows for two or more alternate paths to reach an objective, then failure to reach the objective will occur only if *both* paths fail. On the other hand, if the system provides no alternates or backup systems, then the failure of *any* event in the system could logically lead to the failure of the principal objective.

This point can be illustrated by comparing success analysis with failure analysis. Figures 10 and 11 show the comparison when events in a system must proceed serially, with events A, B, C, and D being prerequisite conditions to achieving objective O. The functional flow chart of Figure 10 shows the events depicted for success analysis—that is, for the *success* of O, a single thread of events is necessary from A to B to C to D to O. The fault tree branch of Figure 11 shows the same events depicted for failure analysis— that is, *failure* of O can be caused by failure of *either* A *or* B *or* C *or* D *or* any combination of them. The events are all related through an OR logic gate.

Figures 12 and 13 show another configuration of events, using both concurrent and prerequisite conditions for success.

Figure 10. Flow Chart of Serial Events for Success Analysis.

Figure 11. Fault Tree Branch for Failure Analysis of Figure 10.

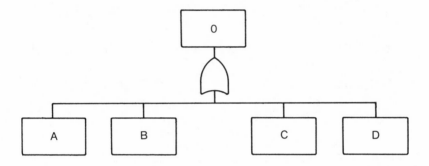

Figure 12 is a functional flow chart for success analysis. For *success* of objective O, the flow of events must proceed from A to B, then to C *and* D *concurrently* before O can occur. Figure 13 shows a fault tree branch for failure analysis of the same events. As in Figure 11, all events in this system are related through OR logic gates. *Failure* of O can be caused by failure of C *or* D *or both*. Failure of C can be caused by failure of A *or* B *or* both; failure of D can also be caused by failure of A *or* B *or* both.

Figure 13 clearly shows the "faulty" nature of a system in which *all* events in the system *must* occur, either serially or concurrently, in order to achieve the objective, or system success. In such a system design, *any* event at the bottom of the fault tree becomes the same as the top UE—that is, any event by itself could cause the failure of the objective, (except as constrained by importance and frequency factors determined in the quantitative analysis). For example, in an education system, such a configuration occurs when academic success can be achieved only if students must

Figure 12. Flow Chart of Serial and Concurrent Events
for Success Analysis.

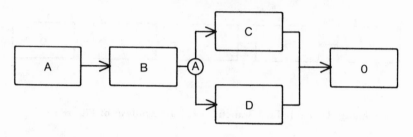

Figure 13. Fault Tree Branch for Failure Analysis of Events in Figure 12.

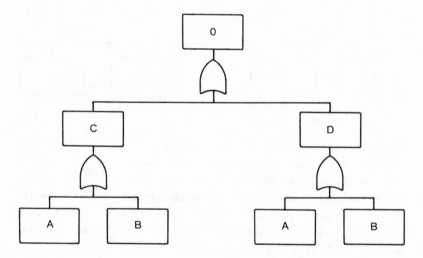

proceed through specified activities or channels, with no alternatives offered for those who have difficulty with the prescribed
activities. This is particularly serious when the system does not
provide an alerting or monitoring mechanism, causing problems to
multiply before corrective action can be taken.

Figures 14 and 15 look superficially like Figures 12 and 13,
but the two systems have important design differences. Figure 14 is
a success analysis of a system that provides an alternative at a certain

**Figure 14. Success Analysis of a System That Provides
an Alternative.**

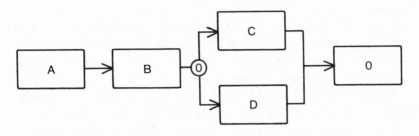

Figure 15. Fault Tree Branch for Failure Analysis of Events in Figure 14.

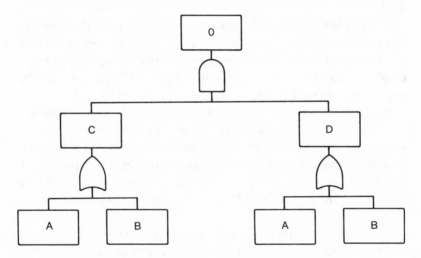

point. For the success of objective O, the flow of events must be from
A to B. But the next stage provides an alternative, *either* through
C *or* D, to reach objective O. Because of this, the fault tree of the
system, shown in Figure 15, has inputs at the first level combined
through an AND gate instead of an OR gate. *Failure* of O will thus
occur *only* if failures of C *and* D coexist.

At the next level, however, the situation is different. In
Figures 13 and 15, failures of both C and D could be caused by

failures of A *or* B *or* both. The importance of events A and B is enhanced, since they are prerequisite to two branches of events, with no alternatives provided. Because of the difference in logic gates at O, however, the fault tree of Figure 15 will have a different strategic path value (and therefore a different probability of failure occurrence) from that of the tree in Figure 13, even if other values assigned to events are the same in both trees. The occurrence of the AND gate for inputs to objective O in Figure 15 makes it less likely that the failure of O will occur. The alternative paths provided by events C and D make this system safer or less likely to fail than the one represented by Figures 12 and 13. Event O in Figures 11, 13, and 15 are all UEs. In other words, the failure of the objective to be reached in success analysis becomes the undesired event in failure analysis.

The logic of success and failure analysis can be illustrated by a simple example. If, in order to qualify for a job, an individual must have certain credentials *and* pass a written test *and* pass an oral interview, then failure of *any one* of the three criteria—credentials, test, interview—will cause failure to qualify for the job. On the other hand, if alternates are provided, the chances of failure are fewer. Thus, if *either* credentials *or* specified life experiences are acceptable, then failures of *both* credentials *and* experiences must coexist in order to cause failure to qualify for the job. Similarly, if either a written test or an oral interview is acceptable, then two failures would have to coexist at that stage to cause the primary failure.

Figure 16 depicts a rudimentary fault tree using the basic event and logic symbols. Inputs to the UE and event B are related through OR gates, but inputs to event A are related through an AND gate. The tree is read as follows: The UE can be caused *either* by event A *or* event B, or *both*. Event A can be caused *only* by the coexistence of events AA *and* AB. Event B can be caused *either* by event BA *or* BB or *both*. Event AB is a primary or basic failure event. Events AA, BA, and BB require no further analysis. The depiction of events by the circle or rhombus shows that those branches occur at the bottom of the tree. In the example of Figure 16 there are two branches and three levels of development. Even without quantitative analysis, inspection shows that the most likely mode of occur-

Figure 16. Rudimentary Fault Tree.

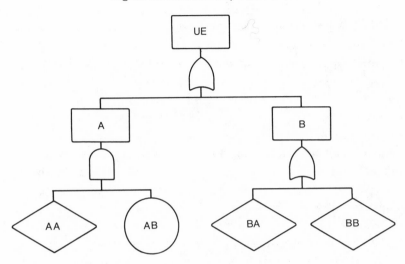

rence of the UE is through branch B since the OR logic gate below
event B indicates no alternative paths or back-up system.

Generating Events to the Tree. Fault trees of complex
systems often have several hundred events, all related through logic
gates. The generation of inputs at each level continues until the
causal factors are sufficiently delineated, in the opinion of the fault
tree analyst(s), to provide the basis for later recommendations as to
priority of needs.

The rules used in systems-safety analysis for generating
causal events at different levels are difficult to apply to analysis of
social systems. One method that has been found acceptable is to
derive events by systematically asking questions regarding input,
processing, and output failures for each event in turn. That is,
failures of a given component or subsystem may be attributable to
failures of input from another part of the system or from the
environment, failures of processing within the component or subsystem itself, or failures of output to another part of the system.
Inputs may be internal or external to the system, but the more
proximate the inputs in time or space to the event being analyzed,

the more powerful the analysis. If internal failure events are really due to events external to the system, they will usually appear at the points of interface between the system and its environment.

It might appear from the foregoing examples that analysis for failure is simply the reciprocal of analysis for success. To an extent this is true in that reduction of the likelihood of a UE occurring—through changing or monitoring the sequences of events in primary or secondary strategic paths (high-priority need areas)—increases the likelihood of system success and thus of meeting client or system needs.

Data from analysis of complex systems, however, reveal that, for any system, FTA gives perspectives that go beyond the simple inversion of success to failure analysis. The latter usually generates causal events that are not apparent from success analysis. In fact, FTA methodology has heuristic value both for those participating in the analysis and for managers and other decision makers to whom the results and recommendations are communicated. It raises questions about the system that do not occur under the usual conditions of success planning or in the stages of needs assessment that precede the causal analysis. Even a preliminary analysis can identify potential problem areas at interfaces or boundaries between systems or subsystems, where managers often have little control of events. Where the success of a venture depends to any degree on inputs or cooperation from people outside the system, critical failures often occur due to lack of attention to the linkages at the interfaces.

Quantitative analysis to derive strategic paths and priorities is described in the next section. Even if no quantitative analysis is performed, however, it should be apparent from inspection of the flow charts and fault tree illustrations of Figures 8 through 16 that they provide important qualitative information about the system. The success analyses show immediately whether the system contains alternatives or backup systems, and the fault trees show all possible modes of occurrence of failure under those conditions. It should be understood, however, that a full FTA is both qualitative and quantitative, even though policy makers can derive information on critical needs at any stage from a success or concerns analysis through fault tree construction.

FTA Methodology—Quantitative Analysis

Fault trees are analyzed mathematically to find strategic paths—those sequences of events that have the highest probability of causing the UE to occur. The method described here was developed by Stephens (1972) for use in systems where empirical evidence is weak or there are no established probabilities. The establishment of priorities of failure event sequences is a function not only of a given event's frequency of occurrence, but also of its contribution to and interaction with other events. The method relates every event in the system to every other event, so that the analysis functions in the context of a network rather than a simple linear cause-and-effect sequence.

A fault tree is constructed in such a way that any or all events shown *could* happen, given certain conditions and relationships. If the system is functioning perfectly, none of them will occur. Occurrence of failure events anywhere in the tree contributes in some way to the potential for failure of the top UE. The quantification procedure makes it possible to postulate which modes of occurrence are more likely than which others, in the order of their likehood. Unlike the method used in engineering systems-safety analyses, however, this procedure does not furnish probability estimates of the occurrence of the UE. It combines the use of expert judgments of key informants and Boolean equations to derive subjective estimates of probability and criticality. Informants may be brought together in groups to be given explanations of the procedure, but each person makes judgments individually. The analysis proceeds in four steps.

1. *Determine the relative contributions of failure events to the more general failures.* Beginning with the highest-level UE, decide on the relative contribution of each input event. For example, given a UE with inputs A, B, and C, each rater estimates the relative importance of A, B, and C to the occurrence of the UE. At the next level below A, with inputs AA, AB, and AC, raters estimate the relative contribution of each to the occurrence of A. The same

is done for inputs to B and C. This step is repeated for all inputs to each failure event, working systematically down through the tree. Each set of relative contribution estimates must sum to 100 percent, and each set is independent of every other. Thus, the percentage contributions of A, B, and C to the UE might be 30 percent, 10 percent, and 60 percent, respectively. At the next level, the contributions of AA, AB, and AC to the occurrence of A might be 15 percent, 50 percent, and 35 percent. The percentages are derived from the best judgments of the raters. Wherever statistics are available, they can be used to validate judgments, but the importance of each event is judged *only* in relation to its possible causation of the event above it in the tree, combined with other events at the same level.

2. *Determine the degree of confidence in the ratings of relative contribution made in step 1.* For each event separately, raters record how confident they are of their judgments, whether strong, moderate, or weak. This acts as a qualifier to the subjective estimates of percentage contribution. Experience with large numbers of raters has shown that, although they may be quite confident that one event is more important than another in contributing to a specified failure event, they are often less confident about their decisions on percentage contributions. The confidence ratings are taken into consideration in the final mathematical analysis of the tree.

3. *Determine the frequency of occurrence of each failure event at the bottom level of each fault tree branch.* Bottom failure events are those for which no further analysis has been done. Regardless of the number of events that occur below a given logic gate, each event is rated separately. Raters judge the frequency of occurrence for each bottom event as frequent, periodic, or rare. The frequency judgments are made independently of the relative contribution judgments. Thus it is possible for an event to be highly important but of rare occurrence, and vice versa.

4. *Determine the difficulty of rectification for each failure event at the lowest level of each fault tree branch.* Like the judgments in step 3, each of these ratings is made independently of the others. The rater decides whether, if the event should occur, it would be easy, difficult, or impossible to rectify. This rating, like the one on

strength of confidence, is used as a qualifier on the other judgments.

The ratings from steps 1 through 4 are combined to produce strategic paths—that is, sequences of causal events that can be traced visually from the top UE to the bottom of the tree. The strategic-path values are derived from weighted probability estimates, taking into account the importance and frequency ratings, as well as how the events interact through the AND and OR logic gates (for the formulas, see Stephens, 1972). The primary strategic path is found by tracing events having the greatest value at each level of the tree. First, determine which major branch has the greatest value, then read down through that branch finding the event with the highest value at each level. Secondary and tertiary paths are determined in the same way. Since the data are ordinal, the strategic-path values supply a rank ordering of possible modes of occurrence of the top UE. The method does not establish statistical probabilities of occurrence either of the major UE or of strategic paths. The rank ordering of strategic paths does, however, give data for establishing priorities of event sequences that have contributed to the need or prevented it from being met.

In a well-designed system of the kind for which FTA was originally intended, such as an aerospace system, the probability of a catastrophic failure is usually very low. In social systems, however, serious failures have a much higher likelihood of occurrence. When FTA is used to determine causal factors for needs assessment purposes, the rank ordering of strategic paths is sufficient to supply a rational basis for determining priorities, regardless of the probability of occurrence of any of the causal sequences.

Using Causal Analysis to Derive Priorities of Need

Causal analysis is generally used for analyzing needs previously identified by other means. FTA may also be used to *identify* critical needs as part of a comprehensive analysis of a system. The highest strategic paths indicate actual or potential high-priority needs, about which additional data may then be gathered by means of surveys, social indicators, or group processes. For long-range planning, trends or predictions derived from futures methods may also be incorporated in the FTA. Regardless of the method, causal analysis contributes to decisions on priorities for meeting the needs by attacking either their causes or the barriers that prevent their being met.

In general, the highest priorities should be given to developing programs to attack those causes (1) that are highly critical, with potentially serious consequences if the need is not addressed, and (2) that also have the greatest likelihood of reducing or eliminating the need.

Priorities may be established from a qualitative FTA alone if resources do not permit quantitative analysis. Key informants and managers can pinpoint individual events or sequences that on their face would have serious consequences if they occurred. These informants should also note redundant events—those occurring in two or more places in the tree, thus multiplying their potential as inputs to other fault events. In addition, a paucity or lack of AND gates indicates a system with few or no alternatives, and some system redesign should be considered.

What is the depth necessary for the analysis of causes—for example, how many levels down should the tree be constructed? FTA for systems-safety engineering has in recent years developed short cuts for identifying the most important branches at the top of the tree and for amalgamating events to analyze them in the most parsimonious fashion (see Lambert, 1975, and Roberts and others, 1980, for explanation of cut sets). Although these procedures are not applicable to FTA of social systems, there is a useful rule of thumb: On any branch of the fault tree that shows a preponderance of OR gates, it is not necessary to carry the analysis to more than three or four levels since any event occurring at the bottom of the branch is the same as the top UE. In the absence of coexisting, conditional, or inhibiting events, the occurrence of any event in that branch will cause the occurrence of the event above it, and so on up to the top.

Scheidel and Crowell (1979, pp. 31–32) offer other criteria for causal analysis in their guidelines for group discussion:

> Causes are like slippery eels. As you grab one it slips away. Since a group can always find a deeper cause springing from a still deeper one, it must ask where to stop and at which level it should work. . . . [You] will have to move down the chain of causes and

conditions *to the level at which you can do something
about it.*

It is important for groups not to name attitudes
as causes; the social, economic, political, and personal
causes that produce these attitudes should be uncovered. . . . In social problems, causes are not absolute
and invariable; we are dealing with *probabilities* and
generalizations. Knowing that we are hazarding
guesses, we can but make our lines of reasoning the
best possible [Scheidel and Crowell's emphases].

FTA analysts also caution their informants not to name
attitudes as causes, but to cite observable events, behaviors, and the
like—and to make them specific to the system being analyzed not
to society in general.

Applications of Causal Analysis

FTA and other kinds of causal analysis provide an important
bridge from the identification of needs to the development of
solutions. Without causal analysis it is all too easy to settle for
simplistic solutions and to install programs that do not really meet
the needs. The survey mentioned at the beginning of this chapter,
in which counseling was confused with need, is a case in point.

Going Beyond Symptoms. Three other examples illustrate
the desirability of going beyond symptoms of need to causes. In a
comprehensive interagency needs assessment (see Chapter Twelve
for description of the LINC project), FTA was used for in-depth
analysis of two need areas—childcare for working parents and
employment of young people and minorities—both of which were
already known to be serious unmet needs. The childcare analysis
uncovered the common tendency to jump from needs to solutions.
A concerns analysis revealed a strong desire in the community for
a licensed childcare center. The FTA, however, showed that the
most critical need was for evening and early morning care, when
childcare centers are not normally open. A corroborating strategic
path showed the barriers that prevented parents from arranging
their work schedules to take advantage of childcare at times it might
be available. The predisposition on the part of childcare center
advocates to consider only one solution had prevented them from

considering other measures that could be taken to meet the actual needs.

The employment analysis also revealed factors present in the local school system and in industry that could be ameliorated through cooperative action in a three-way partnership—the schools, the city government, and the industry-education council. This possibility had previously been unrecognized. In both the childcare and employment cases, acceptable solutions to the needs might have been found by other means. But the FTA methodology was persuasive to the decision makers, largely because of two factors: (1) Key informants, representing those with the needs and those who had power to find solutions, were involved in all stages of the analysis in ways that prevented any one group from monopolizing or biasing the inputs, and (2) the graphic displays of the fault trees made it possible for the policy makers and managers to trace for themselves the strategic paths and to see the relationships of salient factors.

A typical experience with a problem-solving group in a large high school furnishes a third example. A group of teachers, administrators, and students were working together as one of several teams in a district-wide effort to sharpen goals, identify needs, and make recommendations for a long-range master plan. One problem they grappled with was that of single-period absences from class, which had reached alarming proportions. Jumping from the data to a solution, they concluded that there was a need for stricter discipline and that the solution was to get tough by imposing various punishments for unexcused class absences. A couple of sessions of causal analysis showed that the absences were just one symptom of a complex set of needs and that the proposed solution was unlikely to meet the needs although it might reduce the absences for a short time. The causal analysis led to consideration of alternatives that were more likely to solve the problem in the long run.

Design and Management of Needs Assessment Projects. After the plan for assessment has been designed, FTA may be applied prior to the implementation of the plan in order to predict problems that might arise or to anticipate how the analysis could fail to identify the real needs. The UE could be caused by either failures of design or failures of implementation. Failures of design could be caused by failure to identify the right data to collect or to design adequate data collection methods or to use adequate instruments. Each failure mode could be analyzed to the depth necessary to specify how it could occur in the specific setting of the needs assessment, given its resources, expertise, and constraints of policy, time, funds, and the like. A second branch could analyze failure to implement the needs assessment as designed, given the specific setting and operating conditions.

Many needs assessment manuals and kits contain detailed instructions about designing and managing a needs assessment. The needs assessor and committee chairpersons will find it useful to apply the principles of causal analysis to predicting how their best-laid plans might go wrong or how the assessment could fail to produce the desired results. The needs assessor will also find in Chapters Eight through Eleven many concepts dealing with methodology that could be applied to causal analysis of project design and management. For example, the assessor might anticipate problems that could arise in communicating with key groups while planning or implementing the needs assessment, or factors that could prevent adequate and timely use of the results. Then the causal analysis data could be applied to redesigning and/or monitoring key aspects of the needs assessment in order to prevent the problems or mitigate their impact.

8

Setting Priorities

No needs assessment is complete until someone uses the data to make decisions about priorities for action planning. Yet little attention has been paid to the validity and reliability of priority-setting methods or to the problems and issues that are often encountered—theoretical, technical, or political. Priority setting is one of the knottiest procedural problems in needs assessment. The most valid methods are the most time-consuming and often the least acceptable to participants. In fact, the most simplistic and least valid methods of deriving priorities are those in widest use in educational systems (Witkin, 1976c).

Methods for setting priorities should be built into the needs assessment from the very beginning. Best results are obtained when those who plan the needs assessment establish clear criteria for analyzing and converting the data to priorities, using decision rules and systematic procedures to establish levels of need that are deemed critical for immediate and long-term action, that integrate quantitative and qualitative data, and that take into account both the costs of implementing solutions to the needs and the consequences of ignoring them. If the needs assessment is being instituted as part of an ongoing management information system, the procedures should also include criteria for periodic review and updating of priorities.

Ideally, priorities should be set first on *primary* needs—those of service receivers—before setting them on *secondary* needs—those of service providers. The two sets of priorities should not be confused and should clearly identify whose needs are being assessed.

In some settings, such as research and development (R&D) organizations (which must satisfy the requirements of sponsors or funding sources), the question of whose needs is difficult to answer "because they typically serve qualitatively different audiences—the sponsor who is paying for the R&D and the intended user who typically does not pay for the R&D. . . . An R&D organization is primarily accountable to the sponsor [and] the sponsor's needs could be met through fulfilling the contractual obligations in a fiscally responsible manner. A direct mandate for meeting the needs of the ultimate intended user is less frequent" (Adams, 1983, p. 56). The problem is made more difficult because the intended users are actually a chain—intermediate users of R&D products, such as universities, which in turn use the R&D information to meet the needs of local schools. Nevertheless, keeping in mind the distinction between primary- and secondary-level needs assessment is essential in setting criteria for differing levels of priorities.

Methods of setting priorities are both quantitative and qualitative. The needs assessor or analyst can apply formulas to the data, but statistics alone are not enough. Priority setting entails considering the data on needs and their implications in context and integrating all factors in a systematic procedure.

Setting Priorities from Survey Data: Single Data Sets

Category Scales. Priorities are often decided on the basis of one set of data, such as ratings of importance of goals or objectives, or desirability of programs or services. The most common methods are to determine rank orders of items from surveys that use category scales, using the mean, median, or mode; to rank the means of clusters of related items; to rank items directly; or in a large set, to indicate the three most important and the three least important items.

A more precise method is the forced choice (such as the budget allocation method described in Chapter Three) in which a specified number of points is allocated among the items. Mean ratings of items are then used to determine rank order. Another forced-choice method is the card sort, in which items are written separately on cards and the cards in each pack are sorted into piles (typically five) to represent degrees of importance. This method is often used with large numbers of goals or objectives; usually a minimum number of items must be allocated to each pile.

Needs cannot really be determined from one set of data, however. Data and perceptions on both standards and status are necessary. In addition, there are serious flaws in basing priorities on mean ratings from category scales or variants such as the card-sort method because of two faulty assumptions: that the scale values represent intervals of equal or approximately equal magnitude and that the majority of respondents have essentially the same referent for each scale point—that is, that each point will mean about the same thing. Research has shown that these assumptions are erroneous. Three major criticisms have been leveled at category scales: (1) that the limited resolution of the categories causes important information to be lost, (2) that the scales represent only an ordinal level of measurement, so analyses based on them cannot use the powerful statistical methods appropriate for interval measurement (although many researchers erroneously treat the scales in interval fashion), and (3) that the researcher inadvertently affects the response by offering a fixed number of categories (Lodge, 1981).

Most category scales in needs assessments employ adjectives that are arbitrarily selected for the anchor points, with no validation of the selections. In addition, observation of hundreds of needs studies that derive priorities of goal importance from category scales shows two other difficulties: severe compression at the high-importance end of each scale and highly similar mean ratings among the most important items, obscuring any real differences among the items.

Magnitude Estimation Scaling (MES). A more precise method of measuring the relative importance of objectives and of making comparisons of preferences among reference groups is magnitude estimation scaling (Dell, 1973a; Dell and Meeland, 1973; Lodge, 1981). The procedure elicits and displays the range, diversity, and strength of feeling of respondent groups as well as the modal or central viewpoint of each group. The scaling technique uses ratio scales rather than rankings or categorical ratings. MES derives from the paradigm of sensory psychophysical scales. When subjects are presented with a series of sensory stimuli, such as varying light or sound intensities, they are able to make very accurate judgments of the ratio of each stimulus relative to the first (or reference) stimulus, which is usually of low- or middle-intensity level. From these responses, ratio scales of sensation can be constructed. Ratio scales are a highly reliable way to derive judgments on social stimuli for which there are no objective measures. Since many questions about needs involve subjective opinions and values, the reliability of those opinions is an important consideration for deriving priorities from needs surveys.

When MES is used in needs assessment, each respondent is presented with a statement of a goal, objective, or condition, and told that it has an arbitrary value, let us say 50. For each subsequent item presented, the respondent assigns a value of importance relative to 50. If the objective is twice as important as the referent, it is given a value of 100. If it is half as important, the value is 25; if three times as important, the value is 150. Any value may be assigned, and there is no upper limit. The numeric estimates are converted to logarithms, then to the arithmetic mean of the logs, and finally to the geometric mean. The ratio scales can be graphed as curves, with ten subjects being sufficient to produce an interpretable curve (Lodge, 1981).

Judgments of social stimuli made with ratio scaling produce much more information about the relative importance of items than do category scales. Lodge found that "when magnitude scales are compared to category scales in direct matches against metric stimuli on a quantitative continuum, the relationship between types of scales is almost invariably curvilinear" (p. 16). He offers as a rule of thumb that "the greater the disparity between the subjective range of the stimuli and the arbitrary range of the category scale, the greater the deviation from interval assumptions, the greater the loss of information, and the greater the distortion of the response" (p. 17). There is no feasible method for deriving interval data from category-rating scales because "the subjective range of social stimuli varies from individual to individual from issue to issue over time, while the response range of the category scale is arbitrarily fixed. Almost invariably, magnitude scales prove superior to category scales because category scaling artifactually constrains people's judgments, while the magnitude measures are relatively free of this constraint. . . . [The] major substantive effect of using category scales to measure social beliefs and preferences is to truncate strong opinion" (p. 72).

Lodge recommends that ratio scales be validated using either cross-modality matching or a single calibrated response measure. Researchers have used the cross-calibration method to determine scale values of fifteen adjectives, ranging from absolutely perfect to disgusting (Lodge and others, 1975). Further research found that adjectives frequently used in category scales, such as excellent, very good, good, and bad, are by no means equidistant from the referent or from each other. Excellent is about 4.6 times the strength of the neutral adjective so-so, with very good at 2.8 times, very bad at 25 percent of the support for the referent, and poor at 20 percent. If polar adjectives such as good-bad, very good–very bad, adequate-inadequate, excellent-terrible, or first rate–second rate are compared, in no case are they equally distant from the reference standard. Also, the popular polar adjectives provide a very narrow range (Lodge, 1981).

In needs assessment surveys that use category scales, mean ratings of importance typically bunch close together so that it is difficult to discriminate among them. For example, on a five-point scale, three goals might have mean preference values of 3.8, 3.9, and 4.1. Even if tests show those values to be statistically different from each other, the data do not give any indication of the real strength of opinion about the goals, or whether the differences have any practical significance. On a ratio scale, it might be found that the goal with the 4.1 value is 1.5 times or 2.0 times as important as the one with the 3.8 value.

The MES method was tested in a California school district by staff at Stanford Research Institute (SRI) using parents and faculty to rate forty objectives (Dell, 1973a). A standard for determining priorities was established by plotting the relationship of the evaluation scores for each major objective category against a geometric mean scale. All objectives falling above the referent point of 55 were deemed of enough importance to warrant attention. MES can also be used to set a standard for need by deriving a special emphasis value for each objective from consensus of respondents (Dell, 1973b).

Dell (1973b) found that MES provided greater specificity than do category scales for interpreting findings, for comparing different objectives, and for comparing the ratings of subgroups on the same objectives. Figure 17 shows how four subjects in the science curriculum were rated for importance by parents, faculty, and two subgroups of parents. Neither a simple ranking procedure nor category scales would have shown the real differences between faculty and parents or the strength of the difference in ratings between objectives 2 and 3. Also, although a category-scaling method might possibly have shown some differences between ratings by male and female parents, the strength of those differences could not be determined, as it could by MES. Other studies have verified the power of ratio scales over category scales to reveal large differences in strength of feeling among different groups, such as those who perceive the quality of education to be low, moderate, or high.

The rigorous methods used for MES in social-survey research, such as calibration and cross-modality estimates, are not feasible for most needs assessments and may not be necessary. The SRI group, which did not calibrate the items, found the procedure easy to administer and acceptable to respondents (Dell and Meeland, 1973). The task was not time consuming—it took about thirty minutes to rate forty-nine objectives. The groups had little difficulty understanding the procedure and making the estimates.

Paired-Weighting Procedure (PWP). The paired-weighting procedure described in Chapter Five is another method for determining priorities that to some extent overcomes the drawbacks of category scales and simple ranking. PWP, also called paired-comparison rating, is a forced-choice method of establishing group judgments about importance or standards in which every goal or item is rated as more or less important than every other, with the ratings done in pairs. PWP is more discriminating than category scales, and the results are easier to score and analyze than in MES. But it is possibly harder to administer than MES since the latter requires that only one reference goal be kept in mind, while PWP requires constant reminders of the entire set of goals. PWP is also not practicable for more than about fifteen items.

Figure 17. Magnitude Estimation Scaling: Science Objective
Evaluation Scores.

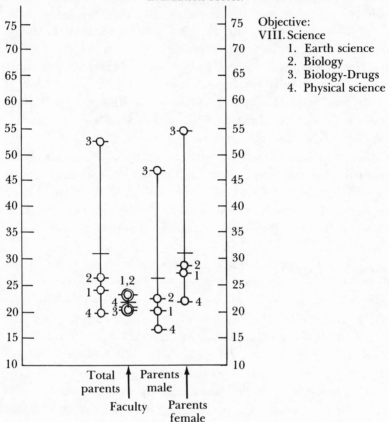

Objective:
VIII. Science
    1. Earth science
    2. Biology
    3. Biology-Drugs
    4. Physical science

Source: Dell, 1973b. Copyright SRI International (Stanford Research Institute), 1973. Used by permission.

Setting Priorities from Survey Data:
Multiple Data Sets

As discussed in Chapter Three, many surveys use written questionnaires designed to elicit two or more responses to individual questions, and priorities are derived directly from comparisons of those responses. The basic concept derives from the discrepancy formula "what should be" minus "what is" equals "need." Following are typical discrepancies sought from surveys:

- between goal importance and perceived attainment
- between desired/expected performance and perceived performance
- between desired services and perceived adequacy of existing services
- between services/resources required to meet a specified need and perceived adequacy of existing level of services/resources
- between desired level of job competencies and present competencies, as perceived by the self or others

Sometimes the discrepancy formula is followed literally. But there are many variations that have improved on the formula. Two steps are usually taken: (1) show the relationship between *should* and *is* (standards and status) and (2) rank those relationships in priority order. Following is a summary of the most common as well as less frequently used techniques for these two steps and a discussion of their adequacy. Discrepancy data from surveys can be verified from nonsurvey sources such as indicators of performance, attainment, existing services, and resources. The statistics derived in the methods described here are then integrated with other data to identify priorities of need.

Rank-Order-of-Difference Scores. In two-response surveys, each goal, objective, or other item is rated twice—once for its desired state and again for its perceived present state. The scaled responses are converted to mean scores, the difference in means between each item is calculated, and the difference scores are arranged in rank order. To illustrate, here are mean scores for three items in a discrepancy survey where both the desired state (defined as goal importance) and actual state (perceived attainment of the goal) were rated on a five-point category scale, with 5 as the highest rating:

Goal	Importance	Attainment	Difference
A	4.2	3.8	.4
B	4.8	2.7	2.1
C	3.9	3.2	.7

Ranking the difference scores, the priorities of need are goals B, C, and A, in that order.

Although this method is widely used, it is the least valid of any discussed here. There are three reasons for this: (1) It is illogical to subtract status from importance. Survey questions are usually on the order of "How important do you think this goal/objective is?" and "How well do you think the objective is being achieved?" The two questions are not comparable, and one estimate cannot be subtracted from another. The fallacy in the method is additionally compounded by the limitations of category scales. (2) Deriving priorities from rank-orders-of-difference scores is also fallacious because the method does not take into account the relative importance of the goals themselves. That is, large discrepancy in a goal rated of low importance may not be as critical a need as a smaller discrepancy in a highly important goal area. (3) In surveys where nearly all goals are rated of high importance (which is often the case) the difference scores are frequently so close as to be essentially meaningless for practical purposes.

A variant of this method uses the discrepancy between mean ratings of ideal and actual *performance,* rather than between importance and performance. Questions in this type of survey are often worded "How well do you think this goal/objective should be achieved?" rather than "How important do you think this goal/ objective is?" On the face of it, this type of discrepancy makes more sense than the importance-achievement discrepancy since the two parameters being compared are similar. But the data are not really helpful for establishing priorities since the means of the scales tell nothing about *level* of achievement, either ideal or real.

Instead of basing priorities on ranks of numerical discrepancies, the developers of APEX surveys for secondary schools (described in Chapter Three), recommend employing bar graphs to display the relationship between present levels of skills or knowledge and the desired standard for those skills or knowledge (Witkin and Richardson, 1983). Figure 18 shows results on the first thirty-three items from a school that used the surveys with students in grades nine and ten. (Items 1 through 4 of the survey are displayed in Figure 6, Chapter Six.) Data from the survey of parents and teachers of the same students can be entered on the same graph for comparison purposes.

Figure 18. Comparison of Discrepancies Between Status and Standards on Thirty-three Behaviorally Anchored Scale Items in the APEX Student Survey.

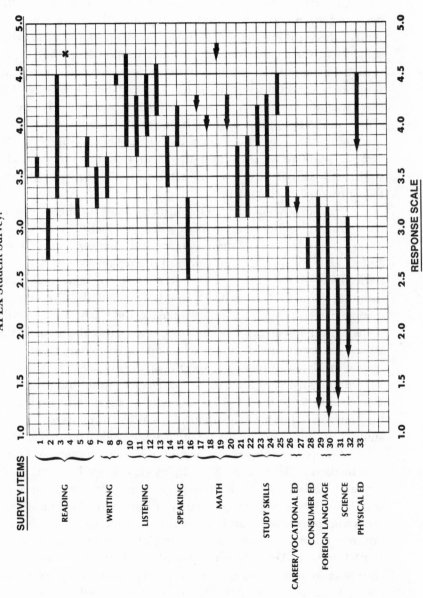

Source: Adapted from Witkin and Richardson, 1983.

The items are on five-level, behaviorally anchored scales, with 5 being the highest level; the statistic used is the median response to each item. The left end of each bar represents the median response of what students say they *do* (their perceived status); the right end represents their median response as to what students in their grade *should do* (their proposed standards). On item 3, for example, the median status response is 3.3, and the mean standard is 4.5; the discrepancy is 1.2. The X on item 4 indicates that there was no discrepancy between status and standards. Where an arrow on the bar points to the left, the median response for status was higher than for standards on that item. Thus, on item 32, the median standard was 1.7 and the median status was 3.1. The students perceived themselves as achieving at a higher level than their proposed class standard.

For purposes of identifying priority items for improvement, the graphs give information of a different quality than simple numerical magnitudes of discrepancies. For example, items 10, 16, and 22 all have similar magnitudes of discrepancies—.9, .8, and .8 respectively—but the discrepancies do not have the same qualitative meaning because of the differing levels of standards. The graphic display makes it easy for parents, students, and teachers to compare items within and among respondent groups. Since the items in the scales are statements of observable student behaviors, those who review the data can judge the specific areas needing improvement. The quantitative data are used as one element in setting priorities. The results on status can be corroborated by performance indicators for some skills, but for many items, such as listening, speaking, and study skills, there are usually no other schoolwide data available.

Priority Need Index. An improvement on the simple subtraction method is the Priority Need Index (PNI) used by Lane, Crofton, and Hall (1983). Their discrepancy survey has two nine-point scales: one of respondents' estimates of importance of educational goals and programs (I) and one of degree being met (D). The importance estimate is used as a weighting factor as well. The formula is PNI = $I \times (I-D)$. Data are reported on eleven goals judged by educators, parents, students, and the community for importance, degree being met, discrepancies, and PNI, with rankings for each. Comparison of the tables of discrepancies and their ranks with the

PNIs and their ranks for each respondent group shows that little is gained by using PNIs over simple discrepancies when rankings alone are considered. (The rank orders were extrapolated from the discrepancy and PNI data since the respondents did not directly rank the goals.) Most of the goals ranked in the same order on the discrepancy measure as on the PNI. But goals with nearly identical discrepancies, based on estimates of two different parent groups, ranked quite differently in within-group rankings. And goals ranked at the same level by different groups often had very different magnitudes of discrepancies and/or PNIs.

This analysis illustrates the fallacy of deriving priorities from rank orders alone. For purposes of setting priorities and synthesizing responses from different groups, the *magnitudes* of the PNIs seem to be of more value than within-group *rankings*. For example, community respondents perceived much larger gaps between ideal and actual attainment than other groups perceived on the same goals. As an instance, on the human relations item, educators' ratings produced a discrepancy value of 2.99, with a PNI of 24.19, and community ratings produced a discrepancy value of 4.56 and a PNI of 37.03. But both ratings resulted in a priority ranking of 1 for that goal.

Three-Factor Formulas. The Westinghouse Learning Corporation used the following formula for deriving priorities from the data in their survey, which contains three category scales for each objective: importance, perceived student attainment, and the school's responsibility for the goal:

$$\text{priority ranking of needs} = \frac{\text{importance} \times \text{responsibility}}{\text{attainment}}.$$

The Center for the Study of Evaluation also considered three factors in deriving priorities from their needs assessment model (Hoepfner and others, 1971). The priority value was derived from goal *importance* measured on a scale of perception, *attainment* measured by performance on standardized tests directly related to goals and then corrected for selected local conditions, and *probable increase in utility* measured by utility of improving student performance and the probability of improving student performance. The probable increase in utility in each goal area was computed using a differentiated school percentile from results of the standardized tests directly related to the goals. The formula was:

priority = rated importance × probable increase in utility.

Matrix Analyses. Hershkowitz (1973) proposed a *criticality function* that uses a 2 × 2 matrix to relate perceptions of goal importance to perceptions of goal attainment. Treating each respondent group separately, the analyst calculates mean scores of importance and mean scores of attainment to establish criticality levels on the X and Y axes of the graph. This procedure corrects for the excessive clustering of importance scores toward the top of the scale, which is characteristic of many discrepancy surveys that use category scales.

The two criticality levels plotted on the graph divide it into four quadrants: (S) successful program, for goals falling above the mean in both importance and attainment; (U) low-level successful program, for goals falling below the mean in importance but above the mean in attainment; (L) low-level need, for goals falling below the mean in both importance and attainment; and (C) critical need, for goals falling above the mean in importance but below the mean in attainment. The distribution of scores for all goals for each respondent group is plotted. Figure 19 shows a criticality function graph for one respondent group in a survey of television needs in Maryland.

Four goals are plotted in Figure 19. Goal 16 is a critical need, goal 23 is a low-level need, goal 1 represents a successful program, and goal 37 a low-level successful program. Goals 1, 37, and 16 cluster together in mean ratings of goal importance, and although goal 16 is in the C quadrant, it is close to the mean in goal attainment.

In Hershkowitz's study, priorities for action were given to those goals to which four or more of the nineteen subgroups assigned a critical need, but others using the method have used other decision rules. The graphic displays are helpful to needs assessment committees making recommendations about priorities. The method can be used not only for goal ratings but also for educational and human services programs or services and for

**Figure 19. Completed Criticality Function Displaying the
Level of Program Need for the School Staff Respondent Group.**

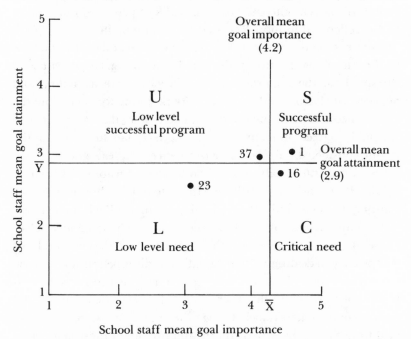

School staff mean goal importance

Source: Hershkowitz, 1973.

Note: For each specified goal statement the mean scores for goal importance (horizontal axis) and mean scores for goal attainment (vertical axis) are plotted as a point. The numbers 1, 16, 23, and 37 refer to goal statements. The axes $\overline{X}$ and $\overline{Y}$ indicate "criticality axes." After plotting the goal points and deriving the axes, the quadrants are assigned a level of program need. Thus, the goal associated with goal point 16 is considered to have a "Critical Need" while the goal associated with goal point 1 is considered to be a "Successful Program." The process is repeated for each respondent group.

making decisions about allocation of program effort. For example, goals or programs in the *C* quadrant could be given priority for program improvement or specific intervention. Items in the *L* quadrant could be given a secondary priority, perhaps for later action. Those in the *S* quadrant could be monitored for maintaining excellence, and those in the *U* quadrant could be reexamined for possible retrenchment.

A similar two-way criticality function was employed for a statewide public opinion survey in New Jersey, which produced ratings of sixteen outcome goals on scales of perceived importance and excellence (Opinion Research Corporation, 1972). The quadrants were established not by setting the vertical and horizontal axes at the means of the two scales but by adopting 60 percent as a threshold for the importance axis and 40 percent as a threshold between satisfactory and unsatisfactory performance. Therefore the critical needs were in the quadrant where more than 60 percent of the public agreed on its importance and less than 40 percent of the public considered the schools' performance as at least good.

A quadrant analysis based on three dimensions was used by Gable, Pecheone, and Gillung (1981) to establish priorities for training teachers and other school personnel. Their model was tested with a sample of 569 classroom teachers who rated themselves on a discrepancy survey of their present and desired levels of competency in dealing with minimally handicapped children in the regular classroom. In their 2×2 matrix, one dimension was the self-reports of teachers on the discrepancies between their present and desired competencies (labeled *need*); the other dimension was generated from ratings by experts on the importance of those competencies (labeled *priority*). The four cells in the quadrant were (1) high discrepancy, high priority, (2) high discrepancy, low priority, (3) low discrepancy, high priority, and (4) low discrepancy, low priority. Differences among the cells can be further analyzed through analysis of variance or t-tests. Those competencies falling within cell 1 constitute priorities for in-service training, but those falling in cells 2 and 3 should be discussed and reinforced. They might also be integrated into the training program.

This method collapses two dimensions—present competency, and desired competency—into one for the quadrant analysis. It thus provides a way to use importance as a qualifying factor in deriving priorities and avoids the fallacy of basing priority decisions on simple discrepancies.

Many variants of the matrix method are found, most of them using simple 2×2 tables with quadrants of the same size rather than basing the divisions on mean scores or percentages of the respondents. Other approaches use larger matrices to show the relationships among more elements.

Proportionate Reduction in Error (PRE). The PRE approach has been used to derive a single statistic to describe an educational need, where either two or three parameters are used (Misanchuk, 1980, 1982a, 1982b; LeSage, 1980a, 1980b). In contrast with the descriptive approaches described earlier, the PRE is predictive of "the probability that certain combinations of a joint distribution will occur, then tests to see how closely the prediction matches the observations" (Misanchuk, 1982a, p. 4). The method has been tested in identifying priorities of need for training, with the dimensions being three need components: "the competence or ability of the individual to perform the task or skill, the relevance of the task or skill for the individual's particular job role, and the individual's desire to undertake training in the task or skill" (p. 2).

> The procedure yields a single statistic which succinctly describes the need as defined on both dimensions [job competence and job relevance] simultaneously, permitting the immediate and intuitively obvious comparison of various skill needs by comparing single numbers, each representing one single need. It also permits statistical tests for determining the significance of difference . . . [p. 5].
> The adaptation of the PRE approach to needs analysis involves predicting a high educational need for each skill, then using the computed value of [the PRE index of need] to determine the validity of the prediction. A high value [of the index] indicates high validity of the prediction, hence high educational need for the associated skill [p. 10].

Misanchuk developed the procedure in order to overcome the deficiencies associated with deriving priorities of need from other analytic methods, including ordinal and nominal data, two-by-two tables, measures of correlation, and others. He maintains that reduction of data by these means causes loss of information and serious possibilities of misinterpretation. Misanchuk (1982a, p. 4) notes:

> Even if one were willing to subject the data to parametric statistical analysis (a somewhat dubious

procedure, given the ordinal nature of the data), there is no convenient way to incorporate consideration of both the within-item variance and the between-item variance in a way that permits the eventual ranking of items (skills) in descending order of educational need. Misanchuk and Scissons (1978) attacked this problem in a less than satisfactory way by converting all average item responses to z-scores, using the pooled inter-item variance, then identifying those items as high need for whom all joint z-scores were over a certain arbitrary cutting point. The use of the cutting-points (for each of competence, relevance, and desire) was problematic, since, at best, it yielded only groups of items whose approximate need was the same; there was no satisfactory way to differentiate with respect to need among items within such a group.

The explanation of the method of deriving and using the PRE is beyond the scope of this chapter. But the rationale for the statistic does address the many problems associated with the most commonly used means to analyze needs data and set priorities.

Goal Framework Model

In their goal framework model for communitywide adult education, Kemerer and Schroeder (1983) use both qualitative and quantitative procedures to derive priorities. The framework has three levels—goal states, attributes of each goal state, and indicators of each attribute. In the qualitative stage, raters use the paired-comparison method to place relative values on the items at each level. (1) *Each goal state's relative value* is measured and a percentage is computed to reflect the proportion of times each goal state is selected over its alternative. (2) *All attributes within a goal state* are rated to determine the proportion each attribute contributes to the definition of the goal state. (3) *All indicators within each attribute* are rated to determine the proportion each indicator contributes as a descriptive measure of the attribute. The proportionate values for each of the three levels of the goal framework are multiplied to yield a final qualitative estimate for each indicator. Thus, if a given goal state is valued at 60 percent of the goal framework, an attribute within that goal state at 25 percent of the goal state, and

an indicator at 40 percent of that attribute, the qualitative estimate
for that indicator (I_{qe}) is:

$$I_{qe} = \frac{60}{100} \times \frac{25}{100} \times \frac{40}{100} = .06 \, .$$

The same process is used to derive a qualitative estimate for
every indicator of every goal state in the framework. All indicators
are then rank-ordered for their relative value, with those of highest
expressed value having the highest qualitative priority.

The model uses two quantitative estimates—size of present
discrepancy and size of future expected discrepancy. The formulas
are

$$\text{present discrepancy} = \left[\frac{\text{current level} - \text{desired level}}{\text{current level}} \right] \times 100$$

and

$$\text{percentage change} \atop \text{in current level} = \left[\frac{\text{current level} - \text{projected level}}{\text{current level}} \right] \times 100.$$

The second estimate refers to the discrepancy predicted to
occur at some time (say five years) in the future if no intervention
occurs to satisfy the need. The percentage change is then combined
with the present discrepancy size. If the future discrepancy is
assumed to be larger than the present discrepancy, the need is
greater and intervention becomes more urgent.

Qualitative and quantitative estimates are integrated in a
four-quadrant matrix, with the qualitative estimate of a need
indicator along the vertical axis and the quantitative estimate along
the horizontal axis. The needs with the highest priority are those
falling in the quadrant having the highest qualitative and quantitative estimates. To reduce ambiguity, a decision rule is imposed:
Where one estimate is higher than the other, priority is given to the
qualitative estimate. Therefore, those indicators having high qualitative and low quantitative importance are given priority over
those having low qualitative and high quantitative importance.

The model has been used to train people in community
services and has been tested for reliability, clarity, and acceptability,

among other things. It was found that two groups ranking the same need statements prior to exposure to the goal framework procedures produced two unrelated lists, whereas intergroup agreement using the model procedures was highly significant. One operational problem is that the paired comparisons become voluminous as one moves down through the model. Kemerer and Schroeder suggest that design of priority procedures must take into account three closely interwoven factors: the reliability of the procedures, the latitude given to practitioners in making decisions, and the final acceptance of the output.

Setting Priorities from Nonsurvey Data

The previous sections described procedures for setting priorities from quantitative analyses of surveys and variant techniques used to elicit opinions. Different methods are used to set priorities when other sources (such as test scores, social indicators, and group-process methods) form the sole or major data base.

Tests. When achievement tests are used to identify status in educational needs assessment, the test results must be compared with norms or other standards in order to set priorities. A method widely used is that a committee of educators and parents sets an objective stating the percentage of students who should be achieving at a specified level as measured by specified norm-referenced tests. The committee may also set criteria for determining priorities of need. Criterion-referenced tests are also used, either in place of or in addition to norm-referenced tests. Priorities are determined by ranking the magnitude of discrepancies between the test results and the criteria set for achievement.

There are many problems associated with using test scores alone to establish priorities of need:

- Although test data are accessible in school records, making them an attractive source of available data for needs assessments, most school systems do not test a wide range of objectives, such as oral communication or many objectives in the cognitive and affective domains. With a few exceptions, there are no satisfactory tests for most of the goals and objectives used in educational needs assessments. In a study comparing published tests with a set of 106 goals that were validated in a nationwide study, Hoepfner (1974) found only a small proportion of tests that related to the goals. Some needs-assessment models, such as the one distributed by Phi Delta Kappa, furnish tests keyed to educational objectives, but they use other means to establish priorities as well.

- Even when satisfactory tests are found, there are no agreed-upon standards against which to measure educational progress. Norms on which tests are based generally relate to national samples of students. Assumptions underlying the tests may not be appropriate to the experiences and cultural and linguistic backgrounds of the local students, the school curriculum, and the like.

- Tests are used to provide global evaluations of student achievement, but they may not accurately reflect achievement due to differences in motivation, possible test anxiety, and so on. Nor do they give information about the strengths and weaknesses that students bring to the assessment task, and thus they lack a sufficient basis for setting priorities. The latter may be more related to matters of information processing than to the areas of knowledge or skill in the test. Significant negative correlations have been reported between test anxiety and grades. Although test anxiety may improve performance with some people under certain conditions, it often interferes with information processing and performance (Sarason, 1983).

- A further issue is whether criterion-referenced tests are more valid than norm-referenced tests for needs assessment. There is some evidence that certain methods of aggregating and interpreting results of criterion-referenced tests cause problems in using them for program evaluation (Barta, Ahn, and Gastright, 1976), which raises a question as to their usefulness in setting priorities of need.

As one source of need indicators, the Native Hawaiian Educational Assessment Project used data from the standardized testing program of the state's Department of Education, plotting the curves of percentages of students scoring in each of the nine stanines on a given test administration. The degree to which the curve representing Hawaiian students differed from the normal distribution represented the degree to which they were not "at parity" with the national norming group in educational outcomes. Needs were also inferred from trends, grade level comparisons, and other analyses of the data (Kamehameha Schools . . . , 1983. See Chapter Two for description of the model.). The project staff found at least three ways of defining educational need based on the curves: (1) The most in need are those scoring lowest on the test. (2) Any disparity from national norms indicates need. Thus there could be a need area *above* the national mean, if too few students score there. (3) Even if Hawaiian students achieve national parity, the need is to achieve parity with the highest achieving local ethnic group.

If used with other indicators and information sources to encompass an adequate range of objectives, test data can assist in establishing general areas of need in basic skills and certain subject-matter areas. Causal analysis should then be used to probe below the surface of the test scores to the factors contributing to the strengths and weaknesses indicated by the test scores.

Social Indicators. Service-based needs assessments often set priorities on the discrepancies between the numbers of clients presently being served by certain programs and the number that would be expected to need the services, from analysis of population statistics. Other needs assessments that rely on social indicators use a problem-solving rather than a discrepancy model. Their priorities are then set on perceived magnitude of the problems rather than on ranking discrepancies based on norms. Still others compare the indicators to established norms in areas such as health, income, or housing.

As has been mentioned elsewhere, social indicators alone are rarely sufficient to order priorities of need, and in any event, they should be used within a conceptual framework that includes criteria for selecting the indicators and establishing a basis for inferring needs and ranking them in order of criticality for allocating resources.

Group Processes. Most of the group processes described in Chapter Five have built-in procedures for determining priorities. These take the form of consensus-formation methods, often through such forced-choice techniques as card sorts, the paired-weighting process, ranking by the rule of three, or the budget-allocation method. The processes usually rely on successive stages of group work to refine lists of needs or problems and to rank them for importance. Some of the group methods involve integrating data from existing records with perceptions of importance of goals or concerns. Whether the group methods include ways of clearly formulating desired states and criteria for determining priorities, depends on the model being followed as well as on the skills of the group facilitators and their understanding of needs assessment.

Setting Priorities in Human Services Planning

Many reports of human services needs assessments, whether based on surveys or social indicators, fail to identify priorities. Presumably, the data are presented to managers and policy boards who then determine priorities for resource allocation by means of their usual budgeting and decision-making processes.

Most of the quantitative refinements for determining priorities that have been discussed in this chapter were developed for educational needs assessments in schools and colleges or for staff training in a variety of organizational settings. Few reports from such sources mention difficulty in achieving consensus on goals. Identifying priorities for needs assessment in human services is a somewhat different matter, made more difficult by the fact that the delivery of human services is highly pluralistic. Bolen (1977, p. 23) notes that many communities find it very difficult to agree on the basic goals of the system:

> Power and authority is diffuse, interest groups abound, and the competition for resources is high. . . . For the general public, it is an arena of confusion, costliness, and ineffectiveness.
>
> Most goals center around vague concerns with adequate social functioning, optimum independence, and good health. Yet the means to achieve these is seldom clear-cut. Indeed, the ways to observe and measure whether the goals are being achieved by any means are not always available. Since goals are essentially statements of values, they are continually subject

to change and adjustment. Goals often conflict with each other. Changing techniques of service delivery or funding create changes in goals and priorities.

Whereas decisions on educational and training priorities often require changes in program emphasis rather than reallocation of funds, human services planners must generally deal with hard questions of funding for services and translating assessed needs into required funding. Kamis (1981), describes three approaches for comparing need and available programs for deinstitutionalized clients in order to make inferences about allocations. Briefly, they are

1. Rank the areas on assessed need, assessed amount of available resources, and service utilization, with the assumption that high need indicates high priority for funding. This method is the simplest and least informative, and it accounts only for the order of priorities not the extent of the differences.
2. Translate the assessed need into required funding: (a) Ascertain the number of people with umet need in each area. (b) Detail the unmet need in terms of specific services. (c) Estimate the number of units of service required for an average recipient. (d) Insert the cost of each relevant unit of service. (e) Calculate needed funds for each area.
3. This procedure uses statistics to provide for equitable division of funds according to need without the necessity to determine the exact numbers of people with unmet needs. Three types of data are compiled and transformed into standardized scores: assessed needs of all service areas, available resources (available beds, staff, funds), and service-utilization data. The three types of data are then compared and contrasted to reveal possible barriers to services, and all data are integrated. Finally, the standardized need scores are applied to available funds to derive the proportion of total funds to be allocated to each area. The formula is

$$\frac{\text{area score}}{\text{total score}} \times \text{available funds} = \text{funds allocated to area.}$$

Kamis-Gould and others (1982, p. 23) developed a method for combining composite need scores, performance indicators, and data on past funding "to produce a formula for the allocation of the mental health portion of the 1982 Federal Block Grant to Community Mental Health Centers" in several counties. Taking into account the reduction in federal funding of 32.5 percent from the base allocation, the reallocation was calculated on the basis of direct allocation of 50 percent of the reduced funds, 40 percent based on a weighted factor derived from need data and 10 percent based on performance indicators—services provided to high-priority target groups.

The allocation formula was intended to "assure continuity while introducing new factors of assessed need and performance assessment. Though expected to weigh more heavily in the future, the new factors were derived from imperfect data and therefore determined only 40% and 10% of the allocations" (p. 25).

Integrative Procedures

Regardless of quantitative methods used to identify and rank the most critical needs, setting priorities involves combining the data on needs with other factors and with the values and judgments of planners and policy makers. Priorities should be based on careful analysis and interpretation of all data and their implications.

Kaufman and English (1979) observe that "the quality, direction, and weight of various administrative decisions will be (or should be) in proportion to the perceived and stated importance and priority of educational goals" (p. 148). They suggest setting a criterion for ranking a number of alternative possible objectives: What does it cost to meet the need? What does it cost to ignore the need? In the latter case, cost is used in the sense of opportunity lost. In other words, what are the social and economic consequnces of ignoring educational and social needs? They further suggest that the present and anticipated gaps between current survival/contribution levels and desired/required levels be placed in priority order, "perhaps ranked on the basis of the 'cost' to close the gap *and* the 'cost' to ignore the gap. 'Cost' here is in societal terms, not the dollar figures to obtain the methods-means for actually closing the gaps"

(p. 190). The final priority of needs, however, is arrived at only after negotiation among the "partner groups" on their disagreements and the collection of such additional data as they deem necessary.

Societal costs, either to meet the need or to ignore the need, are difficult to determine and are rarely dealt with in needs assessments. This is an area where some of the predictive tools mentioned in earlier chapters would be useful. Since one cost of ignoring a need in the present is a potential future need of some magnitude, futures scenarios and cross-impact matrices constructed for the critical need areas would be appropriate. The cause-consequence analysis described in Chapter Seven or decision trees (Archibald and Villoria, 1967) are also helpful in projecting consequences of present actions. Trends analysis of the needs assessment data will also supply indicators of the potential for increasing or decreasing needs.

A manual to guide assessment of needs in adult and continuing education in British Columbia (Lund and McGechaen, 1981, pp. 16–17) offers these criteria for setting priorities, which can be adapted to any needs assessment setting:

> Does the target group recognize this need?
> How many people are affected?
> What would be the consequences if this need is not met?
> Is this a need that can be met by an educational activity?
> Does this need coincide with your department or institution's program policies? If not, what are the reasons for the present policies? What procedures are available for influencing needed change?
> Can you rely on co-sponsorship or cooperation with another agency?
> Is this a critical need that should be met before other educational needs are addressed?
> Will resources (funds, staff) be adequate to meet those needs?

A Systematic Process Model. Sork (1979) developed and validated a model for determining priority of need in community adult education, where the need statements represented measurable discrepancies between a present condition and a more valued future condition and most of the needs were based on economic and social indicators of well-being. A subsequent refinement of the model resulted in a generic process for determining priorities that provides a conceptual framework yet leaves many choices to those involved in the process (Sork, 1982b).

1. *Select appropriate criteria.* The people who will make the priority decisions select and clearly define the criteria for setting priorities. The model suggests two general categories of criteria—importance and feasibility. Examples of importance are number of people affected by the need, degree to which meeting the need would contribute to organizational goals, immediacy, instrumental value, and magnitude of the discrepancy between present and desirable future states of affairs. Examples of feasibility criteria are educational efficacy (degree to which an educational intervention or program can contribute to eliminating the need), availability of resources, and commitment to change. Other criteria could be selected consistent with the value system of the institution.

2. *Assign relative importance to each criterion.* All criteria could be weighted equally or assigned any value from 1 to 10, first identifying the criterion that should carry the least weight in priority decisions. A factor of 2 carries twice the weight of a factor of 1 in the final decision, and a factor of 10 carries ten times the weight.

3. *Apply each criterion to each need.* This results in a separate list of priorities for each criterion used. All priority values are expressed in the same type of units, such as numerical values or descriptors (high, medium, and low). Alternatives are suggested for ranking or rating the needs to derive individual priorities.

4. *Combine individual values to yield a total priority value for each need.* Sork offers a number of techniques for this step, including plotting judgments of importance and feasibility on a quadrant chart or using an additive aggregation rule to combine weighted ranks into a mean rank for each need.

5. *Arrange needs from highest to lowest total priority value and indicate how priorities will be used.* The group should state clearly how the specific needs will be used to allocate resources.

For example, will the organization begin work simultaneously on the "top" group of needs, or will the organization work on meeting one need at a time, beginning at the top, until available resources are exhausted? Will a group of needs at the "low" end of the list be ignored, or will some attempt be made to address all identified needs? And how will newly identified high-priority needs affect the allocation of resources to established, ongoing programs?

. . . Be forewarned—procedures for determining priorities can be manipulated to produce a result which supports someone's personal priorities. Safeguards should be employed to reduce the chances of individuals using the priority-setting process as a means of furthering their own self-interests at the expense of others in the organization or community. Open communication and involvement in decision making are two factors which should reduce the chances that the process will be abused [Sork, 1982b, p. 9].

Decision Matrix. The ACNAM model for elementary schools (Witkin, 1979a) employs a 37 × 52 decision matrix to synthesize data from many different sources in order to set priorities. First, on a 3 × 3 matrix, importance estimations are plotted against actual data on attainment in all instructional and support components in the schools. Data from this analysis are entered into the decision matrix and synthesized with other data to establish priorities. Information from the ACNAM surveys, tests already in the school records, fourteen socioeconomic and demographic factors for the school profile, and ratings of importance of objectives are recorded for each instructional and support component in the needs assessment. Educators and parents review the data and decide whether the findings are of high, medium, or low importance in indicating a critical need in the component. They then make qualitative judgments about the meaning of the data.

In the ACNAM model, priorities are set *within* each of the components—such as reading skills, or library services—since they are all an essential part of the school program. That is, not the components but the elements and objectives within each component are ranked for priority. However, the importance estimates for components can be used as a weighting value. Thus, the action plan for the following year is based on many kinds of data that describe and evaluate standards, performance, and services within each component.

Issues-Based Model. In the issues-based, cyclical model for secondary schools described in Chapter Two, priorities are established by comparing student performance data of many kinds with standards for both adequate and excellent performance that provide cut-off points for defining needs (Witkin, 1979c; Kenworthy and others, 1980). Each curricular department develops a set of expectancies for student performance based on critical issues related to departmental goals and sets three levels as benchmarks: a satisfactory or adequate level, a level of excellence, and a need level, which is defined as any performance below that of adequacy. Priorities for focusing program and staff resources are given to those areas where performance falls the farthest below the minimal standards. Priorities are established for needs *within* departments; they do not compete *across* departments, except in schoolwide issues. Since the standards and levels are specific to each issue, the model supplies criteria both for immediate action and for long-term planning. The latter could include steps to raise standards as well as to enhance the qualities of excellence found in the assessment.

Interagency Priority Setting. Converting masses of data from many different sources into priorities for broad community-based decisions is a complex process. Raw data must be reduced to manageable proportions, and the integration must include alternative implications of the meaning of the data. One approach can be illustrated by the methods used in the last phase of a needs assessment and planning project conducted jointly by a city and a school district (Witkin, Richardson, and Wickens, 1979).

The study assessed needs in five areas that preliminary analysis had identified as critical communitywide concerns. Perceptions on standards for each area were gathered by means of key-informant surveys. Data on status came from the surveys, social indicators, and the compilation of a regional resource directory. Critical needs were further analyzed by means of Fault Tree Analysis.

Priorities were determined as follows. (1) The project staff wrote summary reports for each area of concern, integrating data from all sources and presenting results in a standard format. (2) An

independent evaluator interviewed key people who had been actively involved in one or more aspects of the project, seeking both
their reactions to the needs assessment and suggestions for priorities
for future action. (3) The project director presented data summaries,
the fault trees, the evaluation report, and staff recommendations to
the city council and school board during an action-oriented work
session, during part of which small groups examined the analyses
from individual concerns areas and made specific proposals for
joint action. (4) As the final step in the work session, the full board
and council synthesized the small group recommendations,
achieved consensus on a single priority for immediate action
planning, and proposed a first-stage action plan with a target date
for specific accomplishments.

Issues in Setting Priorities

Although setting priorities is the stage that provides the
essential bridge from gathering data to selecting and developing
solutions to meet the needs, the potential for making "wrong"
decisions begins with the design of the assessment and the validity
of the procedures and instruments used. The issues are not only
technical; they are also practical and political.

Acceptability of Methodology. Regardless of the technical
adequacy and validity of the procedures, there is a danger that
practitioners who must implement the needs assessment will find
them boring, too time consuming, difficult to understand, or
confusing in vocabulary and procedures.

Foster and Southard (1982) conducted a comparison study to
determine the usefulness of various criteria for setting priorities on
needs from the viewpoint of school personnel who participated in
one or more needs assessments in twelve districts in Florida. Four
districts used a model developed in the Florida state department of
education, one used an adaptation of Kaufman's (1972) systems
model, and the remaining seven did not follow any specific published model. "All districts used ranking of goal importance and
size of discrepancy between attained and desired outcomes as the
main criteria for prioritizing needs. Other criteria . . . included cost

of meeting the need, number of persons directly affected by the need, and the probability of success in alleviating the need" (p. 5).

Of the four groups surveyed—board, staff, principals, and teachers—the only criteria on which at least 70 percent of each group agreed were ranking of goal importance, probability of success if the solution were implemented, and feasibility of time and personnel for solving the need. Also highly rated were number of persons affected and cost to meet the need. Foster and Southard (p. 7) note, "Surprisingly, 'Size of discrepancy . . . ,' which is central to most, if not all needs assessment models, ranked eighth out of nine alternative criteria." They make two recommendations: to include causal analysis in the needs assessment process as a prerequisite to setting priorities and to involve in the process of setting priorities school personnel who have the responsibility to design and implement solutions.

They conclude that there is a clear discrepancy between the perspective of those who develop needs assessment models and "the more pragmatic perspective of those who implement needs assessment studies" (p. 7). This is borne out by another study that found that personnel in five districts using the same model to conduct a year-long needs assessment encountered many serious problems (Lewis, 1978). Activities most often cited as problems were obtaining a reasonable response rate from a community survey, identifying educational goals, determining subgoals, and preparing the survey instrument. The technical and administrative problems resulted in serious slippage of time lines; two districts failed to complete five activities of the assessment. Yet the conditions were nearly ideal; the districts had funds, consultant assistance, and commitment from school officials. Nevertheless, they considered the process difficult, expensive, and time consuming.

Ambiguity of Goals. One reason for the low ranking given to the discrepancy criterion in the Foster and Southard study was the variability in the quality of the goal-attainment measures, which disturbed many participants (G. R. Foster, letter to the author, Dec. 9, 1983). A national study of the feasibility of using existing data as information for educational research and development found that the goals and problem statements were so general and inclusive that the implied needs were usually vague and ambiguous (Sikorski, Oakley, and Lloyd-Kolkin, 1977). "We are in the ridiculous situation of having agreed upon a number of broad, vaguely defined goals which now, once they are being implemented, become tremendously controversial" (p. 15). They add, "We must develop ways of discovering and understanding educational problems which do not cloud reality or lead to apparent but in reality *false* consensus" (p. 16, their emphasis).

This ambiguity of goals is often matched by the ambiguous nature of survey responses, the confounding of primary and secondary needs, inadequate analysis of data, and confusion of goals or solutions with needs. Technical adequacy of methods of setting priorities may be of little avail under such circumstances.

Validation of Survey Instruments. The validity of data-collection methods and instruments has not always been a high priority with needs assessors. A few research studies have compared the merits of different data-gathering procedures. No reports have been found of studies to validate the information collected—for example, by comparing respondent opinions of student performance on specific parameters with data from other sources, such as tests and teacher evaluations.

One of the first sets of needs assessment instruments evaluated for face validity and feasibility of administration through field tests was the elementary school kit developed by the Center for the Study of Evaluation in Los Angeles (Hoepfner and others, 1971). Others were the ACNAM model for elementary schools (Witkin, 1979a), the final version of which was based on factor analyses and a statewide field test to evaluate clarity and feasibility of administration, and the HumRRO school problem surveys (Taylor, Vineberg, and Goffard, 1974). In the latter, priorities of needs can be inferred from profiles of student problems by respondent groups based on item clusters developed by the researchers on an a priori basis. Later, factor analyses based on data in two large high schools indicated that the items might well be regrouped into other clusters for purposes of analysis and of identifying critical need areas (Lehnen and Witkin, 1977b).

Examples of other validation studies are factor analyses of instruments to identify in-service training needs of teachers working with handicapped children (Pecheone and Gable, 1978) and the needs of early childhood–elementary school teachers (Hanley and Moore, 1981), reliability studies for college survey instruments (Educational Testing Service, 1974), reliability of an instrument to assess needs and obtain indicators for evaluation utilization (Crane, Crofton, and Kandaswamy, 1982), and validation of an instrument for analyzing needs for training activities in complex organizations (Crumpton, 1974).

The question of reliability of ratings of curricular goals was investigated by Brittingham and Netusil (1976), who found high stability within and between groups of raters in seven rural school districts over a four-month period. Since it often takes a school system two to three years to implement a change following goal rating, priorities based on such ratings must take reliability into consideration. The authors felt that the high reliability may have been due to the stable nature of the communities involved, the lack of unrest or dissatisfaction with the schools, and the specificity of the goal statements in the study. More information is needed about both short-term and long-term change.

Comparability of Methods. An important consideration in deciding whether to choose one method of data collection over another is whether different strategies would yield comparable results. Clifton (1969) found that assessments based on different types of information—such as surveys, job performance ratings, and course work taken—yield noncomparable needs. In a different type of study, Suarez and Cox (1981) found that three methods of data gathering—on-site interviews, telephone interviews, and self-assessments without assistance from the needs assessor—were essentially comparable in identifying service needs of clients of a Technical Assistance Center. In their research, however, they used the same instrument in the three different methods of administration.

Suarez and Cox accept similarity of needs among clients of the center in different locales as evidence of comparability of the methods. Yet there is no good rationale for assuming that different clients should have the same priority of needs. In fact, if the needs assessment considers the context of the location or organization, it would be surprising if different clients did not have different priorities.

The criteria of specificity to the context and avoidance of false consensus on goals, and thus on priorities, are illustrated by the results of a series of needs assessments conducted in several communities in a western state. The communities were very different from each other—one was a large urban school district, another was rural, another had a large proportion of Native Americans, and so on. Goals and need statements were generated through group processes with local stakeholders. Despite the demographic, geographic, and cultural differences among them, the districts came up with priority rankings of needs that were surprisingly similar. Yet the similarities were probably spurious. Not only were the goals and need statements at too high a level of abstraction to be meaningful but also the agreement on priorities appeared to reflect a deference on the part of parents and other lay people to the expressed or implied values of the educators who were leading the meetings rather than a real indication of need.

Priorities Without Resources. Sork's (1982b) process model for determining priorities includes the criterion of availability of resources to meet the need. But many needs assessors raise the issue as to whether needs should be assessed at all in areas for which the organization has no present resources. Whether to do so depends somewhat upon the conceptual basis of the needs assessment— whether it is service-based or population-based. Ideally, needs assessments should be conducted without specific solutions or programs in mind. Service providers should be free to consider many alternative solutions, leaving open the possibility of deriving resources to meet the needs in the future from new quarters, including interagency cooperation. The priority-setting process should certainly consider present resources when selecting need areas for immediate action. But long-range planning might well incorporate methods for acquiring additional resources to meet high-priority needs.

Cutting-Edge Priorities. Adams (1983, p. 56) notes the difficulty of using needs-sensing information to set priorities in settings such as R&D organizations, which "tend to work on the front end of problems before they are perceived as needs. A need such as improving handicapped individuals' access to job training programs may not be perceived as a priority need by educators until well after legislation is passed and programs are in operation. Another problem is that cutting-edge priorities are themselves elusive and tend to fluctuate with changing political priorities and initiatives."

It is not only R&D organizations that seek to be on the cutting edge of priority setting. Many who have worked with needs assessments of various kinds for years are dissatisfied with methods that serve only to identify the obvious, that ignore signals of future needs, employ inadequate or inappropriate data analysis, and arrive at conclusions so general that the priorities are of little value. Adams (p. 56) also observes that "needs sensing may bury controversial needs. Needs sensing typically ranks needs using measures of central tendency. This 'democratic' calculation process often brings widely popular needs to the top of a priority listing (e.g., ensuring that all students master basic skills) while leaving more controversial needs (e.g., ensuring that the curriculum is free from sex role stereotyping) toward the bottom."

The Question of Values. In the last analysis, decisions about priorities must deal with values and outcomes—in fact, strategic decisions. Policy makers weigh needs assessment findings in the light of both internal and external environmental press; this would include changes in the public's expectations and goals, availability of federal funding for programs with high national priorities, and the current hopes and anxieties about human services. Public opinion polls and national commissions often send conflicting messages. The media play a significant part in sounding alarms about educational and social needs on the national level, which may or may not be relevant to local needs.

In examining challenges affecting priorities for continuing education agencies, Knox (1982, p. 13) notes, "Most decisions about priorities seek to achieve an agreement that some outcomes are more desirable than others. A strong commitment to efficiently serving as many adult basic education participants as possible with available funds almost eliminates the possibility of attracting and retaining many of the hardest-to-reach adults." Although directors want to influence the goals and directions of an agency, "there are many possible goals and many influences on the priority setting process. . . . Effective strategies for priority setting typically include . . .

other people, such as policy makers in the parent organization and in the larger society, resource persons, and the participants themselves. Specific strategies typically recognize competing expectations and values and emphasize consensus building with all that implies in the form of bargaining and compromise. Such strategies may appear more political than rational" (p. 18).

9

Improving Organizational Planning

An organization may undertake a needs assessment for two different purposes: to identify and assess client needs or to assess the needs of the organization itself. After a brief discussion of the impact of the organization on the assessment of client needs, the remainder of this chapter is devoted to elements and issues pertaining to the assessment of organizational needs.

Client-centered needs assessments are primary-level, concerned with ends, or gaps in outcomes; organizational assessments are secondary-level, concerned with means, or gaps in inputs. Once specific client needs are identified, the organization should consider alternative methods to meet those needs and then assess its own and its network resources. Frequently used methods of assessment are resource inventories, program budget reviews, analysis of staff capabilities, and appraisal of facilities and equipment. In effect, the secondary or institutional level of a client-centered assessment consists of identifying and analyzing the gaps between actual and desired status of the organization's resources.

The structure and planning capability of the organization have a powerful effect on the needs assessment. Five principal influences are (1) the technical expertise of the needs assessor, (2) the adequacy of the needs assessment concept and plan, (3) the commitment of top management and the board to implement the plan and to utilize the findings, (4) whether the assessment is part of long-range planning or a one-shot study for the short term, and (5) whether or not the organization has looked to external referents for the what-should-be dimension. Much of the impact on the needs assessment of the organization itself is related to its internal communication structure and climate and its internal and external communication strategies, which are discussed in Chapter Ten.

The validity and efficacy of a primary-level assessment is also constrained by the organization's view of its mission and its role in fulfilling client needs and by the political context in which it operates. Most organizations have constituencies they cannot deny regardless of need. Once a service, program, or product has been established, many organizations find it hard to change. It is in those spheres that an organization can profit by an assessment of its own needs as an organization.

Purposes of Organizational Needs Assessment

Organizational needs assessment may take place at the level of the entire organization or by units or departments. Typical purposes are to clarify organizational goals, to identify new directions for the organization, to redefine a company's product line, to set up a new curriculum or restructure an existing one, to analyze present and potential responsiveness to changing societal conditions, or to assess needs related to staff performance and competencies. (Note that "training" or "staff development" is a possible *solution* to an organizational need, the advisability of which could be the focus of an assessment.)

Organizational needs assessment is appropriate both at the beginning of a planning cycle and as part of the evaluation process. Evaluation data alone—such as status reports on an organization's progress, effectiveness of a new program, or reports of earnings—do not in themselves indicate needs. But when the data are linked to organizational or program goals and objectives, need areas can be identified and assessed further. Ideally, the organization would have a continuous sensing mechanism that is responsive to both internal and external information about needs. Needs assessment is then an element of an ongoing organizational-planning capability, and the data are an integral part of the management information system.

Planning Capability

The effort to return planning to state and local governments has meant that public and private agencies at the community level have increased planning responsibilities (Bolen, 1977). Questions as to who should deliver services, what types of services should be delivered, and how resources should be allocated must be answered by local governments that previously had little or no voice in those decisions. Bolen (p. 122) sees five prominent issues for local planners: "the need to integrate methodological development; the lack of agreement on objectives and priorities; increasing problems of coordinating planning; roles and functions in human services planning; and equity and justice in the delivery of human services." These issues are interdisciplinary and interagency, making the organizational factors more complicated.

In order to resolve some of the problems (particularly, the differences in roles between the service provider and the planner), the planner often looks to the management sciences for methodological assistance, "thereby uncovering again the traditional conflict between expertise and organizational hierarchy noted frequently in the literature of organizational studies" (p. 123). Bolen further notes, "The contemporary American community has an entirely new array of needs and a completely new array of providers attempting to meet those needs. City hall is being asked to perform tasks that federal and state governments could not previously handle themselves" (p. 124). That statement has become even more pertinent since the "new federalism" and the Reagan initiatives of 1981 and later.

Despite the importance of planning, many writers are skeptical about the capability of organizations for this task. In 1970, Wholey observed, "Most human services programs can be characterized as having: (1) no clear and objective goals; (2) no identifiable output measures; (3) either no or a poor reporting system; and (4) no system to utilize evaluation results" (cited in Demone, 1978, p. 74). Kells (1981), basing his strictures on in-depth work with more than 300 colleges and universities and contacts with several hundred more, found serious problems with coherent planning and self-assessment.

> At the *institutional* level . . . leaders are rarely able to sort out the demands for study and planning imposed by external sources, and they certainly have difficulty developing a local agenda for study, planning, and action amid these constant and often conflicting demands. . . . The same band of hard-working folk on the campus are dragooned into service in a seemingly never-ending sequence of studies, planning efforts, "commissions to chart the future," mission and goals efforts, management by objectives, superimpositions, and program reviews. Few institutions have decided to collapse it all into a logical, cyclical sequence of locally centered study, planning, and doing. . . . [On the most vulnerable and potiticized campuses] it seems as if an institutional evolution occurs in which self-selection or entrapment results in a type of leadership and a cadre of professionals which defy and deny the principles of organizational health such as openness, effective communication, and ability to recognize and solve problems [p. 18, Kells's emphasis].

Kells believes that those in charge of assessments have no clear sense of how to go about their task. "They have neither a usable theory nor a model which they call forth to be the basis of the effort, nor do they seem to have a reasonable level of technical expertise." As a result, they "grasp at the first plausible approach that is suggested. . . . They do not seem to bring the same level of professionalism to tasks like assessment or planning that they surely must apply in the pursuit of knowledge in their own discipline" (p. 19). Kells did, however, find some institutions that have developed useful processes of assessment under sensitive local leadership.

Kells's comments reflect on the institution's capability for self-assessment or self-study, "a continuous, objective system of monitoring educational quality which a college uses to understand and plan the development of its programs and the operations which support them" (Tritschler, 1981, p. 31). Although its principal purpose is not needs assessment, in well-designed self-assessment or other evaluation processes much information is routinely gathered that indicates gaps between goals and present outcomes—that is, needs. This information is directly usable for feeding into a process for determining priorities, although it may not be recognized as such.

The effort to establish systems of self-assessment that support growth encounters many obstacles: institutional inertia, safety of the status quo, difficulty of being objective, and difficulty of sustaining an effort added on to what staff already do (Tritschler, 1981), external rather than internal motivation, poor design and lack of knowledge of design requirements, and overloads on staff time (Kells, 1981). Kells (p. 18) recommends collapsing all the varied efforts into a "logical, cyclical sequence of locally centered study, planning, and doing."

What is the relationship between self-assessment and needs assessment? Kells (p. 20) recommends using two basic, complementary strategies to assess an institution's effectiveness: "the relationship between goals and goal achievement and how well the institution seems to function as an ongoing responsive, vital organization." The first part of that statement is needs assessment; the second part is evaluation. He adds a perspective that enriches the needs assessment aspect: "The goal-achievement studies cannot prove that the institution caused the outcomes which are ascertained, because of the lack of controls and the variation in input and intervening (external) variables. . . . But if the studies are undertaken for improvement purposes, the studies can look for patterns of outcomes that should occur but do not—and then basic elements of focal points for examination, development, and change have been created" (p. 20). He adds the necessity for setting locally determined and usable criterion levels for each measure of goal achievement or process functioning.

In such loosely coupled systems as school districts, planned change to facilitate organizational growth is even more difficult. As part of a long-term research program on planned change at the Ontario Institute for Studies in Education, Leithwood and Montgomery (1982) propose a three-dimensional framework that relates growth, the system, and strategies. They hypothesize that seven conditions are necessary to produce effective planned educational change. Three of these actually define needs assessment: "knowledge of preferred images, outcomes, or behaviors; knowledge of present behaviors or outcomes actually achieved; identification of the discrepancy between present and desired status" (p. 161).

Planning Models

If needs assessment is seen as the front end—the first step—in planning, one may well ask what shape that planning should take and what role that needs assessment should play. This section presents three views of planning: strategic planning, the role of the chief executive officer in a system approach, and Hirschhorn's core/network design.

Strategic Planning. This book has several times emphasized the role and importance of needs assessment in long-range planning. The concept of strategic (sometimes called open-system) planning challenges many of the assumptions and practices of long-range planning. The difference has been summed up as: "Long-range plans focused upon institutional goals and objectives five years from now; strategic planning asks what decision is appropriate today based upon an understanding of where the critical external variables will be five years from now" (Cope, 1981, p. 1). Strategic planning stresses *effectiveness* (doing the right thing) rather than *efficiency* (doing things well). It involves the capacity to see the organization as a whole and to be concerned with the basic character of the organization.

Cope compares conventional long-range planning with strategic planning on several attributes. The perspective of strategic planning is external rather than internal; the system view is open rather than closed; data are qualitative rather than quantitative; strategic planning functions as participative integration in the whole system rather than as a separate office; the process is inductive rather than deductive; its basis is art, rather than science; and the results are a process, a stream of decisions, and today's decisions *from* the future (rather than blueprints, plans, and decisions *for* the future).

Certain aspects of strategic planning are in essence needs assessment. For example, when it is used in review of university programs in a time of budget cutbacks, "The important questions are less about satisfactory program performance and more about future fit. The key questions become, How important is this program to the mission of the institution? and How important is it to your program?" (pp. 43, 45). Need can be determined by such factors as student demand, graduate employability, importance for the university's profile, the support it provides to other programs, type of clientele service, quality of program, program efficiency, and resource needs. For the plan from such a review to be strategic, one important element is synergy (collaboration among different groups). Another is the use of creative, holistic, and intuitive conceptual processes. Strategic planning involves both vertical and horizontal integration in the institution. The emphasis is on change; the process is dynamic, rather than static.

Strategic planning is consonant with the system approach as well as the external referent element in Kaufman's Organizational Elements Model (OEM). "The essence of strategic planning remains the matching of internal resources (values, programs, facilities, staff) with opportunities to both serve and advance the social good" (Cope, p. 55).

Role of the Chief Executive Officer (CEO). A crucial factor in planning with the OEM is the proportion of attention that a CEO gives to the what-is and what-should-be elements. Herman and Kaufman (1983) argue that a school superintendent who wishes to take a successful leadership role in planning should devote primary planning efforts to identifying what should be and needs, instead of focusing only on what is. They apply the model to delineating twelve possible roles that a superintendent might play in the organization, each role being defined by the percentage of time committed to each element in the model. There are two ideal roles. In the first, the superintendent would attend only to the higher-order planning elements of products, outputs, and outcomes, delegating to others the elements of inputs and processes. In the second, or pragmatic ideal role, the ideal time allocation is modified to emphasize time and effort on the higher-order elements and to minimize, but not omit, attention to inputs and processes, except under special circumstances.

In other, less effective roles, the superintendent puts much more time on the what-is dimension. A crisis-planning perspective, for instance, is one in which the administrator focuses almost exclusively on inputs and processes—such as budget and facilities—

and not upon the outcomes of the system. The configurations vary according to the willingness of the superintendent to take risks, be a change agent, or work for organizational renewal; the superintendent's skills in dealing with higher-order planning perspectives; the level of experience and maturity of people in the organization who must be relied on; and the degree of autonomy possible in the leadership role.

It is obvious that the leadership role of the CEO can strongly influence both the types of needs assessments that take place in an organization and the organization's degree of commitment to doing the needs assessment and taking the priorities seriously in planning. An organizational commitment to periodic review of organizational goals in relation to external societal referents and to planning in terms of organizational outputs and outcomes puts needs assessment in its proper place in organizational functions.

Core/Network Model. Hirschhorn (1983, pp. 122–123) proposes that social agencies "develop organizational designs that balance their need to ensure a stable framework for service provision with a need to create new delivery systems based on new missions and resources." In his *core/network* design, all program functions and allocation of resources can be described along two dimensions: the core/network dimension and the central/compensatory dimension.

The *core/network dimension* refers to the location of a particular activity in the organization. The core consists of activities that lie entirely within the domain of the organization. The network consists of other organizations and stakeholders who participate in the service processes of the agency. For example, schools may furnish vocational assessment, mental health, or hearing-screening services to students by means of agreements with other agencies; in such cases, the school and the agency are each in the organizational network of the other. Network functions may be subcontracted, or agencies may share equipment and other resources. Network resources are mobilized by core staff members to reduce either fixed costs or the uncertainty of conducting agency business. Figure 20 shows the relationship of core to network functions between an agency and two other organizations.

Figure 20. Relationship Between Core and Network Activities.

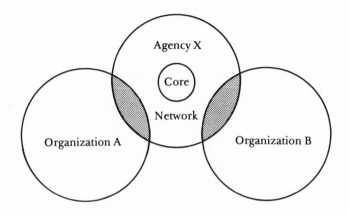

Source: Hirschhorn, 1983. Used by permission.

The *central/compensatory dimension* refers to the relationship between an activity and the mission of the organization. "A central activity is one that the agency *must* perform if it is to fulfill its mission. A compensatory activity, however, is one that an agency organizes in order to keep a program it cannot fully sustain" (p. 125, Hirschhorn's emphasis). For example, teachers might participate in family therapy seminars at a mental health clinic to compensate the schools for a cutback in school consultation services. Compensatory activities can represent either a past or future commitment to clients or community.

Hirschhorn's model suggests an alternative framework to traditional needs assessment methods for assigning priorities to organizational or agency programs and activities. His concepts offer a new way of thinking about organizational structure and program planning. If needs assessments are to be meaningful as well as cost-effective, they must be planned and conducted with understanding of the organizational context. As needs assessors recognize the network relationships, they can expand their thinking to identify needs that cannot be met solely with the organization's own resources. Many school systems object to gathering data on needs they cannot meet because they have no appropriate staff (nurses, for example, to perform certain health screenings and make referrals).

The identification of needs is constrained in their minds by the lack of immediate resources to meet them. But needs should first be analyzed without regard to solutions. By focusing on services, programs, or resources, rather than on client needs, the needs assessment may completely overlook critical problems that are susceptible to nontraditional solution strategies.

The core/network and central/compensatory dimensions are also valuable in helping an organization set priorities for allocating resources among many needs, all of which could be important or highly critical. Considering "central" activities first, the core would focus its own resources on activities of its primary mission and use the network to share resources to continue important activities. Thus, a school system could address an identified need in the area of vocational assessment and counseling with curriculum guidance and general career counseling by core (regular teaching) staff, but comprehensive vocational assessment and training could be offered through arrangements with outside agencies. Then, considering "compensatory" activities, the core would use its own resources to keep a "foot in the door" of past or potential future activities, and at the same time, through the network, maintain former programs and develop new ones using shared resources.

An example is a community service center that served a large county on Long Island and offered a sheltered workshop for adults with learning disabilities as a core/compensatory function (Butler, Witkin, and Mercer, 1982). By means of a state-funded project, the center developed a model of in-depth, comprehensive vocational assessment and counseling for adults with learning disabilities to fill a need that was not met by other agencies in the region. But the only way it could continue to perform the service in the future was to maintain a steady flow of referrals of clients on a fee-for-service basis. This could be done by means of an interagency network with schools, the state and local vocational rehabilitation agencies, boards of cooperative educational services, and organizations for parents of children with learning disabilities. At the same time, the agency had to reexamine its past compensatory activities, such as the sheltered workshop, and modify its program to meet the needs of its client population more realistically and to use its own resources more efficiently.

Elements of Organizational Needs Assessment

Goal Orientations. One aspect of needs assessment at the organizational level is the establishment of priorities of system goals. But organizations often fail to identify the actual degree of staff agreement regarding goals. When conducting surveys of perceptions about educational goals, for example, needs assessors typically look for agreement or differences of opinion *between* constituencies, such as students and instructional staff. Yet little attention has been paid to differences that may exist *within* each constituency. In a study at a large university, Rugg, Warren, and Carpenter (1981) found similar goal orientations among faculty from five different disciplines toward goals ranked high in importance, but there was much less agreement among the groups on lesser-rated goals. Business faculty, for instance, were more concerned about excellence in intercollegiate athletics and program accountability and efficiency than were sciences and mathematics faculty. Such differences among faculty groups have important implications for using needs assessment in planned change: "As institutions attempt to compensate for declining enrollments of the traditional college-age student, greater attention is being directed toward expansion of the service role of colleges and universities and toward broadening of the instructional function to include nontraditional modes of education, particularly off-campus programs. Results of this study suggest that faculty members in the education discipline may be more inclined to support such developments than faculty in the liberal arts . . . [due to] the ease with which their courses, programs, and services can be 'exported' to off-campus locations" (p. 171).

They also found differences among the different disciplines' support for special programs and opportunities for minorities and women, with business and sciences faculties being much less sympathetic than those from education. "Such findings appear to be related to the degree to which the different academic disciplines are people-oriented" (p. 172). There seems little doubt that any university wishing to form a consensus around institutional goals for planned change must take into account potentially sharp differences among faculty groups and should expect different levels of support and resistance from them. The same factors apply to secondary school faculty as well and to different departments within other types of organizations.

Staff Development/Training. Assessing needs for staff training arises out of concern for increasing the effectiveness of the organization and the services or products it delivers. It begins with the assumption that there is a gap or discrepancy between knowledge or skills required for a position and the actual knowledge or skills held by staff persons. Analysis of training needs often leads to specific in-service training offered by the organization, although recommendations may be made for individuals to pursue college courses or relevant workshops on their own initiative.

As fewer new teachers are hired in elementary and secondary schools, due to declining birth rates and concomitant drops in student enrollments, it is likely that there will be an increasing need for in-service training. Organizational needs assessments should, but often do not, identify staff needs in relation to actual learner needs. The typical survey instrument might more accurately be called a "wants assessment" than a needs assessment: staff are asked directly what kinds of courses or training they would like, or feel that they need. It is better to establish a discrepancy between specified skills necessary for job performance and staff members' perceptions of the degree to which they have the skills. But asking teachers to rate their own competencies is sometimes threatening.

One solution, while not ideal, avoids the dilemma by taking a somewhat indirect approach, while still employing a gap analysis of outputs. The staff development section of a survey for secondary schools contains thirteen items on which teachers do a self-assessment: communication skills, stress, subject-area planning, discipline, individualizing instruction, confidence in teaching reading skills, confidence in teaching math skills, helping students meet competency standards, using a multicultural approach in their teaching, coping with decreased resources, managing paperwork, assisting with schoolwide planning, and evaluating programs. Teachers rate each item on two five-point scales—amount of help they are now receiving and amount of help they would like to receive (Witkin and Richardson, 1983). The survey does not indicate possible solutions, nor does it request preferences for such.

The matter of finding feasible and acceptable ways of identifying staff development needs and establishing priorities among them raises a practical question. Who is in the best position to know one's needs, oneself or other persons? Staff members' desires for help are not necessarily good indicators of areas in which they are less competent, as measured by independent observers or performance indicators. Yet it can be argued that adults in a job setting know their own needs best; and in any case, if they do not, they are not likely to accept others' appraisals of what they need and so would not be ready for in-service training that does not meet their own perceptions. Staff who have the most need for improvement in certain areas often feel the most threatened by attempts on the part of others to help them improve.

One answer to this is provided by the multicomponent training model described in Chapter Two, which uses three criteria to establish need: relevance of a skill to the job, competence in the skill, and desire for additional training (Misanchuk, 1982b). Schwier's (1982) extension of the model delineates how each of the possible configurations of the three components indicates not only degree of need but also kinds and acceptability of training that could be offered. Another solution is to employ instruments containing behaviorally anchored scales such as those discussed in Chapter Three (Landy, 1974). In fact, one of its early uses was to measure work motivation (Landy and Guion, 1970). The scales are more difficult and time consuming to construct than the typical staff development survey, but instruments using the scales could be used in the organization on a cyclical basis to establish changing levels of need.

Barriers to Needs Assessment in the Organization. Managers often encounter difficulties in conducting assessments to identify or verify training needs. Employees may perceive the assessment as disrupting their operations; those in charge of gathering data may be inadequately prepared; people at the operational level may not see the desirability of conducting the assessment. Fidler and Loughran (1980) found that a systems analysis helped overcome employee resistance at the British Columbia Telephone Company, where "The needs assessment process is conducted to ensure that valuable educational resources are deployed to design and deliver educational programs *only when education is a reasonable solution in overcoming a performance discrepancy"* (p. 51, Fidler and Loughran's emphasis). The training model relies heavily on needs assessment. Any member of the organization may bring a problem to the attention of the company's education center and request that a course be designed. About fifteen to twenty requests a month are submitted on a companywide basis. The program design calls for a needs assessment to be conducted for every such request. It had been found that the company could save at least $900,000 annually because "the consistent application of needs assessment to requests for education reduces the number of educational programs developed by roughly 50 percent annually" (p. 56). In response to a lack of acceptance of such needs assessments, the company conducted a discrepancy analysis between the system design for the needs assessment and the ways in which the design was being implemented.

Three classifications of discrepancies were identified: in skills, in the environment, and in motivation and incentive. Several alternative solutions were found for all three problems, and cost-effective recommendations were made. Thus, although it was originally thought that a new training program was required for staff of the continuing education department—in order to overcome resistance of line managers to the needs assessments—a separate needs assessment of that problem resulted in a much better range of alternative solutions.

Selected Methods of Organizational Needs Assessment

Organizational History Analysis. Analysis of organizational needs can take several forms. Leach (1979) postulates that organizations have careers just as individuals do and that analysis of an organization's needs must take into account the stage in its career history. Leach finds a number of failings related to needs analysis of organizational training:

- Failure to distinguish between what the firm says it wants and what it really needs.

- Failure to distinguish between training needs and organizational needs—failure to relate training to the organization's goals and objectives.
- Failure to use needs analysis in designing training programs.
- Failure to consult line organization for their perceptions of needs.

Leach uses an organizational history instrument, which is completed individually by a representative sample of people in the organization at different levels. In the exercise, each person sorts the organization's history into stages, writes a paragraph or two about each stage, notes how changes in the career line have affected members of the organization, predicts the next step in the organization's career, recalls what human resources and planning mistakes the organization made in the past and why, suggests human resources and planning strategies for the next stage, and reflects on implications of the historical analysis for the training needs of the individual and others in the organization. The method can be used in connection with other needs assessment techniques. Leach suggests it as a useful first step, to provide insight into where to look for additional data for training and other organizational needs.

Situation Analysis. A somewhat similar approach is situation analysis, which was developed as part of a five-year planning model (King and Beevor, 1978; Beevor, 1981). The strategy can be applied to whole organizations or to units or subsystems. Situation analysis takes an in-depth look at the present and the recent past and speculates about the future of the organization and its environment. The questions to be answered by the analysis are (1) What characterizes the organization today? (2) What has happened in the recent past? and (3) What is predicted and what is desired for the future? Analysis of the present might include measures of employee morale, product or service quality, competition, staff turnover, and social value. People at several levels of the organization are involved, as well as outsiders such as the public or consumers.

Snapshots of the recent past, from two to five years previous to the analysis, identify both positive and negative perceptions of what the organization has been doing, including what has changed and what has improved or worsened. For predictions of the future, the organization identifies key environmental elements such as the community, politicians, teacher organizations or labor unions, taxing bodies, training institutions, federal and local governments, and customers or clients. Changes are predicted for each of the prime environmental elements, as well as changes that are likely to come about in the organization itself through retirements or other system changes; and finally, predictions are made of new or continuing needs.

The trustees or policy board (who use the information for the long-range plan) and the senior staff examine the analysis in the light of the organization's mission and determine areas of emphasis for long-range planning. Further identification of system policy needs is a later step in the implementation plan for each area of emphasis. The situation analysis is repeated yearly, with the subsequent analyses often producing changes in the long-range plan (Beevor, 1981).

OEM. Where planning within an organization is fragmented—at the work-group or departmental level—there is often a failure to relate changes and improvements to the total organization's effectiveness and goals. The Organizational Elements Model (Kaufman, 1981) offers a framework for relating organizational efforts, organizational results, and societal effects. Analysis of current status is done first by individuals, then by units, sections, and so on, moving up the hierarchy to bureaus, departments, divisions, and finally the entire organization. Each group compares its analyses with the next higher group, achieving consensus at one level before moving to a more inclusive one. Next, the same individuals should list the "what should be's," working back from outcomes to products, processes, and inputs. This model has also been applied extensively to training needs in organizations. (See also Kaufman, Johnston, and Nickols, 1979, and Kaufman and others, 1981.)

Organizational Communication Audit. A special type of organizational needs assessment is the organizational communication audit, which employs a discrepancy analysis of key communication factors in the system, comparing the present state to the optimal state derived from the organization's statements of its objectives (Sincoff, Williams, and Rohm, 1980). The audit employs a variety of methodologies to assess vertical and horizontal communication patterns; topics, sources, and channels of communication; quality of communication relationships; bottlenecks or gatekeepers of information; communication roles; internal and external networks and linkages; and identification of underloads or overloads in the system. The audit may be carried out at any level or within any unit of an organization.

Analysis of communication structure often reveals a hitherto unrecognized organizational structure that bears little resemblance to the formal, hierarchical structure of an organization. The communication networks, linkages, and problems throw light on other needs of the organization that affect its ability to achieve its goals. Any needs assessment at the organizational level should include some appraisal of communication needs and identification of problem areas as well as strengths, whether or not a full scale audit is possible.

An audit model developed and field-tested in public and private organizations in the United States and several other countries by the International Communication Association uses five data-gathering tools: a questionnaire survey, confidential interviews, network analysis, critical incident analysis, and the communication diary. Among the outputs from the audit are an organizational profile of communication factors and relationships, a map of the operational communication network, and recommendations for continuation, modification, or elimination of the practices and skills studied (Goldhaber and Rogers, 1979).

Needs Assessment in Times of Retrenchment

Needs assessment in a time of shrinking budgets and retrenchment takes on a somewhat different character from assessment in times of expansion. At the present time, human services agencies are reappraising the role of organizational planning in the light of profound changes in the economy and the reduced role of the federal government in supporting local or regional programs. Cohen (1982) points out that, because retrenchment planning takes place in a context very different from the growth planning of the 1960s and 1970s, many human services agencies resist developing explicit retrenchment plans even when cutbacks are imminent.

Cohen notes five major environmental or contextual shifts taking place: (1) from a period of growth and expansion toward one of stability or decline; (2) from a means orientation to one of ends, determining what should be the role of government, the private sector, and the agency; (3) from an internal focus on a single agency to an external focus, the unit of analysis being multiple, often dissimilar agencies; (4) from low or moderate uncertainty to high uncertainty about the future, and (5) from a moderate- or long-range planning horizon to a short planning horizon. (These changes apply in varying degrees to educational systems as well.)

In order to move from retrenchment planning that is driven by events—such as a key person leaving the organization or a significant cutback in funds—Cohen proposes that the organization's leaders make an early decision as to what the *core program* is that the agency will cut back to. He recommends both collective planning, which addresses the future of the whole organization, and individual planning by staff members to consider their own futures and career needs. Techniques for collective planning have been developed and implemented by a research team at the Management and Behavioral Science Center at the University of Pennsylvania. The team has provided technical assistance to agencies engaged in retrenchment planning, including giving intensive planning and problem-solving sessions that last two or three days.

Hirschhorn (1982, p.1) observes that the present crisis of the social services must be seen in the context of a "long wave of social service reorganization which began in the Sixties and will continue into the Eighties. . . . Schools, public hospitals, libraries, museums, and settlement houses, the bulwark of the industrial social service system, faced competition for resources from a new wave of social agencies whose activities were rooted in women's needs and rights . . . new concepts of learning and education . . . and community economic development and job training." However, it is a crisis not only of decline but also of organization and renewal. A central cultural issue for education is now the question of *what schooling is:* "The rise of adult education on the one side, and the spread of computer technology and new electronic learning systems on the other, has raised critical issues about *how* young people learn, where they learn, and the *rate* and *pace* at which they learn" (p. 2, Hirschhorn's emphasis). Similarly, new relationships between services and society are posed by new agencies, such as those based on women's needs and community development processes.

There is little doubt that the forces Hirschhorn and Cohen cite must bring about a rethinking of the role of needs assessment in the organization. If meaningful priorities are to be established, there must be much more conscious awareness of the role of the organization, what its core functions are or are likely to be in the future, its relationships with other organizations, and how to use renewal and reorganization to accomplish its (redefined) goals. Superficial assessment procedures that are based on traditional assumptions as to what schools or human services agencies or businesses are all about will miss the mark.

10

Communicating Relevant Information Before, During, and After Needs Assessment

Communication strategies must be considered during four phases of a needs assessment: planning the assessment, gathering data, disseminating information on results of the assessment, and utilizing the results in action planning. The first three are discussed in detail in this chapter. Communication strategies for utilizing the results are considered here in connection with communicating of results; they are addressed further in Chapter Eleven.

It is helpful to think of those who assess needs, those whose needs are being assessed, and those who have the power to make decisions about programs to meet the needs as being linked in an information network. The potential for appropriate and timely information flow always exists. Whether the flow is successful depends to some extent on whether key people in the network have an awareness of salient factors of communication and information processing.

If information systems in society are conceived of as "networks of information flow linking nodes to one another" (Danowski, 1975), then the groups of individuals mentioned above could be considered as forming nodes in the network, and all are linked in important ways through information channels. The information can flow in any direction through the network. Factors the needs assessor must consider are selection of communication channels, types of information to seek, timing and amounts of flow of information, and the possibility of information underload or overload—that is, too little or too much information occurring at the wrong time or wrong place.

From a system perspective, communication linkages for needs assessments have inputs, processes, and outputs. Inputs define the types of messages to be received that will furnish opinions or data on what should be and what is—the raw materials from which needs can be inferred—and the internal and external sources from which the messages will come. Needs assessors in the system receive and process the messages (either through interactive or noninteractive channels) and organize the results into outputs consisting of messages to internal or external receivers. Table 3 summarizes potential communication components and linkages in a system context.

Each phase of the needs assessment can benefit from using the most effective means of communication. The needs assessment literature generally lacks guidelines on communication strategies in the four phases, nor has research been reported on the comparative effectiveness of different methods. The discussion in this chapter is based on both theory and practice in organizational and interpersonal communication and small group processes as well as on observation of the effectiveness of various strategies in actual needs assessments.

Communication Strategies in the Planning Phase

The purpose of communication in the planning phase is twofold: to provide the best possible planning and to communicate the plan to those who need the information. To meet the first objective requires a nice balance between planning by experts and participatory planning with others. For that reason, it is wise during the planning stage to include, in addition to service providers, representatives of service receivers and stakeholders, either as members of a formally constituted needs-assessment committee or in an advisory capacity. The principal means of communication is the informal, small group process. The focus group process

Table 3. Communication Linkages of Needs Assessment in a System Context.

Sources	Inputs → Messages	System Processes → Noninteractive	Interactive	Outputs → Messages	Receivers
Internal Sources: Board Management Staff Internal service receivers *External sources:* People: —external service receivers —stakeholders —legal bodies —other agencies —community Records: —existing needs studies —statistical reports	*Opinions:* Goal statements Judgments of goal importance Judgments of system responsibility to implement goals Perceived status of goal attainment Expectations of future states Values Concerns *Data:* Social indicators Data on student performance Demographic data	Written surveys Delphi studies Critical Incident Technique Rating scales Magnitude estimation scaling Individual card sorts Written futures scenarios	Public forums Concerns conferences Community "speak-ups" Nominal group process Small group discussions Individual and focus group interviews Games Group card sorts Group scenarios (futures games) Modified Delphi (interactive) Fault Tree Analysis Telecommunications, two way Committees	Goals ranked for importance Goals ranked for attainment (perceived or actual) Statements of discrepancies: —quantitative —qualitative Ranked client needs (primary) Ranked institutional needs (secondary) Analysis of causes Recommendations for action	*Internal receivers:* Policy: —board —management Operational: —service providers —internal service receivers *External receivers:* Service receivers Stakeholders Professional community External governing and legislative bodies

Source: Adapted from Witkin, 1977a.

described in Chapter Five is useful for tapping the group's present knowledge of needs and establishing a focus for the assessment—to explore what is already known and where to go from there. In general, it is best for the needs assessor to have alternative proposals for the committee to consider, using the small group processes for discussion of their merits and for bringing to bear a variety of points of view from the stakeholders.

Both internal and external communication factors should be considered in planning the needs assessment. Within the system, managers and policy makers must decide (at least in a preliminary fashion) on the purpose, focus, and scope of the assessment; resources to be allocated; time and personnel requirements; criteria for establishing priorities for action planning and solutions; and commitment of top and middle management to utilizing the results.

As to the second objective—communicating the plan to those who need to know—the locus of initiation of the needs assessment determines to a large extent the kinds and amounts of communication necessary within the system. If, for example, the effort was initiated at the board or chief-executive-officer level, the early communication should include large and small group meetings to announce the general purpose and to invite feedback before plans are firmed up. The size of the organization, management style, degree of communication normally taking place among departments or units, and the sense of ownership of system goals present in the organization all influence the extent and kind of horizontal and vertical communication in the planning phase.

If the impetus for the needs assessment comes from a planning department, communication strategies will likely be directed toward obtaining commitment and cooperation at all levels of the organization—toward persuading policy makers and implementers alike about the value of the effort. It is no good to have one unit plan and do the needs assessment and then to expect others who did not participate in the planning to use the results.

Participatory planning and interactive communication strategies are more important for a first-time needs assessment or formal update than for ongoing assessments that are part of an organization's management information system. In the latter instance, internal communication is important to inform policy makers and managers of the results of the assessment, especially if the data indicate the desirability of a major shift in priorities.

Communication Strategies for Gathering Data

A decision to be made when planning the needs assessment is what type of communication strategies will be the most effective for obtaining data from key informants or other respondents. Factors of time, costs, training of data gatherers, potential for misunderstanding, comparability of methodologies, and cultural bias are important considerations. In general, strategies for obtaining information or opinions from people can be categorized as interactive or noninteractive.

Noninteractive Methods. The most widely used method is the written questionnaire, either mailed or administered in person to large or small groups, such as students and faculty in a school. The Delphi and Critical Incident techniques are also typically administered in writing, although interactive adaptations have been developed.

Noninteractive methods are often less costly and more efficient in use of time than interactive methods. Advantages of written communication are (1) one can survey many people over a wide geographical area; (2) large amounts of data can be gathered in a relatively short time; (3) with structured instruments, there is less chance for sidetracking and irrelevant inputs; (4) the process is relatively easy to manage; (5) no special training of data gatherers, such as interviewers or group leaders, is required; and (6) survey data can generally be analyzed by computer. Disadvantages, aside from the technical issues of survey construction and data analysis, are (1) possibility of respondents misunderstanding items; (2) high rate of nonreturns on mailed surveys; (3) difficulty of using complex methods of assigning priorities, such as paired-weighting procedures or magnitude estimation scaling; and (4) failure to take into account cultural and/or linguistic differences in respondent groups that could affect the data and their interpretation.

Interactive Methods. Interactive methods are face-to-face and telephone interviews, nominal group processes, the modified Delphi, community speak-ups and forums, focus group interviews, concerns conferences, and games and simulations. Futures techniques, such as scenarios and cross-impact analysis, often use a combination of interactive and noninteractive approaches.

Interactive communication strategies are recommended for involving people in thinking actively and creatively about problems and needs. Advantages of interactive processes are (1) respondents can ask for clarification of questions, as in interviews; (2) clients and stakeholders who participate in interactive processes are more likely to feel that they have an important part to play in the needs assessment and that the sponsoring organization cares what they think; (3) some strategies enlist the expertise of participants to assist in gathering relevant facts and indicators, such as in the "Games People Oughta Play" process described in Chapter Five (Wickens, 1980); and (4) adjustments in methodology can be made to accord with communication styles of different ethnic and linguistic groups when such differences might affect the needs assessment.

Major disadvantages of interactive processes are: (1) time and costs of training interviewers or group leaders; (2) time taken to plan, schedule, and carry out the interviews or group processes; (3) possible difficulty of obtaining a representative sample of people to attend meetings; (4) possible distortion of data inputs and interpretation by group leaders who advocate their own ideas as to needs and priorities; and (5) reluctance of parents or community representatives to attend meetings because of work schedules, lack of transportation, inability to get childcare for small children, or shyness or dislike of personal involvement in groups. In comparison with noninteractive methods, two additional disadvantages are (6) greater difficulty in analyzing and interpreting the data and (7) the more limited numbers of respondents (participants in group processes are generally fewer than respondents to written surveys and are generally confined to a smaller geographic area).

Interactive group processes are highly recommended for exploratory phases of a needs assessment—to define problems, identify areas of concern that warrant further analysis, and solicit support for planning and implementation from key groups. The written survey can then be used to validate needs and causes with a representative sample of constituent groups.

Sociolinguistic and Cultural Factors. In a comprehensive study of the state of the art of needs assessment in educational systems, Witkin (1977a) found almost nothing in the models, kits or research studies that took account of issues of sociolinguistic and cultural fairness or bias. The principal considerations were

1. Availability of foreign language translations of needs assessment materials.
2. Use of the most appropriate methods of interaction and involvement for people of minority cultures.
3. Concern for adequate representation of all cultural and ethnic groups in the needs assessment process.
4. Appropriateness of the educational goals and the focus of the assessment to the multicultural world of the future.
5. Adequacy of existing performance tests and other measures of "what is" [p. 125].

Since that study, there has been some improvement in regard to items 1 and 5 in the above list. More written questionnaires are now available in languages other than English. Spanish is the most widely used language, but in a model widely used in California instruments have also been translated into Cantonese and Tagalog for students and their parents (Witkin, 1979a). The Educational Planning Model developed and disseminated by Phi Delta Kappa includes both Spanish and English versions of the Educational Goal Attainment Tests (E.G.A.T.), which assess the attainment of goals used in the planning model. The E.G.A.T. were developed under the auspices of the Puerto Rican Congress of New Jersey. In addition to providing a Spanish-language edition of the nine test booklets, a tenth booklet (on Latin America) tests three bicultural goals. Half of the test items in the tenth booklet are in English and survey general knowledge of Latin American cultures; the rest are in Spanish to test Spanish-language facility. The authors also recommend that Spanish-speaking students be given the English-language tests to assess their facility in English (Tuckman and Montare, 1975).

Although some schools and human services agencies are becoming more sensitive to the need for having adequate versions of written instruments in the language respondents know best, there is little indication that needs assessors are aware of the desirability of providing communication settings where clients or stakeholders who speak little or no English can participate effectively in group needs assessment processes. For that matter, it is rare that provisions are made for participants with physical handicaps—limited mobility, or severely impaired hearing or vision—to be accommodated in group meetings.

In regard to item 2, there is little research reported on the best methods of involving people of different cultures in needs assessment. The literature on intercultural communication, however, is rich with descriptions of the verbal and nonverbal factors, including situational, that must be taken into consideration when people of different cultural backgrounds need to work together. Factors such as spatial relationships and distances that are tolerated between speakers, preference for oral or written modes of expression, assertiveness or shyness in groups, relations to authority figures, eye contact or lack of it, gestures, status factors and roles, and willingness to challenge or defend points of view are some of the variables that should be considered when planning the needs assessment. Communication factors play an important role in choosing interactive or noninteractive methods. If group processes are chosen, the needs assessor should make sure that the communication methods to be used not only will encourage participation of all those present but also will not violate deeply held cultural norms that are different from those who do the planning.

The Center for Northern Educational Research at the University of Alaska conducted a study to develop a method to promote more open communication between two populations: the white teachers and administrators in the schools and the other non-Caucasian children who comprised the bulk of the student population.

It was the intent of the project to establish needs assessment as the first step in breaking the pattern of inter-ethnic non-communication which

was instilled in all Alaskan public educational systems. A method was developed which openly solicited
contact and communication between the educational
establishment, usually dominated by personnel and
value orientations of the white American majority,
and Native parents, whose voices are rarely heard by
the institution but who are the so-called recipients of
services of the total educational establishment. The
project's community participation approach to needs
assessment differed from the educational needs assessments previously exercised in that it attempted to
build working relationships between school people
and community people as needs were identified, rather
than simply gathering data and turning them over to
policy-makers or record keepers [Moore and Senungetuk, 1974, p. 1].

The center set up six regional workshops with a core staff of
three: a well-known Eskimo artist and writer, a Tlingit Indian
teacher with a master's degree in school administration from the
University of Alaska and teaching experience in the Peace Corps,
and a white teacher with a master's degree in elementary teaching.
The staff considered appropriate physical surroundings for the
meeting areas, how to group people, the degree to which the agenda
was structured, and the direction taken by speakers and consultants.
They used various methods of involvement with large and small
groups, shared meals, role playing, and watching films.

They also paid close attention to the verbal and nonverbal
communication factors mentioned earlier. For example, many
whites regarded the native people as nonverbal, because the latter,
in the presence of white people, would begin by keeping quiet, and
when they did speak, would speak quietly whereas the white people
began by talking and did most of the talking, even when they were
in the minority. Keeping quiet in a threatening situation is a
cultural response not limited to Alaskan natives, just as talking in
a threatening situation is a cultural response. The center staff
concluded that the fostering of communication channels was difficult, painful, arduous, and frustrating for staff members, consultants, and participants, but that it was necessary.

The United States is a nation of minorities. Yet our ethno-
centrism is such that the planners and evaluators in school systems,

service agencies, and government—whatever their own back-ground—rarely pay attention to cultural differences or preferences in communication.

Needs assessors can prevent occurrence of social bias or inappropriate communication strategies by seeking representation of minority groups on the needs assessment or planning committee. Those members can give valuable advice not only on language and the more obvious cultural barriers but also on the best methods of involvement to ensure active participation of clients and stake-holders both during the needs assessment and later in implementing the results. In communitywide surveys, care should be taken that the sampling technique ensures representation of all groups who have a stake in the needs assessment.

Communicating Results of the Needs Assessment

Communication factors are important not only in the con-duct of the needs assessment but also in dissemination of the results. It is essential that the appropriate information be conveyed to the proper people at the right time, in the right amounts, and in the most effective ways. In Chapter Eleven we discuss the communica-tions gap that exists between researchers and policy makers and is crucial to understanding and utilization of the results. In his study of the use of social science research in government, Rich (1981, p. 131) found that the second most important factor in the utilization of research knowledge is that the information must be written so that it is understandable: "The form in which information is passed through the decision-making channels is often of greater impor-tance than its content." This section discusses written and oral methods of communicating needs assessment findings both within the organization and to external constituencies.

The standard form for recording and communicating results of a needs assessment is the long, comprehensive written report that typically contains narrative and tabular material showing the results of surveys, tests, and other data-gathering procedures. It may also include copies of the instruments used, explanations of meth-ods of analysis, and priority rankings of needs. The reports some-times append copies of letters sent to parents or other groups surveyed as well as documents that substantiate the procedures used.

Distribution of the reports depends on the nature of the organization, who requested the needs assessment, and how the findings are intended to be used. Generally, copies go to policy-making bodies (school boards, boards of trustees) and top management (school superintendent, principals, agency directors). Occasionally, results are disseminated to the general public through newspaper articles or through school or agency newsletters. The written report may also be supplemented by oral presentations to policy boards. If a procedure was built in for utilization of the results, the needs assessor also provides reports to and discusses the results with the individuals or committees charged with taking action on high-priority needs.

The following summarizes the individuals and groups most likely to receive information about the assessment and the purposes for disseminating the information to them.

Funding agency—accountability

Policy makers or school board—policy-level decisions and practices

Top management—program decisions based on priorities

Middle management, staff—program decisions, action planning, utilization in management information system

Professional colleagues (in conferences, journal articles)—sharing technical information on methodology, critical appraisals, recommendations for others' use, unusual findings

Practitioners—sharing practical information on details of methodology, instruments, planning and managing the assessment, recommendations for adaptation to other settings

Needs assessment informants and stakeholders—feedback on results, priorities, and action that is planned to meet the needs; for maintaining good will and credibility

General public—general information about the process and the results; for good public relations

Adequate communication of needs assessment results may facilitate subsequent utilization in program planning; some writers have mentioned effective reporting style as an important factor in utilization in specific projects. Hints for communicating results of a needs assessment can be taken from studies of the use of research and evaluation findings, which indicate that their reception and use can be improved by using more effective methods of communication. As part of a programmatic effort to improve the practice of evaluation, for example, the Northwest Regional Educational Laboratory in Portland, Oregon, compiled descriptions of several alternative strategies for communicating alternative evaluation results (Smith, 1982a). Following are some that are useful for needs assessment.

Research Briefs. These are written, condensed statements that give only the most important information. They may be in the form of a *report summary* found at the end of the entire report; the *executive summary*, which appears at the beginning of the report—usually immediately after the title page; short *memos* to people who need to know the results; and *abstracts*. The research brief can also be adapted to make the information in the comprehensive report more easily accessible to the casual reader through the use of *embedded quotations*. These are abridgments or direct quotations of important findings that are set apart within the text of the report by means of capitalization and lines above and below the quotation, or other visual means. Embedded quotations can constitute a complete overview of the findings and thus be equivalent to a report summary (Macy, 1982).

Graphic Displays. Many needs assessment reports can be improved as communication devices through careful page formatting and the selective use of graphics throughout the text. Important information is signaled by different typefaces, boxes, use of white space, simple flowcharts, tables, graphs, illustrations, and photographs. Hathaway (1982) provides excellent illustrations of graphic methods for evaluation reports. The same displays can also be used for oral reports to groups, using slides, the overhead projector, or videotapes. Although graphic techniques require more time and often more money than simple typed reports, they generally pay off in greater use of the reports and in acceptability, particularly by lay audiences (any groups other than the researchers who performed the assessment). As word processors come into greater use in school districts and service agencies, also, the potential for good graphic displays increases, even if there is no in-house graphic artist.

Histograms, which are often provided with a data processing package to show the distribution of results for each item on surveys with nominal rating scales, can also be used in graphic displays in final reports. Although it would be too cumbersome to include all the histograms from a survey in a written report, a judicious selection of those conveying the most important information can do much to clarify the findings. For example, histograms displaying items that have a pronounced bimodal or skewed distribution provide an effective basis for discussion of the implications. The histogram is also useful for presenting data to a group in an oral briefing.

If graphics are to be presented to large groups by means of slides or transparencies on an overhead projector, it is crucial that letters and numbers be large enough for the audience to read easily. Although it should not be necessary to mention this point, researchers are notorious for presenting audiovisual reports in which information on tables and charts is entered in pica or elite type. Even with very great enlargement, such material can scarcely be read past the first couple of rows. If primary-sized type is not available, it is much better to provide hand-lettered visuals, keeping the amount of information on any one visual to five or six points.

Geographic Displays. When needs are found to be related in some systematic way to demographic characteristics, or when the area studied is large enough so that different needs are associated with different parts of the area, geographic displays are useful as a concise and eaily understood way of sharing information with different kinds of audiences. Smith (1979) notes many evaluation problems that are geographic in nature: distribution of academic achievement throughout a region, relationship between the incidence of crime and the distribution of law enforcement resources, relationship between the quality of health care and the distribution of medical clinics, and geographic conditions that influence questions of school busing. Analytic strategies available for the treatment of geographic data are geocode analysis, trend surface analysis, and social area analysis (1982b).

Geocode analysis aggregates individual data over a geographic area by using codes for street addresses or census tract numbers to denote geographic locations. "These procedures have been employed in studies of school redistricting, the identification of Title I students, projections of school enrollments, and comparative reading evaluations. They are particularly useful in settings that have preexisting data files and geographically defined service areas, such as state departments of education and community mental health centers" (p. 235). The analysis produces grids, plots, and contour maps of individual characteristics by geographic location.

Instead of plotting data on a grid, *trend surface analysis* produces contour maps by using statistical procedures to estimate data that appear at irregular intervals. It is less costly, but also less detailed than geocode analysis. The analysis involves selecting points (such as elementary schools) in a geographic region, assigning certain values to each point, producing a surface equation with statistical modeling procedures, and using the equation to construct a contour map. Further steps include regression analysis and analysis of variance to determine local and regional trends. Finally, multiple-surface maps can be overlaid to illustrate the geographic interactions between variables of interest.

Social area analysis focuses on groups as "organized wholes that can be characterized by their patterns of behaviors and attributes. [It] is not a discrete procedure, but a collection of techniques used to study characteristics of groups within defined geographic areas" (p. 236). Social area analysis for needs assessment in human services was discussed in Chapter Four. The analysis includes the collection of data on conditions of interest and studies the relationships between the data and indices of characteristics in the catchment areas (geographic regions) of interest in the needs assessment.

The three types of geographic analysis described above require highly technical procedures using computers, statistical programs, and mechanized plotting facilities. But *maps* are also useful to present descriptive information in a meaningful form. They can depict the areas participating in a needs assessment, patterns of location of existing educational or human services delivery programs of interest, comparisons of goal preferences or importance ratings among different areas in a school district or different districts in a state or region, or the need for new patterns of delivery of services to elderly citizens in a large urban or metropolitan area.

Still another use of maps, both for analysis and for communication to decision makers, is to determine needs for expanded or reduced services for community college or adult continuing education in an area where there has been considerable population mobility or demographic change and where existing courses and services are being underutilized. Smith provides an example of an analysis of a similar problem—the evaluation of the computer services delivery system of a large university. This was "a basic needs assessment service delivery question calling for a kind of market analysis" (p. 242). The use of a series of campus maps enabled him to answer the question in part and communicate the results to administration of the computer center and to station managers.

The needs assessor who wishes to use maps to communicate findings must select the right scales and grouping of data, being careful not to overload the detail or to present data in possibly misleading ways. Although maps provide information that cannot be as well portrayed through narratives, tables, or graphs, they must often be accompanied by oral or written commentary to qualify and clarify the visual display.

Oral Briefings. Oral presentations to policy makers are very useful in presenting highlights of the needs assessment results, clarifying questions about procedures or data, and stimulating commitment to action planning and utilization of the findings. Hendricks (1982) makes specific suggestions for creating a successful presentation, based on four years of experience with oral policy briefings for Service Delivery Assessment, an innovative form of program evaluation created in 1977 by the U.S. Department of Health and Human Services. Some of Hendricks's suggestions are also applicable to needs assessment briefings. The most pertinent are discussed in the following paragraphs, with specific references and adaptations to needs assessment added by this author.

Material for the briefing should be carefully chosen. Questions to be asked are: What information is necessary to understand the needs assessment? What are the implications for program planning? What can the audience do with the findings? What are the highlights? An outline should be made that provides a logical presentation but allows flexibility for answering questions. The person who presents the briefing should be the one most knowledgeable about the needs assessment and should also "possess sufficient dynamism to capture the audience's attention, an effective speaking voice, the interpersonal skills to relate to the audience, and the confidence and poise to handle the distractions that inevitably occur" (p. 252).

If the briefing is to be given to a very high-level policy group, Hendricks recommends practicing as much as possible before a wide variety of audiences first. The practice sessions also give the opportunity to refine the use of audiovisual aids, which might include the kinds of graphics discussed above. Hendricks also favors using a set of large, high-quality briefing charts that focus the attention of the audience and provide a summary of the findings. Letter-sized handouts of the charts can also be prepared for distribution to the audience so that they can follow the presentation easily and make marginal notes for their own use.

Hendricks cautions that it is important to set the stage properly for the briefing. This includes having a back-up staff person present to give additional information or clarification if necessary. He recommends that the audience be kept to a "small, select group of persons with the ability to act on the findings" (p. 253) and that there be a high-ranking liaison to bridge the gap between the presenter and the audience. (This would be particularly true if the audience were composed of top-level management or policy makers in a large organization with whom the needs assessor/presenter normally would have very little contact. There are crucial differences in perspective between the planning/researcher/ evaluator types who conduct needs assessments and the managers and policy makers who must use the findings.) Advance materials may be sent out to the audience; they may include a summary of the presentation as well as the full draft report (although the latter might better be given out after the oral briefing is concluded).

The formal briefing should take no more than one third of the time allotted for the entire meeting, leaving plenty of time for questions and discussion. The presentation should include a brief background of the needs assessment; how, when, and where it was conducted; a nontechnical description of the findings; and an interpretation, including implications for action planning. If the needs assessment established clear priorities, a nontechnical explanation should be given of how they were derived and the amount of confidence that can be placed in them. For example, if a number of priorities cluster closely together, policy makers should know that they can confidently choose among them for immediate action. On the other hand, if a need that the policy makers are interested in is far down the list, that fact should be made clear. If, for political or economic reasons, they choose to act on that need in preference to other, more critical needs, they should do so with the full knowledge of the place that it holds in the perspective of the entire needs assessment. Interpretations of the findings, as distinct from descriptions of the results, should be presented as informed judgments of the needs assessment director or committee, so that the presenter will not be viewed as biased. As to style, the presenter should be informative, understandable, realistic, and objective. Language should be simple and direct, avoiding technical jargon and long discussions of complex statistics.

Insofar as possible, the presenter should include suggestions for follow-up during the oral briefing. Although the presenter may not have the authority to do this, previous consultation with the liaison person can facilitate its inclusion. The briefing should lead naturally into consideration of steps that can be taken to utilize the findings; and at the very least, the meeting should conclude with people assigned to specific tasks and with a date set for a follow-up meeting to initiate specific program planning.

Television Presentations. When it is desirable to disseminate results of a needs assessment widely to the public, such as in a large school district or in a regional or statewide study, a television presentation can be effective. Shoemaker (1982) reports on a nationally televised four-part miniseries sponsored by the National Institute of Education that explored the pros and cons of minimum competency requirements. The series grew out of an evaluation study that was designed to provide information to state and local decision makers using a nontraditional evaluative technique. She notes that "the use of television in education has consistently lagged behind its use in business and industry" (p. 291) to inform or influence educational decision makers.

Television is useful for making information available to business people, parents, and other community stakeholders who are unlikely to see the needs assessment report or to attend briefings. A good presentation distills the important points, highlighting the findings and informing the public of steps that will be taken to act on the results to improve the educational enterprise. Closed-circuit television from a central facility to all the schools in a district is also an option when faculty and students are the audience for the report. It is particularly desirable to use mass media to disseminate results of needs assessments that surveyed hundreds of people. Timely feedback to them of the most important findings and of critical priorities enhances the credibility of the institution that did the needs assessment, especially if the presentation includes a report of plans for using the findings in a meaningful way.

There are several drawbacks to the use of television for communicating needs assessment results—the costs of production, the necessity of having participants who are both informed and effective speakers, and the time and energy that must be given to preparing for the telecast. In cities where there is a regular program on which a trained person interviews educators or human services providers, an interview format with a key policy maker or a small panel can usually be arranged with little cost and preparation. The television presentation is most effective when the information is presented in a simple, nontechnical manner. It is not suited to conveying statistical information or to complicated discussion of results, although well-designed and produced visuals can be used to clarify and enhance the presentation. A panel discussion of the significance of the findings or a phone-in question-and-answer session with a top administrator can be both lively and informative.

Shoemaker offers a scenario for a videotaped television program presenting the results of a naturalistic evaluation study, much of which is applicable to reporting a needs assessment. After an introduction, using charts or other graphics to explain the purpose of the study and the questions it addressed, she suggests:

> Show how important audiences for the evalua-
> tion were involved in the planning and implementa-
> tion of the study (panel meetings or advisory groups).

> Explain briefly the data collection techniques used
> (students taking tests, evaluators conducting inter-
> views) and analysis techniques (computer at work,
> evaluators discussing the findings . . .). List each of
> the major findings in chart form (one per frame)
> followed by an illustration of that finding. [For exam-
> ple, if one of the critical needs is for better reading,
> show a student reading aloud.] . . .
>
>   The television segment could end there or
> could continue with policy and program recommen-
> dations. . . . The videotape itself could lead to a
> discussion by viewers of implications for their school
> district. . . . [Policy recommendations] could be illus-
> trated through interviews with outside experts or
> school administrators [Shoemaker, 1982, p. 298].

Regardless of supplementary oral or written reports, it is
understood that there must be full, written documentation of the
needs assessment. The foregoing communication techniques are
indicative of methods that are useful for disseminating the results
to various constituencies. The value of any of them must be weighed
against the criteria of effectiveness and feasibility. The form must
also be compatible with practices currently in use by the intended
audience. School systems that do not use television will have neither
the capability for producing televised or videotaped programs nor
the inclination to watch reports on them. If managers or policy
makers are accustomed to receiving important information orally,
the oral policy briefing is more effective than written reports. On
the other hand, some decision makers prefer to read reports rather
than to hear them, and for them the executive summary and other
brief reports are essential. Whether the form is oral or written,
however, needs assessment reports are enhanced and clarified by the
selective use of well-designed and constructed graphics.

   Prior to the needs assessment, and regardless of the methods
or instruments chosen, the whole process should be examined in the
light of communication factors. Is the purpose clear? Are questions
unambiguous? Has the difference between wants and needs been
clarified? Are interviewers and group facilitators aware of their
communication roles and trained for them? Have the communication norms of culturally or linguistically different groups been
considered? What are the communication factors in the organiza-

tion (such as lateral and vertical channels, bottlenecks, and the like) that should be taken into account in planning and managing the needs assessment and in utilizing the results?

Communication strategies for disseminating results of the assessment are a vital link in moving the whole effort into the utilization phase. No amount of written reporting or formal oral presentation will ensure that the priority needs will result in concrete plans and programs and that the information will become a part of the organization's management information system. Chapter Eleven discusses communications gaps and other communication factors that either inhibit or facilitate the utilization of needs assessment by organizations.

11

Facilitating the Use
of Needs Assessment Results

A needs assessment is not complete until policy makers and managers translate the identified priorities into specific action, such as improved programs or delivery of services. There is little evidence of the extent to which needs assessments data actually affect program planning. Published reports of specific needs assessments rarely include information on how the data were used in the following year or two since the reports are usually intended for immediate presentation to policy makers. Kimmel (1977), whose critique focused mainly on programs supported by federal funds for health and human services, found little evidence of utilization and scanty documentation of the use of the thousands of needs assessments that had been conducted up to that time. The situation is analogous to that in program evaluation. In a review of the literature, Thompson (1981) found a failure of evaluation to affect decision making significantly and a widespread frustration with the use of research reports by school administrators for "door stops" and "swatting flies." He observes that nonuse is costly—an enormous waste of money, effort, and failure to provide clients of programs with optimally effective services.

Although information on incidence is lacking, a few studies, to be discussed later, have identified patterns of utilization and factors that facilitate or inhibit use. In addition, for understanding organizational factors that affect utilization, we can draw some inferences from research on evaluation, change agentry, organizational structure and communication, and studies of the dissemination and utilization of research knowledge.

What Is Utilization?

The extent to which needs assessment data are perceived to be utilized depends somewhat on the interpretation of *utilization*. The evidence is often scanty for a direct link between the needs assessment and specific decisions. Perhaps utilization should be defined by decision makers in ways that are useful to them. Writers who have investigated the concept of research utilization found that local, state, and federal administrators "described utilization as occurring when a study influenced their thinking about a particular issue; assisted them in defining problems, setting goals, and choosing among alternatives; and caused them to reconsider and question existing policy" (Robins, 1982, p. 202). Using a broad definition of utilization based on an administrator's perception of usefulness, Robins found that, while only about one third of the studies were judged to be very useful for decision making, over half were characterized as very useful in the overall operation of the agency.

Another way of viewing utilization is to consider the specific purposes to which the data are put. For example, information from community mental health needs assessments can be used not only for program planning but also for program justification, formative evaluation (including appraisal of accessibility of services) and identifying high-risk groups for prevention programs. Goza, Strube, and Fennimore (1982) discuss specifically how data from community needs assessments can be used for each of these purposes and recommend disseminating the results early and in many ways to "milk the data for all it's worth" (p. 20).

As a framework for thinking about utilization, one can ask the following questions about levels of utilization of needs assessment results, going from the most general to the most specific levels as well as from immediate to later postassessment periods:

Were the findings adopted as policy? If so, with or without modifications?
Did the findings lead to *general* recommendations for change, renewal, program improvement, or service delivery?
Did the findings lead to *specific* recommendations for

change, renewal, program improvement, or service delivery?

Was a mechanism or procedure established for *incorporating* general or specific recommendations in policy statements or program plans? Were program objectives and activities delineated? To what extent did the objectives and program activities relate to the needs established by the assessment?

Were the recommendations *implemented?* If so, with or without modifications?

Was the implementation *evaluated* as to whether the plans were carried out as specified?

To what extent were the needs *met* or ameliorated by the program as implemented?

Leviton and Hughes (1981) identified three broad categories of utilization of evaluation research (of which needs assessment is often considered a subcategory): *instrumental,* making decisions or solving problems; *conceptual,* influencing a policy maker's thinking about a particular issue; and *persuasive,* defending or supporting a position or policy. Rich (1981, pp. 14–15), however, found that "the principal purpose served by knowledge utilization is not to provide objective fact gathering and analysis of high-quality, relevant information bearing on a substantive policy issue, but to reinforce the using agency's information policy and to maintain and strengthen the bureaucratic interests for control associated with the acquisition and processing of information in accord with that policy."

Knowledge Utilization Studies

The use of needs assessment results by an organization is a specialized case of knowledge utilization, as is the transference of research findings to policy and practice. Clues to factors that facilitate or inhibit utilization can be inferred from studies of dissemination and utilization of knowledge. Since information in the form of an individual's expertise is the foundation of a power base for any given bureaucracy, only policy makers who are technically trained tend to make use of available research. Rich analyzed the uses government agencies made of social science research information generated through the Continuous National Survey (CNS). In the eighteen-month experiment, the National Opinion Research Center at the University of Chicago provided policy-relevant survey data to federal domestic service agencies interested in receiving them. Data were collected thirteen times a year and reported every three or four weeks to agencies such as departments of Agriculture, Labor, the Interior, Housing and Urban Development, Transportation, and Health, Education, and Welfare.

The research design analyzed the behaviors and attitudes of four major groups that interacted in the knowledge-inquiry system: sponsors, researchers, decision makers, and the Office of Management and Budget, which must approve all requests for information by federal agencies. The analysis also investigated the roles played by the four groups at four developmental stages: funding, research, analysis and reporting, and summative evaluation. Finally, it related policy decisions to the agencies' use of the CNS data, social science information as a whole, and information in general.

Rich found two waves of information utilization, with very different profiles, that could be equated to some extent with short- and long-term utilization. The first wave, occurring approximately in the three-month period after information is received, was *instrumental,* characterized by a flow of information upward through the decision-making hierarchy. The use was documented through memos, discussions at cabinet meetings, or at congressional briefings and in drafting legislation. In eleven out of twenty-six policy areas, however, no use was made of the information—it "simply sat on the desk of the staff member who initially received it" (p. 117).

That same information, however, might be used in the second wave, which generally occurred from three to six months after initial reception and sometimes later. In the second wave, the flow was primarily lateral or downward in the hierarchy, and the information was used *conceptually* rather than instrumentally. It often profoundly influenced policy makers' thinking about an issue as well as their methodological planning. "By far, the most prevalent form of utilization was a memo to subordinates in the decision-making hierarchy concerning general notions and ideas that had been teased out of the CNS results. . . . [There were] a significant number of cases in which the respondents' thinking was affected by the results of the survey . . . [and] a significant number of journal articles and papers were written on the basis of the CNS results. . . . Finally, [in thirty-four policy areas] the respondents had concrete plans for utilizing the CNS results in the future" (p. 119).

One must be cautious about generalizing Rich's study to the utilization of needs assessment information. Yet his findings about the conceptual impact of the information, rather than its strictly instrumental use, are confirmed by Robins's (1982) findings, mentioned earlier, on the use of needs assessment information in human services agencies. In the Rich study (1981, pp. 130–131), the six most important factors affecting use of social science research information are also applicable to needs assessment:

1. The information supports the policy position that the decision maker is predisposed toward.
2. The information comes directly to the decision maker from a trusted staff aide.
3. The information is on a timely topic that is of interest and need.
4. The objectivity of the producer is unquestionable.
5. The information is written up in a manner that is understandable.
6. The information does not challenge the budget or staff allocations of the agency.

Regarding the last point, a needs assessment probably *should* challenge budget and staff allocations, although in practice, such challenges are often disregarded in order to preserve existing organizational priorities and programs. Respondents in Rich's study felt that the most important factor for understanding utilization was that the information comes directly to the decision maker through a trusted staff aide (since objectivity and timeliness of the information were assumed). This finding, and the one regarding conceptual and instrumental use, "provide evidence for the argument that information is used or not used depending on whether its use would violate organizational interests within the limited context of purely administrative factors" since "policy makers consciously try to minimize risk in relation to their own position and the position of their organization. They cannot afford to be embarrassed by the results of a study or other information that has been submitted to a superior. . . . This notion of risk also implies that trade-offs are consciously made in policy decisions" (130–131).

To what extent do such observations apply to the typical needs assessment within an organization? There is little evidence on this point. Nevertheless, some generalizations can be drawn from reports of needs assessment as well as from personal observation and discussion with many researchers and policy makers.

To the extent that needs assessment data are general, such as results from the typical one-shot educational assessment that relies heavily on surveys of goal preferences and perceptions of student achievement, the findings usually pose little risk to administration and policy boards. On the one hand, if the questions are at a high level of abstraction and the rankings of priority needs are close, a board can safely act in accordance with its own preconceptions, if indeed it takes any action on the data. On the other hand, policy boards often make decisions directly contrary to the findings of a needs assessment when political or economic considerations seem more important than objective data or community perceptions of needs. The point can be illustrated by noting what happened in three communities.

1. A medium-size city conducted a survey of recreational needs, polling residents through the local newspaper. Disregarding the results, which highlighted a need for neighborhood recreation centers, the city council decided to build a community swimming pool, to which respondents had given a low priority.

2. A large city undertook a multilevel, comprehensive needs assessment, engaging the total community through surveys, interviews, group meetings, and television, as well as gathering extensive social indicator data. After a three-year period of data-gathering, the city council failed to act on any of the recommendations. Rather, it continued to allocate resources on the same political and economic bases as before the needs assessment.

3. In a survey for a high school in an upper-class suburb, parents
    rated the after-school competitive athletics program as having
    the lowest need, in terms of importance and achievement, of all
    the areas studied. Yet that finding did not lead to a reallocation
    of resources in line with new priorities of need.

The Two-Worlds Model

   To explain problems of utilization of research in organizations, Rothman (1980) offers a model of two worlds—the world of
research and the world of administrative practice—that have "essential differences in language, values, methods and points of view" (p.
12). Researchers tend to be more concerned with quality of information while policy makers are more interested in organizational
factors. Rothman's premise is that the manager and the researcher
must pay attention to the process of research utilization and must
build linkages with each other. Noggle (1982) also finds these two
worlds in regard to formative and summative evaluation. The
evaluator is typically concerned with methodology—the adequacy
of instruments, sampling, analytic strategies, and the like. None of
these decisions "have anything whatsoever to do with the planning,
implementation, and outcomes of educational programs, materials,
or strategies. These decisions may not affect education at all" (p. 1).
Educational decision makers tend to be concerned with the sound
of the evidence—if it sounds reasonable, they will use it to their
advantage and interpret the data in the direction of their beliefs.
   A similar point is made by Rich (1981) as a factor in
utilization of social science information. "Policy makers and research personnel (both in and out of government) tend to have
distinct vocabularies and languages, which hinders the coordination of their work" (p. 7). "The identification of specific information needs is dependent upon articulated goals, projections for
future information needs, and projections identifying future problem areas" (p. 9). But policy makers have great difficulty in
communicating the information they want, and "the reports that
they do receive are abstract, full of jargon, and seemingly irrelevant
to the operational needs of managers" (p. 10). They prefer known
and familiar methodologies as well, especially the survey.

The communications gap between researchers and policy makers has been studied as a prime factor in utilizing knowledge (Rothman, 1980; Rich, 1981). Gaps are found between expected and actual uses of information, which becomes greatly attenuated as it passes up the line from the researcher's full report to the policy makers. Complexity of findings and nuances of methodology (which often affect the findings) must be greatly simplified for users of the information, and the information is often not seen as useful to short-term needs. Rich, however, found that "the fact that a piece of information is not utilized for the purpose expected does not substantiate the argument that a communications gap is the most important factor in an understanding of utilization" (p. 134) and that organizational and administrative factors must also be taken into consideration. The findings of Rich and of Rothman should give pause to those who ignore organizational and communication factors when planning a needs assessment. In the CNS experiment, Rich found that utilization did not follow, even when all the conditions deemed necessary were met. "Instead, levels of utilization seem to be controlled by a preoccupation of public officials with issues of ownership and control of information" (p. 159). The factors of timeliness, cost, and relevance "are necessary but not sufficient conditions" (p. 159). He found the "sufficient conditions" to be the factors of bureaucratic organization, which influenced selectivity more than any other factors. Utilization is much more likely to be influenced by budget allocations and staff resources than by data bearing on the formulation of policy. Rich, however, could not document instances in which research was deliberately misused to serve purely political ends.

General Factors in Utilization

A key factor in utilization is the degree of commitment to the needs assessment by top agency officials. Robins (1982) found, however, that commitment alone is not sufficient to ensure utilization. Both access to funding and autonomy of the agency to modify programs influenced the degree to which the needs assessment was used in making decisions, although these factors were not as important in influencing other agency activities. She did not find that utilization of needs studies was related to the soundness of the assessment methods. In-house assessments were perceived as more useful than those done by outsiders, and the assessments that produced surprising findings had higher rates of utilization than those that did not. Further, "an assessment was more likely to be utilized if it was tied in some way . . . to the broader planning process, if it included specific procedures for addressing the study's major findings, and if it was part of an ongoing assessment process carried out by the agency," with the tie to planning being the most important (p. 205). She emphasized that the organizational factors that facilitate utilization warrant attention and that "designing assessments which include an outline of procedures for *addressing* unmet needs and which have clear and direct ties to the development of plan objectives may pave the way for greater utilization" (p. 207, my emphasis).

Basing their work on a small group of intensive case studies, Alkin and Daillak (1979; also Alkin, Daillak, and White, 1979) found that the degree of utilization of data from program evaluations was associated to a large extent with certain characteristics of the evaluation situation. They derived an analytic framework to explain the most important factors: (1) preexisting evaluation bounds, (2) orientation of the users, (3) evaluator's approach, (4) evaluator credibility, (5) organizational factors, (6) extraorganizational factors, (7) information content and reporting, and (8) administrator style. The categories were found to overlap—for example, the evaluator and the user can work together to tailor information-reporting formats and methods to the needs and preferences of the user.

Alkin (1982) reports that, at the stage of problem recognition, evaluation data in education play a prominent role in identifying a situation that requires attention and that their use is greatest when both administrators and teachers are involved in decision making. He also found evaluation data more useful for instructional and curricular decisions than for administrative and personnel decisions.

The Joint Committee on Standards for Educational Evaluation (1981, p. 47) set a standard for evaluation impact that is applicable to needs assessment: "Evaluations should be planned and conducted in ways that encourage follow-through by members of the audience." Evaluators should help their audiences take "such beneficial actions as improving programs, projects, or materials; selecting more cost-beneficial products or approaches; or stopping wasteful, unproductive efforts." Evaluators should play an important role—that of a change agent—in stimulating and guiding such improvements. The Joint Committee's guidelines for achieving this standard include demonstrating to key audiences at the beginning of the evaluation how the findings might be useful to them, involving representatives of the evaluation audience in planning and implementing the evaluation procedures, reporting interim results, using both written and oral communication, and assisting the audience to interpret and apply the findings after the submission of the final report.

The impact of needs assessment on educational policy is difficult to ascertain, partly because "public policy decisions are made incrementally and . . . no single set of findings can hope to influence major decisions by itself" (Hendricks, 1981, p. 17). Educational policy is usually stated in such broad terms that specific findings of a needs assessment might not have any effect on the goals and objectives of the organization or of a given program. School districts that employ goal preferencing surveys as the core of the needs assessment often leave the impression that changes might be made in the focus of allocation of resources to goals on the basis of input from parents, educators, and the community. In actual fact, this is rarely the case. A school system committed to particular programs for target student groups rarely drops the programs simply because constituent groups consider them of lower importance than other programs. Also, state regulations normally require certain subject matter to be taught regardless of whether a local needs assessment indicates that some of the subjects are considered of low importance.

The limitations of the usual goal importance/goal attainment discrepancy surveys were discussed in previous chapters. Given the fact that most priority-setting methods for such surveys are methodologically weak, priorities cannot generally be interpreted in such a way as to have an effect on policy. On the other hand, a needs assessment that is undertaken in the context of a comprehensive systems approach or one that uses Hirschhorn's (1982) program planning model described earlier might affect policy as well as program decisions.

Factors Inhibiting Utilization

In preparation for this book, I conducted a telephone survey of selected needs assessment projects that had taken place during the past decade in different parts of the country, to find out what had happened in the organization or the community as a result of those studies. The projects represented a wide range of contexts and methodologies. Although there were impressive instances of successful utilization, many organizations made little or no practical use of the data, methods, or products after the project period was over. Typical reasons were

- The project lacked strong administrative support, often because of arrival of a new principal or superintendent who was not familiar with the assessment and who had other priorities.
- The project director left and no one remained to sustain the effort.
- During the life of the project, no one had developed clear plans for utilization.
- The needs assessment was never seen as an integral part of the overall administrative decision-making function.
- In an interagency project that had specifically provided for utilization, the plans broke down because high-level elective officials and executive officers were recalled or fired.
- The assessment was done mainly for public relations; actual priorities were set by political criteria.
- Sometimes school-district-wide assessments with good plans for implementation were thwarted at the school-site level because of poor leadership by the principal or poor communication between the principal and teachers. Some principals felt threatened by the needs assessment process itself—having to share decision-making power with teachers, parents, and students in planning committees. And teachers who resisted implementing the findings felt they had had little real input to the study and were cut off from power or influence in the school.

- When the study was done by an external consultant, or when a project director and staff were hired for the purpose and were not a permanent part of the agency or the school system, the reports often vanished into the system when the staff departed. Two or three years later it was difficult to find administrators or staff who remembered the needs assessment.

- So much effort was put into the needs assessment over a long period that little energy or motivation remained to implement the recommendations. In one long and costly project, the final report was drafted but never completed or published. People were tired of meetings and discussions. Managers remarked that if they had to do it over again, they would confine the assessment to one or two manageable areas rather than trying to assess the full range of human needs in the community.

- Changes of administration and phasing out of project funding left projects with no money for implementation. This factor was often found when the needs assessment had been backed by an outside grant rather than funded by the organization's own resources.

- The most crucial variable, and the one that occurred most often, was the continuity of administrators and researchers in the system who provided support for the original study and who continued to use the data in planning and implementing programs. Without this continuity there was no organizational memory, no mechanism for institutionalizing the findings in ways that affected priorities and allocation of resources for the benefit of service receivers. In fact, considerable detective work was often required to track down the outcomes of needs assessment studies after the project director and key administrators had left. (The solution was to locate an administrative secretary with long tenure and an infallible memory. Needs assessors might consider building this factor into the design for utilization!)

This informal study corroborated factors frequently mentioned by other observers; these included staff turnover, political factors, and costs of implementation. Baumheier and Heller (1974), who obtained data on factors in utilization from more than a hundred sites that used needs assessment for human services planning, found that major barriers to utilization were financial rather than methodological—that lack of funds reduced the quality of the studies and limited the dissemination. Additional variables found by others were computer-related delays, weaknesses of the needs assessment design, or failure of the study to produce data that covered an adequate time period or were of sufficient quantity for making decisions.

Reviewing the literature on needs assessment, Rossing (1982) identified five factors to explain the limited use of needs assessment data in decision making: the diffuse, interrelated, and dynamic nature of the needs addressed; the lack of effective solutions to meet the needs; the political nature of the decision-making process, which favors marginal changes in the existing pattern of resource allocation; the nature of participation and involvement of those who identify needs and set priorities; and failure to take into account elements, such as costs and staff, that affect the translation of needs into programs.

Organizational barriers to adequate needs assessment and to utilization of the results in effective planning often arise from the fact that accountability is fragmented within the organizational structure (Kaufman, Johnston, and Nickols, 1979). In the typical systemwide needs assessment in school districts and universities, for example, consensus is reached among various constituencies as to the importance of broad goals and of needs related to them. But specific planning (usually not based on a systematic needs assessment) is done at the departmental level, with little attempt to relate individual departmental goals, needs, and problems to the whole curriculum or to student needs as a whole. It is not unusual to find that a large percentage of students in a high school do not have the requisite reading skills to cope with the demands of courses such as science and social studies; yet no department has the responsibility for diagnosing their needs and planning appropriate interventions.

Another organizational barrier is related to the two-worlds concept discussed earlier—it is the gap between research and applier "comprised of intellectual, social, emotional, and (usually) physical distance, with numerous barriers to knowledge transfer and few facilitating linkages" (Rothman, 1980, p. 20). Linkage can be analyzed on the basis of the source of initiation of communication—the researcher, the user, or a third party. But communication alone cannot be relied on to achieve utilization.

Anxiety and stress are factors that inhibit utilization of needs assessment data in classrooms, as is often the case when teachers are required to integrate test results with their instructional planning. Administrators use a wide variety of strategies to stimulate teachers to use test and evaluation information. A by-product is the "high correlation between administrators' emphasis on improving test scores and teachers' felt anxiety" (Kennedy, 1982). Teachers respond to such stress in ways that vary from trying to develop meaningful plans to complying on paper and waiting for the system to go away to trying to undermine the whole testing system. The need for incentives to change teacher behavior (toward using evaluation and needs assessment data) must be balanced against the danger of engendering a level of anxiety that interferes with productive work. Data-based instructional improvement systems are easy to circumvent. "It is relatively common to define and implement a solution to educational problems, and then turn the other cheek to evidence of its malfunctioning. If the solution itself is broken, it should be fixed, and it certainly can't be fixed with rhetoric about how it *should* work" (p. 9, Kennedy's emphasis).

Factors That Facilitate Utilization

There is less information on factors that facilitate utilization of needs assessment results than on barriers to utilization. Based on his review of needs assessments, Rossing (1982) makes the following recommendations:

- Be aware of real-world decision-making processes and the political aspects of program development.
- Be clear about the purposes of the assessment—whether educational, programmatic, or for accountability.
- Be more critical of needs assessment methods and processes.
- Include information needed for decision making, such as analysis of interrelationships and causes.

- Reinforce the connection between needs assessment and program evaluation.
- Involve key clientele and other participants in the needs assessment.
- Identify the requirements for a systematic needs assessment and be more judicious about doing assessments which consume significant resources.

Baumheier and Heller (1974) suggest that findings are more likely to be used when the study is user-based, when it is conducted by an independent research team involved in technical assistance or capacity building with the users, when the data will be used to expand rather than limit existing resources, and when the data are congruent with values held by decision makers. The recommendation about using an independent team should be accepted with caution, however. Unless the external group really does have a continuing relationship with the sponsoring organization, including effective communication links with key levels of the organization structure, there may not be the sense of ownership on the part of management and staff necessary to ensure commitment to utilization.

In his review of federally funded needs assessments, Kimmel (1977) found that "focused problem statements are better points of departure for action than general and lengthy statements of undifferentiated need" (pp. 29–30) and that "results which fit the political predispositions of policy makers are more likely to be used than those that do not" (p. 33).

A factor frequently mentioned as a barrier to implementing recommendations is the cost of the solutions, particularly for nonprofit organizations with tight budgets. Sugarman (1982) describes how top administrators have successfully used a networking method to find people who could act as "facilitators" for particular needs. Their assistance included finding equipment, providing expertise, using contacts to open doors where support was needed, and other forms of support such as corporate gifts of cash.

Needs assessors usually assume that they have a responsibility to disseminate the findings appropriately and to interpret them to policy makers, but they rarely see their role as one of persuasion to accept and act on the data. In order to cope with the widespread nonuse of evaluation findings, Thompson (1981) suggests that evaluators should be more willing to consider evaluation as a persuasive process instead of clinging to an image of objectivity at any cost. Drawing on the principles of classical rhetoric, he argues that evaluators should pay more attention to factors of rhetorical proof—logic, credibility, and the ability to dispose an audience favorably toward a message (reason, ethos, and pathos). Other important dimensions are the levels of self-esteem of the evaluator and clients, awareness of values and beliefs of clients, tapping group norms, and awareness of elements of group dynamics that militate against the use of data. Although needs assessment results do not necessarily carry the same affective load as evaluation findings, needs assessors would find it helpful to use the principles of effective communication to persuade decision makers—not to accept certain points of view but to follow up the needs assessment by developing and adopting specific plans of action.

The following examples of successful use of needs assessment results offer clues as to factors that facilitate utilization.

Needs assessments are more likely to be used when they are built into a regular program-planning cycle. The Lansing, Michigan, school district has been conducting needs assessments annually for the last decade, involving parents, teachers, administrators, and when appropriate, students, in a systematic, cyclical planning and budgeting process; administrators and staff are familiar with the process and expect that the results will be used. Curriculum and advisory committees examine data of various kinds, including test data supplied by the research and evaluation department, and establish priorities at each school site. Data from individual buildings are aggregated to establish broader priorities for all elementary schools, all secondary schools, and finally the whole district, although the last level may include using data not considered at the building level. When goals are changed, added, or eliminated, the decisions are not random; they are a matter of conscious choice (Lansing School District, 1977, 1979, 1983). The leadership of the superintendent, who has a strong background and interest in planning, is no doubt a critical factor in the utilization.

In the Lake Washington (Washington) school district, at the beginning of each school year, building principals receive a packet of planning materials to help them identify training needs. The packet contains demographic information on students and staff, cost factors, data on absenteeism of students and staff and on accidents and vandalism, and percentage of instructional time spent on reading and math at primary and intermediate levels. Data collected from the building profiles are summarized in categories according to school factors, school climate, and achievement factors. The needs identified in the building assessments lead to the development of plans to meet those needs. Trends such as an increase in vandalism are watched. The Lake Washington approach tries to develop better decision making by prescribing elements of the process and using common definitions and common components (Lehman, 1981).

The Seattle school district has been involved in a long-range school improvement project that began with a comprehensive district needs assessment and proceeded through several stages to school-based planning. The project was initiated by a new superintendent (with strong support from the board) and was funded in part by a Ford Foundation grant. After districtwide priorities were established, the planning office developed guidelines so that each school could do its own in-depth needs assessment and follow through with specific action plans. The community needs assessment was conducted in 1981, with the years 1982 to 1984 designated for implementation of the strategies and evaluation. Ninety-seven school communities, including eleven special programs, developed action plans, which at this writing are in various stages of implementation (Morgan, 1982).

The probability of utilization in Seattle was strengthened through the use of teacher-parent-student-citizen planning committees at each site (1,839 individuals participated) and the detailed planning manuals and illustrative materials the district supplied to the schools (Burton, Toews, and Birnbaum, 1982). For each concern area that was potentially a need at the school site, the manuals give specific instructions as to what to read or whom to call for more information. Interest during the communitywide assessment phase was kept high through frequent news releases and interviews with the superintendent on local television stations. The key factor in utilization was undoubtedly the superintendent's commitment and the school-based, broadly participative implementation design that was built into the project from the very beginning. The project also illustrates the importance of having a key administrator who can bridge the two worlds of research and practice. The superintendent had previously headed the Toledo, Ohio, school system, where he initiated the comprehensive needs assessment and research project that resulted in the Toledo Catalog described in Chapter Four (Nowakowski, 1983). As this is written, however, the superintendent has resigned to join a private institute, and further implementation will depend on the inclination of the new superintendent.

The Pittsburgh school district, working closely with the Learning Research and Development Center of the University of Pittsburgh, successfully followed through on a needs assessment that used surveys and an analysis of an existing five-year data base (Bickel and Cooley, 1981, 1982). Results were disseminated over a two-month period by means of brief written reports and interactive slide show sessions with the board, teachers, and building administrators. The four different written reports varied the content, amount of detail, and format according to the audience and the uses they would make of the information. A memo to the superintendent summarized specific suggestions from the surveys. Utilization activities included news releases from the administration, a board resolution that adopted two priorities and six specific needs, establishment of task forces that prepared detailed action plans, and adoption of the plans by the board. This series of events illustrates the *instrumental* use of evaluation information (Leviton and Hughes, 1981). A further result was the beginning of intensified focus upon reading instruction in the primary grades as a means of preventing serious reading problems that were showing up in the fourth grade. Bickel and Cooley offer this as an example of Leviton and Hughes's *conceptual* utilization, since the needs assessment data helped refocus district managers' attention on the primary grades.

Bickel and Cooley note that no single variable ensures utilization. They identified the following factors that increased the probability of utilization of the Pittsburgh data: right timing for district initiatives, clear identification of a single client (the super-intendent), a design that encouraged utilization at various levels in the district, the strong motivation and research background of the superintendent, avoidance of political land mines, the combination of survey and existing data-analysis strategies, the advantage of having substantive knowledge about the educational structure and politics of the district, adequate pilot testing of survey instruments, credibility of the data, and the interactive reporting style. They suggest that sophisticated analytical techniques are probably less important in influencing utilization than substantive knowledge of the realities of the district.

The Atlanta Assessment Project illustrates how a well-designed and adequately supported needs assessment study can produce products and resources that encourage utilization of the findings. The seven-year project was funded by an innovation (ESEA Title IV-C) grant through the Georgia State Department of Education, and major components were tested statewide (Sweigert, 1973; Atlanta Public Schools, 1980). The project used a series of Delphi studies to validate state educational goals for the future, then developed objectives, test instruments, and procedures related to the goals (see Chapter Six). The instruments were field-tested with more than 10,000 twelfth-grade students in sixty-one school systems throughout Georgia, under auspices of the statewide testing pro-gram of the department of education.

Subsequently, the test instruments were adopted for state-wide use in selected goal areas, and many items were incorporated in data banks. In addition, the project provided ten other school systems in Georgia with assessment materials and technical support for conducting their own assessment studies. To a considerable degree, the project was the forerunner of the Competency-Based Education program later adopted by the state board, which sets requirements for high school graduation. No doubt the commit-ment of state resources, the high visibility of the project, and the continuance of the project director as a staff member in the Atlanta school district after the project was phased out were factors encou-raging utilization of the results, although they were not as com-pletely implemented as planned.

Community-based efforts that use participants in the needs assessment as members of planning teams also provide a design for building utilization into the needs assessment process. This method has been successfully demonstrated in projects to develop community responses to alcoholism (Jackson, 1981b) and violent crime (Jackson, 1981a). The group decision processes used in these projects also encourage key informants and stakeholders to follow up with programs to meet the needs that they have identified and given priorities.

Sometimes needs assessment results are successfully used on a partial basis when circumstances preclude full implementation. Teaching staff in several departments at Saratoga (California) High School actively participated in developing and testing a model for cyclical needs assessment (Kenworthy and others, 1980; and see Chapter Two). The developmental stage, funded by an ESEA Title IV-C grant, took two years, after which no money or staff were available for further steps required for the implementation. However, with encouragement and support of the vice-principal, who had initiated and directed the project, the foreign language teachers continued to work and implemented as much as possible of the original design. They had previously established standards (what should be) related to critical issues of student performance, and they used the data from the needs assessment to identify current status, or what is. The school had installed several minicomputers and a computerized test-scoring program that were helpful in implementing the needs assessment. At this writing, the department has a test bank for its data and continues to update the needs assessment on a cyclical basis. An important factor in the implementation is the interest and leadership shown by the department chairperson, who was enthusiastic about the needs assessment from the beginning.

The foregoing discussion of patterns of utilization and of factors that facilitate or inhibit use of needs assessment findings points to one conclusion. Utilization is a management responsibility. If the study is to be worthwhile and the data useful, the assessment must be carried out as an integral part of a systematic process of cyclical program planning, implementation, and evaluation. Utilization of results cannot be considered apart from the structure and management of the organization conducting the assessment.

12

Interagency Cooperation in Needs Assessment: A Case History

In a time of shrinking resources and retrenchment in education and public services, there is growing interest in interagency planning. Taxpayer revolts, such as the property tax limitation of California's Proposition 13 and similar efforts in other states, are viewed by many as an indication that managers of human services must undertake realistic assessments of needs and resources and overcome barriers caused by guarding their own turf (Agranoff and Pattakos, 1979).

Interagency planning can take many forms. At the simplest level, agencies supply data for sharing resources through a regional resource directory (Witkin, 1979b, 1979c; Curtis, 1981; Terrill, 1982). A needs assessment for Santa Clara County, California, was carried out through the cooperation of city and county governments, special districts, public and private resource allocators, service organizations and agencies, and citizens in the community (Rutland, 1977). In Woonsocket, Rhode Island, the city government contracted with a nonprofit agency to plan and deliver social services that received government funds (Bolen, 1977). Many regional planning agencies also assess needs and programs in metropolitan or multicounty areas.

The concept of interagency cooperation among organizations with similar purposes and constituencies is not new. But joint needs assessment and planning among unlike agencies is much

300

rarer, and there are few models. One type, which is limited in both goals and time, is that of indirect human services, such as mental health consultation to schools (Taylor and Vineberg, 1975, 1977; Taylor, Vineberg, and Goffard, 1974). Planning begins with a survey of school needs conducted by or with the help of a mental health agency. The survey, using interviews and written questionnaires, is done by a consultant working with a planning group composed of the principal and staff members and includes a "systematic and comprehensive analysis of the school by reviewing strengths, weaknesses, and systemic constraints upon solutions to problems" (Taylor and Vineberg, 1977, p. 447.). The consultant gathers information on general characteristics of the school and the community, extrinsic factors such as community support for the school, specific school characteristics such as curriculum and student achievement, staff characteristics, and the principal's appraisal of major school needs and problems. The needs assessment leads to selection of intervention procedures based on the problems identified.

The concept of services integration came into use in the 1970s to describe activities intended to bring some coordination to the vertically organized federal-state system of allocating resources. The need to coordinate and build linkages among human services programs led to such developments as Community Action Agencies, regional commissions, and the Intergovernmental Cooperation Act of 1968 (John, 1977). Interagency linkages and networks have been much more common in human services administration than in education, except in attempts to improve dissemination and utilization of research findings. The latter has been spearheaded by the National Institute of Education, working with regional research and dissemination centers and networks and with regional educational laboratories.

By the mid 1970s, when both school systems and human services agencies relied heavily on categorical grants from federal and state sources to establish and maintain supplementary programs to meet varying needs, the concept of integrating social services was gaining currency. But there was no analogous concept for education programs and almost no communication about services between social agencies and school districts or between city governments and the schools. It is true that when cities performed communitywide needs assessments they usually included preschool and adult education as one of the social elements on which to focus data collection (League of California Cities, 1975, 1977). Conversely, school districts usually sought the opinions of the community in setting educational goals and in general surveys of needs and often used advisory boards representing business, labor, and consumer groups to assist in needs identification. But there were no instances of full-scale needs assessments undertaken jointly by a city and a school district to identify common goals and needs and to develop an ongoing capability for joint program and facilities planning.

The case study described in the next section was designed as a test of the desirability and feasibility of such a joint effort. It is followed by a review of more recent models and examples of interagency needs assessment and planning, discussion of related problems, and suggestions for some solutions.

The LINC Project

The venture reported here illustrates a synthesis of divergent methods of needs assessment from different perspectives. LINC (Local Interagency Needs Assessment Capabilities) was a four-way partnership project designed to develop and demonstrate a model for interagency needs assessment and program planning between city governments and school districts. The major partners were the city of Elson and the Elson Unified School District (fictitious names). The supporting partners were two county agencies: the County Office of Education (COE) and the County Community Action Program (CAP), which was prime sponsor of many federally funded projects in the county. The project was funded by a partnership grant from the Community Services Administration of the United States Department of Health, Education, and Welfare, with substantial support from the four partners.

The principal objectives of LINC were to identify and analyze critical needs of common interest to the city and the school district and to develop a joint planning capability between the two major partners that would continue after project funding was withdrawn. The project operated for fifteen months in 1977 and 1978. Information on follow-through on the needs assessment recommendations was collected during the following year (Witkin, 1979b; Witkin, Richardson, and Wickens, 1979).

The project was intended to supply the "missing LINC" in a setting where it was badly needed. Although the city and the school district shared many problems and cooperated informally on a few specific matters, there had never been any official joint planning. The four-way partnership was to function during the life of the project, with COE and CAP providing project management and technical assistance, performing the needs asessment for the city and school district, and assisting them to develop the capacity for joint planning to meet common needs. When the project was completed the two county agencies would withdraw as active partners, and the city and school district would continue joint planning on a regular basis.

Participating Agencies: Roles and Relationships. Elson was a city of about 5,000 population in a large metropolitan area and flanked by two much larger cities. The school district enrolled some six hundred students in two elementary schools and one high school. The district's boundaries were coterminous with those of the city. The school district and the city had separate governing boards—a five-member school board and a five-member city council, with the mayor as one of the members. The COE provided direct services and technical assistance to the school district, and CAP provided technical assistance to the city. These services were part of ongoing relationships that the two county agencies had with the city and district. An earlier proposal by the city to conduct a needs assessment with the help of CAP laid the groundwork for a natural extension into joint assessment and planning with the school district.

Elson appeared to be a good site for a demonstration project. The city was small enough in both geography and population to provide a manageable setting, yet it had many of the characteristics of inner cities in large urban centers and therefore could serve as a laboratory for joint planning on typical urban problems. But in some respects it was like an isolated rural community. At the time of the project, the city provided no social services to its residents, nor did it have parks, libraries, or childcare centers. There was a need for full-day care for more than a hundred preschool children and before-and-after school care for at least fifty-five youngsters. Such recreational facilities as existed were supplied for the whole community by the school district. This *ad hoc* cooperation, limited as it was, indicated that more systematic planning might be possible on an ongoing basis.

The community offered some interesting paradoxes. Although the city was largely industrial, with an excellent tax base, it had one of the highest unemployment rates in the state. Similarly, although the school district's per-pupil expenditures ranked in the ninety-ninth percentile in the state, its scores on the state testing program fell in the lowest five percentiles. The two problems were related. Although 93 percent of the unemployed were high school graduates, there was a serious lack of both academic and vocational preparation of students for employment. For this and other reasons, the majority of employees in the city's businesses and industries came from outside the city. The population was divided about equally between the older residents (mainly poor blacks, and other minorities) and a newer group of white, middle-class residents who occupied an expensive apartment complex. Since the apartments were for adults only, most of the school children came from the poorest segment of the population.

Project Management. There were four operational groups: a Core Team of three, a twelve-member Management Team, a community-based Needs Assessment Committee (NAC), and an *ad hoc* committee formed to plan and create a minipark. The Core Team, composed of a project manager, a COE administrator, and a technical assistance and planning specialist from CAP, carried out the project management and supervised a staff of part-time clerk-typists, research interns, and technical specialists. The Management Team, representing all four partners, met monthly to decide policy matters. The NAC, which represented community groups and associations, met weekly to assist in various aspects of the needs assessment and to gather information on progress of activities that they could report back to their own groups. Members also received training related to needs assessment and interagency planning. The minipark committee consisted of members of the LINC management team, school board, city council, involved city departments, and the community.

Needs Assessment Plan. Needs assessments done independently by cities and school systems typically differ in focus of concern, types of data collected, and methods used to set priorities. It would be unusual if separate assessments were to uncover needs that could or should be met by joint planning and use of resources. In order to guide the collection of data, the LINC administrator and CAP specialist devised a plan that drew on disparate approaches and provided a synthesis useful for guiding decisions on priorities and interagency planning. It consisted of the following phases:

1. *Areas of need* were identified by city council and school board members at a joint work session, using an adaptation of the group process "Games People Oughta Play" described in Chapter Five. The five areas deemed most critical for joint planning were chosen for the focus of the assessment. They were childcare, education, employment, recreation, and health, including mental, physical, and public health.

2. Data were gathered on both *status* and *desired states* for discrepancy analyses of the five areas. Status was determined by means of social indicators. Perceptions of both status and desired states were gathered by (a) interviews with selected business leaders in Elson and service providers in Elson and adjoining communities, (b) a mail questionnaire to key informants in the city and the school district, and (c) meetings of the NAC and other community groups.

3. Information on *resources* available to students and the community in Elson and adjoining cities was collected and organized in a resource directory that presented it in a standard format.

4. A *causal analysis* (Fault Tree Analysis) was performed to identify the major barriers preventing the meeting of needs and to indicate priorities for action. The two areas analyzed in depth were inadequate childcare and unemployment. Less formal causal analyses were also used to evaluate the project management and procedures and to help design a structure for ongoing interagency planning.

5. At the second work session, which closed the project, the school
    board and city council members set *priorities of needs* and
    made decisions for *joint action* in program planning.

Table 4 summarizes the major steps in the model, and
indicates the participants, methods, and outputs for each step.

The plan sought to avoid the heavy reliance on discrepancy
surveys and over-simplistic approaches to setting priorities that
were currently in vogue in educational needs assessments and to
improve on the use of social indicators so as to permit comparison
of human services and educational indicators. Surveys were used to
corroborate other data and to provide supplementary information
and perceptions rather than as the primary data source. The
collection of social indicators was guided by a conceptual model
and reported in a standard matrix to facilitate synthesis of the data.
Criticalities of need and priorities for joint action were derived
through group decision-making processes that took into account
and synthesized the data on needs, the strategic paths of the Fault
Tree Analyses, current and potential resources in the community,
and the political and economic realities in the city and school
district. Both formative and summative evaluation of the needs
assessment process and its results were an integral part of the
project.

Special Features. The two joint work sessions held for the
project were innovative for the community. In addition to the
council and school board, the initial meeting was attended by some
fifty community members who participated in identifying major
areas of concern for the needs assessment. After presentations by the
project director, all present engaged in a paired-weighting procedure to set priorities on major areas of concern, from an initial list
of about twenty. Results from the elected officials and the community were later analyzed separately by the Core Team, additional data
were gathered from a preliminary search of social indicators to
verify critical importance, and the final selection of five areas was
made at a meeting of the Management Team. *Thus the needs
assessment was focused from the beginning on areas that were
known to be critical. The task of the assessment was to analyze each*

Table 4. Model of Interagency Needs Assessment.

Steps	Participants	Methods	Outputs
1. Identify major areas of joint concern	City Council and school board facilitated by LINC Core Team	Group processes	List of major areas of concern
2. Collect data and perceptions on "what is" for major areas of concern	LINC researchers (one for social indicators, one for questionnaires and interviews)	Social indicators, interviews, questionnaires to key informants	Social indicator report; report on "Elson Perceptions"
3. Collect perceptions on "what should be" (concurrent with step 2)	LINC researcher, Core Team	Interviews, key-informant questionnaires, NAC and community meetings	Report on "Elson Perceptions"
4. Identify resources available	Part-time LINC staff member	Extrapolate and update information from existing service directories of neighboring cities	Service directory; resource hot line to LINC project office
5. Perform Fault Tree Analysis on two concern areas: childcare and unemployment	FTA consultant and Core Team; quantification by key informants from the community	Qualitative and quantitative Fault Tree Analyses	Two Fault Trees, in graphic displays with major strategic paths drawn; narrative documents
6. Synthesize data	LINC Core Team and researchers	Analyze data from all written reports for each major concern area	Executive summaries of each major area of concern
7. Evaluate the needs assessment	External evaluator	Interviews with people who had been actively involved with LINC	Narrative report summarizing "Perspectives of LINC"
8. Select priorities for joint school-community action	City council and school board, facilitated by external consultant	Review of FTA and written reports; group decision-making processes	Specific priorities for action on unemployment

area in depth to identify needs that could and should be met by joint planning and action.

The major needs assessment activities were carried out by two graduate school interns with backgrounds in public administration and market research, who were recruited through the Western Interstate Council on Higher Education (WICHE). They received stipends from WICHE and graduate credit for their work from their universities. They collected and reported the social indicator data, designed the questionnaires and interview protocols, and trained five students from a nearby community college to be interviewers. The Core Team assisted the researchers with analysis and interpretation of the data.

Concurrently with the data gathering, the Core and Management teams worked to develop a structure for ongoing joint planning between the school district and the city and to establish permanent linkages so that the joint planning process could be incorporated into the organizational structures of the two prime partners.

Qualitative FTAs on the joint planning structure and on the project management and operations identified present and potential hazards, which the Core Team attempted to deal with by securing additional resources, restructuring some activities, and alerting the Management Team about corrective action that could be taken. Problems regarding future joint-planning capability, however, could not be dealt with until the final meeting of the city council and school board.

Results. All planned activities were carried out, with the exception of some in the school-based assessment that had to be sharply curtailed for reasons that will be explained later. In particular, a focus group process with educators, parents, and students, was canceled. The massive social indicator and "Elson Perceptions" reports were supplemented by executive summaries that highlighted the need areas, synthesized major corroborating data, and made recommendations for action. In addition to the five areas of major concern, the survey reports included perceptions on city identity, housing, and transportation.

There were several spin-offs to the project. The local newspaper carried articles about the resource directory, copies of which were available in school district and city locations, and also publicized a hot line that was established in the LINC project office to provide an information and referral service to the community based on the directory. The service was maintained for three months toward the end of the project but had to be ended due to lack of funds.

The needs assessment reports and resource directory were compiled by LINC staff and consultants. The only formal joint planning effort undertaken between the school district and the city was to develop the community's first minipark for children. The school district supplied the land, the city furnished funds, and both contributed ideas and resources for planning. Once the project focus had been identified, the park was built in a remarkably short time—about three months from planning to public dedication.

Informal cooperative efforts initiated by the NAC also paid off in concrete action. For example, during the project year the school district had closed off playgrounds after school hours due to lack of money to pay supervisory staff. Children were climbing over the fences, getting hurt, and causing disturbances. A committee of concerned NAC members asked the city council for funds to keep the playgrounds open since there were no other recreation sites in the city at that time. The council appropriated funds, two community members were hired, and the school district supplied the general supervision.

The impetus of LINC also stimulated the city to apply for a grant to set up a childcare center, for which the school district offered a site. The application was made before the childcare FTA was completed and therefore did not reflect some of the critical needs that emerged from the analysis, especially the need for night and early-morning care for children of parents who worked the night shift. Nevertheless, the center was funded, and was in operation by the time the project was ended.

At their final joint work session, the school board and city council reviewed the needs assessment data and fault trees, heard recommendations from the LINC project staff, and engaged in structured activities to help them set priorities for action. The result: a decision to continue joint planning (adding the city's Industries Association as a third partner) with a focus on reducing local unemployment and better preparing youth for the world of work. A follow-up meeting was scheduled for January 1979.

Nothing came of that decision. By January, both the city and the school district, which had undergone traumatic dislocations of various kinds throughout the project, faced political and operational problems that fully engaged their attention. The joint planning capability was never institutionalized, and the LINC appeared to sink without a trace.

What Went Wrong? In some ways, LINC was a prime example of the workings of Murphy's law: Whatever can go wrong, will! If ever planners and researchers were faced with maddening obstacles, delays, and events beyond their control, this was the time.

The influence of Murphy's Law came in two forms: those things that went wrong with the project implementation per se and those events that occurred within the school district and the city that were internal to their own operations but impinged on the project and effectively put an end to any immediate hopes for a continued partnership. The main problems were:

- During the first three months of the project, the city governance structure underwent a major reorganization. The position of city manager (who was of crucial importance in the original LINC plan) was abolished and new departments were created, with department heads forming an administrative cabinet that reported to the city council. At the same time, the school district sustained major personnel changes, losing an administrative assistant to the superintendent who had previously performed important liaison functions with the project. These changes necessitated revisions in the interrelationships among the four LINC partners and the establishment of new lines of communication with project management, causing a four-month delay.
- The Management Team lost its city council member after six months and never gained a replacement. This seriously hampered getting high-level input and support from the city.
- There were three project managers: the first became ill after four months, the second was injured after three months, and the third manager was abruptly reassigned by her agency to another project, later returning part-time.

- The project office was moved three times. Office space was cramped and noisy. Office equipment had to be rented, which contributed to unanticipated costs.
- Efficient half-time clerical assistance could not be located in the community. CETA (Comprehensive Employment Training Act) employees required extensive training and supervision to complete assigned tasks, detracting from other project activities and adding to the load on the project manager.
- The school superintendent was involved in a widely publicized legal battle involving a former teacher and failed to attend many meetings. There was no other district-level administrator to replace him on the Management Team.
- The loss of high school accreditation from the Western Association of Schools and Colleges occupied the attention of school officials for several months.
- The high school principal became ill in the fall, which delayed and curtailed the high school data collection. She refused to schedule the focus group meetings for reasons that were never clear.
- Although a search was begun early through WICHE for two graduate interns, qualified and willing candidates were not located for six months. The needs assessment had to be compressed within a three-month period toward the end of the project. One intern did not complete her report, which was finished by the CAP Technical Assistance Unit.
- The project's closing date had to be extended three months, without additional funds, in order to complete needs assessment activities and reports.
- School administrators made all sorts of excuses to thwart gathering crucial educational data. The final assessment was heavily skewed toward analysis of city needs, with gaping omissions in the school-based data.

Why Things Went Wrong. Initially, striking geographical, sociological, and economic factors operating in the city and the school district made it appear that the setting would be ideal for an experiment in interagency planning. It was a microcosm, almost a laboratory situation—a small urban inner-city enclave that functioned like a remote rural area in many respects. It had large problems, but small and (it was thought) manageable governance bodies.

This felicitous combination blinded the Core Team to cues that should have alerted them to the pitfalls awaiting LINC, conditions existing prior to the project. They included:

- *Unstable organizational structures and personnel.* The school district had had five superintendents in ten years and little continuity in management. As for the city, the Core Team knew it was considering a reorganization plan but did not know the details.
- *Use of external consultants instead of staff.* Both the city and school district typically retained consultants to perform tasks that should normally have been done in-house. Therefore, they had no staff available to do planning. This way of operating carried over to LINC in that they expected the project teams to do all the needs assessment and planning tasks, involving city and school district staffs only minimally.
- *Inadequate funding.* Key project tasks had to be carried out by unskilled CETA employees, volunteers, and part-time professional help. Objectives were in some respects wildly unrealistic, given the level of funding and staffing.
- *Lack of mutual trust and communication.* There was considerable suspicion among important figures connected with the schools and the city. Furthermore, the school superintendent and the president of the school board were scarcely on speaking terms.

Many other things went wrong that could not have been foreseen. As soon as the project was funded and the Core Team realized the problems arising due to the reorganization of the city's governance structure and the various upheavals in the school district, the team took several steps. They did failure predictions on project management and attempted to set up alternatives and backup systems. They explored new lines of communication with the city staff because the major original supporters of the project (the city manager and his assistant) were gone after three months. And they endeavored to anticipate problems in building the joint planning capability.

These efforts were only partially successful. As the year wore on, the project administrator and staff found themselves reeling from one crisis to another. When it was over, they could appraise the effort. LINC accomplished its short-range goal of needs assessment and demonstrated that school-community planning on specific issues could yield very good results in a short time frame. But it failed to meet the long-term goal—to utilize the findings in meeting critical needs and to institutionalize a permanent interagency planning capability.

The Missing LINC One Year Later. One year after termination of the project, there was evidence of continued *informal* interaction among many groups involved with LINC, including increased cooperation between the Neighborhood Improvement Associations and the Industries Association. Also, based on the needs highlighted by LINC, the city itself funded a job development and placement element in its Job Bank, which had previously been limited to training. The childcare center and minipark were still operating, and the needs assessment data base and resource directory were available to substantiate funding requests. LINC also demonstrated successful processes for public, focused work sessions with a school board and city council. An external consultant who developed the city's reorganization plan (and who later acted as a management consultant to the school district) reviewed the LINC reports and made specific recommendations to the city council, addressing the areas of greatest unmet need in the field of human services.

Since Murphy and his cohorts continued to strike, these recommendations were not implemented. After a year, the community was still smarting from a series of traumas that occurred following the project phase-out. Among the developments:

- The school superintendent was fired and there was no replacement for several months. In the interim, the district was run by the two elementary school principals, acting as joint superintendents.

- Due to a community uproar over a condominium conversion, two city council members lost their seats in a recall. Both of them had been staunch supporters of LINC and interagency planning. The city council had only three members for a year, and a suit was filed contesting the recall election.
- The chief of police served briefly on the school board, long enough to help get the district's accreditation back. He then resigned, leaving a power vacuum.
- Due to loss of revenues following the passage of a law restricting property tax revenues, the school district dismissed the recreation director, who had been the only staff member actively involved in the interagency planning. The district then wanted the city to assume responsibility for recreation, but the city refused to do so. The former LINC administrator offered to bring in a consultant (who had worked with the project earlier) to facilitate dialogue and joint planning to meet this immediate need, as well as to consider what could be done on the serious unemployment and vocational education issues. But the staff members concerned were not interested, and the time was not right to approach the council and school board.

In short, although there was a crying need for continued joint planning to solve critical problems of mutual concern, the people who should have been most supportive of such an effort were apparently too overwhelmed by continued crises to take the necessary steps.

Recommendations for Other Planners. Although the LINC setting had peculiar and possibly unique characteristics, there is evidence from later research that Murphy's Law in interagency planning might be circumvented to a large extent by keeping the following in mind:

1. The organizations and agencies involved should have a stable governance structure, with continuity of management over a long period of time.
2. Agency staffs should be large enough so that people can be assigned specifically to the tasks involved in the interagency planning. Banathy (1978, p. 22) points out that "if personnel

are operating at peak level simply to meet the basic survival needs of the organization, they may balk at being asked to assume an additional work load to effect linkage, unless the linkage process or program itself actually eases the work load necessary for maintenance."

3. In order to institutionalize the process, interorganizational linkages should be established on at least three levels: (a) with elected officials, (b) with top management, and (c) with lower-level staff who have permanent positions. Although the actual work will probably be accomplished at the third level, it is essential to get official support, understanding, and active involvement at the highest levels (Banathy, 1978).

4. As early as possible, identify the informal power brokers operating and involve them in supporting the interagency efforts. These people are often *not* elected or appointed officials. They can find resources, give good advice, and help or hinder your efforts. (For starters, the city clerk and police chief should have been actively engaged with LINC.)

5. Success is more likely if the agencies cooperate on specific, short-term projects and issues and move from there to more general planning, as was done in the case of the minipark, rather than starting with a planning structure and working down to specifics.

6. Success is probably more likely when the impetus for interagency planning comes from one of the prime partners, rather than from outside, as it did on the LINC project. It is often necessary, however, to have a third party act as facilitator to the joint planning efforts until linkages and processes have been firmly established (Banathy, 1978).

7. Visible products are necessary early on in order to maintain interest. So much energy went into data gathering for the LINC needs assessment that less was available for channeling directly into joint planning activities; but the needs assessment reports were necessary in order to establish credibility and to provide incentive for continued efforts.

8. Involve community and grass roots groups as early as possible and keep them interested. As long as the community-based NAC met regularly, interest was high and the members in-

itiated many informal liaisons that resulted in specific action benefiting both the city and the schools. When meetings became less frequent and finally stopped because of excessive demands on LINC staff time, that initiative was irretrievably lost.

Such groups should do what they are best suited for, however. Many city planners feel that community groups and citizen organizations can assist with technical questions, data collection, and professional expertise on needs assessment and social planning efforts (League of California Cities, 1975). The LINC staff found, however, that NAC members felt most comfortable with providing communication linkages and general community support for the project. Although the NAC had intended to help with data collection through conducting interviews and assisting with fault tree construction, those efforts were not successful. But some NAC members did provide expert judgments that were used in the quantification process of the two fault trees.

9. If joint planning is undertaken on a programmatic scale, there should be two kinds of staff involved—one for data collection and technical aspects such as needs assessment and another to facilitate meetings and planning processes. Technical and facilitator roles are very different, and there should be trained people available to do both.

Models and Research on Interagency Cooperation

Although little has been written on needs assessments conducted jointly by and for agencies with widely different constituencies and goals, some recent work on interorganizational linkage is relevant. Banathy (1978) proposed a generic model and guidelines for planning and implementing a linkage program based partly on a project that linked formal and nonformal education sectors in advancing environmental education. He defined linkage as "a negotiated, authoritative arrangement between organizations . . . whose internal components allow for a mutual coordination and/ or exchange of resources or activities" (p. 1). The initiation of a linkage between two or more independent organizations can be

made by either organization, although it might be facilitated by a
third party—as was done in the LINC project. Coordinating roles
are common in health care and social welfare delivery systems but
less common in education. There the role is often taken by an
agency that is in an intermediate position between local districts
and the state—the office of a county superintendent of schools (as
in California and many other states), for example, or an intermediate educational service district (as in the state of Washington) or
a Board of Cooperative Educational Services (BOCES, as in New
York State). Banathy's model provides three phases of activity:
prelinkage, a trial cycle of linkage activity, and formalized cooperative arrangements. In the final stage, the linkage facilitator with-
draws as an integral part of the activity, as both COE and CAP did
after the LINC project was phased out.

An important aspect of Banathy's model is his specification
of the roles and activities of three categories of individuals necessary
to the linkage process:

(a) *Boundary Personnel:* These individuals *represent the participating organizations* and as such
have the authority to go beyond each organization's limits or boundaries to *perform communication and negotiation roles regarding the
linkage process.* . . .

(b) *Linkage Coordinator:* One of the boundary personnel should be appointed to this position. It
will be the responsibility of this individual *to
coordinate the linkage process within the participating organization.*

(c) *Linkage Facilitator:* The linkage facilitator represents the third party who may play a role in
initiating and maintaining the linkage arrangement. . . . The . . . facilitator may . . . provide
training for boundary personnel, particularly
the linkage *coordinators,* so that planned activities can be carried out effectively [pp. 3–4,
Banathy's emphases].

The linkage roles can be illustrated by the LINC project. The
Management Team was composed of three boundary personnel
from each of the four partners. The linkage coordinator for the
school district was the superintendent of schools; the city represen-

318   **Assessing Needs in Educational and Social Programs**

tative was a staff person, but the personnel changed several times because of city management reorganization. The facilitator role was handled jointly by the two people who had initiated the LINC venture—the research administrator from COE and the CAP planning specialist who constituted one member of the Core Team and who became the third project manager.

Banathy's model and role delineation throw light on the successes and failures of LINC, although the model was not available to the COE and CAP facilitators when the project was planned. The boundary personnel and facilitator roles worked very well, enabling the needs assessment activities to be carried out as planned. But the linkage coordinators were the weakest elements. And since they were responsible for promoting the joint planning capability between the city and the school system and for institutionalizing the planning process, the ineffectiveness of the linkage coordination seriously hampered major aspects of the project.

In recent years several interesting examples of interagency cooperation in the United States have been reported. The Division on Aging of King County (Washington), with a service area of about 1.2 million people, is administered as a partnership between the city of Seattle, King County, and United Way (Dudley, 1980). Human services delivery systems have been integrated in places as diverse as rural areas in Utah (Mitchell and Gallegos, 1980), and in the Louisville/Jefferson county area of Kentucky (Delahanty, 1980).

Delahanty and Atkins (1981) propose a collaborative planning model based on a system approach, which was used in the Louisville project. Their model provides alternative implementation paradigms to fit the preferences and requirements of the groups that are collaborating. The three alternatives utilize varying degrees of voluntary or coercive interagency cooperation in identifying problems and developing program plans.

Terrill (1982) reported a countywide needs assessment project that was done as the first step in a four-stage planning process of a public/private partnership. The vehicle was the Metropolitan Human Services Commission (MHSC) of Summit County, Ohio, which operates with a staff of three and a board of trustees composed of twenty-four members representing business/industry, government, United Way, labor, education, and health. MHSC planning involves twelve major human services funders in the county, and the seventy-eight key agencies that they support. The needs assessment, carried out by telephone survey, elicited community perceptions and actual incidence of problems in fifty-one areas, identified the most important, and compared the needs with available services to identify priorities. MHSC also designed a computerized countywide service inventory.

Terrill points out that the current planning environment includes factors of uncertainty about levels of funding and relationships of service providers with their funders; community ambivalence toward human services, where the desire to be accountable conflicts with the desire to help people; and reluctance on the part of agency boards to give up territoriality. She also notes an emerging factor that many communities will have to face: "Selecting priority areas of services has less to do with effectiveness of service provision and more to do with addressing unmet community need," yet "as resources continue to shrink . . . choices between like agencies within priority services will be made" (p. 3). But there is evidence that "joint planning ventures such as MHSC cost the community less, and have the potential of ensuring that higher quality services will be offered to the community" (p. 4).

Researchers at the Center for Governmental Studies at Northern Illinois University produced a major study of human services integration (Agranoff and Pattakos, 1979) in which they identified four dimensions of organization: the services-delivery approach, development of interorganizational community linkages between independent agencies, reorganization of large bureaucracies that deliver human services, and the attempt by government officials to develop and manage more coherent public policies. They note the difference between small, focused networks that work on a single problem area, and communitywide networks that develop linkages for planning and delivering services across agencies: "The original purposes for which a set of agencies agree to develop integrative linkages are highly diverse. Although all such attempts to build bridges between programs start with a need to improve agency interactions, the way a set of agencies will define problems, and hence the solutions that stem from the problems, will necessarily be different. The aims of a network will vary with the number and type of agencies involved. Generally speaking, a network made up of a small number of agencies focusing on a problem or two will look different from a community-wide set of agencies that cuts across a number of categorical areas. It is therefore difficult to speak in general terms of how program linkages are developed in services integration" (p. 45). Their services-integration model, which incorporates the four dimensions cited earlier, illustrates different ways in which needs assessment can be incorporated into the planning process, depending on which of the four dimensions is the focus of the integration.

Curtis (1981) describes a "mediated model" of interagency cooperation, in which the voluntary action of local agencies creates a human services organization. "This model recognizes the autonomy of its participants, but it formalizes their interdependence through a collective umbrella organization" (p. 13). Although each agency manages its internal environment independently, the agencies are tied to one another through a host of planning and linking mechanisms. Needs assessment in the mediated model appears in two places: as input from the general population to the human services *information* system and again within the human services *planning* system, in which an interagency planning information team receives planning information from the aforementioned information system. The needs assessment is in turn modified by input on systems goals from the governance body and on citizen goals from citizen groups. The population studied (in Louisville, Kentucky) was geographically based rather than based on existing services, clients, or agencies, as is usually the case.

In contrast with needs assessments that are done *after* interagency linkages and relationships are established is the identification of need *through* analysis of interagency relationships, including the extent of collaboration among human services resources. Siegel, Attkisson, and Carson (1978) suggest that inquiries conducted by skilled interviewers on site visits to agencies should explore (1) underutilized resources, (2) how the resources are perceived and used by peer agencies, (3) the extent to which continuity of service exists and degrees of service duplication and integration, and (4) which agencies or service providers maintain collaborative ties and thus would work well in a collective effort.

A needs assessment through analysis of interagency relation-ships is relatively low in cost, the information is readily available, and the survey "tends to increase communication between human service agencies and providers, [and] often leads to a greater sensitivity to the needs of community residents and . . . to a more adequate integration of human services" (p. 236). The strategy also facilitates the compilation of a general inventory of community resources, which is useful for integrating information from needs assessment into program planning. There are two main disadvan-tages to this type of need identification, however—the difficulty of obtaining reliable data and drawing conclusions about the popu-lation based solely on utilization of services:

> One must proceed with caution when attempt-ing to estimate the needs of an entire community on the basis of information obtained from an analysis of information about a sample of persons receiving ser-vices from the community's public and private care providers. In the mental health field, for example, there is a great deal of research which suggests that there is a wide gulf between the mental health needs of a community as determined by field prevalence surveys and the number of persons receiving mental health care in the same community [because many residents are receiving services outside the commun-ity]. A systematic need identification and assessment program must always include data concerning (a) the extent to which identified needs are being met by resources within or outside the social area being studied, and (b) the appropriateness of reliance on external resources to meet social area needs [Siegel, Attkisson, and Carson, 1978, pp. 236–237].

Curtis (1981) also considers the limitations of needs assess-ments based on service information as a major reason for carrying out geographically based population studies of need.

The ways in which each agency in a network guards its own turf were studied in eighteen projects that used some form of joint planning or programming (John, 1977). Five of the projects were successful in implementing joint planning or programming, and four were successful in creating meaningful linkages through voluntary participation: "In each of these projects—Glasgow [Montana], New York City, East Cleveland, and Seattle—questions of turf were avoided or postponed by limiting the interagency discussions to joint development of new programs to meet clear social needs. When turf issues did surface in Seattle, they were handled successfully through the voluntary interagency council. In East Cleveland . . . dissension was controlled by the exercise of line authority" (pp. 26-27). In five other projects, which involved multiservice centers, experiences with planning and programming linkages were generally viewed as negative. In each project, "latent or open conflicts over lines of authority within the center made agencies conscious of threats to their turf and reluctant to work cooperatively on planning" (p. 30).

John used a taxonomy of interagency linkages, adapted from one presented by the former Department of Health, Education, and Welfare. The taxonomy has six categories: fiscal, personnel, planning and programming, administrative support service, core service, and case coordination linkages. The Planning and Programming Linkage defines joint planning as "the joint determination of total service delivery system needs and priorities through a structured process" (p. 80). That definition applies to an increasing number of efforts to integrate human services needs assessments, but there is little evidence that much joint planning is taking place between agencies or organizations that are as different as city governments and school systems.

Recently, Delahanty and Atkins (1981) noted that "local planning is assuming the role of 'cutback planning,'" which requires that "decisions must appear to be rational and deliberate" when funding priorities are ranked (pp. 63-64). They predict that collaborative planning is likely to increase in importance. It would provide means for completely researching alternatives for funding existing services and help public officials to negotiate funding reductions through various constituencies. In the long run, "human services will increasingly be funded through multiple sources coming together at the local level. . . . Local governments . . . will be less able to make unilateral decisions influencing the rest of the system" (p. 64). Local governments may continue to initiate collaborative/comprehensive planning in order to provide a rational decision-making process on program cutbacks, to assure accountability in use of public funds, and to provide changes rapidly in human services, since "someone must remain concerned about how these changes influence the availability and effectiveness of services to those most in need" (p. 65).

In many communities where there is considerable overlap in the provision of certain services, agencies may be reluctant to cooperate in a communitywide needs assessment because they are competing for the same tax or foundation dollars. A case in point is adult education, which ranges from bringing adults up to a basic functional literacy level to offering avocational and recreational courses and opportunities to providing "life skills" in the five official adult-performance levels recommended by the federal government—job-seeking, health, using community resources, consumer education, and knowledge of government and law. Some of the agencies that offer courses, services, or counseling in these areas are adult basic education, community education, university and community college systems (both in courses and in labs), alcoholism and drug education and prevention programs, vocational rehabilitation, and organizations that deal with specific groups such as disabled adults, teenagers, displaced homemakers, and senior citizens.

An example of where lack of comprehensive, collaborative planning leads to failure to identify real needs in critical areas is in youth-training programs such as those formerly operated under CETA. Lefkowitz (1982) conducted a national study of such programs, interviewing nearly 300 people in seventeen cities. His major conclusion was that "few, if any, of the hundreds of youth-training programs in the United States are prepared to respond to the underlying problems [of youth] whose personal lives are so debilitating that no conventional job-skill program is likely to change their prospects" (p. 12). Their histories include parental abuse and neglect, leaving home and school as preadolescents, "sleeping in cellars and doorways, [and] long-term dependence on alcohol or narcotics" (p. 12). For a large segment of the disadvantaged youth population who may not have such problems, improving their reading levels or teaching computer skills is not enough. Youngsters have been found to suffer from undiagnosed hearing and visual problems, learning disabilities, or emotional or physical problems that had not been previously detected in the schools. A comprehensive, interagency assessment approach would identify the most serious problems and would lay the groundwork for programs involving not just job training, but also "medical treatment, basic and remedial education, psychological and social counseling, family intervention, skill development, attitudinal preparation for employment, and counseling and support once a job is found" (p. 14). Obviously, single-agency or school-system needs assessments are not likely to produce that kind of planning and service implementation in spite of the critical needs.

A different model of needs assessment involving the cooperation of many agencies is that by which United Way allocates its funds each year. United Way of King County (Washington), for example, has a Planning and Allocations Committee (PAC) that is responsible for reviewing recommendations from other planning and allocations committees and making final recommendations to its board of directors. The PAC identifies community needs and sets priorities, and recommends allocations to agency programs (United Way of King County, 1982).

Information on community problems, existing services, and ideas for solving social service problems come from eleven conference panels, each concerned with a specific field (aging, mental health, developmental disabilities, youth and family support services, and the like). Typically, each panel reviews the work of ten or eleven agencies. In 1982, 170 volunteers served on the conference panels, meeting for more than 2,200 hours to review and assess their programs and to review other program trends within their areas of service. Each report contains a historical perspective on the service area, program planning issues, observations on unmet needs and trends, and recommendations to United Way and other agencies or governmental bodies. The needs assessment component of the planning process also includes data on client characteristics, population changes, employment trends, changing value of money, community resources, and constraints. Input to that phase of the process (which takes place early in the year, prior to the conference panel meetings) comes from consumers, technicians, professionals, agencies both within and outside of United Way, and government, labor, and management groups.

Further interagency cooperation in identifying community concerns is exemplified by the Council of Planning Affiliates (COPA), a service of United Way. COPA is an association of voluntary and public agencies, community organizations, and government units that seeks to improve health and social services in King County. It is directed by an elected board of volunteer citizens.

The growing awareness of the importance of public/private partnerships and intergovernmental cooperation in coordinating human services at the local level was attested to at two recent conferences sponsored by the National Network for Coordinating Human Services (Institute for Information Studies, 1981a, 1981b). At the first, representatives of community associations, financial institutions, local governments, unions, business and industry, voluntary agencies, foundations, state departments of social services, and the media led workshops and addressed plenary sessions. They discussed issues of reduced funding for human services programs, the role that the corporate sector might play, and activities of coalitions of business, unions, and the private voluntary sector. The second conference dealt with issues of intergovernmental relationships, the impact of block grants on local roles and responsibilities, and the changing role of the corporation and foundation sector, among others. Noting that recent administrations had emphasized the desirability of using private resources to meet public needs, one speaker ironically observed that both providers and recipients could take encouragement from the fact that they had already begun to do by choice what they now must do of necessity.

A skill essential to obtaining community support for collaborative planning is the ability to identify key political and civic leadership allies and to maintain their support (Mastrine, Elder, and Delahanty, 1981). Although elected officials must gain and maintain public exposure, agency directors feel that "professionals concerned with human services coordination are better off to maintain lower profiles and support positive exposure for elected officials" (p. 25). Since the prime concern of the elected official is continuing electability, collaborative efforts must seem compatible with this concern.

The LINC case study noted that the only feasible method for initiating joint planning appeared to be through a specific action project such as the minipark. (The needs assessment activities were conducted by the project staff and consultants, whereas the joint planning necessitated active involvement of elected officials and/or staff of the city and the school district.) The LINC project was not unique in this regard. Mastrine, Elder, and Delahanty (p. 25) observe that a lack of action focus is a problem for organizations responsible for coordination of human services: "Long-range planning functions are, often, not as valued by community leadership as the ability to take on a shorter-range action-oriented approach to current problems. This approach, in turn, runs the risk of 'moving from one crisis to another.' . . . [It] is important to maintain a balance between the long-range policy issues on an organization's agenda and the short-range problem issues."

They also emphasize the importance of clear, concise communication skills in gaining and maintaining community support and the necessity to foster win-win situations, to compromise and negotiate—"even though the 'right' solution and the 'best' solution are not necessarily one and the same" (p. 25).

There is a clear trend toward interagency cooperation in planning, including needs assessment, particularly among human services agencies and to a lesser extent between the public and private sectors, although problems of governance, protection of turf, and accountability sometimes present barriers. Interagency needs assessment and planning among dissimilar organizations, such as that illustrated by the LINC project, however, are still rare. It remains to be seen whether the pressure for quality education and human services in a climate of severe funding cutbacks will stimulate city governments, agencies, and school boards to consider interagency planning as an alternative way to identify and meet critical needs of all in the community.

13

Uses of Needs Assessment for Community Programs and Services

The major tools for communitywide needs assessment and planning are the same as for other types of needs assessment—namely, the survey, social indicators, large and small group processes, and variants such as outreach and forecasting. But the key factors in community needs assessment are not so much the methods as the purposes and scope of the effort. Communitywide needs assessment is generally used by service providers to clarify their goals, expand the scope of their efforts to reach those previously not served, or to identify problem areas that have not been addressed. Other motivations are to test models or guidelines for community assessments and to increase citizen participation and intergovernmental cooperation. Such assessments are conducted by cities or counties, human services agencies, and school systems or universities. Community needs assessments may also be initiated by stakeholders, often in volunteer community-action groups, to analyze and develop programs for recognized problems, such as alcohol and drug abuse among youth, or inadequate recreational facilities. This chapter describes different approaches to community needs assessment by service providers and stakeholders.

Communitywide planning is sometimes undertaken to obtain a more coherent and complete picture of community needs when previous assessments by many agencies have focused on specific need areas or target populations. For example, between

1973 and 1982, planning agencies and funding bodies in and near Summit County, Ohio, conducted nineteen different studies with a needs assessment component. The studies used a variety of data sources—secondary data from the census, agency records, and other research and new data generated from community surveys, client and provider interviews, and input from advocacy groups. Although there was a good deal of excellent needs data in specific areas, none of the studies addressed the wide range of human services needs and resources in the county until the Metropolitan Human Services Commission made a countywide survey of the general population (Clough, 1982; Terrill, 1982).

The diversity of community needs assessments can be exemplified by the following:

- A study that assessed the social and economic problems of recently arrived Cubans and Haitians in Dade County, Florida (Metropolitan Dade County Department of Human Resources, 1981). Interviews were conducted with entrants applying for cash assistance, involved in social service programs, and in jail, as well as with key informants. The study identified immediate and long-term problems, educational needs and resources, and the entrants' use of the transportation and legal systems.
- An assessment of problems in major cities in Virginia, undertaken as part of a five-year program to examine human services delivery systems and to design a new statewide system. The assessment included determination of needs, gaps, and constraints in human services delivery programs in the public and private sectors (Virginia Division of State Planning and Community Affairs, 1973).
- A needs assessment conducted to improve the coordination of human services in Duluth, Minnesota. Needs were determined by surveying a sample of households in the Model Neighborhood area. The assessment was one phase of a demonstration project that also included an agency survey of human services resources in the community. The needs survey measured one aspect of the demand for human services and was tied to program objectives and problem areas (Dobmeyer and others, 1972).

- A regional study by the New England Municipal Center, for five New Hampshire municipalities, undertaken to improve the capabilities of the municipalities to do human services planning and management. The assessment used three methods: a human services opinion survey to tap citizens' attitudes toward local human services programs; socioeconomic data, with comparisons among the municipalities; and a resource inventory of programs and providers (Gundersdorf, 1975).

Community Planning Models

Community needs assessments often use more than one method of gathering data and generally choose approaches that emphasize citizen participation, particularly of those groups presumed to need education or social services.

Community Impressions Approach. This is a procedure for involving groups with the greatest human services needs both in the assessment phase and in subsequent planning and evaluation activities directed at establishing programs to reduce their needs (Siegel, Attkisson, and Carson, 1978). The procedure has three steps: (1) *Key-informant interviews,* with ten or fifteen individuals who live or work in the community and who have extensive knowledge of both the human services needs and the demographic characteristics of the population. Information about where various target groups live, their transportation links to service centers, and the like are recorded on a map. (2) *Integration of existing information,* in which existing data from the widest possible range of needs assessment methods are integrated with the community impressions to develop a convergent analysis of needs. The additional information is added to the map derived from the interviews. (3) *Community forum,* in which each group or section of the community identified as having significant unmet human services needs meets in a community forum to validate or invalidate those needs. The forum also offers the opportunity to explore the nature and causes of the needs in greater depth and to establish priorities.

The community-impressions model can be carried out with less expenditure of time and resources than other methods, and it offers a broad-based approach to needs assessment. As in other approaches, the validity and reliability of the information gathered by the three methods, as well as its synthesis, must be considered when setting priorities.

Outreach. Needs assessments can also be accomplished through outreach, a form of case finding. Its purpose is to locate individual members of a target population, tell them of the availability of a service, and inform them of their entitlement to the service or benefit. Salvatore (1978) considers outreach a human services marketing process that generates a demand for services by persuading potential consumers that the service will meet their needs. Although the primary purpose of outreach is to share information and not to gather data, it may be used to discover what members of a target population need or want and to gather unobtrusive data through observation. It can also be used in connection with a survey.

An advantage to using outreach in needs assessment is that it can yield data on needs from people who are unaware of services or who for some reason do not seek aid. Disadvantages are that outreach staff may try to engage in informal service delivery and that the informants in the target area or group may not be representative of those in need (Salvatore, 1978).

An outreach program designed for one purpose may also turn up information indicating needs not met by the current program, resulting in a change of program focus for a service agency. Sometimes the changed view of the need comes about because workers who have been providing a service become aware that the real need is something other than the one being addressed. This alters the character of the service or the intervention.

A case in point is reported by a counseling center serving children and adolescents in the Milwaukee metropolitan area. In the early 1970s it operated a crisis intervention/drug abuse outreach program that provided services in the school setting to adolescents "whose abusive use of drugs and alcohol caused highly dysfunctional behavior" (Burke-Peterson, 1982, p. 1). The students were referred through their schools, and sessions were led primarily by staff of the counseling center. Eventually the program changed its focus from drug abuse intervention to prevention of any social problems that might prove hazardous to youth. The new program,

Positive Alternatives for Youth (PAY), was designed to help students find positive alternatives for coping with problems of stress and depression, making decisions, and developing positive self-image (McClellan, 1975; Burke-Peterson, 1982). The programs, which took place at school sites, involved the cooperation of the school district and site administrators, a community counseling center, and several other agencies.

Although no formal needs assessment appears to have been done to bring about the changes in emphasis, it is clear that the alertness and expertise of the counseling-center staff, coupled with frustration about several aspects of the original program, resulted in reappraisals that produced a much more effective program. In effect, the needs were redefined in such a way that the most appropriate response was no longer crisis intervention and drug abuse outreach but rather a multifaceted program designed to assist youngsters to find positive alternatives to satisfy their needs. PAY has three goals: prevention of problems that might affect a child's growth, helping students acquire basic communication and coping skills, and working cooperatively with other agencies "to create conditions in the school systems that promote well-being and reduce the need for remedial treatment" (Burke-Peterson, p. 1).

The change in focus altered not only the content of the program but also the type of participants, shifting the emphasis from teenagers alone to include elementary school children and preteens in a separate program. Curriculum and personnel also changed, with teachers being trained to conduct PAY classes that are incorporated into the curricula at their schools. The new program involves the public school system of Milwaukee, the Junior League, the Archdiocese of Milwaukee, and local businesses. Thus the program shifted from being run by a single center to a cooperative, interagency project.

A similar shift in program emphasis has happened on the national scene. Whereas in the late 1960s and early 1970s, methods of coping with drug abuse were to provide factual information, crisis intervention, and treatment, it was later felt that drug abuse and the rising incidence of alcohol and other substance abuse were symptoms of other problems that had at least some roots in low self-esteem. This redefinition of the problem and the recognition of the role of peer pressures resulted in new program emphases. New curriculum materials and staff training focused on enhancing basic decision-making, communication, and interpersonal skills for all children and young people in schools.

Considered from another angle, it may be that the trend grew out of a solution seeking a problem/need. In the 1970s many movements arose to help people with "self-awareness," "fulfilling one's potential," and "improved self-concept." Encounter groups, sensitivity training, humanistic approaches to education, and exploration of alternative lifestyles were the order of the day. Nevertheless, the recognition that substance abuse and other forms of self-destructive behavior were not isolated phenomena but were related to the individual's concepts about self and others and the power to make choices did serve to change the focus of many educational/mental health programs. Subsequently, needs assessments were designed to elicit information and opinions about a much broader range of behaviors and attitudes than the incidence of ingestion of drugs or alcohol.

Targeted Community Needs Assessments. Many community or regional assessments are made to identify needs of target groups. Two examples are studies done in the interests of children and the elderly. The School of Architecture and Urban Planning of the University of California at Los Angeles was instrumental in developing a model for needs assessment and planning of daycare services. The Child Care Referral Service (CCRS) was begun to assess daycare needs in a low-income inner-city community of Los Angeles. The CCRS served as the basis of a survey that resulted in a demographic profile of the community, information on the availability and nature of childcare services, and data on the needs, preferences, and characteristics of parents seeking childcare in the community. The profile of parent preferences and use patterns was compared with availability of childcare services to identify a range of serious unmet needs. The model is replicable in other communities (Hill-Scott, 1977).

The Area Office on Aging of Northwestern Ohio undertook a four-pronged study of the problems and needs of older persons in northwestern Ohio. The components were a telephone survey exploring the problems and magnitude of needs in eight areas of life, a key informants survey, a study of utilization of services by the elderly in the area, and a spatial analysis of the entire study area, which examined the current delivery system. The outcome of the assessment was an optional system design for the total system area (King and others, 1980).

The model for a youth needs assessment described in Chapter Two also provides a comprehensive approach to a targeted community needs assessment.

A Group Process Model

A combination of nominal group process and other small group approaches has been used successfully in California, Arizona, and other western states for identifying and analyzing community problems. The process enlists active participation of stakeholders in the community, who are organized into task forces and who meet for five sessions of two hours each. The following steps are taken (O. Jackson, interview, Sept. 14, 1981):

1. The task forces establish a service goal.
2. They generate effectiveness criteria for the data to be collected—for example, recency, validity, or nonbias.
3. They then generate feasibility criteria, such as availability of data, cost, and time.
4. They generate potential data types and sources, such as dropout rates, test scores, or other indicators.
5. After testing the data types and sources against the criteria on effectiveness and feasibility, the task forces decide what data should be gathered.
6. The same groups that met in the preliminary sessions assist in gathering the data, which might be collected by means of a survey of key informants.
7. The staff of the sponsoring agency and outside consultants present that data in another group session, and the group decides how important the data are in addressing the goal.
8. The task forces develop program objectives designed to make an impact on the problems associated with the data collected and to accomplish the goal.

9.   Finally, they set priorities on the program objectives based on
the relevant data.

The group processes used are brainstorming, clustering,
advocacy, paired-weighting, and other consensus procedures (see
Chapter Five).

The process can be illustrated by a needs analysis and
planning project carried out in Phoenix, Arizona, under the egis of
a nonprofit umbrella service-delivery system for alcohol abuse. The
board of directors selected the service goal: "to reduce the negative
impact of alcohol problems on the personal, social, and economic
lives of the residents of Maricopa county through alcohol prevention, education, treatment and control efforts" (Jackson, 1981b, p.
6). Indicators already available were number of deaths from cirrhosis, incidence of drunken driving arrests, alcohol-related crimes,
economic costs for treatment, and number of clients in alcohol
treatment centers.

The task forces reviewed current services and matched them
with objectives. A two-by-two grid was developed in which one
dimension was the impact the objectives would make and the other
was the performance of current services. The cells then were (A)
high services, low impact; (B) high services, high impact; (C) low
services, low impact, and (D) low services, high impact. Those
objectives falling in cell D—high impact of objectives, but low
performance where the objectives were not being addressed by
current services—became the priorities for action planning.

Additional data were gathered by a survey of key informants.
Each member of the task force conducted two interviews among
clergy, educators, service providers, police, and people in the
alcohol industry. There were eight task forces, one in each catchment area, with a total of 128 task force members. The catchment
areas covered Scottsdale, an Indian reservation, and a Chicano
community.

Since each task force did its own needs assessment and
planning and collected its own data base, it had a strong sense of
ownership both of the process and of the results. In this model, there
should be no problem with nonutilization of data since the same
people who assess the needs are also responsible for following up

with objectives and plans for improving services or instituting new ones.

The foregoing model has been used extensively to actively involve communities in needs assessment and planning. A key concept in the method is "community empowerment," which is based on the premise of encouraging open participation of diverse ethnic/cultural and age groups in the decision-making process (Jackson, 1981a, 1981b).

Community Planning for Mental Health

A Consumer Model. Another model of community needs assessment is the consumer model, which is used for assessing community mental health needs. The consumer—defined as "any community member who resides within a given geographic area"— is the major source of input (Rossi, Freeman, and Wright, 1979, p. 93). The model supplies information on the priorities of need for additional services by target problem, age group, and geographic area. The consumer groups surveyed are mental health agencies, secondary related agencies that make referrals to mental health services, high-risk individuals, community and civic groups that are organized around a common goal or for a specific purpose, and a random sample of the community-at-large in the area.

In this model, each source contributes a different perspective on the same general problem. The model was tested in a subregional area of San Diego county, California. Questionnaires were sent to thirteen mental health agencies and thirty-three secondary related agencies, such as schools, the probation department, Juvenile Hall, and a hospital. Each agency ranked the target problems that required the first, second, and third most immediate attention within three age groups: youth under eighteen, adults, and those over sixty years of age. The agencies also answered questions regarding the quantity and types of programs already existing in the area.

A different questionnaire was sent to ten community and civic groups, which were asked to check the services that should be made available to a greater number of people in the area for the three age groups. Demographic information about the members of the groups was also requested. A similar questionnaire was mailed to a random sample of 16 percent of the households in the area. An additional open-ended question was included in the community-at-large questionnaire, where consumers were asked to list the people to whom they would go for help if they had a personal problem.

Finally, data were gathered from high-risk individuals by means of interviews using the same questions about rankings of services as in the mailed questionnaires. The individuals interviewed were selected from fourteen mental health agencies and secondary related agencies in the target area (Weiss, 1975, cited in Rossi, Freeman, and Wright, 1979, pp. 93-95).

Researchers and agency planners who are interested in analyzing needs in a community may encounter sharply differing perspectives on what the needs are, their importance, and how they should be met. Rossi, Freeman, and Wright note that "a variety of sources may be needed to encompass the several perspectives of agencies, youths, and parents in determining the needs for youth services" (p. 95). When surveys show widely varying or contradictory perspectives, the authors suggest that it may be necessary to reconceptualize the problem or the prospective intervention or even to abandon an intended program. They cite the fate of the urban renewal program, which in many cities foundered on the conflict that was occasioned by sharply divergent views as to what constituted dilapidated and obsolete housing. "The criteria used by planners often did not correspond with those held by residents" (p. 97).

Institutional Planning. Large-scale community assessments can be used not only to identify mental health needs and the size of populations to be served but also to serve institutional planning, evaluation, and research purposes. Goza, Strube, and Fennimore (1982) report on a community needs assessment that was done by the research and evaluation units of three mental health centers in the Salt Lake City area prior to their reorganization into one center. They surveyed a 1 percent random sample of households within each Salt Lake City census tract. Trained interviewers conducted the needs assessment using a basic survey instrument for 75 percent of the respondents and an extended instrument with five additional measures for the other 25 percent. The basic survey sought information on demographics, perceived community and personal needs, and why respondents might not turn to a community mental health center. There were also questions on quality of life and measures used to identify psychiatric impairment in children and adults. Items in the extended questionnaire included additional measures of psychiatric symptoms and questions on social network support systems, coronary-prone behavior, patterns of attribution of success or failure, and recent life changes.

Data from the assessment were used for program justification by identifying percentages of the population who could be considered at risk for physical and mental health impairments. The data on problems in the neighborhood, in the county, in daily life, and in school were useful for indicating potential for collaboration with other agencies. Other data yielded information on accessibility of services, barriers to treatment at community mental health centers, decisions regarding staffing patterns for therapists dealing with children's issues, and variables related to prevention programs.

Projects of this scope are time consuming and costly. Goza, Strube, and Fennimore recommend that a project leader devote approximately one and a half years, full time, to the work. Collaboration within the agency (between the research/evaluation unit and other units) and among agencies is essential. Other communities wishing to do a similar large-scale study, however, might be able to lower the costs and shorten the time needed by focusing on the needs assessment without the research elements.

City Planning

Comprehensive community needs assessment can be exemplified by a study undertaken in the mid 1970s by the city of Hayward, California, which at the time had a population of about 110,000. The needs assessment was designed as a joint effort of the Hayward Human Relations Commission, which gave initial impetus to the study; the staff of the city's human services department; and staff of the League of California Cities. The Hayward Needs Assessment Committee—composed of members from three Human Services Commissions, a Citizens Advisory Commission, a Human Relations Commission, and a Social Development Commission—

was formed to develop and implement the process. The committee identified eight areas of social need for examination: social environment, safety and justice, recreation, transportation, education, housing, health, and income/employment. There were three stages—problem identification, resource identification, and problem analysis. The total needs assessment process took more than three years (City of Hayward, 1978).

In the problem-identification stage, the needs assessment committee gathered and analyzed data from the census, a community conference, neighborhood census tract meetings, records of the school district, police records, election statistics, reports from the Social Security Administration, and statistics from the Alameda County Health Service Agency. Resources were identified through an update of the city's social service directory, which yielded information regarding availability of services to Hayward residents. In the third stage, in order to obtain information about community and social needs that did not surface from the analysis of existing data and to assess the adequacy and effectiveness of resources, the city contracted for a social needs assessment survey of a representative cross-section of adult Hayward residents. The survey was completed in a three-and-one-half month period (Reimer, Wahl, and Lathrop, 1977). As the last step, the committee compared the social problems with existing and potential resources and identified significant gaps between problems and services that suggested need for action.

Citizen involvement was heavy in all stages of the process including the development of the survey instrument. A special public meeting was held to obtain community reaction to the questionnaire draft, which was a joint effort of the needs assessment committee, city council members, staff of the Human Services Department, and the consultants. The questionnaire was pretested under field conditions, and translated into Spanish for administration to Spanish-speaking residents. The survey sample was drawn from households listed in the city directory, and the seventy-six-item questionnaire was administered by trained interviewers. In addition to eliciting facts and opinions from people who would not be reached otherwise, even through public hearings or neighborhood meetings, the survey provided estimates on current rates of unemployment, handicap, and poverty that would not be available until after the 1980 census. Questions probed all eight categories of social need.

All citizens had further opportunities for involvement through attendance at citywide and neighborhood meetings. The Community Resource Conference, the first major public activity of the needs assessment, had two purposes: to provide an opportunity for residents to learn of the resources of the social service agencies in the area and to elicit service-provider and community input to the assessment through a workshop format. The two-day conference was sponsored jointly by the needs assessment committee, the League of Women Voters, and the Eden Area Information and Referral service. Participants met in workshops of eight to ten, each group reflecting the diversity of residents in terms of age, sex, and race/ethnicity. Using the nominal group process developed by Delbecq (Delbecq and Van de Ven, 1971; see also description in Chapter Five), on the first day the groups created lists of priority needs and on the second day they identified resources and possible solutions to each problem area. Ten members of the Human Services Commission were trained to act as leader/recorders for the workshops. Staff also provided assistance for monolingual Spanish-speaking participants.

The conference was widely publicized through many channels. Some 3,000 fliers were distributed; most public service offices posted announcements in English and Spanish for clients and staff, agencies sent fliers to their clients, and sixth-grade students of the Hayward school district took fliers home to their parents. The area's major newspapers carried notices with a general invitation to all interested residents to attend. Additional notification was made through publications of the Area Agency on Aging and the California State University at Hayward. A local cable television station hosted an hour program discussing the conference and the needs assessment and aired spot announcements as well.

After the first day's session, the needs assessment committee and Human Services Department staff categorized the information into the eight need categories that had been chosen for the assessment. These categories served as the basis for forming the small groups in the second day's workshops. In most instances, however, the groups were not able to identify available resources, due to lack of knowledge; nor were they able to identify possible solutions for the need areas, due to both lack of time and the structure of the nominal group process, which provides for only minimal interaction and clarification.

The data from the conference were difficult to quantify and so were treated as qualitative inputs and considered in conjunction with the social indicators and results of the survey. The committee was also cautious about interpreting the data as being representative of the residents since, in spite of the wide publicity prior to the conference, most of those attending were agency staff or their clients.

Supplementing the Community Resource Conference, neighborhood meetings were held in elementary schools in nineteen census tracts. Some tract areas were combined because of geographic and demographic characteristics. Some thirty human services commissioners were trained to act as facilitators of the meetings, working in two-person teams at each location. A broad publicity campaign included announcements in daily and weekly newspapers, on network and cable television, and on major radio stations; personal letters were sent to key community leaders; and students delivered fliers to every household in the city.

The census-tract meetings attracted from five to forty people each. The nominal group process was used except in very small groups, where a general discussion was held and consensus derived. Only problems and needs were identified, however, and not resources or possible solutions. In eight census-tract areas that had been previously identified as target neighborhoods for community development, the participants performed two tasks. Once they had identified and set priorities on an initial set of needs, they discussed and ranked for priority those needs that would be appropriate for community development projects.

The information from the census-tract meetings was qualitative, like that from the community conference, but an additional analysis was made by comparing the perceptions of high-priority needs in each tract with statistical information. For example, analysis of the data could show whether residents of an area with a relatively high crime rate were correspondingly concerned about crime. Although the census-tract meetings suffered from the same problems of self-selection as the community conference, the needs assessment committee considered that the findings indicated the pulse of the community.

In addition to analysis of statistical and demographic data, the community conference and census-tract meetings, and the community survey, the final source of information was from in-depth interviews with ninety-eight key informants: sixty men and thirty-eight women. The consultants conducted the interviews with the mayor and representatives of the city council, city and agency administrators, all city commissions and boards, selected service providers, educational administrators, counselors, university professors, religious leaders, business and industrial managers, hospital and clinic directors, newspaper personnel, leaders of nonethnic advocacy groups, and members of advocacy groups for the Latino, black, Asian, and Portuguese communities.

Four major topics were covered: problem identification, resource identification, problem analysis, and problem solution. The focus on topic areas rather than on specific questions permitted maximum flexibility in eliciting information. Interviews were open-ended and lasted from one to two hours, except for four telephone interviews that lasted from fifteen to thirty minutes. With the permission of the respondents, interviews were taped and their content categorized immediately after each interview.

The example of Hayward's needs assessment shows how a city can mobilize all its resources to conduct a truly comprehensive study. Every resident had the opportunity to voice concerns and to participate in seeking solutions—through the community conference, neighborhood meetings, or the community survey. The needs assessment was modeled on ideas that had been developed and disseminated through the League of California Cities, and the city government committed three years of staff time and other resources to the project. The city's effort was initially designed in part for guidance in allocating revenue sharing funds. It later was expected to provide input to annual policy budgeting as part of the city council's ongoing information process.

In contrast with Hayward's multifaceted effort to define community needs, many cities approach the social dimension of planning from the point of view of goals, frequently using a citizen-oriented goals-study process. The city of Alameda, California, carried out a citizen participation process for a whole year. Techniques included a mail questionnaire, citywide meetings, task forces, and an interview survey. The citizen task forces produced long-range goal statements on crime prevention, economic development, education, housing and physical planning, human services, planned growth, recreation and cultural facilities, and transportation (Schoenberger and Williamson, 1977). A goals steering committee was assisted by a management consulting firm.

The process was conducted in seven stages:

1. Questionnaires designed to determine the problem areas were mailed to every household in Alameda.
2. Preliminary results of the survey were presented to the community at a citywide congress at which task forces were organized around the crucial issues.
3. Each task force met at least weekly for three months to consider its problem and to develop preliminary goal statements. Graduate students in urban planning provided staff support.
4. Preliminary goals were presented to a second citywide congress.
5. Personal interviews to validate the goals were held with 1,000 randomly selected residents.
6. Each task force used the results of the validation survey to refine and modify its work and to prepare a final report.
7. The reports were consolidated into a single document and adopted by the city council.

Altogether, several thousand residents participated in the congress, task forces, and the surveys.

Community Education

Postsecondary institutions such as community colleges frequently do community needs assessments to identify unmet educational needs in the adult community that they can address. Their needs assessments often resemble market surveys in that they aim to identify potential students for both regular programs and for continuing education or nondegree courses. San Diego Community College District, which has four colleges, developed a model and a survey questionnaire aimed at various publics in the county and designed to gather preferences for goals, population statistics, and data on courses that the respondents might enroll in (Morgan, 1975). The model has been widely used by other college districts in California and elsewhere. The Piedmont Virginia Community College used key informants to analyze *future* trends as a major part of a longe-range community-based needs assessment model in the college's five-county service area (Askegaard, 1982). The intergovernmental data analysis model developed by a consortium of community college districts in Florida is another approach (see Chapter Two and Tucker, 1973, 1974).

For many years, several Canadian provinces have been actively engaged in assessing educational needs of their communities. The University of British Columbia and the Ministry of Education of the province collaborated on developing a six-stage model to identify and reach learners in the community (Lund and McGechaen, 1981). They remind college planners to consider these points before undertaking any form of needs assessment:

> [Some] groups have little or no contact with educational services.
> . . . some individuals or groups . . . have little occasion to define their [educational] requirements.
> While some needs and problems within the community relate directly to the services of an educational institution, others, because of their complexity and scope need the co-operation of several private and governmental agencies before any effective educational program can be organized.
> While some educational needs are clearly identified and recognized as urgent by the target group, an analysis is still necessary in order to assess the scope and nature of the need in order to plan a meaningful program.
> No educational need can be assessed effectively without the participation of the target group. A major part of any needs assessment is how the target group perceives its need.
> Sometimes a community need is identified which cannot be solved through an educational

> program. A thorough needs assessment will often
> help you to reach this kind of conclusion and
> provide some indication of an alternate solution
> [Lund and McGechaen, 1981, p. 1].

A Continuing Education (CE) programmer's manual details the six stages of the needs assessment. In the first stage, the needs assessor determines the structure and organization of the community where the needs assessment is to be done, listing what is already known about the community and what other information should be gathered. Four sources of information are suggested: (1) community resources (such as government and private agency services, business associations and trade unions, recreational and religious organizations, and educational services other than the institution conducting the study), (2) demographic information (from Canada Census, provincial annual reports, and municipal and local records), (3) channels of communication within the community (media, publications of churches and businesses, informal networks), and (4) transportation systems (bus routes, locations where people gather, such as churches and shopping centers).

The second stage is to consult with community representatives. In the third stage, planners are encouraged to participate in community activities that will give background for the assessment, including how the resources of the institution could contribute to the needs of various community organizations and groups. In stage four, the planners review existing sources of information and identify new information that should be gathered. The analysis of existing sources gives information important for planning a formal survey. At this stage, a decision is made as to the type of survey to use—whether a mailed questionnaire, personal interview, or telephone interview—and the survey is then designed and tried out with a test group. In the fifth stage data are gathered to identify community needs, and the sixth stage is determining priorities.

Lund and McGechaen note that "much of continuing education involves responding to needs which are identified by both the CE planner and the community" (p. 12). Other ways to identify needs are:

> Where CE planners perceive a need that the learners have not identified. In this case, the CE planner's role is one of social animation.
>
> Where learners identify needs which are previously unknown to the planners. Here planners must create avenues so that potential communities of learners can reach them with their needs.
>
> Where needs exist which have not yet been identified by either the planners or the learners. In this case, a needs analysis such as a survey of the community is in order [p. 12].

In addition, CE administrators from different communities in the region can meet and compile a master list of needs of which they are already aware. To supplement their perceptions, needs-identification workshops can be held with citizens of the communities, using large and small group sessions to generate lists of needs and differentiate between those that are and are not being met by existing resources. In the final stage, priorities are determined, and Lund and McGechaen recommend consulting with the director of the institution to see if the list of priority needs is realistic and congruent with the policy of the institution.

Since 1973, the communities of Saskatchewan have used a community education brokerage model in which several hundred contact committees of local citizens assist in identifying needs and setting priorities (Province of Saskatchewan, 1972). The province developed a system of community colleges with an emphasis on community development and community service. The community is defined as a social dimension produced by the interaction of individuals who share similar concerns. Community education includes both formal learning, which is normally directed toward a diploma or degree and conducted in a classroom, and informal long- or short-term learning experiences, which are in the interests of personal or community enrichment and often occur outside the formal classroom. Continuous needs assessment is carried on in local communities, with CE personnel assisting organizations in joint planning to achieve maximum use of their educational resources. Local leaders as well as professional educators are part of the community education teams in this model.

Informal and Indirect Methods

With the growing trend toward informal networks of all kinds in the United States (Naisbitt, 1982), many communities are developing grass roots groups and coalitions outside the structure of agencies and government that perform a variety of needs assessment functions although they are not necessarily labeled as such. These groups sometimes evolve into regularly constituted organizations, cooperating with both the public and private sectors to sense community needs and to advocate for better services, schooling, or community programs.

One such group is Citizens Education Center Northwest (CECN), a nonprofit organization in Washington state that works with a state and national network of citizens and educators to make public education more effective (Austin, 1982). CECN began in 1979 as a small group of women meeting informally in the Seattle area to discuss educational issues. In 1981, CECN and the Seattle school district, with support from the Ford Foundation, launched a project to enable parents, students, school staff, and community members to work together at the school-site level to design and implement school-based improvements. An outgrowth of this project was a community survey CECN conducted in the spring of 1982, using telephone and on-site interviews and a written questionnaire. The survey studied 21 of the 110 schools in Seattle. The results were organized into comprehensive profiles for each of the 21 schools, and a districtwide profile. The community survey was one aspect of a comprehensive needs assessment of the district.

CECN continues to function as a community-based organization studying the programs and funding needs of the schools of Washington state, providing information to citizens and the schools, and offering research services to the schools as well. Support comes from individual memberships as well as businesses and foundations.

In some cities, the residents have set up coalitions of organizations to act as research and advocacy groups for public education. Although they do not engage formally in needs assessment, their focus on educational priorities alerts citizens to educational issues, particularly those related to the budget. In January 1982 a coalition of fifteen civic organizations in Chicago launched the Chicago Panel (Chicago Panel on Public School Finances, 1982). It published a study reviewing the education budget for the years 1979 to 1983 and made specific recommendations to improve both the format and review process for the budget. The purpose was to increase the understanding and participation of the citizens of Chicago in decisions about raising, spending, and cutting money for education and to ensure that the most educational dollars go to direct services to students.

The Chicago Panel was modeled on the Educational Priorities Panel of New York City, which within six years redirected some $300 million to students. Other cities have been studying the Chicago Panel as a method of involving the community in educational decision making.

In Placentia, California, a town of 36,000 about thirty miles southeast of Los Angeles, the city manager and some twenty-five top-ranking administrators did a personal needs assessment by visiting every home and business in the town, asking for complaints and suggested improvements. Each official spent two to three hours a week for eight months going door to door. When no one was home, the callers left their business cards, a letter from the city manager, and a brochure explaining how to contact city leaders. Most of the 370 requests that were logged during the first four months of the project asked for specific services that were fairly easy to fulfill, although some needed reallocation of personnel, such as more police patrols on residential streets to cope with speeding teen-age drivers. The project director believes the method will work in any size city that takes it seriously (Ingwerson, 1983).

Two districts in New York City that used a district manager to tailor municipal services to the needs of their communities employed citizens to assess city services and communicate to the city administrators the perceptions of problems and needs of community residents. Representative groups of local residents met in small panels to discuss similar concerns. Project funds paid for their cooperation. Project coordinators led the panels, which were conducted in an informal, fairly unstructured atmosphere. Each study had two phases, in each of which different problems were discussed. An important finding was the fact that the existence of a resource is no guarantee to a target group, such as senior citizens, that the resource is available to them (Berrill, 1974).

A town-hall approach to citizen involvement was used in Casa Grande, Arizona. This was a voluntary association of involved citizens of the city and surrounding areas "who meet to discuss community problems, study alternatives, and make recommendations to appropriate legislative and authoritative bodies" (Bolen, 1977). The association had a board that included the mayor, city manager, president of the chamber of commerce, president of the board of trustees, president of the local college, school board superintendent and president, and fifteen citizen members. The association sponsored a town-hall conference every year with voting delegates representing various ethnic and socioeconomic groups in the community. The conference used smaller discussion groups to develop policy and implementation suggestions for the coming year.

Issues in Community Needs Assessment

Communitywide needs assessment and planning are often undertaken to identify needs of groups that could not be reached otherwise. Demone (1978) notes that the network of social relationships among people seldom cluster neatly in neighborhoods and that neighborhood boundaries in urban areas are often unclear. Sometimes the most vocal advocacy group in a neighborhood represents a minority of the population. I have called attention elsewhere to the fact that assessing needs of target groups (such as the elderly or those with mental health problems) or clients of social service agencies fails to account for a great many people and their needs.

Burdine and Gottlieb (1980) have raised the issue that certain practices of community health assessment may actually subvert community need. They explore three models of community organization and social change—community development, social planning, and social action—each of which includes a community health assessment in some form and to some degree. They view the social-planning approach of the 1980s as an instrument of government or of elites to impose order on society through planning and thus to obtain social control over certain segments of society.

Any groups planning to conduct a community assessment should give thoughtful consideration to these issues, although as with any type of needs assessment, there is no one best approach. The effectiveness depends on the factors discussed in previous chapters—degree to which those involved represent the community, adequacy of the data-gathering and analysis methods, attention to causal factors, effective use of communication, consideration of differing ethnic and linguistic backgrounds, and commitment to follow through with action plans and implementation of the priority recommendations. Above all, leaders and participants must keep firmly in mind the difference between wants and needs. Unless needs and problems are sufficiently discussed and analyzed before solutions are considered, the needs assessment may very well lead to programs that do not really address the needs, and that therefore are a waste of resources.

14

Implications
for Needs Assessment
in Education, Health,
and Human Services

A distinguished computer scientist, the inventor of the first natural-language processing system, observes, "We can count, but we are rapidly forgetting to say what is worth counting and why"(Weizenbaum, 1976, p. 16). In a nutshell, that is what needs assessment is all about—to disentangle means from ends, and to determine what is worth doing. Planning without needs assessment focuses on solutions, on means. It helps the organization determine how something *can* be done, but not whether it should be done in the first place. Planning with needs assessment focuses on ends, on defining and analyzing the problems that the solutions are supposed to solve.

But to be effective, needs assessors must pose the right questions, look beyond the obvious. A case in point is a large school system that recently found itself in a dilemma. As the result of a comprehensive school-community needs study, it set priorities on improving basic reading skills and discipline, and threw major resources into solutions to those needs. Two years later it discovered, from external inputs, that it was failing to prepare its graduates with a well-rounded education, and particularly, that there were alarming deficiencies in its music and foreign languages programs. Now it is scrambling to find adequate teaching staff and to shore up curricula that had suffered erosion of support for many years. The needs study, although large in scope, relied too heavily on opinions from stakeholders whose attention was riveted on the squeaky wheel.

This chapter makes a case for increased attention to *effective* needs assessment concerned with quality of life, long-range goals, and the interaction of the organization with the larger environment. It then summarizes some predictions of future trends and their implications, especially for setting priorities and planning in the public sector.

There are several cogent reasons why needs assessment is more important and more useful than ever.

- *Reduction in resources.* With the enactment in 1981 of Public Law 97–35, categorical aid and entitlements gave way to block grants; federal mandates, to decentralization and increased state and local responsibilities; and rising expectations, to retrenchment. Cuts in monies allocated to the states averaged 20 to 25 percent. Thus, at the same time as states have been given primary responsibility for setting their own priorities and solving educational and social service problems, they have had fewer resources with which to meet the challenge.

    This reduction in resources came at a time coincident with a high rate of unemployment and a greatly depressed economy. Although the economic outlook has improved, changes in federal priorities and assistance to states have put a considerable strain on state and local resources, and careful planning is more important than ever before. Most public agencies and government units find themselves in a period of retrenchment likely to continue for several years. Needs assessment provides the tools for analyzing both present and future needs and for developing a data base for a more equitable allocation of scarce resources. It also gives direction for setting priorities on services to eliminate, add, or modify.

- *Increased competition for funds.* The combination of block grant funding with reduced funds has led to sharply increased competition among local agencies. Health and human services agencies as well as school districts will find it profitable to take a serious look at needs and priorities and to do a more competent job of documenting their requests. In spite of the gloom and skepticism with which educators and human services providers greeted block grant funding and budget cutbacks, many people have seen opportunities for rethinking needs and priorities. Some educators believe that the categories for funding were conceived more on the basis of social theory or politics than on an evidential base of what children needed. "Schools unabashedly scrambled for grant money because it was there, not because it would enable them to develop or enhance their own local programs in an orderly, coherent fashion. . . . Program evaluations, though commonly required, seemed to be operationally unrelated to continued program funding. . . . [Now] it behooves decision makers to have a pertinent data framework within which to make and defend the decisions" (Laurent, 1982, p. 3). Similarly, social service providers now have the chance to reexamine their programs and to consider assessing the needs of people in the community rather than of programs or services.

- *Opportunity for improved service delivery.* Better identification and analysis of needs, including causal analysis, will lead to better methods of meeting those needs, such as through interagency cooperation. Communitywide needs assessments, for instance, that include evaluation of present methods of delivering health services can point the way to better use of community resources to hold down the rising costs of health care. Combining needs assessment with the core/network approach to organizational planning can also lead to a better use of resources.

- *Responsiveness to changing societal needs.* Needs assessments should provide periodic assessments of environmental factors that are likely to affect the organization and the clients it serves—such factors would include shifts in demographics, in trends in related services, and in economic climate. Thus the organization can operate in a proactive rather than reactive mode, anticipating new needs or changes in the criticality level of previous ones.

- *Reconsideration of organizational goals.* Needs assessments can furnish data necessary for formulating issues facing an organization, which in turn can lead to reconsideration of organizational goals and objectives. The needs assessment component promotes a reality-based planning process. Given the kinds of structural changes that have been occurring, the dislocations in the economy, and the changes in expectations for all public services, those who are responsible for educational and human services planning will have to rethink their goals and where their organizations are likely to be going. The needs of the 1970s, as well as the methods for identifying and setting priorities on those needs, may not be applicable.

Each state or territory receiving funds under block grants is permitted wide discretion in how the funds will be used. Both state and local agencies can choose their own priorities in cutting up the pie, perhaps adding resources to a previously underserved population or need area and reducing or eliminating others. This flexibility and local discretion offer opportunities for reexamining priorities and for taking a second look at programs that have become entrenched but are no longer needed. On the other hand, there is always the danger that needs of certain populations may be ignored if local values do not support national goals having to do with equity.

Several years ago, in a time of expansion rather than retrenchment, Bolen (1977) observed that "the return of planning and decision making to the local level can do much to overcome the abstract quality and large gaps of understanding and insensitivity that comes from a planning process too highly centralized. The transfer of decision-making power casts an extremely large shadow of responsibility on local government. But only at the local level can the ordinary citizen really sense that he or she is a vital part of the process and has the power to effectuate change that can meaningfully improve the quality of life" (pp. 124–125).

The following sections consider some of the projections of major national trends that have been made by futurists and the possible implications of those trends for needs assessment. Naisbitt (1982), as well as Toffler (1980) and other writers, contend that we are in the midst of a major shift in society. During this period there is bound to be considerable tension between our expectations of events, based on past experience, and occurrences that contradict those values and expectations. Naisbitt's trends are based on an extrapolation of the present to the future—a method with which some futurists disagree. Nevertheless, certain concepts and movements that are clearly present now and that, according to most indicators, will be here for the forseeable future have relevance for the identification of needs and the needs assessment process.

Trends Affecting Public Education

1. *Increased demand by parents and the public to have a voice in educational decisions.* Even though formal needs assessments are no longer mandated for many funded programs, this trend provides an impetus for school administrators to continue to involve parents and other stakeholders in formal and informal methods to identify needs and set priorities. Advisory councils representing educators, students, and the public may well play an even greater role in this process than they do now. Many sections in the new block grant legislation contain provisions that state agencies have advisory committees broadly representative of the educational interests and general public of the state to advise on the planning, development, support, implementation, and evaluation of state programs assisted under the act. (Likewise, chapters dealing with human services contain mandates for significantly involving parents and residents of the area affected by the program.)

   Recently, many large cities have used public opinion surveys to elicit opinions of the public on educational goals and needs. As this is written, a special committee of the legislature of the state of Washington has just released the results of a statewide poll of citizens, the findings of which are expected to guide state policy and to "help shape the future of public education" in the state (Angelos, 1984, p. C1). The survey, which in part assessed the public's reaction to proposals that the committee made in an interim report last year, will be used along with two more surveys and several regional meetings to influence the committee's final recommendations to the legislature next year.

2. *Increased preference by parents for private schooling or home
    tutoring for their children.* From time to time, in order to link
    school financing with more freedom of choice, initiatives are
    brought forth to provide education vouchers to parents. The
    uncertainty of financing for public education that would
    ensue, as well as the probable changes in the nature of the
    school population as a consequence of large shifts from public
    to private schooling, must be taken into consideration in
    assessing future needs.

    This trend arises in part from an erosion of confidence
    in public education. In 1979, the Gallup Poll (Gallup, 1979)
    found that respondents expressed very little confidence in the
    schools and that, for the first time, adults considered themselves
    better educated than young people. School enrollment de-
    creased 16 percent in the 1970s. "Partly because of fewer
    students, the schools faced enormous financial problems. In
    some communities, for example, only a small percentage of
    taxpayers had children in the school system. The result is an
    erosion in local financial support, coupled with the effects of
    a generalized taxpayer revolt" (Naisbitt, 1982, p. 143). The
    revolt against high property taxes has had disastrous conse-
    quences on school financing in many states, as Californians
    can attest since the passage of Proposition 13.

    Disillusionment with the school system has fostered
    various self-help responses: parent activism, dramatic increases
    in private school enrollments, and development of new alter-
    native schools. Many parents have tried to move the education
    process from the schools into the home, either as a supplement
    or as "an outright threat to the compulsory education laws"
    (p. 143). Naisbitt cites John Holt, whose criticisms of public
    schooling have increased sharply in the last decade: "I used to
    say reform the schools. Then I said start your own school. Now
    I say take the children out entirely" (p. 144). He adds, "Several
    years ago, Holt estimated there were at least 10,000 families
    educating their children at home. In 1982 the figure was
    estimated at one million" (p. 144).

    What are the implications of these two trends? School
systems will have to reassess their goals. Most large-scale needs

assessments that engaged parents and the community in setting goals and priorities were done in the decade from about 1968 to 1978, and in many cases they have not been reviewed or modified since that time. Although it is not necessary that every needs assessment begin with a goal-preferencing stage, schools should review previous goal studies to decide whether a new one is in order—or if, in fact, anyone has been paying attention to the earlier ones! They might find, as did one fine high school that undertook a comprehensive needs assessment, that certain district and school goals were not being implemented by any department or service in the school.

3.   *Networking—the "communication that creates the linkages between people and clusters of people"* (p. 192). "Networks exist to foster self-help, to exchange information, to change society, to improve productivity and work life, and to share resources. They are structured to transmit information in a way that is quicker, more high touch, and more energy-efficient than any other process we know" (pp. 192–193). Networks offer horizontal and diagonal links among people, whereas organizational links are usually largely vertical; and because networks are nonbureaucratic, they cut across hierarchical levels. Needs assessors should take advantage of informal networks in addition to formal organizational sources and random sampling of a community to acquire data or opinions. Naisbitt points out that by using networks, we can cut down on information overload, by being able to "select and acquire only the information we need as quickly as possible. Networks cut diagonally across the institutions that house information and put people in direct contact with the person or resource they seek" (p. 197).

4.   *Changes in management styles and ages within organizations.* The new management styles will be based on networking concepts, such as informality and equality. "Its communication style will be lateral, diagonal, and bottom up; and its structure will be cross-disciplinary" (p. 198). Naisbitt believes that this change will come about because networking is the dominant management style of people who were a part of the

activist baby-boom generation. "By the late 1980s, 80 percent of total management will be under forty-five" (p. 199). The women's movement, antiwar movement, and environmental movement all grew through networks, and Naisbitt argues that "it is irrational to think they will quietly blend into the hierarchical structure once they reach the executive suite" (p. 199). Further, "Some 40 percent of the baby-boom workers during the 1980s will be college educated" (p. 199). Quality circles and Theory Z (a hybrid of American and Japanese management styles) will be more congenial to them than the past and present rigid hierarchical structures. As these management concepts become incorporated in human services and education systems, they could influence both the content and the methods of needs assessment in the future—leading to more flexibility in methods, closer attention to organizational links and needs, and willingness to engage in strategic planning.

5. *The fast growth of small towns and rural areas, based partly on decentralization of large business.* According to the 1980 census, rural areas and small towns are pulling ahead of cities in population growth for the first time since 1820. In the decade from 1970 to 1980, small towns and rural areas grew 15.5 percent faster than cities, although about 60 percent of Americans still lived in cities or suburbs. Apparently, however, the move is not back to an agricultural life but to a thinning out or deconcentration of population in counties near large metropolitan areas—a phenomenon recently labeled "ruburbia." Just as their lifestyles differ from those of the established residents, so the incoming populations will doubtless have somewhat different values and concepts of their needs for educational, social, and health services.

This trend reverses one from the preceding decades, when the large flows of people in the United States were from farms to cities and then to nearby suburbs. If the trend to move to small towns and rural areas continues, there will be many implications for needs assessment—identifying the characteristics of new populations, their needs for services and for educational opportunities, and the strains that a larger population will put on existing services and facilities. Concomitantly, this trend should be watched by cities and suburbs that stand to lose large numbers of residents.

6. *The shift in population centers from the northeast to the southwest and west.* There is an age factor in this shift, as well, since the median age of the population in the northeast is 31.8, nearly two years higher than the national average of 30. This fact holds implications for planning by postsecondary institutions because the college age population declines in some areas and rises sharply in others.

7. *The growth of service (information) jobs.* This trend has important implications for vocational educational planning and career counseling. On the face of it, the advent of the information society, with its widespread use of computers in homes, schools, and offices, would indicate the desirability of an even higher level of literacy in the population than ever before. Newspapers and magazines regularly publish articles on the need for computer literacy to be taught in the schools. In fact, it might be inferred that there will be even less place in society than there is now for the functionally illiterate, who now number one out of five adults in the United States.

Trend seven could encourage schools to limit needs assessments even more than they do now to identifying deficits in a narrow range of reading and mathematics skills, ignoring student needs related to higher-order cognitive and information-processing skills as well as to the rest of the curriculum. True, a major goal of public education is to prevent illiteracy in children and to vastly reduce illiteracy in the adult population. But too narrow a focus in needs assessment leads to overlooking other elements essential to preparing students for satisfying and productive adulthood. Furthermore, a whole new vista may open for the functionally illiterate adult, as Toffler (1980, p. 189) suggests in his description of the "Third Wave" world of the future:

> Today millions of people are excluded from the job market because they are functionally illiterate. Even the simplest jobs demand people capable of reading forms, on-off buttons, paychecks, job instruc-

tions, and the like. In the Second Wave world the ability to read was the most elemental skill required by the hiring office.

Yet illiteracy is not the same as stupidity. We know that illiterate people the world over are capable of mastering highly sophisticated skills in activities as diverse as agriculture, construction, hunting, and music. Many illiterates have prodigious memories and can speak several languages fluently—something most university-educated Americans cannot do. In Second Wave societies, however, illiterates were economically doomed.

Literacy, of course, is more than a job skill. It is the doorway to a fantastic universe of imagination and pleasure. Yet in an intelligent environment, when machines, appliances, and even walls are programmed to speak, literacy could turn out to be less paycheck-linked than it has been for the past three hundred years. Airline reservation clerks, stockroom personnel, machine operators, and repairmen may be able to function quite adequately on the job by listening rather than reading, as a voice from the machine tells them, step by step, what to do next or how to replace a broken part.

If Toffler's predictions of life in the Third Wave world are on target, educators will have to broaden their concepts of student needs and relate them more closely to the rich variety of potentials in individuals, rather than to narrow concepts of basic skills. It is interesting to note Toffler's observation that listening could well replace reading in many jobs since that communication skill is almost never assessed, let alone taught.

Trends Affecting Higher Education

Needs assessment in higher education must take account of possible futures for universities. Although universities no longer experience turmoil such as that of the late 1960s and 1970s, the university will never be the same as it was during the years following World War II, when it was "a community of relative peace, stability, and continuity" whose members shared mutually held goals (Bunzel, 1980, p. 391). Today, higher education is confronted with serious and complicated troubles.

The whole society is now in transition—but to what? It is a paradox of our times, Clark Kerr has observed, that as more and more Americans from all walks of life are able to obtain an education at some postsecondary institution, knowledge has come to be seen "as less of a source of good and more a potential source of evil." Besides, many people no longer believe that going to college will improve their prospects of getting a job. One reason educators do not know what our colleges and universities will look like in ten or twenty years is that there is little agreement among them about what education should be or do. We exalt education throughout the land, but are we developing the kinds of knowledge and attitudes of mind we want to see passed on from one generation to another? Is vocational training a substitute for education? What is our idea of an educated person [p. 392]?

Those questions are exactly related to the aspect of needs assessment that considers goals and values. In addition, establishing priorities in institutions of higher education will necessitate taking cognizance of the changes that the entire society, as well as the universities, are undergoing and will continue to undergo in the next two decades. "The future of the university will depend on how it adapts to a society that is in the process of redefining itself. It will also depend on what it conceives its basic mission and purposes to be. In the most practical terms, our institutions of higher education have a dual obligation: to expand the principle and practice of equal access and to preserve standards of excellence. The university's future will depend on how it accommodates both. In the words of former University of Chicago president Edward Levi, we must reach more minds without deserting the mind" (p. 392).

Bunzel notes several trends that will affect higher education: drops in enrollment, rising tuition and other educational costs, a substantial slowing of the growth rate of the enrollment of women, decrease in fulltime enrollment, and slowing of growth rate for professional schools (except in independent law and medical schools and in engineering, technological, and business schools). "Between now and 1985 college graduates are more likely to be employed below the level of skill for which they were trained, resulting in job dissatisfaction, high occupational mobility, and perhaps (for the first time) unemployment" (p. 394). Colleges and universities are producing a surplus of chemists, food scientists, meteorologists, oceanographers, physicists, political scientists, psychologists, and teachers.

Other factors are lower public confidence in higher education, impact of collective bargaining, shifts in power to make policy decisions away from university presidents toward contractual arrangements (part of the shift to power of the faculty as a result of union vs. management roles), diminishing of authority of boards of trustees, conflicts over tenure, and extreme competition for students, resulting sometimes in compromises of integrity. Bunzel also sees less freedom of inquiry in the biological and medical sciences because of more regulation.

Still another trend is the increase of foreign students, who may constitute 10 percent of enrollment in American colleges by 1990. Some colleges have already changed their curricula to accommodate these students. Also attempting to influence college policy are student activists who demonstrate against regents' policies of investing funds in certain businesses—American companies doing business in South Africa, for example, where apartheid is practiced by the white minority. Bunzel raises the question, "whether colleges and universities in this country have either the responsibility or the obligation to act as institutions of political action and social reform" (p. 403).

In the context of such trends as well as the demographic changes and population shifts noted by Naisbitt, which will affect higher education as well as the common schools, reevaluating priorities through needs assessment will greatly benefit institutional planning. But narrowly conceived needs studies undertaken by single colleges and universities may be of minimal use to identify priorities based on client needs. As noted in Chapter Twelve, regional and multiagency studies can do a far better job of assessing population needs, whether for education or for social services. Institutions trying desperately to survive will probably not take kindly to this view. Nevertheless, in some areas in the United States and Canada, regional needs assessments undertaken by consortia of community colleges have identified differentiated roles that the several colleges could play in serving large numbers of potential adult students who were not served by existing programs.

Trends Affecting Health and Human Services

Many of the same trends that affect needs assessment and planning in education (such as geographic shifts in population centers and changing demographics of cities and rural areas) also have an impact on human services and all community planning. There is also an increasing desire on the part of the public to have a voice in setting priorities for public services, or at least to make clear what kinds of programs they will *not* support. A study of public opinion regarding support for social services—with growing numbers of persons claiming to be in need but decreasing budgets for social welfare—found that the general public would support certain needy groups more than others: the disabled more than the poor, the elderly more than children and adults under age sixty-five, and chronic disability conditions rather than acute conditions (Cook, 1979). The degree of support for certain groups was modified, however, when the support was contingent on a particular service. For example, poor adults of working age had highest priority for support for job-related educational services but were not supported for most other services. To the extent that community needs assessments seek to marshall support as well as to identify needs, contingency factors should be built into needs surveys in order to derive a more accurate view from stakeholders.

In addition, needs assessment for health care in the future will have to take account of changes in concepts of sources of medical help, moving from reliance on the medical establishment— annual physical examinations, drugs, and surgery—to programs of self-help and preventive health care through appropriate diet and exercise and changes in life styles. Naisbitt considers that the changes in personal habits are central to medical self-help. In 1982, about half the population was exercising in some way, Americans had reduced their fat intake by about a quarter since 1965, smoking was down substantially, there was a switch from hard liquor to wine, the number of health food stores in the United States had increased from 1,200 in 1968 to more than 8,300 in 1981, and the business community was strongly supporting fitness programs (Naisbitt, 1982).

For reasons of cost as well as the interest in self-care, the health care focus was shifting from medical facilities to the home. More than half a million self-help medical groups have been formed to support home self-care. "Central to the whole self-help concept is the redefinition of health from the mere absence of disease to the existence of a positive state of wellness in the whole person" (p. 137; also see the May/June 1983 issue of *The Center Magazine* for a symposium on wellness by prominent representatives of several branches of the health care field).

The self-help trend in medicine is somewhat analogous to the desire of parents to have alternatives to traditional schooling for their children. If this trend continues, then needs assessments based solely on service statistics will identify neither target groups in need of health care nor the actual type and scope of their needs.

Implications for Communitywide Planning

If service providers are serious about serving the real needs of populations, communitywide or interagency assessments make more sense than single-agency needs studies. The area of adult basic education is a prime example of a situation in which many agencies have the responsibility and authority to provide essentially the same services. The mission of adult basic education is to bring adults up to a basic functional literacy level, as well as to provide them with life skills in five areas: job seeking, health, using community resources, consumer education, and knowledge of government and law. Many agencies with federal, state, or private foundation grants offer services, courses, and counseling in some or all of these areas— these agencies include adult basic education, community education, parks and recreation departments, community college systems and universities, alcoholism and drug education and prevention programs, vocational rehabilitation, and organizations dealing with specific groups, such as disabled adults, teenagers, displaced homemakers, and senior citizens.

It is surely in the interest of service receivers, as consumers, to have their needs known and the services provided in the most effective (as well as the most cost-effective) way. In most cases, consumers have little interest in the nature of the organization providing the service or program. But many of these organizations are competing for the same dollars, and it is to their interest to protect their territory. In communities where some of the service providers are quite small, interagency needs assessment can supply them with information they could not obtain otherwise. As resources for planning dwindle, the future should see more use of community needs assessments, with perhaps a willingness on the part of organizations to eliminate unnecessary overlapping while still maintaining enough of a plurality of offerings to give community members a wide range of choices.

Methodological Trends

In recent years, there has been a growing awareness among planners and evaluators of the inadequacy of many popular methods of assessing needs. Previous chapters have discussed strengths and shortcomings of models, data-gathering procedures, and methods of analysis and of setting priorities. Planners in the health and human services fields are strongly advocating population-based rather than service-based needs assessments. In education, a review of the history of surveys and educational planning in the public schools of the United States has identified five new or continuing patterns (Ignasias, Henkin, and Helms, 1982). They note "an assumption critical to the value system of most policy makers; that is, information, systematically gathered and organized, is prerequisite for better decision making" (p. 176). There is no reason to suppose that the trends they identify do not apply, in some degree, to needs assessment and planning in fields other than education. These trends are

1. *A focus on futurism.* "Proposed school plans and forecasts often are projected anywhere from five to twenty years into the future, and sometimes include alternate scenarios (educational

futures). Increasingly, surveys contain alternative approaches to current and future problems expressed through short- and long-term plans with contingency provisions for educational program and facilities development and funding" (p. 176).

2. *Widespread use of attitudinal surveys* with both internal and external constituencies, with the purpose "to reconcile needs of school systems with expectations of its constituencies. These efforts implicitly recognize the bargaining component and the need for compromise within the planning environment" (p. 176).

3. *The use of computer technology* to facilitate the planning process in data storage and retrieval, data analyses, and enrollment projections.

4. *Cooperative and multiagency planning,* requiring coordination of educational planners and policy makers with citizens' groups and external consultant advisors. (Ignasias, Henkin, and Helms do not, however, mention multiagency planning between school systems and other kinds of agencies.)

5. *The institutionalization of planning* through maintenance of information systems for ongoing evaluation and planning. A related aspect "is the need for continuous consultation between school officials and outside experts during documentation as well as implementation phases" (p. 177).

They add, "The importance of planning in education may reside less in its technical adequacy of vision than in the processes it conditions and the political environment within which it functions. Planning processes may yield rationalized strategies which delineate relationships between means and ends" (p. 177).

Needs assessment as a vehicle for making planning and evaluation decisions arose out of specific political and social forces and contexts. It eventually came to have a life of its own with value systems, methodologies, advocates, and critics. Those interested in systematic, rational methods of identifying and analyzing needs and setting priorities in the public interest have a rich array of processes and technologies from which to choose, with the potential for both theoretical and practical improvements in the future. In view of the foregoing social and methodological trends, organizations will find it to their advantage to incorporate needs assessment as a permanent element in a management information system, with provisions for using both internal and external information to sense trends and changing needs over time, and to use the *process* itself as a potent source of both information and organizational renewal.

References

Adams, K. A. "Needs Sensing: The Yeast for R&D Organizations." *Educational Evaluation and Policy Analysis*, 1983, *5* (1), 55–60.

Agranoff, R., and Pattakos, A. *Dimensions of Services Integration: Service Delivery, Program Linkages, Policy Management, Organizational Structure*. Human Services Monograph Series, No. 13. Washington, D.C.: Project SHARE, Department of Health and Human Services, 1979.

Alkin, M. C. "Patterns of Evaluation Use in Schools." *Evaluation Comment*, 1982, *6* (3), 9–10.

Alkin, M. C., and Daillak, R. "A Study of Evaluation Utilization." *Educational Evaluation and Policy Analysis*, 1979, *1* (4), 41–49.

Alkin, M. C., Daillak, R., and White, P. *Using Evaluations: Does Evaluation Make a Difference?* Beverly Hills, Calif.: Sage, 1979.

Alwin, D. F. (Ed.). *Survey Design and Analysis: Current Issues*. Beverly Hills, Calif.: Sage, 1978.

Anderson, S. B., and Ball, S. *The Profession and Practice of Program Evaluation*. San Francisco: Jossey-Bass, 1978.

Angelos, C. "Stiffer Public Education Demands Favored In Poll." *Seattle Times*, April 11, 1984, C-1.

Archibald, R. D., and Villoria, R. L. *Network-Based Management Systems (PERT/CPM).* New York: Wiley, 1967.

Arizona Department of Education. *Educational Needs Assessment Handbook.* Phoenix: Arizona Department of Education, 1976.

Ascher, W. *Forecasting: An Appraisal for Policy-Makers and Planners.* Baltimore, Md.: Johns Hopkins University Press, 1978.

Asher, H. B. *Causal Modeling.* Beverly Hills, Calif.: Sage, 1976.

Askegaard, L. "A Methodology for Long-Range Community Assessment Using Key Informants." Paper presented at annual conference of Evaluation Network/Evaluation Research Society, Baltimore, Md., Oct. 1982.

Atlanta Public Schools. *The Atlanta Assessment Project.* End-of-Budget-Period and Final Report. Atlanta, Ga.: Atlanta Public Schools, 1980.

Austin, S. *Involving Citizens in Seattle Schools: Highlights of a Community Survey.* Seattle, Wash.: Citizens Education Center Northwest, 1982.

Ayres, R. U. *Uncertain Future: Challenges for Decision-Makers.* New York: Wiley, 1979.

Banathy, B. H. *A Guide to Interorganizational Linkage in Education.* ITS Monograph Series, Report No. 78-1. San Francisco: Far West Laboratory for Educational Research and Development, 1978.

Bank, A., and Morris, L. L. *A Needs Assessment Kit: Guidelines and Resources for Educators.* Los Angeles: Center for the Study of Evaluation, University of California, 1979.

Barta, M. B., Ahn, U. R., and Gastright, J. F. "Some Problems in Interpreting Criterion-Referenced Test Results in a Program Evaluation." *Studies in Educational Evaluation,* 1976, *2* (3), 193–202.

Baumheier, E. C., and Heller, G. A. *Analysis and Synthesis of Needs Assessment Research in the Field of Human Services.* Denver, Colo.: Center for Social Research and Development, Denver University, 1974.

Beatty, P. T. "The Concept of Need: Proposal for a Working Definition." *Journal of the Community Development Society,* 1981, *12* (2), 39–46.

Beatty, P. T., and others. *Addressing Needs by Assessing Needs: A*

Handbook for Adult Education Program Planners. College Station: College of Education, Texas A&M University, 1980. (ED 218 493)

Beers, J. S., and Campbell, P. B. "Statewide Educational Assessment." In *State Educational Assessment Programs.* (Rev. ed.) Princeton, N.J.: Educational Testing Service, 1973.

Beevor, W. G. "Long-Range Planning: An Effective Management Strategy." Paper presented at annual meeting of International Society for Educational Planning, Toronto, Ontario, October 1981.

Bell, R. A., and others. "Service Utilization, Social Indicator, and Citizen Survey Approaches to Human Service Need Assessment." In C. C. Attkisson and others (Eds.), *Evaluation of Human Service Programs.* New York: Academic Press, 1978.

Benham, B. J., Giesen, P., and Oakes, J. "A Study of Schooling: Students' Experiences in Schools." *Phi Delta Kappan,* 1980, *61* (5), 337–340.

Bentzen, M. M., Williams, R. C., and Heckman, P. "A Study of Schooling: Adult Experiences in Schools." *Phi Delta Kappan,* 1980, *61* (6), 394–397.

Berrill, A. V. "Citizen Feedback Project. An Experiment in Community Participation." New York: New York City Office of Neighborhood Government, 1974.

Bickel, W. E., and Cooley, W. W. "The Utilization of a District-Wide Needs Assessment." Pittsburgh, Pa.: Learning Research and Development Center, University of Pittsburgh, 1981.

Bickel, W. E., and Cooley, W. W. "A District-Wide Needs Assessment: How It Worked and Why." *Discrepancy Digest,* 1982, *5* (1), 4–7.

Blackwell, P. J., and Joniak, A. J. "Conflict and Consensus Among Parents About Goals for High School Education." Paper presented at annual meeting of American Educational Research Association, Chicago, April 1974. (ED 092 817)

Blair, J. W., and Brewster, E. O., (Eds.). *Long-Range Planning for School Improvement. Resource Guide 3: Programs and Services Needs Assessment.* Harrisburg, Pennsylvania Department of Education, 1981.

Bolen, R. S. "Social Planning and Policy Development in Local

Government." In W. F. Anderson, B. J. Frieden, and M. J. Murphy (Eds.), *Managing Human Services.* Washington, D.C.: International City Management Association, 1977.

Brittingham, B. E., and Netusil, A. J. "The Reliability of Goal Ratings in a Needs Assessment Procedure." *Journal of Educational Research,* 1976, *69,* 184–188.

Bronfenbrenner, U. *the Ecology of Human Development.* Cambridge: Harvard University Press, 1979.

Bunzel, J. H. "Higher Education: Problems and Prospects." In P. Duignan and A. Rabushka (Eds.), *The United States in the 1980s.* Palo Alto, Calif.: Hoover Institution, Stanford University, 1980.

Burdine, J. N., and Gottlieb, N. H. "Community Health Assessment: A Closer Look." *Texas Rural Health Journal,* Dec. 1980, 7–24.

Burke-Peterson, K. "Positive Alternatives for Youth." *Sharing,* May/June 1982, *6* (4), 1–2, 5.

Burns, R. J. "Skyline Wide Educational Plan: The Decade of the 1980's." Dallas Independent School District, Dallas, Tex., 1974.

Burton, N., Toews, E., and Birnbaum, D. *School-Based Planning Manual.* Report No. 82-1. Seattle, Wash.: Seattle Public Schools, 1982.

Butler, K. G., Witkin, B. R., and Mercer, F. "Evaluation of Suffolk and Nassau County Projects: Demonstration Project Serving NI/LD Persons, Long Island, NYC." Syracuse, N.Y.: Syracuse University, 1982.

Butz, R. J. "Enroute Social Indicators: A School/Community Measurement of Organizational Outcomes." *Performance and Instruction Journal,* 1983, *22* (8), 28–31.

California State Department of Education. *California Assessment Program. Profiles of School District Performance 1982-83. A Guide to Interpretation.* Sacramento: Office of Program Evaluation and Research, California State Department of Education, 1983.

Campbell, J. P., and others. "The Development and Evaluation of Behaviorally Based Rating Scales." *Journal of Applied Psychology,* 1973, *57* (1), 15–22.

Canadian Commission for UNESCO. "Report of the Secretary-

General 1981-1982." Occasional paper No. 40. Ottawa: Canadian Commission for UNESCO, June 1982.

Capoccia, V. A., and Googins, B. "Social Planning in an Environment of Limited Choice." *New England Journal of Human Services,* 1982, 11 (2), 31-36.

Carlin, E., and others. *Human Resources Assessment Project.* Seattle: Clinical Training Unit, Child Development and Mental Retardation Center, University of Washington, 1981.

Cates, C. "Using Citizen Surveys: Three Approaches." *Municipal Management Innovation Series,* No. 15. Washington, D.C.: International City Management Association, February 1977.

Center for Statewide Educational Assessment. *State Educational Assessment Programs: 1973 Revision.* Princeton, N.J.: Educational Testing Service, 1973.

Chicago Panel on Public School Finances. "Recommendations for Improvement: The Chicago School Budget and Budget Process." Chicago: Chicago Panel on Public School Finances, Oct. 28, 1982.

City of Hayward Social Services Needs Committee. "Hayward Needs Assessment." Unpublished final report. Hayward, Calif.: Human Services Department, City of Hayward, 1978.

Clark, T. N. "Community Social Indicators: From Analytical Models to Policy Applications." *Urban Affairs Quarterly,* 1973, *9* (1), 3-36.

Clifton, O. B. "Methods of Determining Inservice Training Needs of Beginning County Extension Agents." Unpublished doctoral dissertation, Texas A&M University, 1969.

Cloud, R. B. "The Opinions of Selected School Personnel and Involved Citizens Regarding Secondary Curriculum Development Needs, Processes and Procedures in the L'Anse Creuse Public School District in Macomb County, Michigan." Unpublished doctoral dissertation, Department of Education, Curriculum Development, Wayne State University, 1973.

Clough, L. *Summit County Needs Assessment: A Preliminary Report.* Akron, Ohio: Metropolitan Human Services Commission and Institute for Futures Studies and Research, University of Akron, 1982.

Clough, L., and Gappert, G. *Long-Range Planning Research for the Summit County Children Services Board.* Akron, Ohio: Institute for Futures Studies and Research, University of Akron, 1981.

Cochran, N. "On the Limiting Properties of Social Indicators." *Evaluation and Program Planning,* 1979, *2,* 1-4.

Cohen, B. J. "Do You Really Want to Conduct a Needs Assessment?" Philadelphia: Management and Behavioral Science Center, University of Pennsylvania, 1981.

Cohen, B. J. "Managing Retrenchment in Human Services Agencies." *Sharing,* 1982, *6* (2), 4-5.

College Entrance Examination Board. *Academic Preparation for College: What Students Need to Know and Be Able to Do.* New York: The College Board, prepublication copy, 1983.

Colorado State Department of Education. *Colorado Adult Needs Assessment Survey Instruments for Citizens, Employers, and Agencies, 1974.* Denver: Colorado State Department of Education, 1974. (ED 128-401)

Commission on Educational Planning—Phi Delta Kappa. *Educational Planning Model.* (Rev. ed.) Bloomington, Ind.: Phi Delta Kappa Center for Dissemination of Innovative Programs, 1978.

Consulting Services Corporation. *An Assessment of the Educational Needs of Indian Students in the State of Arizona.* Phoenix: Arizona State Department of Public Instruction, 1969. (ED 066 275)

Consulting Services Corporation. *Phase II: An Assessment of Educational Needs for Students in Washington State.* Prepared for Title III ESEA Advisory Council. Seattle: Consulting Services Corporation, 1970. (ED 082 311)

Cook, F. L. *Who Should Be Helped. Public Support for Social Services.* Sage Library of Social Research, Vol. 83. Beverly Hills, Calif.: Sage, 1979.

Cope, R. G. *Strategic Planning, Management, and Decision Making.* AAHE-ERIC/Higher Education Research Project No. 9, 1981. Washington, D.C.: American Association for Higher Education, 1981.

Cox, J. *Basics of Questionnaire Construction in Educational Settings.* Los Angeles, Calif.: Division of Program Evaluation, Research, and Pupil Services, Office of the Los Angeles County Superintendent of Schools, May 1976.

Crane, L. R., Crofton, C., and Kandaswamy, S. "Needs Assessment for Evaluation Utilization Training." Paper presented at annual meeting of American Educational Research Association, New York, March 1982.

Crouthamel, W. and Preston, S. M. *Needs Assessment Resource Guide.* Atlanta: Research and Development Utilization Project, Georgia Department of Education, 1979.

Crumpton, J. "A Needs Analysis Instrument for Focusing Training Activities in Complex Organizations." Paper presented at Adult Education Research Conference, Chicago, April 1974.

Cummins, C. C., Jr. "A Fault-Tree Analysis of Computer Support Services: Utah State Board of Education Division of Data Processing." Unpublished doctoral dissertation, Department of Educational Administration, Brigham Young University, 1977.

Cunico, G. "A Delphi Approach to the Future of Industrial Education." Unpublished doctoral dissertation, Department of Industrial Education, Utah State University, 1973.

Curtis, W. R. *Managing Human Services with Less: New Strategies for Local Leaders.* Human Services Monograph Series, No. 26. Washington, D.C.: Project SHARE, Department of Health and Human Services, 1981.

Dajani, J. S., and Murdock, M. S. *Assessing Basic Human Needs in Rural Jordan.* Contract No. AID-278-322. Washington, D.C.: U.S. Agency for International Development, 1978.

Danowski, J. A. "Informational Aging: Implications for Alternative Futures of Societal Information Systems." Paper presented at annual meeting of International Communication Association, Chicago, 1975. (ED 020 611)

Delahanty, D. S. "Service Coordination: An Introduction to the Louisville/Jefferson County, Kentucky System." In *Coordinating Human Services at the Local Level: Proceedings of the First National Network Building Conference.* Falls Church, Va.: Institute for Information Studies, 1980.

Delahanty, D. S., and Atkins, G. L. *Strategic Local Planning: A Collaborative Model.* Human Services Monograph Series, No. 23. Washington, D.C.: Project SHARE, Department of Health and Human Services, 1981.

Delbecq, A. L., and Van de Ven, A. H. "A Group Process Model for

Problem Identification and Program Planning." *Journal of Applied Behavioral Science,* 1971, 7, 466–492.

Dell, D. L. "Magnitude Estimation Scaling Procedures of Patron Assessment of School Objectives. Illustrative Brief." Menlo Park, Calif.: Stanford Research Institute, 1973a.

Dell, D. L., "Patron Assessment of School Objectives for M—— School." Menlo Park, Calif.: Stanford Research Institute, 1973b.

Dell, D. L., and Meeland, T. "Needs Assessment Scaling Procedures." Menlo Park, Calif.: Stanford Research Institute, 1973.

DeLorme, H. L. *Pupil-Perceived Needs Assessment.* Philadelphia, Pa.: Research for Better Schools, 1974.

Demaline, R. E. *An Overview of Needs Assessment.* Portland, Oreg.: Northwest Regional Educational Laboratory, 1982.

Demaline, R. E., and Quinn, W. D. *Hints for Planning and Conducting a Survey and a Bibliography of Survey Methods.* Kalamazoo: Evaluation Center, Western Michigan University, 1979.

Demone, H. W., Jr. *Stimulating Human Services Reform.* Human Services Monograph Series, No. 8. Washington, D.C.: Project SHARE, Department of Health and Human Services, 1978.

Dickinson, G. *Getting to Know Your Community: Data for Community Adult Education Programming in British Columbia.* Victoria: Continuing Education Division, Ministry of Education, Province of British Columbia, July 1981.

Dobmeyer, T., and others. "Improved Coordination of Human Services: Final Report." Vol. 3. Needs Survey: A Technical Report. Minneapolis, Minn.: Institute for Interdisciplinary Studies, 1972.

Driessen, G. J. "Cause Tree Analysis: Measuring How Accidents Happen and the Probabilities of Their Causes." Paper presented at 78th annual convention of American Psychological Association, Miami Beach, Fla., Sept. 3–8, 1970.

Dudley, D. "Partnerships in Human Services: Experiences of the Seattle-King County Area." In *Coordinating Human Services at the Local Level: Proceedings of the First National Network Building Conference.* Falls Church, Va.: Institute for Information Studies, 1980.

Duignan, P., and Rabushka, A., (Eds.). *The United States in the*

1980s. Palo Alto, Calif.: Hoover Institution, Stanford University, 1980.

Eastmond, J. N., Jr. "The Implementation of a Model for Needs Assessment in Higher Education." Unpublished doctoral dissertation, Department of Educational Psychology, University of Utah, 1976.

Eastmond, J. N., Sr. *Needs Assessment: A Manual of Procedures for Educators.* Salt Lake City, Utah: Worldwide Education and Research Institute, January 1974.

Educational Testing Service. *Institutional Goals Inventory.* Princeton, N.J.: College and University Programs, Educational Testing Service, 1974.

English, F. W., and Kaufman, R. A. *Needs Assessment: A Focus for Curriculum Development.* Washington, D.C.: Association for Supervision and Curriculum Development, 1975.

Ericson, C. "System Safety Analytical Technology—Fault Tree Analysis." Seattle, Wash.: The Boeing Company, 1970.

Evashwick, C., Oatis, S., and Herriott, M. *Health and Social Service Needs of the Elderly: A Comparison of Residents of Public Housing and Residents of the Neighboring Community.* Seattle: University of Washington Institute on Aging, Dec. 1980.

Ferguson, S., and Ferguson, S.D. (Eds.). *Intercom: Readings in Organizational Communication.* Rochelle Park, N.J.: Hayden, 1980.

Fidler, J., and Loughran, D. R. "A System Approach." In F. C. Pennington (Ed.), *New Directions for Continuing Education: Assessing Educational Needs of Adults,* no. 7. San Francisco: Jossey-Bass, 1980.

Flanagan, J. C. "The Critical Incident Technique." *Psychological Bulletin,* 1954, *54,* 327-358.

Foster, G. R., and Southard, M. "Criteria for Prioritizing Needs: The Practitioner's Perspective." Paper presented at annual meeting of American Educational Research Association, New York, March 1982.

Frey, J. H. *Survey Research by Telephone.* Beverly Hills, Calif.: Sage, 1983.

Frisbie, R. D. "Field Analysis: Something More Than Needs Assessment." Paper presented at annual meeting of Evaluation Network/Evaluation Research Society, Austin, Tex., Oct. 1981.

Gable, R. K. *Special Education Inservice. Needs Assessment.* Hartford: Bureau of Pupil Personnel and Special Educational Services, Connecticut State Department of Education, 1980.

Gable, R. K., Pecheone, R. L., and Gillung, T. B. "A Needs Assessment Model for Establishing Personnel Training Priorities." *Teacher Education and Special Education,* 1981, *4* (4), 8–14.

Gallup, G. H. "The Eleventh Annual Gallup Poll of the Public's Attitudes Toward the Public Schools." *Phi Delta Kappan,* 1979, *61* (1), 33–45.

Glass, T. "What the Community Wants." *Council of Educational Facility Planners Journal,* 1977, *2,* 13–16.

Goldhaber, G. M., and Richetto, G. "ICA Communication Audit of Wichita State University." Report submitted to the Wichita State University Communication Audit Liaison Team. Wichita, Kans.: July 1977.

Goldhaber, G. M., and Rogers, D. P. *Auditing Organizational Communication Systems: The ICA Communication Audit.* Dubuque, Iowa: Kendall/Hunt, 1979.

Goodlad, J. I., Sirotnik, K. A., and Overman, B. C. "An Overview of 'A Study of Schooling.'" *Phi Delta Kappan,* 1979, *61* (3), 174–178.

Gould, J., and Kolb, W. L. (Eds.). *A Dictionary of the Social Sciences.* New York: Macmillan, 1964.

Goza, B. K., Strube, M. R., and Fennimore, D. "Community Needs Assessment for Formative Evaluation and Applied Theoretical Research." Paper presented at annual meeting of Evaluation Network/Evaluation Research Society, Baltimore, Md., Oct. 1982.

Green, T. B., and Pietri, P. H. "Using Nominal Grouping to Improve Upward Communication." In S. Ferguson and S. D. Ferguson (Eds.), *Intercom: Readings in Organizational Communication.* Rochelle Park, N.J.: Hayden, 1980.

Guba, E. G., and Lincoln, Y. S. *Effective Evaluation.* San Francisco: Jossey-Bass, 1981.

Guba, E. G., and Lincoln, Y. S. "The Place of Values in Needs Assessment." *Educational Evaluation and Policy Analysis,* 1982, *4* (3), 311–320.

Gundersdorf, J. *Human Service Needs Assessment Study*. Durham, N.H.: New England Municipal Center, 1975.

Haasl, D. F. "Advanced Concepts in Fault Tree Analysis." *Proceedings, Systems Safety Symposium*, Seattle: University of Washington and the Boeing Company, 1965.

Hacker, A. "Lost Our Census." *Harper's*, April 1983, *266* (1595), 16.

Hanley, P. E., and Moore, K. D. "Development and Validation of an Early Childhood Elementary Teacher Needs Assessment Profile." Paper presented at study conference of Association for Childhood Educational International, St. Louis, Mo., April 9, 1979.

Hansen, B. P., and O'Neill, J. *Educational Needs Assessment Survey*. Pittsburgh, Pa.: Educational Services, Westinghouse Learning, 1973.

Hathaway, W. E. "Graphic Display Procedures." In N. L. Smith (Ed.), *Communication Strategies in Evaluation*. Beverly Hills, Calif.: Sage, 1982.

Heathers, G., Roberts, J., and Weinberger, J. *Educators' Guide for the Future*. Philadelphia, Pa.: Research for Better Schools, Inc., 1977.

Heise, D. R. *Causal Analysis*. New York: Wiley, 1975.

Helmer, O. "The Use of the Delphi Technique in Problems of Educational Innovations." Santa Monica, Calif.: Rand Corporation, 1966.

Helmer, O. *Looking Forward: A Guide to Futures Research*. Beverly Hills, Calif.: Sage, 1983.

Hendricks, M. "Service Delivery Assessment: Qualitative Evaluations at the Cabinet Level." In N. L. Smith (Ed.), *New Directions for Program Evaluation: Federal Efforts to Develop New Evaluation Methods*, no. 12. San Francisco: Jossey-Bass, Dec. 1981.

Hendricks, M. "Oral Policy Briefings." In N. L. Smith (Ed.), *Communication Strategies in Evaluation*. Beverly Hills, Calif.: Sage, 1982.

Herman, J. J., and Kaufman, R. A. "Organizational Success and the Planning Role(s) and Perspectives of a Superintendent." *Performance and Instruction Journal*, 1983, *22* (8), 16–21.

Hershkowitz, M. "A Regional ETV Network: Community Needs and System Structure." Report for Regional Education Service

Agency of Appalachian Maryland. Silver Spring, Md.: Operations Research, Inc., October 1973.

Hershkowitz, M. *Statewide Educational Needs Assessment: Results from Selected Model States.* Silver Spring, Md.: Hershkowitz Associates, 1974.

Hill-Scott, K. "Assessing the Status of Child Care." Los Angeles: Graduate School of Architecture and Urban Planning, University of California at Los Angeles, 1977.

Hirokawa, R. Y. "Group Communication and Problem-Solving Effectiveness: An Investigation of Group Phases." *Human Communication Research,* 1983, *9* (4), 291-305.

Hirschhorn, L. "Core Network: A Program Planning Model for Assessing an Agency's Developmental Potential." Philadelphia: Management and Behavioral Science Center, Wharton School, University of Pennsylvania, 1982.

Hirschhorn, L., and Associates. *Cutting Back: Retrenchment and Redevelopment in Human and Community Services.* San Francisco: Jossey-Bass, 1983.

Hoaglin, D. C., and others. *Data for Decisions. Information Strategies for Policymakers.* Cambridge, Mass.: Abt Books, 1982.

Hoepfner, R. "Published Tests and the Needs of Educational Accountability." *Educational and Psychological Measurement,* 1974, *34,* 103-109.

Hoepfner, R., and others, "Report on the Field Testing of the CSE Elementary School Evaluation Kit: Needs Assessment." *CSE Report No. 70.* Los Angeles: Center for the Study of Evaluation, University of California at Los Angeles, Sept. 1971.

Hofmann, C. M., and Rancer, M. D. "Managing Community Change." *Municipal Management Innovation Series,* No. 28. Washington, D.C.: International City Management Association, Winter 1978-1979.

Houston, W. R., and others. *Assessing School/College/Community Needs.* Omaha: The Center for Urban Education, The University of Nebraska at Omaha, 1978.

Hunt, B., and others. *Conducting a Student Needs Assessment.* Portland, Oreg.: ESEA Title I Evaluation Technical Assistance Centers, Northwest Regional Educational Laboratory, 1982.

Ignasias, C. D., Henkin, A. B., and Helms, L. B. "Looking Back at the Future: Public School Surveys and Educational Planning." *Peabody Journal of Education,* 1982, *59* (5), 170-179.

Ingwerson, M. "A City Where Officials Go Door to Door Asking How They Can Do Better." *Christian Science Monitor,* Jan. 11, 1983.

Institute for Information Studies. *Highlights Report on Developing Public/Private Partnerships in Human Services: A Conference.* Rochester, N.Y., April 1981. Falls Church, Va.: Institute for Information Studies, 1981a.

Institute for Information Studies. *Proceedings of the Second National Network-Building Conference for Coordinating Human Services at the Local Level.* San Francisco, June 1981. Falls Church, Va.: Institute for Information Studies, 1981b.

Instructional Systems Group. *Needs Assessment: A Check-Up on Student Learning.* Huntington Beach, Calif.: INSGROUP, Oct. 1974.

Ish, D. C. *Getting to Know Your Community. A Lower Mainland Supplementary Report on Data for Community Adult Education Programming in British Columbia.* Victoria: Continuing Education Division, Ministry of Education, Province of British Columbia, Aug. 1982.

Jackson, O. *An Assessment for Determining Appropriate Programming to Reduce Homicides and Violent Crimes.* Phoenix, Ariz.: Kunisawa and Associates, 1981a.

Jackson, O. *1981 Alcohol Services Needs Assessment for Maricopa County.* Phoenix, Ariz.: Kunisawa and Associates, 1981b.

Johansson, S. *Mot en teori for social rapportering* [Toward a Theory of Social Reporting]. Stockholm, Sweden: SOFI, 1979.

John, DeW. *Managing the Human Service "System": What Have We Learned from Services Integration?* Human Services Monograph Series, No. 4. Denver, Colo.: Center for Social Research and Development, Denver Research Institute/University of Denver, 1977.

Johnston, A. P. "Proposition Development, Cross-Impact Analysis and Futures History as a Prologue to Long-Range Planning." Paper presented at annual meeting of International Society of Educational Planners, Nashville, Tenn., Feb. 1976.

Joint Committee on Standards for Educational Evaluation. *Standards for Evaluations of Educational Programs, Projects, and Materials.* New York: McGraw-Hill, 1981.

Jordan, W. *The School and Community: Partners in Education.* 2d Ed Fresno, Calif.' Fresno County Department of Education, July 1973.

Jung, S. M. "Evaluative Uses of Unconventional Measurement Techniques in an Educational System." *California Journal of Educational Research,* 1971, *22* (2), 48–57.

Kahn, H., and Wiener, A. J. *The Year 2000. A Framework for Speculation on the Next Thirty-Three Years.* New York: Macmillan, 1967.

Kamehameha Schools/Bernice Pauahi Bishop Estate. *Native Hawaiian Educational Assessment Project.* Honolulu, Hawaii: Office of Program Evaluation and Planning, Kamehameha Schools/Bernice Pauahi Bishop Estate, 1983.

Kamis, E. "Sound, Targeted Compassion: Assessing the Needs of and Planning Services for Deinstitutionalized Clients." In I. D. Rutman (Ed.), *Planning for Deinstitutionalization: A Review of Principles, Methods, and Applications.* Human Services Monograph Series, No. 28. Washington, D.C.: Project SHARE, Department of Health and Human Services, 1981.

Kamis-Gould, E., and others. "A Need-Based Planning Model for Resource Allocation and Management." Paper presented at 90th annual meeting of the American Psychological Association, Washington, D.C., Aug. 1982.

Kaufman, R. *Educational System Planning.* Englewood Cliffs, N.J.: Prentice-Hall, 1972.

Kaufman, R. "Determining and Diagnosing Organizational Needs." *Group and Organization Studies,* 1981, *6* (3), 312–322.

Kaufman, R. *Identifying and Solving Problems: A System Approach.* (3d ed.) San Diego, Calif.: University Associates, 1982a.

Kaufman, R. "Means and Ends: Needs Assessment, Needs Analysis, and Front-End Analysis." *Educational Technology,* 1982b, *22* (11).

Kaufman, R. "A Holistic Planning Model." *Performance and Instruction Journal,* 1983a, *22* (8), 3–12.

Kaufman, R. "Needs Assessment." In F. W. English (Ed.), *Fundamental Curriculum Decisions.* ASCD 1983 Yearbook. Alexandria, Va.: Association for Supervision and Curriculum Development, 1983b.

Kaufman, R. "Planning and Organizational Improvement Terms." *Performance and Instruction Journal,* 1983c, *22* (8), 12–15.

Kaufman, R., and English, F. W. *Needs Assessment: Concept and Application.* Englewood Cliffs, N.J.: Educational Technology Publications, 1979.

Kaufman, R., Johnson, J. C., and Nickols, F. K. "Organizational Planning and Conventional Wisdom." *Training and Development Journal,* 1979, *33* (9), 70–76.

Kaufman, R., and Stakenas, R. G. "Needs Assessment and Holistic Planning," *Educational Leadership,* 1981, *38* (8), 612–616.

Kaufman, R., and Stone, B. *Planning for Organizational Success: A Practical Guide.* New York: Wiley, 1983.

Kaufman, R., and others. "Relating Needs Assessment, Program Development, Implementation, and Evaluation." *Journal of Instructional Development,* 1981, *4* (4), 17–26.

Kay, F. DeW., Jr. "Applications of Social Area Analysis to Program Planning and Evaluation." *Evaluation and Program Planning,* 1978, *1,* 65–78.

Kearney, W. J. "Behaviorally Anchored Rating Scales—MBO's Missing Ingredient." *Personnel Journal,* 1979, 20–25.

Kells, H. R. "Some Theoretical and Practical Suggestions for Institutional Assessment." In M. W. Peterson (Ed.), *New Directions for Institutional Research: Institutional Assessment for Self-Improvement,* no. 29. San Francisco: Jossey-Bass, 1981.

Kemerer, R. W., and Schroeder, W. L. "Determining the Importance of Community-Wide Adult Education Needs." *Adult Education Quarterly,* 1983, *33* (4), 201–214.

Kennedy, M. "Teachers' Stress Reactions to District Use of Test Scores." *Evaluation Comment,* 1982, *6* (3), 8–9.

Kenworthy, M. B., and others. *Needs Assessment—Sustained Cycle.* ESEA title IV-C Developmental/Innovative Projects. 1979–80 End-of-Year Report. Project 3718. Saratoga, Calif.: Los Gatos Joint Union High School District, Saratoga High School, Aug. 1980.

Kimmel, W. A. *Needs Assessment: A Critical Perspective.* Washington, D.C.: Office of Program Systems, Office of the Assistant Secretary for Planning and Evaluation, U.S. Department of Health, Education, and Welfare, Dec. 1977.

King, D. C., and Beevor, W. G. "Long-Range Thinking." *Personnel Journal*, Sept. 1978, *57*, 504–509.

King, J. A., and others. "Profiling the Needs of Older Persons: A Case Study." Toledo, Ohio: Area Office on Aging of Northwestern Ohio, 1980.

Klein, M. F., Tye, K. A., and Wright, J. E. "A Study of Schooling: Curriculum." *Phi Delta Kappan*, 1979, *61* (4), 244–248.

Knox, A. B. "Leadership Strategies for Meeting New Challenges. Priority Setting." In Alan B. Knox (Ed.), *New Directions for Continuing Education: Leadership Strategies for Meeting New Challenges*, no. 13. San Francisco: Jossey-Bass, 1982.

Lambert, H. E. "Fault Trees for Decision Making in Systems Analysis." Unpublished doctoral dissertation, Department of Nuclear Energy, University of California, Berkeley, 1975.

Landy, F. J. "The Development of Scales for the Measurement of Updating." In S. S. Dubin, H. Shelton, and J. McConnell, (Eds.), *Maintaining Professional and Technical Competence of the Older Engineer—Engineering and Psychological Aspects*. Washington, D.C.: American Society for Engineering Education, 1974.

Landy, F. J., and Guion, R. M. "Development of Scales for the Measurement of Work Motivation." *Organizational Behavior and Human Performance*, 1970, *5*, 93–103.

Lane, K. R., Crofton, C., and Hall, G. J. "Assessing Needs for School District Allocation of Federal Funds." Paper presented at annual meeting of the American Educational Research Association, Montreal, Canada, April 1983.

Lansing School District. *Needs Assessment Handbook*. Lansing, Mich.: Lansing School District, 1977.

Lansing School District. *Planning Manual 1979–80*. Lansing, Mich.: Lansing School District, 1979.

Lansing School District. *Comprehensive Planning Report of the Lansing School District*. Lansing, Mich.: Lansing School District, 1983.

Laurent, J. "President's Corner." *Washington Educational Research Association Newsletter*, 1982, *5* (2), 3.

Leach, J. J. "Organization Needs Analysis: A New Methodology." *Training and Development Journal*, 1979, *33* (9), 66–69.

League of California Cities. *Assessing Human Needs.* Sacramento: League of California Cities, 1975.

League of California Cities. *Social Element Planning in California.* Sacramento: League of California Cities, 1977.

Lefkowitz, B. "Training the Troubled Ones." *Psychology Today,* 1982, *16* (9), 12–15.

Lehman, R. "Evaluation of Inservice." Panel discussion presented at annual meeting of Washington Educational Research Association, Seattle, Nov. 6, 1981. In *A SIRS Report on In-Service Education,* School Information and Research Service, 1981, *1,* (3), 25–26.

Lehnen, P. A., and Witkin, B. R. "Focus Group Interview: Report to San Lorenzo High School." Hayward, Calif.: Alameda County Office of Education, 1977a.

Lehnen, P. A., and Witkin, B. R. "Needs Assessment Report: Marina High School and San Lorenzo High School." Hayward, Calif.: Alameda County Office of Education, 1977b.

Leithwood, K. A., and Montgomery, D. J. "A Framework for Planned Educational Change: Application to the Assessment of Program Implementation." *Educational Evaluation and Policy Analysis,* 1982, *4* (2), 157–167.

LeSage, E. C., Jr. "A Quantitative Approach to Educational Needs Assessment." *Canadian Journal of University Continuing Education,* 1980a, *6* (2), 6–13.

LeSage, E. C., Jr. "LeSage Responds." *Canadian Journal of University Continuing Education,* 1980b, 7 (1), 33–34.

Leviton, L. C., and Hughes, E. F. X. "Research on the Utilization of Evaluations: A Review and Synthesis." *Evaluation Review,* 1981, *5* (4), 525–548.

Lewis, J. L. "Problems Encountered in Conducting an Assessment of Educational Needs in Selected Ohio School Districts." Paper presented at annual meeting of the American Educational Research Association, Toronto, Canada, March 27–31, 1978.

Lodge, M. B. *Magnitude Scaling. Quantitative Measurement of Opinions.* Quantitative Applications in the Social Sciences, No. 07-025. Beverly Hills, Calif.: Sage, 1981.

Lodge, M. B., and others. "The Psychophysical Scaling and Validation of a Political Support Scale." *American Journal of Political Science,* 1975, *19,* 611–649.

Long, R. W. "A Fault Tree Approach to the Analysis of Perceived Internal Communication Problems in an Expanding Multi-Campus Community College District." Unpublished doctoral dissertation, Department of Educational Administration, Brigham Young University, 1976.

Lucco, R. J. *Developing and Establishing Local School District Goals.* PERM Handbook Series, Vol. 2. Hartford: Division of Educational Administration, Connecticut State Department of Education, 1980.

Lund, B., and McGechaen, S. *CE Programmer's Manual.* Victoria, B.C.: Continuing Education Division, Ministry of Education, 1981.

McCallon, E., and McClaran, R. Determining an Appropriate Sampling Method. Austin, Tex.: Learning Concepts, 1974.

McClellan, P. P. "The Pulaski Project: An Innovative Drug Abuse Prevention Program in an Urban High School." *Journal of Psychedelic Drugs,* 1975, *7* (4), 355–362.

McCollough, T. *Project Redesign.* Palo Alto, Calif.: Palo Alto Unified School District, 1975.

MacQuarrie, D. "Needs Assessment: What It Is and What It Isn't." Paper presented at meeting of Washington Educational Research Association, Seattle, Wash., March 1982.

Macy, D. J. "Research Briefs." In N. L. Smith (Ed.), *Communication Strategies in Evaluation.* Beverly Hills, Calif.: Sage, 1982.

Maier, N. R. F. "Assets and Liabilities in Group Problem Solving: The Need for an Integrative Function." In S. Ferguson and S. D. Ferguson (Eds.), *Intercom: Readings in Organizational Communication.* Rochelle Park, N.J.: Hayden, 1980.

Maslow, A. H. *Motivation and Personality.* New York: Harper & Row, 1954.

Mastrine, B., Elder, J., and Delahanty, D. "Skills and Techniques for Collaborative Human Services Planning." Summary of workshop presentation. In *Proceedings of the Second National Network-Building Conference for Coordinating Human Services at the Local Level.* Falls Church, Va.: Institute for Information Studies, 1981.

Mattimore-Knudson, R. "The Concept of Need: Its Hedonistic and Logical Nature." *Adult Education,* 1983, *33* (2), 117–124.

Mills, O. R., and Hamilton, D. L. *School Community Climate Survey Guide.* Columbus, Ohio: Battelle Center for Improved Education, 1976.

Misanchuk, E. R. "A Methodological Note on Quantitative Approaches to Educational Needs Assessment." *Canadian Journal of University Continuing Education,* 1980, 7 (1), 31–33.

Misanchuk, E. R. "The Analysis of Multi-Component Training Needs Data." Paper presented at annual meeting of Association for Educational Communications and Technology, Dallas, Tex., May 1982a.

Misanchuk, E. R. "Toward a Multi-Component Model of Educational and Training Needs." Paper presented at annual meeting of Association for Educational Communications and Technology, Dallas, Tex., May 1982b.

Misanchuk, E. R., and Scissons, E. H. *Saskatoon Business Training Needs Identification Study: Final Report.* Saskatoon: University of Saskatchewan, Nov. 1978.

Mitchell, A., and Gallegos, A. L. "Unification of Social Services— The Utah Experience." In *Coordinating Human Services at the Local Level: Proceedings of the First National Network Building Conference.* Falls Church, Va.: Institute for Information Studies, 1980.

Moore, V. R., and Senungetuk, J. E. "Statewide Community Participation in Needs Assessment." Paper presented at annual meeting of American Educational Research Association, Chicago, April 1974. (ED 093 984)

Morgan, K. *Project ACCESS: Summary of School-Based Plans.* Seattle, Wash.: Seattle Public Schools, Aug. 1982.

Morgan, L. *Districtwide Needs Assessment: Final Project Report.* San Diego, Calif.: Office of Planning and Evaluation Services, San Diego Community College District, 1975.

Moroney, R. M. "Needs Assessment for Human Services." In W. F. Anderson, B. J. Frieden, and M. J. Murphy (Eds.), *Managing Human Services.* Washington, D.C.: International City Management Association, 1977.

Myers, E. C., and Koenigs, S. S. "A Framework for Comparing Needs Assessment Activities." Paper presented at annual meeting of American Educational Research Association, San Francisco, April 1979.

Naisbitt, J. *Megatrends: Ten New Directions Transforming Our Lives.* New York: Warner Books, 1982.

Neuber, K. A., and others. *Needs Assessment. A Model for Community Planning.* SAGE Human Services Guide 14. Beverly Hills, Calif.: Sage, 1980.

Nguyen, T. D., Attkisson, C. C., and Bottino, M. J. "Definition and Identification of Human Service Need in a Community Context." Paper presented at National Conference on Needs Assessment in Health and Human Services, University of Louisville, Louisville, Ky., March 1976.

Nichols, J. L. "Needs Assessment." Monograph 6 (2). Pittsburgh, Pa.: Westinghouse Learning Corporation; n.d.

Nisbet, R. "What to Do When You Don't Live in a Golden Age." *American Scholar,* 1982, *51* (2), 229–241.

Noggle, N. L. "Supplementing Summative Findings with Formative Data." Paper presented at annual meeting of American Educational Research Association, New York City, March 19, 1982.

Nowakowski, J. M., (Ed.) *The Toledo Catalog: Assessment of Students and School Administration.* Vol. 1: *Students;* Vol. 2: *School Administration.* Boston: Kluwer-Nighoff, 1983.

Opinion Research Corporation. *Goals for Elementary and Secondary Public Schools in New Jersey. A Survey Among New Jersey Residents.* Trenton: New Jersey State Department of Education, 1972.

Orlich, D. C. *Designing Sensible Surveys.* Pleasantville, N.Y.: Redgrave, 1978.

O'Toole, J. "How to Forecast Your Own Working Future." *The Futurist,* 1982, *16* (1), 5–11.

Pecheone, R. L., and Gable, R. K. "The Identification of Inservice Training Needs and Their Relationship to Teacher Demographic Characteristics, Attitude Toward, and Knowledge of Mildly Handicapped Children." Paper presented at 62d annual meeting of American Educational Research Association, Toronto, Canada, March 1978.

Petrovskiy, S. A., and Khairov, R. I. "Towards a Synthesis of a

Study of the Social Value of Science." *Impact of Science on Society,* 1979, *29* (3), 191–199.

Porter, D. T. "The ICA Communication Audit: 1979." *Norms and Instrument Documentation for Seventeen Audits Using the Survey (1974–1979).* West Lafayette, Ind.: Department of Communication, Purdue University, 1979.

Pratt, D. *Curriculum: Design and Development.* New York: Harcourt Brace Jovanovich, 1980.

Province of Sasketchewan. "Report of the Minister's Advisory Committee on Community Colleges." Regina: Department of Continuing Education, Province of Sasketchewan, Canada, 1972.

Radig, J. E. *Community Education: Need/Resource Assessment Guidebook.* Pitman, N.J.: Educational Improvement Center, South Jersey Region, n.d. (ED 123 769)

Rasp, A., Jr. *Consensus Formation on Educational Outcomes Using a Modified Delphi Technique.* Olympia: Office of the Washington State Superintendent of Public Instruction, 1972. (ED 090 363)

Rasp, A., Jr. "A New Tool for Administrators: Delphi and Decision Making." North Central Association Quarterly, 1974, *48* (3), 320–325.

Ravitch, D. "A Wasted Decade—Urban Educators Have Frittered Away Ten Years Searching for Panaceas." *The New Republic,* 1977, *177* (19), 11–13.

Reimer, D. J., Wahl, J. R., and Lathrop, B. A. *Hayward Social Needs Assessment Survey.* Berkely, Calif.: Planning, Evaluation, Research Corporation, May 1977.

Research for Better Schools. *Planning Schools for the Future: Workshop.* Philadelphia, Pa.: Research for Better Schools, Inc., 1977.

Rich, R. F. *Social Science Information and Public Policy Making.* San Francisco: Jossey-Bass, 1981.

Rindfleisch, N. J., Toomey, B. G., and Soldano, K. *Assessing Training Needs in Children's Services: How to Do It.* Report of the Ohio-Wisconsin Children's Services Training Needs Assessment Project. Columbus: College of Social Work, Ohio State University, 1980.

Roberson, D. R., and Kees, P. W. "Self Study: The Profile of a

System." Paper presented at annual conference of American
Educational Research Association, New York, March 1982.

Roberts, N. H., and others. *Fault Tree Handbook*. Report for
Probabilistic Analysis Staff, Office of Nuclear Regulatory Re-
search, U.S. Nuclear Regulatory Commission, Washington,
D.C., 1980.

Roberts, W. K., Daubek, K. M., and Johnston, J. C. "The Use of
Needs Assessment Techniques for Establishing Training Programs Responsive to the U.S. Army's Role." *Educational Technology*, 1977, *17* (11), 41–42.

Robertson, D. L. "English Language Needs Assessment for Foreign
Students." Paper presented at annual meeting of Evaluation
Network/Evaluation Research Society, Baltimore, Md., Oct.
1982.

Robins, B. J. "Local Response to Planning Mandates: The Prevalence and Utilization of Needs Assessment by Human Service
Agencies." *Evaluation and Program Planning*, 1982, *5*, 199–208.

Rossi, P. H., Freeman, H. E., and Wright, S. R. *Evaluation: A
Systematic Approach*. Beverly Hills, Calif.: Sage, 1979.

Rossi, R. J. "Social Indicators and Social Area Analysis: Demographic Profile System." *Social Indicators*, March 1979.

Rossi, R. J., and Gilmartin, K. J. "Social Indicators of Youth
Development and Educational Performance: A Programmatic
Statement." *Social Indicators Research*, 1980, *7*, 157–191.

Rossi, R. J., and Gilmartin, K. J. *The Handbook of Social Indicators: Sources, Characteristics, and Analysis*. New York: Garland
STPM Press, 1980a.

Rossing, B. E. "The Gap Between Need Assessment and Program
Implementation." Paper presented at annual meeting of Evaluation Network/Evaluation Research Society, Baltimore, Md., Oct.
1982.

Roth, J. E. "Theory and Practice of Needs Assessment with Special
Application to Institutions of Higher Learning." Unpublished
doctoral dissertation, Department of Education, University of
California, Berkeley, 1978.

Rothman, J. *Using Research in Organizations: A Guide to Successful Application*. Beverly Hills, Calif.: Sage, 1980.

Rubenson, K. "Adult Education and the Distribution of Individual

Resources." Paper presented at Conference on Economic and Social Indicators, sponsored by the Ministry of Education, Province of British Columbia; New Westminster, B.C., Canada, Nov. 1982.

Rugg, E. A., Warren, T. L., and Carpenter, E. L. "Faculty Orientations Toward Institutional Goals: A Broken Front with Implications for Planned Change." *Research in Higher Education,* 1981, *15* (2), 161–173.

Rutland, S. P. "Human Services and Needs Assessment Capacity Building Project: General Report. An Integrated Approach to Human Service Planning, Delivery, and Resource Allocation." San Jose, Calif.: Santa Clara County, 1977. (SHR-0001956)

Salem, S. L. "A Computer-Oriented Approach to Fault Tree Construction." Unpublished doctoral dissertation, Department of Nuclear Engineering, University of California, Los Angeles, 1976.

Salvatore, T. *Needs Assessment in Community Planning: An Evaluation of Ten Approaches.* Media, Pa.: Delaware County Area Office, Health and Welfare Council, Inc., 1978.

Sapone, C. "CURMIS. Curriculum Management Information System (and) Prospectus of a Design to Assess a High School Staff in Evaluation of Its Program." Madison, Wis.: Madison Public Schools, Nov. 1972. (ED 075 281)

Sarason, I. G. "Understanding and Modifying Test Anxiety." In S. B. Anderson and J. S. Helmick (Eds.), *On Educational Testing.* San Francisco: Jossey-Bass, 1983.

Scarborough, B., Fraser, J., and Witkin, B. R. *Social Indicators: Emeryville.* Hayward, Calif.: Alameda County Training and Employment Board/Associated Community Action Program, 1978.

Scheidel, T. M., and Crowell, L. *Discussing and Deciding. A Desk Book for Group Leaders and Members.* New York: Macmillan, 1979.

Schneider, R. M. "Using the Modified Delphi to Determine Research Priorities." Frankfort: Bureau of Vocational Education, Kentucky State Department of Education. *Kentucky Research in Vocational Education Series, No. 3,* 1975. (ED 128 558)

Schoenberger, E., and Williamson, J. "Deciding on Priorities and

Specific Programs." In W. F. Anderson, B. J. Frieden, and M. J. Murphy (Eds.), *Managing Human Services*. Washington, D.C.: International City Management Association, 1977.

Schriner, J. D. (Ed.). *Problem-Solving: A Practical Guide to Attaining Goals*. Lansing: Michigan Department of Education, 1979.

Schwab, D. P., Heneman, H. G., III, and DeCotiis, T. A. "Behaviorally Anchored Rating Scales: A Review of the Literature." *Personnel Psychology*, 1975, *28*, 549–562.

Schwier, R. A. "Applying Multi-Component Training Needs Information." Paper presented at annual meeting of Association for Educational Communications and Technology, Dallas, Tex., May 1982.

Scott, C. "Research on Mail Surveys." *Journal of the Royal Statistical Society*, 1961, *124*, 143–195.

Scriven, M. "The Good News and the Bad News About Product Evaluation." *Evaluation News*, August 1981, *2* (3), 278–282.

Scriven, M., and Roth, J. "Special Feature: Needs Assessment." *Evaluation News*, 1977, *2*, 25–28.

Scriven, M., and Roth, J. "Needs Assessment: Concept and Practice." *New Directions for Program Evaluation*, 1, Spring 1978.

Shively, J. E. *Appalachia Educational Laboratory's Needs Assessment Design for Determining Short-term R&D Service Agendas and a Long-term Programmatic R&D Agenda*. Charleston, W.Va.: Appalachia Educational Laboratory, 1980.

Shively, J. E., and Holcomb, Z. J. *Needs Assessment Project: Factor Analytic Studies*. Charleston, W.Va.: Educational Services Office, Appalachia Educational Laboratory, 1981.

Shively, J. E., and Holcomb, Z. J. "Regional Needs Assessment: A Factor Analytic Approach." Paper presented at annual meeting of American Educational Research Association, New York, March 1982.

Shoemaker, J. S. "Television Presentations." In N. L. Smith (Ed.), *Communication Strategies in Evaluation*. Beverly Hills, Calif.: Sage, 1982.

Siegel, L. M., Attkisson, C. C., and Carson, L. G. "Need Identification and Program Planning in the Community Context." In C. C. Attkisson and others (Eds.), *Evaluation of Human Service Programs*. New York: Academic Press, 1978.

Sikorski, L. A., Oakley, G., and Lloyd-Kolkin, D. *A Report of the Research and Development Exchange: The Feasibility of Using Existing Data as Feedforward Information.* San Francisco, Calif.: Far West Laboratory for Educational Research and Development, November 1977.

Sincoff, M. Z., Williams, D. A., and Rohm, C. E. T., Jr. "Steps in Performing a Communication Audit." In S. Ferguson and S. D. Ferguson, *Intercom: Readings in Organizational Communication.* Rochelle Park, N.J.: Hayden, 1980.

Sizer, J. "European Perspectives Suggest Other Criteria." In M. W. Peterson (Ed.), *New Directions for Institutional Research: Institutional Assessment for Self-Improvement,* no. 29. San Francisco: Jossey-Bass, 1981.

Smith, N. L. "Techniques for the Analysis of Geographic Data in Evaluation." *Evaluation and Program Planning,* 1979, 2 (2), 119–126.

Smith, N. L., (Ed.). *Communication Strategies in Evaluation. New Perspectives in Evaluation,* Vol. 3. Beverly Hills, Calif.: Sage, 1982a.

Smith, N. L. "Geographic Displays." In N. L. Smith (Ed.), *Communication Strategies in Evaluation.* Beverly Hills, Calif.: Sage, 1982b.

Sork, T. J. "Development and Validation of a Normative Process Model for Determining Priority of Need in Community Adult Education." Paper presented at Adult Education Research Conference, Ann Arbor, Mich., April 4-6, 1979.

Sork, T. J. "Adult Education and the Distribution of Resources: Models for Financing." Paper presented at Conference on Economic and Social Indicators, Sponsored by the Ministry of Education, Province of British Columbia, New Westminster, B.C., Canada, November 1982a.

Sork, T. J. "Determining Priorities." Vancouver: University of British Columbia, Vancouver, B.C., Canada, 1982b.

Stanford Research Institute. "Anticipating Educational Issues over the Next Two Decades: An Overview Report of Trends Analysis." Palo Alto, Calif.: Stanford Research Institute, 1973.

Stephens, K. G. "A Fault Tree Approach to Analysis of Educational Systems as Demonstrated in Vocational Education." Unpublished doctoral dissertation, Department of Educational Administration, University of Washington, 1972.

Stewart, R., and Poaster, L. B. "Methods of Assessing Mental and Physical Needs with Social Statistics." *Evaluation*, II (1975), 68, 70.

Stipak, B. Local Governments' Use of Citizen Surveys." *Public Administration Review*, 1980, *40* (5), 521–525.

Straus, M. A. "State and Regional Data Archives (SRDA)." *Social Indicators*, April–May 1980, *25*, 1–3.

Stufflebeam, D. "Forward." In J. M. Nowakowski (Ed.), *The Toledo Catalog: Assessment of Students and School Administration.* Boston: Kluwer-Nighoff, 1983.

Suarez, T. M., and Cox, J. O. "A Comparison of Three Technical Assistance Needs Assessment Strategies." Paper presented at annual meeting of Evaluation Network/Evaluation Research Society, Austin, Texas, October 1981. Chapel Hill, N.C.: Technical Assistance Development System, 1981.

Sudman, S., and Bradburn, N. M. *Asking Questions: A Practical Guide to Questionnaire Design.* San Francisco: Jossey-Bass, 1982.

Sugarman, B. "The Nonprofit Manager as a Guerilla Leader." *Sharing*, 1982, *6* (5), 1–2, 4.

Sweigert, R. L., Jr. "Need Assessment—The First Step Toward Deliberate Rather Than Impulsive Response to Problems." Paper presented at conference of Interstate Project for State Planning and Program Consolidation, United States Office of Education, San Francisco, April 1968.

Sweigert, R. L., Jr. *Goals for Education in Atlanta, 1985—As Seen by Community Leaders, Educators, and Students.* Atlanta, Ga.: Atlanta Assessment Project, Atlanta Public Schools, April 1973.

Sweigert, R. L., Jr., and Kase, D. H. "Assessing Student Needs Using the ESCO Model." Paper presented at annual meeting of American Educational Research Association, New York City, February 1971.

Sweigert, R. L., Jr., and Schabacker, W. H. "The Delphi Technique: How Well Does It Work in Setting Educational Goals." Paper presented at annual meeting of American Educational Research Association, Chicago, April 1974.

Taylor, E. N., and Vineberg, R. *Mental Health Consultant Reports of the Field Trials for Surveying Problems in Schools.* Alexandria, Va.: Human Resources Research Organization, 1975.

Taylor, E. N., and Vineberg, R. "Evaluation of Indirect Services to Schools." In W. F. Anderson, B. J. Frieden, and M. J. Murphy (Eds.), *Managing Human Services.* Washington, D.C.: International City Management Association, 1977.

Taylor, E. N., Vineberg, R., and Goffard, S. J. *Surveying School Problems: Some Individual, Group, and System Indicators.* Alexandria, Va.: Human Resources Research Organization, 1974.

Terrill, A. F. "Planning with Less for More." Paper presented at annual meeting of Evaluation Network/Evaluation Research Society, Baltimore, Md., Oct. 1982.

Thompson, B. "Communication Theory as a Framework for Evaluation Use Research: Evaluation as Persuasion." Paper presented at annual meeting of Evaluation Network/Evaluation Research Society, Austin, Tex., Oct. 1981.

Toffler, A. *The Third Wave.* New York: William Morrow, 1980.

Torres, E. E., and others. "Foreign Language Dropouts: Problems and Solutions. An Examination of the Reasons Why Students Do Not Continue Foreign Language Instruction and a List of Suggested Solutions to the Problem." New York: Modern Language Association of America, 1970. (ED 043 262)

Tritschler, D. "Strategies for Assessing Performance at Your Own Institution." In M. W. Peterson (Ed.), *New Directions for Institutional Research: Institutional Assessment for Self-Improvement,* no. 29. San Francisco: Jossey-Bass, 1981.

Tucker, K. D. *Needs Assessment: Computerized Simulation Model* Gainesville, Fla.: Center for Community Needs Assessment, University of Florida, May 1973.

Tucker, K. D. *A Model for Community Needs Assessment.* Report to Central Florida Community Colleges' Consortium. Gainesville: Institute of Higher Education, University of Florida, 1974.

Tuckman, B. W., and Montare, A. P. S. *Educational Goal Attainment Tests.* Bloomington, Ind.: Center for the Dissemination of Innovative Programs, Phi Delta Kappa, 1975.

United Way of King County. *1982 Planning Report.* Seattle, Wash.: Planning and Allocations Division, United Way of King County, 1982.

Virginia Division of State Planning and Community Affairs. *Human Services Planning, Financing and Delivery of Virginia.* Richmond: Office of Human Resources and Service, Virginia Division of State Planning and Community Affairs, 1973.

Warheit, G. J., Bell, R. A., and Schwab, J. J. *Needs Assessment Approaches: Concepts and Methods.* Rockville, Md.: National Institute of Mental Health, U.S. Department of Health, Education, and Welfare, 1979.

Warwick, D. P., and Lininger, C. A. *The Sample Survey: Theory and Practice.* New York: McGraw-Hill, 1975.

Weaver, W. T. "The Delphi Forecasting Method." *Phi Delta Kappan,* 1971, *52* (5), 267–271.

Weiss, A. T. "The Consumer Model of Assessing Community Mental Health Needs." *Evaluation,* 1975, *2,* 71.

Weizenbaum, J. *Computer Power and Human Reason. From Judgment to Calculation.* San Francisco: W. H. Freeman, 1976.

Wholey, J. S., and others. *Federal Evaluation Policy: Analyzing the Effects of Public Programs.* Washington, D.C.: Urban Institute, 1970.

Wickens, D. *Games People Oughta Play: A Group Process for Needs Assessment and Decision-Making for Elementary and Secondary Schools.* A Manual for the Facilitator. Hayward, Calif.: Office of the Alameda County Superintendent of Schools, 1980. (ED 189 089)

Wisconsin Department of Public Instruction. *Statewide Assessment of Educational Needs.* Madison: Division for Management and Planning Services, Wisconsin Department of Public Instruction, 1977. Draft.

Wishart, B. *TARGET: To Assess Relevant Goals of Education Together.* El Dorado Hills, Calif.: B. Wishart, 1972.

Witkin, B. R. "Fault Tree Analysis as Formative Evaluation of Research and Development Projects." Paper presented at 51st annual meeting of California Educational Research Association, Los Angeles, Nov. 1973.

Witkin, B. R. "Communication Strategies in Public Policy Decision Making: An Analysis of Processes in Major Needs Assessment Models from a Systems Point of View." Paper presented at annual meeting of International Communication Association, Chicago, 1975. (ED 120 848)

Witkin, B. R. "Educational Needs Assessment: The State of the Art." *Educational Planning,* 1976a, *3* (2), 1–5.

Witkin, B. R. "Educational Needs Assessment: Theme and Variations." Abstracts of models presented at National Conference on Educational Needs Assessment, Oakland, Calif., April 1976. Hayward, Calif.: Office of the Alameda County Superintendent of Schools, 1976b.

Witkin, B. R. "Needs Assessment Models: A Critical Analysis." Paper presented at annual meeting of American Educational Research Association, San Francisco, April 1976c.

Witkin, B. R. *An Analysis of Needs Assessment Techniques for Educational Planning at State, Intermediate, and District Levels.* (Rev. ed.) Hayward, Calif.: Office of the Alameda County Superintendent of Schools, 1977a. (ED 108 370)

Witkin, B. R. "Fault Tree Analysis as a Planning and Management Tool: A Case Study." *Educational Planning,* 1977b, *3* (3), 71–85.

Witkin, B. R. "Needs Assessment Kits, Models and Tools." *Educational Technology,* 1977c, *17* (11), 5–18.

Witkin, B. R., (Ed.). *Before You Do a Needs Assessment: Important First Questions.* Hayward, Calif.: Office of the Alameda County Superintendent of Schools, Oct. 1978a.

Witkin, B. R. (Ed.). *Needs Assessment Product Locator. Available Needs Assessment Products and How to Select Them for Local Use.* Hayward, Calif.: Office of the Alameda County Superintendent of Schools, Oct. 1978b.

Witkin, B. R., (Ed.). *A Comprehensive Needs Assessment Module.* (Rev. ed.) Manual, survey questionnaires, statistical and data forms booklet, and guide to analysis. Hayward, Calif.: Office of Alameda County Superintendent of Schools, 1979a.

Witkin, B. R. "Interagency Planning: A Case Study in Murphy's Law." Paper presented at annual meeting of International Society of Educational Planners, Kiawah Island, S.C., Nov. 1979b. (ED 231 021)

Witkin, B. R. "Model of Cyclical Needs Assessment for Management Information System." ESEA Title IV-C Developmental/ Innovative Projects. First Year Report. Saratoga, Calif.: Los Gatos Joint Union High School District, Saratoga High School, 1979c.

Witkin, B. R. "New York Association for Learning Disabilities Project: Formative Evaluation—Fault Tree Component. Final Report." In K. G. Butler, B. R. Witkin, and F. Mercer, "Evaluation of Suffolk and Nassau County Chapter Projects: Demonstration Project Serving NI/LD Persons." Fourth Quarter End of Project Period Report, Syracuse University, 1982.

Witkin, B. R., and Richardson, J. *APEX Needs Assessment for Secondary Schools. Manual.* Hayward, Calif.: Office of the Alameda County Superintendent of Schools, 1983.

Witkin, B. R., Richardson, J., and Sherman, N. *APEX Needs Assessment for Secondary Schools.* (Rev. ed.) Hayward, Calif.: Office of the Alameda County Superintendent of Schools, 1982.

Witkin, B. R., Richardson, J., and Wickens, D. *LINC (Local Interagency Needs Assessment Capabilities). Final Project Report.* Hayward, Calif.: Office of the Alameda County Superintendent of Schools, 1979. (ED 182 560)

Witkin, B. R., and Stephens, K. G. *Fault Tree Analysis: A Research Tool for Educational Planning.* Technical Report No. 1. Hayward, Calif.: Office of the Alameda County Superintendent of Schools PACE Center, 1968. (ED 029 379)

Witkin, B. R., and Stephens, K. G. "A Fault Tree Approach to Analysis of Organizational Communication Systems." Paper presented at annual meeting of Western Speech Communication Association, Honolulu, Hawaii, November 1972. (ED 081 039)

Witkin, B. R., and Stephens, K. G. *Fault Tree Analysis: A Management Science Technique for Educational Planning and Evaluation.* Hayward, Calif.: Office of the Alameda County Superintendent of Schools, 1973a.

Witkin, B. R., and Stephens, K. G. "Solving Communication Problems in Organizations: A Workshop on Fault Tree Analysis." Paper presented at annual meeting of International Communication Association, Montreal, Quebec, April 1973b.

Zangwill, B. *A Compendium of Laws and Regulations Requiring Needs Assessment.* Washington, D.C.: Office of the Assistant Secretary for Planning and Evaluation, U.S. Department of Health, Education, and Welfare, May 1977.

Name Index

Subject Index

A

Accountability, and needs assessment, 1

ACNAM model, 232, 236

Adult education: priority setting for, 230–232; and social indicators, 124

Advocacy, for community needs assessment, 334

Aid to Families with Dependent Children (AFDC), 113, 121

Akron, University of, Institute for Futures Studies and Research at, 167–168

Alameda, California: community needs assessment in, 342; public meetings in, 131–132

Alameda County (California): Health Service Agency of, 338; Office of Education of, 32, 137

Alaska, University of, Center for Northern Educational Research at, 267–268

American Institutes for Research

(AIR) in the Behavioral Sciences, 111

American Library Association, 60

APEX surveys, 82–83, 85, 94, 214–215

Appalachia Educational Laboratory, 6–7

Archdiocese of Milwaukee, 331

Area Agency on Aging, 339

Area Office on Aging of Northwestern Ohio, 332–333

Arizona: community needs assessment in, 333, 334–335, 348; survey scales in, 70

Arizona Department of Education, 70, 368

Atlanta Assessment Project, 155–156, 162–163, 178, 298

Atlanta Public Schools, 162, 298, 368

B

Battelle Institute, 73

Behavioral Research and Evaluation Corporation (BREC), 54–55

National Institute of Education, 21, 32, 276, 301
National Institutes of Health, Demographic Profile System of, 103, 105
National Network for Coordinating Human Services, 325
National Resources Planning Board (NRPB), 158–159
National School Public Relations Association, 71
Native Hawaiian Educational Assessment Project, 51–53, 225–226
Need: ambiguity of, 8–10; categories of, 7; components of, 44; definitions of, 5–14, 64; democratic, diagnostic, or analytic view of, 8; as discrepancy, 6–7, 10–12, 16; formulas for, 10–12; individual level of, 6–7; inferences of, 104–105; motivational, 10; organizational level of, 6–7, 18; in personality theory, 5–6; prescriptive, 10; primary and secondary, 57; priorities of, 201–203; as problem, 7–8, 32
Needs assessment: analysis of role of, 1–28; applications and trends for, 280–366; assumptions about, x; causal analysis for, 180–205; classifications of, 15; and communication, 260–279; community-wide, 327–349; concept of, ix–x; criteria for doing, 18; definitions of, 5, 14–16; futures methods in, 152–158; group processes for, 129–150; history of, 1–2; implications for, 350–366; influences on, 241–242; interagency cooperation in, 300–326; and management information system, 50–51; methodological trends in, 364–366; models of, 29–62; organizational, 241–259; overview of, ix–xi; in planning-implementation-evaluation cycle, 25–28; and priority setting, 206–240; purposes and settings of, 18–25, 241; reasons for, 3, 351–353; scope,

purposes, and variety of, 1–62; self-assessment related to, 245; and social indicators, 100–128; survey methods for, 63–99; terminology and scope in, 2–5; utilization of, 280–299; values in, 16–18
Needs assessor: and communication, 261, 263, 269, 274, 275; concept of, 4; and utilization, 294–295
Needs study, concept of, 4–5
New England Municipal Center, 329
New Hampshire, community needs assessment in, 329
New Hampshire, University of, State and Regional Data archives (SRDA) at, 104
New Jersey: criticality function in, 220; Puerto Rican Congress of, 266
New York City: community needs assessment in, 347–348; interagency cooperation in, 322
New York state: Board of Cooperative Educational Services (BOCES) in, 317; community needs assessment in, 347–348; interagency cooperation in, 322; organizational planning in, 250
Nominal group process: for community needs assessment, 333, 339; for data gathering, 264; in small groups, 133–135
North Carolina at Chapel Hill, University of, data bases at, 104
Northern California Program Development Center, 137
Northern Illinois University, Center for Governmental Studies of, 319
Northwest Regional Educational Laboratory, 271

O

Office of Management and Budget (OMB), 103, 159–160, 283
Ohio: community needs assessment